symmetrical english

by David Cummings

EVERYMAN CHESS

Published by Everyman Publishers plc, London

First published in 2001 by Everyman Publishers plc, formerly Cadogan Books plc, Gloucester Mansions, 140A Shaftesbury Avenue, London WC2H 8HD

British Library Cataloguing-in-Publication Data
A catalogue record for this book is available from the British Library.

ISBN 1 85744 292 X

Distributed in North America by The Globe Pequot Press, P.O Box 480, 246 Goose Lane, Guilford, CT 06437-0480.

All other sales enquiries should be directed to Everyman Chess, Gloucester Mansions, 140A Shaftesbury Avenue, London WC2H 8HD
tel: 020 7539 7600 fax: 020 7379 4060
email: dan@everyman.uk.com
website: www.everyman.uk.com

To Marguerite

The Everyman Chess Opening Guides were designed and developed by First Rank Publishing.

EVERYMAN CHESS SERIES (formerly Cadogan Chess)
Chief advisor: Garry Kasparov
Commissioning editor: Byron Jacobs

Typeset and edited by First Rank Publishing, Brighton.
Production by Book Production Services.
Printed and bound in Great Britain by The Cromwell Press Ltd., Trowbridge, Wiltshire.

CONTENTS

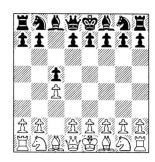

1 c4 c5

	Bibliography	4
	Introduction	5
1	The Hedgehog	7
2	The Double Fianchetto Defence	28
3	White plays an early d2-d4	39
4	Black plays an early ...d7-d5	69
5	Symmetrical English with g2-g3	99
6	Symmetrical English Main Line with 5 ♘f3 ♘f6	124
7	Breaking the Symmetry	141
	Index of Complete Games	159

BIBLIOGRAPHY

Books
Encyclopaedia of Chess Openings vol. A, (Chess Informant 1996 and 2001)
Nunn's Chess Openings, (Everyman 1999)
English Opening A33, Gyula Sax (Chess Informant 1994)
English Opening A34, Beliavsky and Mikhalchishin (Chess Informant 1994)
English Opening: Symmetrical, Vladimir Bagirov (Everyman 1995)
The Symmetrical English, Carsten Hansen (Gambit 2000)
Symmetrical English 1... c5, John Watson (Batsford 1988)
Secrets of Modern Chess Strategy, John Watson (Gambit 1998)
Positional Play, Dvoretsky and Yusupov (Batsford 1996)
Dynamic Chess Strategy, Mihai Suba (Pergamon 1991)
The Hedgehog, Mihai Suba (Batsford 2000)
The Dynamic English, Tony Kosten (Gambit 1999)
Flank Openings, 3rd edition, Raymond Keene (British Chess Magazine 1979)

Periodicals
Chess Informant 1-80
New in Chess Yearbook 1-58
New in Chess Magazine

Databases and websites
ChessBase Mega Database 2001
The Week in Chess

INTRODUCTION

The Symmetrical English (1 c4 c5) is an important part of chess theory, and is played at every level of the game from World Championship to club chess. Soon after starting work on this book, I began to appreciate the wide spread of material categorised under 1 c4 c5. While 1 c4 and 1 ♘f3 are less popular than 1 e4 and 1 d4, any tournament player who neglects to prepare a response to them as Black, does so at his peril. I have tried to be as objective as possible and cover both Black's and White's ideas and interests on an equal footing.

I had the following goals in mind for this book:

1) Give a 'feel' for the opening through games that illustrate recurring themes, some of which often occur deep into the middlegame.

2) Cover the most critical lines and present theory that is up to date at the time of writing, together with suggested improvements over published works. Inevitably, given the huge volume of games available, something had to give, so I compromised on the depth of coverage of non-critical material. For example, if in a certain line there are four different lines that all equalise for Black, I did not try to cover them all in-depth.

3) Give an insight into the move order issues and transpositions (into and out of the Symmetrical English), which are such an important facet of this opening. The fact is that many of the main lines in the Symmetrical English can be reached by almost any permutation of the first 7 or 8 moves! There are also a number of tricks along the way to throw the unwary off their preferred path. At one point I wondered whether to 'sanitise' the move order in the main games to conform to standard categorisations such as the ECO system. I decided against this, since the variety of actual move orders practised by top players is very instructive, even though it makes the subject-matter initially somewhat harder to grasp. However, I have wherever possible explained the 'official' move orders and how the practical material relates to these.

I believe the 'complete games' approach is well suited to this subject matter. There seems little point in presenting the latest 1 c4 c5 theory in encyclopaedic fashion without explaining some thematic examples of, for example, how and when to go for a ...d7-d5 break in the Hedgehog, or what the key plans are in a 'quiet' symmetrical line. At the same time, it is naïve, especially the higher you go, to expect to avoid concrete knowledge in any modern opening. Many lines are as sharp as main-line 1 e4 or 1 d4 openings.

Some chapters have a longer introduction, covering typical ideas, than others. This is no accident. Some lines have positional ideas or common tactics that crop up in a large number of games and across several sub-variations, while others are less systematic. While there are some general principles that can be abstracted, almost every line has its own character and concrete nature.

Who should read this book, and how should the material be tackled?

As a broad generalisation, I have observed two types of player who take up the English as White.

1) The 'system' player. Playing a certain set-up against a wide range of responses has the advantage that you can become finely attuned to the subtleties of the structure, while your opponent will most likely be on less familiar ground. One example would be playing as White, in one order or another, c2-c4, ♘b1-c3, g2-g3, ♗f1-g2 and then either the Botvinnik set-up with e2-e4 and ♘g1-e2 or the regular ♘g1-f3. Life is somewhat more straightforward here; you can choose the approach you like from the Symmetrical English chapters. You will also need something against the 3...d5 line and the Hedgehog.

2) The 'flexible d4 player'. This is someone who takes up the English move order as a way of picking and choosing which Indian defences (or Queen's Gambit lines) they want to entertain, e.g. for the days when you realise you don't have an opening against the Grünfeld. Such players will be concerned with the nuances of move order and transposition, and commonly start 1 ♘f3 (avoiding 1 c4 e5 but allowing 1 ♘f3 d5) as often as 1 c4. These players will benefit from studying the full range of material.

For Black, the Symmetrical English is a mainstream and reliable response to 1 c4. If you don't like 1 c4 e5 or have been thwarted from playing your favourite Benoni or Benko by 1 d4 ♘f6 2 c4 c5 3 ♘f3, then the Symmetrical English is ideal. One approach is to choose your main or target system as Black (e.g. Hedgehog, Double Fianchetto or an early ...d5 with the Rubinstein set-up), and then study the other games that branch from your preferred move order.

If you are looking for a role model, then on the White side, the games of Korchnoi and Kramnik will repay close study. For Black, both Kasparov and Adams have used various lines of the Symmetrical English as mainstays of their repertoire over the years. Karpov, and to some extent Anand, show up on both sides of the board.

David Cummings,
Toronto,
July 2001

CHAPTER ONE

The Hedgehog

The term 'Hedgehog' is used both to refer to a generic development scheme (based on ...b7-b6, ...♗b7, ...e7-e6, ...d7-d6, ...♗e7) that occurs in several openings (and other variations within the Symmetrical English), and a specific variation which is the subject of this chapter. It is a flexible and resilient defence with a strong counter-punch.

1 c4 c5 2 ♘f3 ♘f6 3 ♘c3 e6 4 g3

The system presented in this chapter depends on White playing g2-g3. If instead he goes for an early d2-d4 (see Chapter 3), then if Black wants a Hedgehog set-up, he has to resort to lines like 3 d4 cxd4 4 ♘xd4 b6 (Game 16). If Black plays 3...b6 (instead of 3...e6) then White has 4 e4 or 4 d4, which are covered in Games 16 and 63.

The Hedgehog is also often reached from a Queen's Indian style move order such as 1 ♘f3 ♘f6 2 c4 b6 3 g3 ♗b7 4 ♗g2 e6 5 0-0 ♗e7 6 ♘c3 c5.

4...b6 5 ♗g2 ♗b7 6 0-0 ♗e7

Black has an important decision to make on move 6. The most popular move is 6...♗e7, but 6...a6 has its supporters, including the Rumanian GMs Suba and Marin. 6...d6 will transpose into one or the other, but is somewhat less flexible. One advantage of 6...♗e7 is that it gives Black more options in response to the dangerous 7 ♖e1,

such as 7...d5 or 7...♘e4 (Games 7-8; these would make less sense with 6...a6 in place of 6...♗e7). On the other hand, 6...a6 enables Black to avoid the line 6...♗e7 7 d4 cxd4 8 ♕xd4 d6 9 ♗g5 a6 10 ♗xf6 (see Game 5).

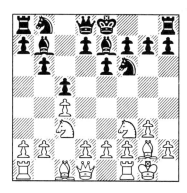

White has several approaches to the opening:

a) Develop the pieces and build up for an attack later (see Game 2).

b) Try and strike early against the d6-weakness, with a view to extracting a positional concession. White can try some combination of ♖f1-d1 with ♗c1-g5 or ♘f3-g5, or b2-b3 and ♗c1-a3. One advantage of these plans is that White can always revert to plan A (slow build up). Black needs to be vigilant against these 'sneaky' move orders, which are covered in Games 3-4.

c) Direct and aggressive play with 7 ♖e1 and the 'Open Sicilian style' continuation (Games 6-7). White aims to achieve something concrete early on, before Black's solid build-up is complete.

7 ♖e1 d6 8 e4 a6 9 d4 cxd4 10 ♘xd4 ♕c7

Black always needs to be wary of tactics along the h1-a8 diagonal, especially when his b7-bishop is undefended. For example 10...0-0 would fall for 11 e5 – a typical trick.

11 ♗e3 0-0 12 ♖c1 ♘bd7

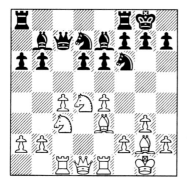

Let's look at this position to discuss some of the key ideas. The character of the Hedgehog is such that, even during protracted periods of manoeuvring, both sides need to be constantly calculating the tactics of the important pawn breaks. Knowing the typical motifs helps you to know what to look for and can save time (but keep an open mind!).

White's Ideas

White has a number of aggressive ideas to make progress:

1) f4-f5 (see Game 7), hitting the potential weakness on e6, or provoking ...e6-e5, which leaves the d5-square in White's hands.

2) g3-g4-g5 to cause havoc with Black's minor pieces, and attempt a kingside attack.

3) e4-e5 (supported by f2-f4) often

threatening to win a piece.

4) The thematic ♘c3-d5 sacrifice.

5) The queenside clamp, for example with a2-a3, b2-b4. This is more appropriate in the long manoeuvring style game. White needs to ensure he has the c4-pawn well defended before playing b2-b4.

A number of these goals are harder to achieve, the later in the opening we go. For example, once Black has played, ...♖a8-c8 and ...♕c7-b8, the ♘d5 sac loses its point, or once Black has played ...♖f8-e8 and ...♗e7-f8, the f4-f5 thrust has less bite. So good advice for White is to maintain concentration during the early stages, and not just aim to get the pieces out.

Black's Ideas

The following are the ideas that Black should keep in mind:

1) A lot of the potential energy in Black's game comes from his harmonious piece formation, particularly the knights on f6 and d7. Most modern Hedgehog players prefer this to the ...♘c6 set-up, though this is appropriate in several situations. Rooks are usually best placed on e8 and c8, while the dark-squared bishop can be routed via ...♗e7-f8-g7 or ...♗e7-d8-c7.

2) Black's 'classic' break is ...d6-d5 (an instructive example of this can be studied in Yermolinsky-Salov below).

3) The advance ...b6-b5 is more double-edged than many people think. Sometimes Black can achieve his 'goal' only to find his b5-pawn is a target (after c4xb5, ...a6xb5, b2-b4 etc.)

4) A well timed ...e6-e5 is also an important weapon – controlling the central dark squares.

5) Occasionally, Black can even fight fire with fire on the kingside, for example answering f2-f4 and g2-g4 with ...h7-h6 and ...g7-g5, attempting to grab the dark-squares. (see Karpov-Csom, Game 3)

It is noticeable that quite a few players

play the Hedgehog as both Black and White, perhaps on the principle that 'poachers make the best gamekeepers'. Or put another way, 'I like to play it from both sides; as White you must always introduce some new tricks because over the years the Hedgehog has proved to be rock-solid. Playing it gives more satisfaction when you are Black – it's like defending truth, justice and the poor simultaneously' – Mihai Suba in *Dynamic Chess Strategy*.

Game 1
Yermolinsky-Salov
Wijk aan Zee 1997

---

1 ♘f3 ♘f6 2 c4 c5 3 ♘c3 e6 4 g3 b6 5 ♗g2 ♗b7 6 0-0 ♗e7 7 d4 cxd4 8 ♕xd4 0-0

8...♘c6 9 ♕f4 0-0 will transpose.

9 ♖d1 ♘c6

Nowadays in the Hedgehog, Black usually develops his queen's knight with ...d6 and ...♘b8-d7. The line with ...♘b8-c6 was the traditional approach, dating back to the 1950s and 60s, before the Hedgehog proper was 'discovered' in the early 70s. However, ...♘b8-c6 still crops up from time to time, and in this game Salov manages to pull off a nice thematic win.

10 ♕f4

The best spot for the queen, eyeing d6 and making way for the rook on d1.

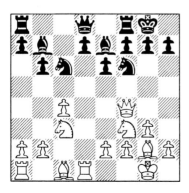

10...♕b8

Offering the trade of queens is the old main line. Alternatively, Black can put up the barricades with 10...d6 and arrange his pieces behind them. This was shunned in the 'old days', perhaps because people were afraid of defending the cramped Hedgehog set-up which we now take for granted. Some of the more recent games with this approach indicate that it is playable for Black, so ...♘c6 may, after all, provide a respectable alternative to the heavily analysed Hedgehog lines (with ...d6 and ...♘b8-d7) to be found elsewhere in this chapter. One example:

10...d6 11 b3 (11 e4 ♕b8 transposes to the main game) 11...♕b8 12 ♗b2 ♖d8 13 ♖d2 (13 ♖ac1 a6 14 ♕e3 b5) 13...a6 14 ♖ad1 b5! 15 ♘e4 ♘xe4 16 ♕xe4 ♘e5 17 ♕e3 ♘xf3+ 18 ♗xf3 bxc4 19 bxc4 ♗xf3 20 ♕xf3 ♕c7 ½-½ Van der Sterren-Van Wely, Rotterdam 1998.

11 e4

a) 11 b3 is also popular. A recent high level game (and a fairly typical example) is 11...♖d8 12 ♗b2 h6!? 13 ♖d2 ♕xf4 14 gxf4 ♘a5 15 ♖ad1 d5 16 cxd5 ♘xd5 17 ♘xd5 ♗xd5 18 ♘e5 ♗xg2 19 ♔xg2 ♖xd2 20 ♖xd2 ♔f8 21 ♖c2 ♗e8 Kramnik-Leko, Linares 1999, and Black should hold this ending.

b) Many games have been played in the endgame that arises from 11 ♕xb8 ♖axb8 12 ♗f4 ♖bc8 and now White can play the forcing 13 ♘e5 (13 ♗d6 leads to an equal position after 13...♗xd6 14 ♖xd6 ♘e7 15 b3 ♘f5 16 ♖d2 d5) 13...d6 14 ♘xc6 ♗xc6 15 ♗xd6 ♗xd6 16 ♖xd6 ♗xg2 17 ♔xg2 ♖xc4. In this position White has tried:

b1) 18 ♖ad1 g5!. White would like to advance his pawns to drive away the knight, which is in a key defensive post on f6. Black's plan pre-empts this. 19 h3 and now:

b11) Black should play 19...h5 20 f3 g4 according to Gipslis, when he should have no trouble equalising.

b12) 19...♖fc8 20 f3 ♔g7 21 e4?! (21 ♘f2 is slightly better for White) 21...b5! with equality, Krogius-Giorgadze, Riga 1975.

b2) 18 f3 may be an improvement, for example 18...♖fc8 19 ♖ad1 ♔f8 (19...g5 20 h3 h5 21 g4 nips Black's plan in the bud) 20 e4 e5?! (creating weaknesses on d5 and e5, but after 20...♘e8 21 ♖6d3 White is still slightly better) 21 ♔f2 ♖4c5 22 g4 ♔e8 23 ♔e3 ♖5c6 24 ♖6d2 and White is much better, Saidy-Andersson, Las Palmas 1973.

c) 11 ♘g5!? ♘a5 12 b3 ♗xg2 13 ♕xb8 ♖axb8 14 ♔xg2 ♖fd8 15 ♗f4 ♖bc8 16 ♖ac1 ♘c6 17 ♘ge4 ♘xe4 18 ♘xe4 d5 19 cxd5 exd5 20 ♘c3 ♗a3 21 ♖b1 d4 22 ♘b5 ♗c5 with a level endgame, Savchenko-Sulskis, Lubniewice 1998.

11...d6

A fighting move. Instead 11...♕xf4 12 ♗xf4 ♖fd8 13 e5! ♘e8 14 ♘d4 ♘a5 15 b3 ♗xg2 16 ♔xg2 d6 17 exd6 ♗xd6 18 ♗xd6 ♘xd6 19 ♖d2 and White is a touch better, Karpov-Petrosian, Milan 1975.

12 b3 ♘e5

Another approach is 12...♘d7!? 13 ♕e3 ♖e8 14 ♗b2 a6 15 ♕e2 ♗f8 with a tough battle in prospect, Korchnoi-Skembris, Beersheba 1993.

Alternatively 12...a6 13 ♗b2 ♕c7 14 h3 ♖ac8 15 ♕e3 ♘e5 16 ♘d4 h6 17 ♖d2 ♖fe8 18 ♔h1 ♘ed7 19 f4 ♗f8 20 ♖f1 ♕b8 21 g4 ♘h7 with a tense position was Kramnik-Leko, Budapest 2001. Leko later achieved the rare feat of provoking to Kramnik to overreach himself, and won.

13 ♕e3

13 ♘xe5? dxe5 is rarely a good idea for White as it gives Black control of d4; 13 ♗a3 probing the d6-pawn, is more critical, e.g. 13...♘g6 (this will be necessary sooner or later, but g6 is not the ideal square for this knight) 14 ♕e3 ♖e8 15 ♗b2 ♗f8 16 h3 a6 17 ♕xb6 ♘xe4 18 ♘xe4 ♗xe4 19 ♕xb8 ♖axb8 20 ♘d4 ♗xg2 21 ♔xg2 (Huzman-Yudasin, Haifa 1996) and White is slightly better.

13...♘ed7

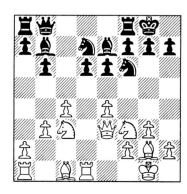

...♘c6-e5-d7 is a common regrouping idea.

14 ♕e2

White gives the impression of drifting. Yudasin suggests 14 ♗b2, with h2-h3, ♖d1-d2 and ♖a1-d1 to follow. At least that would keep more firepower on the d5-square.

14...a6 15 ♘d4 ♕c7

Making room for the a8-rook to come to c8, and also incidentally threatening ...b7-b5, since the c3-knight is undefended.

16 ♗d2

White wants his bishop on e3, but because of the tactic 16 ♗e3? b5! he has to take two moves to achieve it. 16 ♗b2 is more to the point, e.g. 16...♖fe8 17 ♖ac1 ♖ac8 18 g4!?.

16...♖fe8 17 ♖ac1 ♖ac8 18 ♗e3 ♕b8

Black now has the Hedgehog 'Plan A' piece formation. The queen gets out of the line of fire of the White rook, which helps facilitate a future ...d6-d5 or ...b6-b5. The queen also sometimes moves across to a8 to add pressure against the e4-pawn.

19 f3

Another rather pointless move, which reduces White's control of the d5-square. White can try 19 f4!?.

19...d5!

All the pre-requisites for a successful ...d6-d5 break are in place: the e8-rook is vis-à-vis the White queen on e3, Black's queen is tucked away on b8, White's f2-f3 has blocked his g2-bishop's control of d5 and loosened the defence of e3, creating potential tactics on the a7-g1 diagonal. But above all the tactics have to work! These factors just serve as a clue that the break is worth seriously analysing, or as a guide if you can't reach a concrete assessment and have to play intuitively.

20 cxd5 exd5 21 exd5?

The only problem with an early ...d6-d5 is that even after White has made a series of mistakes, he can sometimes still recover and equalise. So here White should play 21 ♗f4! according to Salov, when 21...♗d6 22 ♗xd6 ♕xd6 23 ♕f2! ♕a3 (23...dxe4 24 ♘db5) 24 exd5 ♘xd5 25 ♘de2! is about equal.

After 21 ♘xd5 ♘xd5 22 exd5 ♗c5 23 ♕f2 ♕e5 Black retains the initiative.

21...♗a3!

Pinning the e3-bishop to the queen, with gain of time.

22 ♖c2 ♖xc3! 23 ♖xc3 ♘xd5 24 ♖cd3 ♘c5

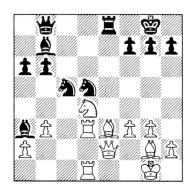

25 f4!

The best chance. Otherwise, 25 ♘c6 ♗xc6 26 ♖xd5 ♗xd5 27 ♖xd5 ♗c1! wins for Black, while 25 ♕f2 ♘xd3 26 ♖xd3 ♘xe3 27 ♖xe3 ♖xe3 28 ♕xe3 ♗c5 also wins.

25...♘xd3 26 ♖xd3 ♗c5 27 ♗xd5 ♗xd5 28 ♘f5

If 28 ♕f2 then 28...♕c8!, threatening to invade on the light squares.

28...♗e4 29 ♗xc5 ♗xd3 30 ♕xd3 bxc5 31 ♕c3! f6 32 ♕c4+ ♔h8 33 ♕f7 ♖g8 34 h4! ♕e8 35 ♕d5 ♕e1+ 36 ♔g2 ♕e2+ 37 ♔h3 h5

Salov analyses 37...♕f1+! 38 ♔g4 h5+! 39 ♔xh5 ♕e2+ 40 ♔g6 ♕g4+ 41 ♔f7 ♕h5+ 42 ♔e6 ♕e2+! 43 ♔d7 ♕e8+ 44 ♔d6 ♕d8+! 45 ♔c6 ♕a8+ 46 ♔xc5 ♖c8+ 47 ♔d4 ♖d8 48 ♘d6 ♕a7+ 49 ♔d3 ♕d7 as winning for Black.

38 ♘d6 ♕g4+ 39 ♔g2 ♖f8 40 ♔f2! ♔h7 41 ♕xc5 ♖d8! 42 ♕c2+ g6 43 ♕c4

43 ♘e4! was a tougher defence.

43...♕d7 44 ♘e4 ♕e7 45 ♕c3 ♔g7

Not 45...♕xe4?? 46 ♕c7+.

46 ♔f3 ♖e8 47 ♕d3 ♕b7! 0-1

Black wins after 48 ♕d4 ♔g8! 49 ♕c4+ ♔h7 50 ♕d4 ♖e7!, followed by ...f6-f5 (but not 50...f5 51 ♕d7+! ♕xd7 52 ♘f6+).

Game 2
Uhlmann-Priehoda
Wattens 1995

1 c4 ♘f6 2 ♘c3 e6 3 ♘f3 c5 4 g3 b6 5 ♗g2 ♗b7 6 d4 cxd4 7 ♕xd4 d6 8 0-0 a6 9 e4

White dispenses with the tricky ♗c1-g5 or b2-b3 and ♗c1-a3 ideas (which are covered in Games 3-5), and settles for straightforward development along Open Sicilian lines.

For 9 ♖d1 ♗e7 10 b3 ♘bd7 11 e4 (which can sometimes transpose) see Game 4.

9...♘bd7 10 ♕e3 ♗e7 11 ♘d4 ♕c7 12 b3 0-0 13 ♗b2

This was the traditional main line (in the 1970s) of the Hedgehog, but in fact has become almost the personal property of GM Wolfgang Uhlmann, who played it for over two decades.

13...♖fe8

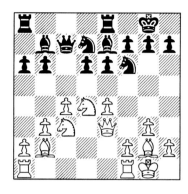

14 ♖fe1

The modern treatment of this line is to keep Black's pawn breaks under close scrutiny, while engaging in intricate manoeuvring. One of White's key ideas is to be ready to answer ...d7-d5 with e4-e5. Alternatively:

a) 14 ♖ac1 was well met by 14...♖ad8 15 ♖fe1 ♕b8 16 ♖e2 ♗f8 17 h3 g6 18 ♖ce1 ♗g7 19 ♕d2 ♘c5 20 ♕c2 ♕a8 21 a4 ♖c8 22 ♘f3 ♖ed8 23 ♘d2 d5 in Karpov-Adams, Wijk aan Zee 1998, and Black is at least equal.

b) In the early days of the variation, White would often throw caution to the winds, sometimes winning with a crushing kingside attack, but other times being stung by the Hedgehog counter-attack. For example Uhlmann-Suba, Bucharest 1979 continued 14 ♔h1 ♗f8 15 f4 g6 16 ♖ae1 ♗g7 17 h3 ♖ad8 18 g4 e5 19 fxe5 ♖xe5 20 ♘de2 ♖de8 21 ♘g3 h6 22 ♕d2 ♖5e7 and White has only succeeded in burdening himself with a weak e-pawn and loose kingside.

14...♗f8 15 ♕d2

Alternatively:

a) 15 h3 was the move used by Uhlmann and others, before the German GM refined his plan and did without this move. A modern example: 15...♖ac8 16 ♖e2 ♕b8 17 ♖ae1 g6 18 ♕d2 ♗g7 19 ♔h2 ♘c5 20 ♖d1 ♕a8 21 ♕e1 ♖ed8 with a typical war of attrition in prospect, Kasimdzhanov-

Bunzmann, Yerevan 1999.

b) 15 ♖e2 ♖ad8 (Uhlmann points out that 15...d5 16 e5 ♘g4 17 ♕f4 ♘gxe5 18 cxd5 is better for White, which means that h2-h3 is not an essential precaution) 16 ♕d2 ♕b8 17 ♖d1 and now:

b1) 17...♕a8 18 ♕e1 ♕a7 19 ♔h1 ♗a8 20 f3 ♕c7 (20...h5!?) 21 g4 h6 22 ♕g3 g5, Uhlmann-Schneider, Debrecen 1988, and here Uhlmann suggests 23 ♖ed2 planning ♘d4-e2 and f3-f4.

b2) 17...g6 18 ♕e1 e5!? (18...♗g7) 19 ♘c2 b5 20 cxb5 axb5 21 ♘b4 ♘c5 22 ♗c1 ♗g7 23 ♗g5 ♗a8 24 ♘cd5, Uhlmann-Ftacnik, Debrecen 1989, and White is on top.

b3) 17...♗a8 18 ♕e1 g6 19 f3 ♗g7 20 ♔h1 ♘c5 (20...h5!?) is equal according to ECO, though Uhlmann-Zsinka, Frankfurt 1990 continued 21 ♗c1 ♘cd7 22 g4 ♖c8 23 ♗a3 d5? 24 exd5 exd5 25 g5, winning the d5-pawn.

15...♖ac8

This is the more natural square for the queen's rook in most lines of the Hedgehog, though in this position ...♖ad8 has been played more often.

16 ♖e2 ♕b8 17 ♖d1

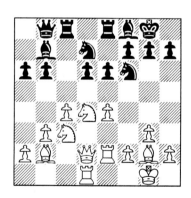

17...g6

Or 17...♘c5 18 ♗a1 ♕a8 19 f3 (this renders Black's last two moves rather ineffectual) 19...♖ed8 20 ♔h1 g6 21 ♕e3 ♗g7 22 ♖ed2 ♖e8 23 ♕f2 and White has a firm clamp on the centre, Uhlmann-Grünberg, Dresden 1985.

18 ♕e1 ♕a8

Or 18...♖ed8 19 f3 h5 20 ♔h1 ♗a8 21 h3 ♗g7 22 ♖ed2 ♗h6 23 ♖e2 ♗g7 24 ♖ed2 ♗h6 ½-½ Novikov-Brodsky, Koszalin 1999.

19 f3

One of the advantages of omitting an early h2-h3 (as seen in several Uhlmann games) is that White can bolster his centre with f2-f3, with a later g3-g4 in mind. In this game, however, Black comes up with a good reply which Uhlmann's earlier opponents had not tried.

19...h5! 20 ♔h1 ♕b8 21 h3

So White is prompted into h2-h3 after all, but now his kingside looks decidedly loose.

21...♗g7 22 ♘c2 ♗a8 23 ♘b4 ♘c5 24 ♖ed2 ♖ed8 25 ♘c2 ♗c6 26 ♘e3

White can no longer prevent ...b7-b5 unless he repeats moves with 26 ♘b4.

26...b5 27 b4 ♘cd7 28 a3 ♘b6 29 cxb5 axb5

Black's b6-knight is eyeing c4 and a4, which in turn keeps the White knights tied down.

30 ♕e2

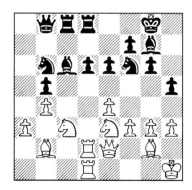

30...d5!?

Sometimes ...b7-b5 and ...d7-d5 breaks are like buses, you wait for hours and then two of them come along in quick succession!

31 e5 ♘e8

Of course not 31...♕xe5 32 ♘cxd5.

32 f4 ♘c7 33 g4

Stopping any ideas of ...f7-f6.

33...hxg4 34 ♕xg4 ♘e8 35 ♘e2 ♘c4

This is a vital resource, otherwise White would get a firm blockade with ♘e2-d4.

36 ♘xc4 dxc4 37 ♗xc6 ♖xd2 38 ♖xd2 ♖xc6 39 ♘c3 ♖c8 40 ♕d1

40 ♘e4 can be answered by 40...♖d8.

40...♕b7+ 41 ♔h2 ♗h6 42 ♖d4 ♘g7 43 ♗c1 ♘f5 44 ♖d8+

White has enough to counter the threats to his weak kingside pawns.

44...♖xd8 45 ♕xd8+ ♔g7 46 ♕d1 ♘h4 47 ♕e2 ♘f3+

Settling for the draw by repetition. It is very risky to go for 47...♕f3 48 ♕xf3 ♘xf3+ 49 ♔g3 ♘xe5 50 ♘xb5.

48 ♔g3 ♘d4 49 ♕d1 ♘f5+ 50 ♔h2 ♘h4 51 ♕e2 ♘f3+ 52 ♔g3 ½-½

Game 3
Karpov-Csom
Bad Lauterberg 1977

1 c4 ♘f6 2 ♘c3 c5 3 ♘f3 e6 4 g3 b6 5 ♗g2 ♗b7 6 0-0 d6 7 b3

A sneaky move order. White waits to see what Black does next, before committing to whether he will recapture on d4 with the queen or knight.

7...♗e7

7...♘bd7 is an inferior move order. 8 ♗b2 ♗e7 9 d4 and here:

a) 9...cxd4 10 ♘xd4 ♗xg2 11 ♔xg2 ♕c7 12 e3 a6 13 f4 is an important idea to know, if you have not seen it before:

a1) 13...0-0 14 ♕f3 (the immediate 14 f5!? was suggested by Yudasin) 14...♖ac8 15 g4 ♘c5 16 g5 ♘fd7 17 ♖ad1 ♖fe8 18 h4 and White is slightly better due to his huge space advantage, Andersson-I.Sokolov, Bilbao 1987.

a2) 13...g6, slowing White's kingside advance and providing an outpost on h5 for the f6-knight, is perhaps Black's best try: 14 ♕f3 ♖c8 15 g4 (perhaps 15 ♖ad1; or 15 e4 0-0 16 ♖ae1) 15...0-0 16 g5 ♘h5 17 ♖ad1 ♘c5 18 ♘e4 ♕b7 with equal chances, Sorokin-Yudasin, USSR Championship 1991.

b) 9...0-0 10 d5 exd5 11 ♘h4 g6 12 cxd5 ♘e8 13 f4 ♘c7?! (White has compensation for the pawn after 13...♗xh4 14 gxh4 ♕xh4 15 e4, according to Kramnik) 14 e4 b5 15 e5 f5 16 a4 b4 17 ♘b5 ♘xb5 18 axb5 ♕b6 19 ♖e1 ♕xb5 20 ♗f1 ♕b6 21 ♗c4 and White has a dominating centre, Kramnik-Topalov, Amsterdam 1996.

8 d4 cxd4 9 ♕xd4

After 9 ♘xd4 ♗xg2 10 ♔xg2 Black has not yet committed his b8-knight, so the c6-square is not as weak as in the line covered in the previous note.

9...a6

Once again 9...♘bd7 is too committal: 10 ♖d1 a6 11 ♘g5 ♗xg2 12 ♔xg2 ♕c7 13 ♘ge4 ♘xe4 14 ♘xe4 0-0 15 ♗a3 ♕c6 16 f3 ♘c5 17 ♗b2 f6 18 ♘f2 and Black came to regret his additional weakness on e6, Andersson-Szmetan, Pinamar 2001.

A quite different idea is 9...0-0 10 ♗a3 ♘a6 11 ♖fd1 ♘c5, when White can initiate a forcing sequence with 12 b4 ♘ce4 13 ♘xe4 ♗xe4 14 b5 ♕c8 15 ♗xd6 ♖d8 16 c5 bxc5 17 ♕e5 ♗xd6 18 ♖xd6 ♕b7! 19 a4 c4 20 ♖c1 ♗d5 21 ♘e1 ♖xd6 22 ♕xd6 ♕b6! 23 ♕xb6 axb6 24 ♖xc4 with a level ending, Yermolinsky-Adams, Elista Olympiad 1998.

10 ♗a3

This is the only way to try and take specific advantage of this move order.

10...0-0

Or 10...♘c6 (this is probably the best, rather than sticking to the ...♘b8-d7 development scheme at all costs) and here:

a) 11 ♕d2 ♕c7 12 ♖ac1 ♘a7 13 ♖fd1 ♖d8 14 ♕e3 0-0 15 ♗b2 ♖fe8 16 h3 h6 17 g4 ♘c8 18 ♔h1 ♕c5 (perhaps 18...♗f8 and, in some circumstances, Black can re-route his knight via ...♘c8-e7-g6 (or -f5), depend-

ing on White's actions) 19 ♘d4 ♗xg2+ 20 ♔xg2 ♕c7 21 f4 ♕b7+ 22 ♕f3 ♕xf3+ 23 ♔xf3 (Petursson-S.Hansen, Copenhagen 1997) and White has a slight edge, though nothing that Black should not be able to handle.

b) 11 ♕f4 with the split:

b1) 11...d5 12 ♗xe7 ♘xe7 13 ♘e5 0-0 14 ♖fd1 ♕b8 15 cxd5 ♘exd5 16 ♘xd5 exd5 17 ♘d3 ♖e8 18 e3 and White has a sizeable advantage thanks to play against the isolated queen's pawn (IQP), Salov-M.Gurevich, Biel 1993.

b2) 11...♕c7 12 ♖fd1 ♖d8 13 ♖ac1 (13 ♕e3 transposes to Petursson-S.Hansen above) 13...♘a7 14 ♘g5 ♗xg2 15 ♔xg2 0-0 16 ♘ge4 ♘e8 17 f3 ♕b8 18 ♗b2 ♕b7 19 ♘f2 b5 and Black is doing fine, Szuhanek-Marin, Romanian Team Championship 1995.

11 ♖fd1 ♘e8 12 ♗b2

Marin suggests 12 ♘e4!? to force further concessions from Black, such as 12...♘c6 13 ♕e3.

12...♘d7 13 e4 ♘c5 14 ♕e3 ♕b8

14...♕c7 is the more modern queen placement.

15 ♘d4 ♘f6 16 h3 ♖c8 17 g4

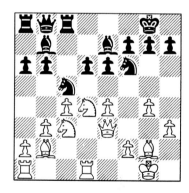

ECO assesses this position as much better for White, but although Black's major piece arrangement is somewhat eccentric, this looks like a fairly normal Hedgehog position for Black.

17...h6 18 f4 ♘h7

It is vital that Black takes measures to avoid being overrun by the white kingside pawns. His idea is to set up a dark-square blockade.

19 ♕f2 ♖a7

Black's rook plays an important defensive role on the 2nd rank.

20 ♖d2 ♗a8 21 ♖e1 ♗f6 22 h4 g5

Implementing the idea started on move 17 and 18.

23 hxg5 hxg5 24 fxg5?!

24 f5 gives a big advantage to White according to Marin. However Black seems fine, e.g. 24...♖e7 25 b4 ♘d7.

24...♗xg5 25 ♖dd1 ♘d7 26 ♖d3 ♘e5 27 ♖h3 ♖e8 28 ♘ce2 ♖c7 29 a4 ♕d8

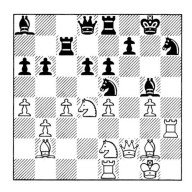

This kind of chaotic position often results from the Hedgehog when White attempts a kingside assault. After some quiet manoeuvring the position explodes, and then anything can happen!

30 ♕g3 ♘g6 31 ♕h2 f6 32 ♖d1 ♖g7

Black has the kingside solidly defended, so White turns his attentions to the d6-pawn. However, his own central pawn falls in the process, and soon the white king becomes exposed.

33 ♘f3 ♗xe4 34 ♖xd6 ♕c7 35 ♗a3 ♗e3+ 36 ♔f1 ♗c5 37 ♗xc5 ♕xc5 38 ♖d4 ♗xf3 39 ♖xf3 ♘e5 40 ♖h3 ♘xg4 41 ♕d6 ♕f5+ 42 ♖f3 ♕b1+ 43 ♖d1 ♕e4

Things have gone badly awry for White. In those days, the reigning World Champion was almost invincible with the White pieces; this game was almost a huge upset.

44 ♖g3 ♘e3+ 45 ♔g1 ♘xg2 46 ♖xg7+ ♔xg7 47 ♘g3 ♕a8 48 ♕c7+ ♔h8

48...♔g6 is also winning for Black.

49 ♖d7

49...♘f8??

49...♘g5 leaves White with nowhere to go.

50 ♘f5! 1-0

Tragic. Black cannot defend against both ♕c7-h2+ and ♖d7-h7+.

Game 4
Zifroni-Kaspi
Tel Aviv 1998

1 ♘f3 ♘f6 2 c4 b6 3 g3 ♗b7 4 ♗g2 c5 5 0-0 e6 6 ♘c3 ♗e7 7 d4 cxd4 8 ♕xd4 d6 9 b3

Another anti-Hedgehog try is 9 ♖d1 a6 10 ♘g5 ♗xg2 11 ♔xg2 0-0 (11...♘c6 is also adequate) 12 ♘ce4 ♖a7, for example:

a) 13 ♘xf6+ ♗xf6 14 ♕g4 ♗e7 (14...♖d7 is preferable and should equalise) 15 h4 ♘d7 16 b3 ♘f6 17 ♕f3 with an edge for White, Adorjan-Lau, Plovdiv 1983.

b) 13 ♕d3 ♘xe4 14 ♘xe4 ♖d7 and now:

b1) 15 ♘c3 ♕c8 16 ♗d2 ♘c6 17 ♕e4 ♘e5 18 b3 ♖e8 19 ♖ac1 f5!? 20 ♕b1 ♕b7+ 21 ♔g1 ♗f6 and Black later launched his g-

and h-pawns forward to attack the white king, Agdestein-Adams, Slough 1997.

b2) 15 ♗f4 ♕c8 16 ♖ac1 ♖fd8 17 ♕f3 ♕b7 18 ♖d2 ♘c6, and Black has everything covered, Csom-Ermenkov, Plovdiv 1983.

9...♘bd7 10 ♖d1 a6 11 e4

White's idea is to strike early, putting pressure on the d6-pawn with ♗c1-a3, and often playing e4-e5, usually with a queen exchange to follow. In the resulting ending, White hopes that his small lead in development, and Black's vulnerable queenside pawns, will enable him to establish a more tangible endgame edge.

11...♕c7

Or:

a) Black needs to avoid 11...0-0, which gives White a superior endgame after 12 ♗a3 ♘c5 13 e5 dxe5 14 ♕xd8 ♖fxd8 15 ♘xe5 ♗xg2 16 ♔xg2 ♗f8 (16...♖dc8 17 ♘a4!) 17 ♗xc5 ♗xc5 18 ♘a4 ♖db8 19 ♘c6 ♖b7 20 ♘xc5 bxc5 21 ♖d3 g5 22 ♔f3 ♖b6 23 ♘e5 – White has a nagging advantage, I.Ivanov-M.Gurevich, Philadelphia 1989.

Because of this, Black realised he should move his queen off the d-file and to defend the b7-bishop. 11...♕c7 is the most natural move, as played in the main game.

b) After Black experienced some awkward moments with 11...♕c7, 11...♕b8 was tried. Although this has scored somewhat better in practice, the nature of the game is similar: Black should equalise, but is in danger of slipping into a slightly worse endgame if he does not play accurately: 11...♕b8 12 ♗a3 ♘c5 13 e5 dxe5 14 ♕xe5 ♘cd7 (if Black is determined to keep the queens on, then 14...♕a7 is playable) 15 ♕xb8+ ♖xb8 16 ♗c1 (16 ♗xe7 ♔xe7 relieves the pressure) 16...♖c8 17 ♗b2 and now:

b1) 17...♖c7 18 ♘d4 ♗xg2 19 ♔xg2 ♘c5 20 ♖ac1 0-0 21 ♘f3 ♘cd7 22 ♘e2 ♖fc8 23 ♘e5 is slightly better for White, Nogueiras-Browne, Taxco 1985.

b2) 17...♖g8 18 ♘e2 (I don't find this ex-

ample, quoted by ECO, entirely convincing; maybe 18 h4!?) 18...g5 19 ♘e5 ♗xg2 20 ♔xg2 ♘xe5 21 ♗xe5 ♘d7 22 ♗b2 ♘c5 with equality, Pelts-Browne, New York 1986.

c) 11...♕c8 is the move to play if Black wants to maintain a complex middlegame position and play for a win. This move was invented by a process of elimination! A fairly normal Hedgehog position is reached, White has an extra tempo, but otherwise his set-up is rather innocuous: 12 ♗b2 (the justification for 11..♕c8 is that White cannot go for 12 ♗a3 ♘c5 13 e5 because of 13...♗xf3 14 ♗xf3 dxe5 15 ♕e3 – 15 ♕xe5 ♘cd7 – 15...♖b8 etc.) 12...0-0 13 ♕e3 ♖e8 14 ♘d4 ♗f8 15 h3 ♕c7 16 ♖e1 (note that we have now transposed into the Uhlmann variation {see Game 2} with both sides having lost a tempo, i.e. ...♕c8-c7 and ♖f1-d1-e1). 16...g6 17 ♖ad1 ♖ad8 18 ♕d2 ♗g7 19 ♘c2 ♘c5 20 ♗a1 h5 21 ♘b4 ♕c8 22 ♕f4 ♕a8 23 ♘d3 ♘fd7 24 ♘xc5 ½-½ Kramnik-Shirov, Dos Hermanas 1997.

12 ♗a3 ♘c5 13 e5 dxe5 14 ♕xe5 ♖c8

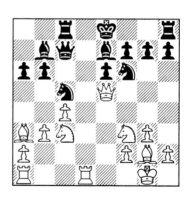

15 ♗c1

This is a refinement over the earlier move 15 ♕xc7 ♖xc7 16 ♗c1 ♘fe4 17 ♗f4 ♖c8 18 ♘xe4 ♗xe4, when White has tried:

a) 19 ♖d2 ♗c6 20 ♖ad1 f6 21 ♗e3 ♔f7 22 ♘e1 ♖he8 23 ♗xc6 ♖xc6 24 f3 ♖ec8 25 ♔f1 ♔e8 with equality, Nogueiras-Short, Montpelier 1985.

b) 19 ♗d6 ♗f6 20 ♘e5 and here:

b1) 20...♗xg2 21 ♔xg2 ♗xe5 22 ♗xe5 f6 23 ♗d6 gave White unpleasant pressure, Ribli-Ambroz, Baile Herculane 1982.

b2) 20...♘b7! 21 f4 ♘xd6 (21...♗xg2 22 ♔xg2 g5) 22 ♖xd6 ♗e7 (Black steers a course to equality with precise moves exploiting the tactical features of the position) 23 ♖dd1 ♗xg2 24 ♔xg2 f6 25 ♘f3 ♗c5 26 ♖d3 ♖d8 27 ♖ad1 ½-½ Andersson-Browne, Naestved 1985.

15...♕xe5 16 ♘xe5 ♗xg2 17 ♔xg2 ♘fe4?!

a) 17...♘cd7 18 ♘xd7 ♘xd7 is equal according to Cvetkovic. After Bagirov's 19 ♘e4 ♘c6 20 ♗f4 f6, Black is not out of the woods yet. I believe White is slightly better.

b) 17...0-0 is recommended by Stohl: 18 ♗e3 ♖fd8 19 ♖xd8+ ♗xd8 20 ♖d1 ♗c7, Schirm-Bethe, Bargteheide 1988, and now 21 f4 would maintain the bind.

18 ♘xe4 ♘xe4 19 ♗e3

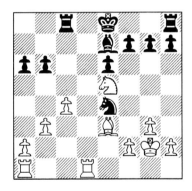

19...♘c5

19...♗f6 is answered by 20 f4.

20 ♖ac1 f6 21 ♘d3 ♔f7 22 ♘xc5 bxc5

22...♗xc5 23 ♖d7+ ♔g6 24 ♗xc5 ♖xc5 25 ♖d6 wins a pawn.

23 ♖d7

This is the problem with this whole line (with 11...♕c7 or 11...♕b8) – without doing anything spectacular, White often gets a nagging endgame edge which he can try and exploit with little risk of losing.

23...♖hd8 24 ♖a7 ♖c6 25 ♖c2 e5 26 ♖d2

Trading Black's only active piece.

26...♖xd2 27 ♗xd2 ♔e6 28 f4 exf4 29 ♗xf4 h5 30 ♔f2 g6 31 ♔e2 ♗d8 32 ♔d3 g5 33 ♗e3 ♗c7 34 a3 ♔f5 35 b4 cxb4 36 axb4 ♔g4 37 ♗d4 ♗e5 38 c5 ♔h3 39 ♗xe5 fxe5 40 ♔e4 ♔xh2 41 ♔d5 ♖c8 42 ♖xa6 ♖d8+ 43 ♖d6 ♖e8 44 ♔e4?

44 c6! is clear cut, e.g. 44...e4 45 c7 ♖c8 46 ♔c6 ♔xg3 47 b5 e3 48 b6 e2 49 ♖e6 winning.

44...♖b8 45 ♖b6 ♖c8! 46 ♖h6 h4 47 gxh4 g4 48 ♔xe5 ♖b8 49 c6 ♖xb4 50 c7 ♖c4 51 ♔d6 g3 52 ♖g6 g2 53 h5 ♖c3 54 h6 ♖d3+ 55 ♔c6 ♖c3+ 56 ♔d6 ♖d3+ 57 ♔c6 ♖c3+ 58 ♔b6??

58 ♔d6 or 58 ♔b7 would still win. Now Black queens with check.

58...♖g3! 59 ♖xg3 ♔xg3 60 c8♕ g1♕+ 61 ♕c5 ♕b1+ 62 ♕b5 ♕g6+ 63 ♕c6 ♕b1+ 64 ♔a7 ♕h7+ 65 ♔a6 ♔g4 ½-½

1 ♘f3 ♘f6 2 c4 b6 3 g3 c5 4 ♗g2 ♗b7 5 0-0 e6 6 ♘c3 a6 7 d4 cxd4 8 ♕xd4 d6 9 ♗g5

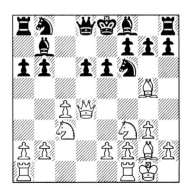

This is a dangerous line, for which Black

needs to be well prepared.

9...♗e7

The advantage of the 6...a6 move order is that Black can now choose 9...♘bd7.

a) 10 ♘d2 ♗xg2 11 ♔xg2 ♗e7 (a big improvement over 11...♖c8?! 12 ♘ce4 ♖c6 13 b4! b5 14 a4 e5 15 ♗xf6 gxf6 16 ♕d5 ♘b8 17 axb5 axb5 18 ♖a7 and Black is being crushed, Pogorelov-Suba, Las Palmas 1994) 12 ♘de4 ♕c7 13 ♖fd1 0-0 (the point – Black does not need to worry about 14 ♘xd6, as after 14...♖ad8 the white queen is embarrassed) 14 ♖ac1 ♖fd8 15 ♔g1 h6 16 ♘xf6+ ♘xf6 17 ♗e3 ♖ab8 18 b3 ½-½ Illescas-Suba, Cordoba 1995.

b) 10 ♖fd1 ♗e7 and now:

b1) An important alternative is 11 ♕d2 which has some sting, though Black should be okay if he is careful: 11...0-0 (11...♕c7?! 12 ♗f4 forces 12...e5, when after 13 ♗g5 White has control of d5) 12 ♗f4 ♘e8 13 ♖ac1 ♕c7 with a further split:

b11) 14 e4 ♖d8 15 ♕e2 ♘ef6 16 ♘d2 ♖fe8 17 h3 ♕b8 18 b4 ♕a8 19 ♘b3 d5! (Bönsch-Ftacnik, Trnava 1988) with complications in which Black should be no worse.

b12) 14 b3 ♖d8 and now:

b121) 15 h4!? was tried in Gritsak-Ftacnik, Kozalin 1999: 15...♘e5 16 ♕c2 ♘xf3+ 17 ♗xf3 ♗xf3 18 exf3 h6 19 ♖d3 ♘f6 20 ♖cd1 b5 and Black was able to hold the balance.

b122) After 15 ♘e1 ♗xg2 16 ♘xg2 ♕b7 17 a4 ♘c5 18 ♕c2 a5 19 ♗e3 f5 20 ♗xc5 bxc5 21 e4 ♗g5 22 ♖b1 f4 Black has the initiative, while his d-pawn is in no danger, Ftacnik-Adianto, San Francisco 1991.

b2) 11 ♘d2 ♗xg2 12 ♔xg2 0-0 13 ♘de4 ♕c7 transposes to line 'a'.

b3) 11 ♗xf6 ♘xf6 12 ♘a4 ♖b8 13 c5 initiates complications, but Black should be fine if he keeps a clear head: 13...dxc5 14 ♕e5 ♗d5 15 e4 ♘xe4 16 ♕xg7 ♗f6 17 ♕h6 ♕e7 (or 17...b5 18 ♘e1 ♘xf2 – Ca.Hansen) 18 ♖ac1 c4! 19 ♕e3, Hergott-

Suba, Sitges 1993, and now Black should play 19...♘c5 (or 19...b5 20 ♘b6 ♕c5).

10 ♗xf6

This move disrupts the co-ordination between Black's pieces and together with further upcoming simplifications, deprives the Hedgehog of much of its dynamism. Black is theoretically okay, but this kind of position is not why many people play this line as Black. In my opinion, this is a strong argument in favour of the 6...a6 move order.

10...♗xf6

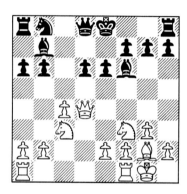

11 ♕d3

11 ♕f4 is an alternative, when:

a) 11...♗xf3 12 exf3!? (instead of the regular 12 ♕xf3 ♖a7 13 ♖fd1 0-0 14 ♖ac1 ♘d7 with a balanced position) 12...♖a7 13 ♖fd1 ♗e7 (Stohl suggests 13...♖d7 14 ♕e3 0-0) 14 ♕d4 0-0 15 f4 g6 16 h4 (the 'crab formation' – compare with Karpov-Topalov, Game 23) 16...♘d7 17 ♖ac1 ♕b8 18 ♘e4 ♖d8 19 h5 and White has a strong attack, Fominyh-Csom, Rimavska Sobota 1991.

b) 11...0-0 12 ♖fd1 ♗e7 13 ♘e4 ♗xe4 14 ♕xe4 ♖a7 15 ♘d4 ♖c7 16 ♖ac1 ♕c8 is another line which is theoretically equal, but easier to play for White, and White scores well in practice: 17 ♖c2 ♗f6 (Black cannot play 17...♖xc4 because of 18 ♘f5) 18 b3 ♖d8 19 ♖dc1 ♖c5 20 e3, Savchenko-Plachetka, Cappelle la Grande 1999. White has good chances of getting a queenside pawn roller going, while Black is rather passively placed.

11...♖a7

a) 11...0-0?! is answered by 12 ♘g5 ♗xg5 13 ♗xb7 when White has the preferable set of minor pieces.

b) 11...♕c7 is safest, e.g. 12 ♖ad1 ♗e7 13 ♘d4 ♗xg2 14 ♔xg2 ♘c6 15 f4 0-0 16 ♖f3 (attempting to save a tempo over 16 ♘xc6 ♕xc6+ 17 ♖f3, which allows 17...b5) 16...♘xd4 17 ♕xd4 ♗f6! 18 ♕xd6 ♕xc4 19 b3 ♕c8 20 ♘e4 ♖d8 21 ♘xf6+ gxf6 22 ♕xd8+ ♕xd8 23 ♖xd8+ ♖xd8 with a level rook endgame, Hergott-Browne, Linares 1994.

12 ♖ad1 ♗e7 13 ♘d4 ♗xg2 14 ♔xg2 ♕c8 15 f4 g6

Or 15...♘c6 (15...♘d7 is similar) and then:

a) 16 f5 ♘e5 17 ♕e4 0-0 18 fxe6 fxe6 19 ♖xf8+ ♗xf8 20 ♘f3 ♘xc4 21 b3 ♘e5 22 ♘xe5 dxe5 23 ♕xe5 was slightly better for White, Dorfman-Psakhis, Lvov 1984.

b) 16 ♖f3 (again this time saving idea) 16...0-0 17 ♘xc6 ♕xc6 18 f5 ♖c7 19 b3 ♖b7 20 a4 ♖bb8 21 ♕e3 and White has uncomfortable pressure, Suba-Nicholson, Malaga 2001.

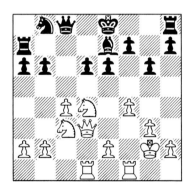

16 f5!?

A true 'Tal-like sacrifice' from the man himself! 16 b3 is a more 'normal' move: 16...0-0 17 h4 b5 (White is only slightly better after 17...♖c7) 18 cxb5 ♖c7 19 ♖f3 e5 20

♘d5 ♕b7 21 b6 and White is close to having a winning position, Greenfeld-Pasman, Beersheba 1984.

16...gxf5 17 e4

White is trying to blast open as many lines as possible before Black gets organised.

17...fxe4 18 ♘xe4 f5!?

Short suggests 18...♖c7 19 ♖de1 ♕b7 20 ♔h3 and assesses this wild position as slightly better for Black. On the other hand, 18...0-0 19 ♘f6+ ♗xf6 20 ♖xf6 is very dangerous.

19 ♘g5

In an earlier game, Tal had tried 19 ♘c3 ♘c6 20 ♕e2 ♘xd4 21 ♕h5+ ♔d7 22 ♖xd4 ♕c5 23 ♖fd1 ♖c7 and a draw was agreed here in Tal-Gavrikov, Tallinn 1985. It's not clear whether or not White has sufficient compensation, but sitting opposite Tal with your king in the middle of the board must have been an unnerving experience!

Other lines don't work for White, for example 19 ♕e2 fxe4 20 ♕h5+ ♔d7 21 ♘xe6 ♕xc4; 19 ♘xf5 exf5 20 ♖xf5 ♕c6 21 ♕f3 ♖f8; 19 ♖xf5 exf5 20 ♘xf5 ♕c6.

19...♗xg5 20 ♘xe6 ♕xe6

Black needs to trade in his queen for assorted material, as after 20...♗e7 21 ♕xf5 Black's king is in big trouble.

21 ♖de1 ♕xe1 22 ♖xe1+ ♖e7 23 ♕d4!

23 ♖xe7+ ♔xe7 24 ♕xf5 ♗f6 25 ♕e4+ ♗e5 doesn't lead anywhere.

23...♖g8!

The best way of safeguarding the h8-rook. Alternatives are:

a) 23...0-0 24 ♖xe7 ♗xe7 25 ♕xb6 ♘d7 26 ♕b7 ♖d8 27 b4 is good for White according to Short.

b) Not 23...♖f8 24 ♖xe7+ and if 24...♔xe7 25 ♕g7+ wins the bishop.

24 ♖xe7+ ♔xe7 25 ♕xb6 ♘d7! 26 ♕xa6 ♖b8 27 b3 ♗e3

Black manages to hold the White pawns in check by piece power.

28 ♕c6

28 ♕a5 is answered by 28...♘e5.

28...♘e5 29 ♕c7+

White has to be careful not to try too hard, e.g. Short gives 29 ♕d5 ♗c5 30 ♕d2 ♘g4 31 ♕b2 ♔f7 32 a3 ♘e3+ 33 ♔h3 ♖g8, with mating threats such as ...♖g8-g6-h6.

29...♘d7 30 ♕c6 ♘e5 ½-½

It's a draw by repetition.

Game 6
Krivoshey-Shipov
Yalta 1996

1 ♘f3 ♘f6 2 c4 c5 3 ♘c3 e6 4 g3 b6 5 ♗g2 ♗b7 6 0-0 ♗e7 7 ♖e1

This is the precursor to the modern main line of the Hedgehog. Play is similar in style to an Open Sicilian, and becomes very sharp and concrete.

7...d6 8 e4 a6 9 d4 cxd4 10 ♘xd4

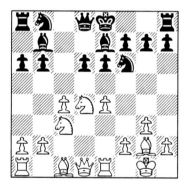

10...♕c7

Black needs to take some precautions to avoid the simple trap 10...0-0? 11 e5!. Note that this tactical possibility (which sometimes occurs in more sophisticated forms!) is made more potent by the rook moving from f1 to e1, so that ...♗b7xg2 does not attack anything.

11 ♗e3

Or 11 b3 0-0 12 ♗b2 and now:

a) 12...♖e8 13 ♖c1 ♘bd7 14 ♘d5! is a good version of the thematic sacrifice, e.g. 14...exd5 15 cxd5 ♕d8 16 ♘c6 ♗xc6 17 dxc6 ♘c5 18 c7 ♕c8 19 e5 dxe5 20 ♗xa8 ♕xa8 21 ♗xe5 ♖c8 (Eingorn-Hobuss, Travemunde 1996), and now Eingorn gives 22 ♗xf6 ♗xf6 23 ♕d6 as very good for White.

b) 12...♘bd7 13 ♖c1 ♖ac8 14 h3 ♖fe8 15 ♔h2 ♕b8 16 f4 ♗f8 17 ♘c2 g6 18 ♕e2 h5 19 ♖cd1 ♖cd8 20 ♕f2 ♗g7 with balanced chances, Stefansson-Hjartarson, Icelandic Team Championship 1997.

11...0-0

Or 11...♘bd7 12 f4 ♖c8 13 ♖c1 0-0 14 f5 (14 g4 is also playable) 14...e5 15 ♘b3 ♕d8 16 ♕e2 h5 17 ♘d5 ♘xd5 18 cxd5 h4 19 ♖xc8 ♗xc8 20 ♘d2 hxg3 21 hxg3 and now:

a) 21...♗g5 22 ♗xg5 ♕xg5 23 ♕e3 gave White a big plus in Akopian-Shirov, Madrid 1997.

b) Black should play 21...♘f6 with an unclear outcome, according to Shirov.

12 ♖c1 ♘bd7 13 f4

Now Black has to choose how to arrange his rooks. There are three main options:

13...♖fe8

Alternatively:

a) 13...♖ac8 transposes to Akopian-Shirov from above.

b) 13...♖fc8 is an unfortunate choice, as it allows another classic ♘d5 sacrifice: 14 g4 ♘f8 15 g5 ♘6d7 16 ♘d5! exd5 17 ♘f5! ♖e8 (17...♕d8 18 exd5) 18 cxd5 ♕b8? (18...♕d8 19 e5 is still strong for White according to Zhu Chen) 19 ♗d4 f6 20 ♕g4 ♘e5 21 fxe5 fxe5 22 ♗e3 ♗d8 23 ♖f1 ♗c8 24 ♕h5 1-0 Zhu Chen-Bischoff, Pulvermuehle 2000.

c) 13...h5!? is an intriguing possibility. In order to achieve g3-g4, White must now play h2-h3 and exchange a pair of pawns. This leaves his kingside exposed as well as Black's: 14 h3 ♖fe8 15 g4 hxg4 16 hxg4 ♘c5 17 ♗f2 d5! 18 e5 ♘fe4 19 ♗e3 dxc4 20 ♘xe4 ♘xe4 21 ♕c2 ♘c5 22 ♕xc4, M.Gurevich-Hoffmann, Dutch League 2000, and now 22...♖ac8 23 ♕e2 ♕d7 is equal according to Gurevich.

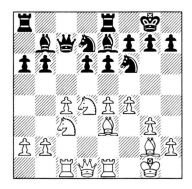

14 g4

a) 14 ♘d5 exd5 15 cxd5 ♕b8 (other possibilities are 15...♘c5 16 b4 ♕d7; or 15...♕d8) 16 ♘c6 ♗xc6 17 dxc6 ♘c5 18 c7 ♕xc7 19 e5 dxe5 20 ♗xa8 ♖xa8 21 b4 exf4 22 ♗xf4 was Ftacnik-Browne, San Francisco 1991, and now Ftacnik gives 22...♕b7 23 bxc5 ♗xc5+ 24 ♗e3 ♗b4 25 ♖e2 b5 26 ♕d4 with an approximately equal position.

b) 14 f5 can be answered by 14...♗d8!, e.g. 15 fxe6 fxe6 16 ♗h3 ♘f8 17 ♗f2 ♘6d7 18 ♕h5?! g6 19 ♕e2 ♘e5, Arsovic-Genov, Belgrade 1994, and Black is in great shape.

c) 14 ♗f2 ♗f8 (14...h6 is also playable) 15 ♕e2 h5!? 16 h3 g6 17 e5 ♗xg2 18 ♔xg2 ♘h7 19 ♘f3 ♖ac8 20 b3 dxe5 21 fxe5 ♖ed8 with good play for Black, Gelfand-Ljubojevic, Belgrade 1997.

14...♘c5

This is currently looking better than the alternatives:

a) 14...h6 15 g5 hxg5 16 fxg5 ♘h7 17 g6 ♘hf8 18 gxf7+ ♔xf7 19 ♘d5! (that move again!) 19...exd5 20 cxd5 ♕d8 21 ♘e6 and White has a huge attack, Pogorelov-Rodriguez Lopez, Mondariz Balneario 1999.

b) 14...g6 15 g5 ♘h5 16 f5 exf5 17 ♘xf5 ♗f8 18 ♘d5 ♕d8 19 ♖c3 ♘c5 20 ♗d2 ♘e6 21 ♕g4 and White is in command, Damljanovic-Annageldyev, Istanbul Olympiad 2000.

15 ♗f2 g6

15...e5 is, for some reason, given by ECO as leading to equality. After 16 ♘f5 ♕d8 17 ♘xe7+ ♕xe7 18 f5 (Yermolinsky-Frias, London 1994) White is slightly better – he has control of d5, and play on both wings.

16 b4 ♖ad8 17 ♕f3!

This is an improvement over 17 ♕e2 ♘cd7 18 ♗f3, Sarno-Shipov, Cappelle la Grande 1995, and now Shipov recommends 18...♖c8 19 g5 ♘h5 20 ♗xh5 gxh5 with an unclear position.

17 g5 ♘h5 18 ♕f3 is also possible.

17...♘cxe4

On 17...♘cd7 Shipov gives 18 ♘d5 exd5 19 cxd5 ♕b8 20 ♘c6 ♕a8 21 g5 ♘h5 22 ♘xd8 ♗xd8 23 ♗h3 ♘f8 24 ♗g4 ♘g7 25 a4 as being in White's favour. All four of Black's minor pieces are boxed in.

18 ♘xe4 ♘xe4 19 ♖xe4 ♗xe4 20 ♕xe4 d5 21 ♘xe6?

White would have been better after 21 ♕e1 ♕xf4 22 ♘c6 ♗g5 23 ♖c2 ♖d6 24 cxd5 ♕xg4 25 h3, according to Shipov.

21...♖c8

Black simply wins a piece, leaving him the exchange up for a pawn.

22 ♕e1 ♕xe6 23 ♕xe6 fxe6 24 ♗xb6 ♖b8 25 c5 ♗d8 26 ♗xd8 ♖exd8 27 a3 a5

Black is clearly better; a technical task lies ahead.

28 c6 ♖dc8 29 bxa5 ♖b5 30 a6 ♖a5 31 ♗f1 ♔f7 32 ♖b1 ♖xc6 33 ♖b7+ ♔f6 34 ♖xh7 ♖xa3 35 a7 ♖c1 36 ♔f2 ♖c2+ 37 ♔g1 ♖ca2 38 ♗h3 g5 39 ♖h6+ ♔e7 40 fxg5 ♖xa7 41 ♖h7+ ♔f8 42 g6 ♖xh7 43 gxh7 ♔g7 44 g5 ♖a6 45 ♗f1 ♖a4 46 ♗h3 e5 47 ♗e6 ♔xh7 48 ♗xd5 ♔g6

Black has one pawn left, which is good enough.

49 ♔f2 ♔xg5 50 ♔e3 ♖h4 51 ♗c6 ♖xh2 52 ♗b7 ♔f6 53 ♗c6 ♖h3+ 54 ♔e4 ♖b3 55 ♗d7 ♔e7 56 ♗f5 ♔d6 57 ♗g6 ♖g3 58 ♗f7 ♖g7 59 ♗h5 ♖g1 60 ♗f7 ♖e1+ 61 ♔d3 ♔e7 62 ♔d2 ♖h1 63 ♗d5 ♖h3 0-1

followed by ...♕c7-b8 and possibly ...♕a8.

13...♗f8 14 f5

Striking at the potentially weak e6-point. Other moves:

a) 14 g4 deserves more attention: 14...♘fd7 (Black vacates the kingside and avoids creating any weaknesses) 15 g5 ♘c6 and now:

a1) 16 ♘xc6?! ♗xc6 17 b4 ♖ac8 18 ♕e2 ♕b8 19 ♕f2 ♗a8 20 ♘e2 b5 21 c5 dxc5 22 bxc5 ♖c7 leaves Black with the advantage, Schwartzman-Marin, Bucharest 1994.

a2) 16 ♘de2 (this is an improvement over the previous line) 16...♖ac8 17 ♘g3 ♕b8 18 h4 ♗a8 19 ♗f1 ♘a7 20 ♕e2 d5? (despite White's build up, Black should continue manoeuvring) 21 cxd5 exd5 22 ♕g4 and White is much better, Davies-Sowray, British League 2000.

b) 14 ♗f2 and now Black can finally play 14...♘bd7, which transposes into note 'c' to White's 14th move in Game 6.

14...h6!

Black has struggled with the alternatives:

a) 14...♘bd7 15 fxe6 fxe6 16 ♗h3 ♘c5 17 b4 e5 18 bxc5 exd4 19 cxb6 ♕xb6 20 ♗xd4 ♕d8 21 ♘d5 ♘xe4 22 ♗f5 turned into a rout: 22...♘g5 23 ♖xe8 ♕xe8 24 ♕g4 ♗xd5 25 cxd5 ♕a4 26 ♗e6+ 1-0 Gawehns-Wojtkiewicz, Bonn 1994.

b) 14...exf5?! 15 ♘d5 ♗xd5 16 cxd5 ♕b7 17 exf5 and White is much better, Vaganian-Bischoff, Walldorf 1998.

c) 14...♕e7 15 fxe6 fxe6 16 ♗h3 ♕f7 was Marin's original suggestion, but the further analysis 17 ♘f3 ♕c7 18 ♘g5 ♗c8 19 ♕b3 gives White the advantage according to Poluljahov.

15 g4 ♘bd7 16 g5

16 fxe6 fxe6 17 g5 hxg5 18 ♗xg5 ♘e5 with counterplay – Komarov.

16...hxg5 17 ♗xg5 ♘h7

Black could try 17...e5!?.

18 ♗h4 ♘e5 19 fxe6 fxe6 20 ♖f1 ♗c8 21 ♗h3 g6!

An improvement over 21...♕xc4 22 ♘d5

Game 7
Komarov-Del Rio Angelis
Italy 1999

1 ♘f3 e6 2 c4 ♘f6 3 ♘c3 c5 4 g3 b6 5 ♗g2 ♗b7 6 0-0 d6 7 ♖e1 a6 8 e4 ♗e7 9 d4 cxd4 10 ♘xd4 ♕c7 11 ♗e3 0-0 12 ♖c1 ♖e8

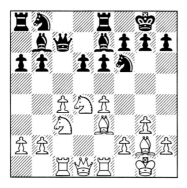

In the previous game, which featured 12...♘bd7, we saw that Black often got into some trouble when his f6-knight was threatened, for example by g3-g4-g5 or f2-f4 and e4-e5. Black's pieces are somewhat congested so these early pawn thrusts are awkward to meet. In addition, the ♘c3-d5 sacrifice is a constant possibility. This sac often works because after the standard forced sequence ...e6xd5, c4xd5, ...♕c7-b8, ♘d4-c6, ...♗b7xc6, d5xc6, the knight on d7 is attacked, which keeps White's initiative going. Because of all this, Marin and others developed the lines examined in this game, where Black makes a number of other developing moves before committing the b8-knight.

13 f4

This is the usual reaction. Also possible is 13 g4 ♗f8 14 g5 ♘fd7 15 b3 ♘c6 16 ♘cb5! ♕b8 17 ♘xc6 ♗xc6 18 ♘d4 ♗b7 19 h4 g6 20 ♕d2 ♘e5 21 ♕e2 (M.Gurevich-Cummings, British League 1998), and now Black should play 21...♕c7 22 ♖ed1 ♖ac8,

---

exd5? (22...♕d3 23 ♕xd3 ♘xd3 24 ♖xc8 and White is still on top) 23 ♖xc4 ♗xh3 24 ♖c7 ♗xf1 25 ♔xf1 dxe4 26 ♘f5 and White is winning, Poluljahov-Ulibin, St Petersburg 1998.

22 b3 ♕g7

Black has all the kingside squares adequately covered, and can use the second rank as a conduit for his major pieces.

23 ♕d2 ♕h6 24 ♕xh6 ♗xh6 25 ♖cd1

Both sides have chances here.

25...g5 26 ♗g3 g4 27 ♗g2 ♘g5 28 ♘de2 ♘gf3+?

Overenthusiastic. Black should keep his d6-pawn defended with 28...♗f8, when Komarov gives the interesting exchange sacrifice 29 ♖xf8+ (29 ♘f4) 29...♖xf8 30 ♖xd6 ♘gf3+ 31 ♔h1.

29 ♔h1 ♗f8 30 ♘g1

This simplification makes Black's kingside easier to get at.

30...♘xg1 31 ♖xg1 ♗b7 32 ♗xe5 dxe5 33 ♗h3 ♖ad8?! 34 ♖xg4+ ♗g7

34...♔f7 35 ♖f1+ ♔e7 was a tougher defence.

35 ♖dg1 ♖e7 36 ♖g6 ♖d6 37 ♘d5!

White gets his ♘d5 move in after all!

37...exd5 38 ♖xd6 dxc4 39 ♗f5 c3 40 ♖d8+ ♔f7 41 ♖c1 ♖c7 42 ♖d3 1-0

Game 8
Akopian-Gulko
Yerevan Olympiad 1996

---

1 ♘f3 ♘f6 2 g3 b6 3 ♗g2 ♗b7 4 0-0 e6 5 c4 ♗e7 6 ♘c3 0-0 7 ♖e1 d5 8 cxd5 ♘xd5

8...exd5 9 d4 transposes to a line of the Queen's Indian. One example: 9...♘a6 10 ♗f4 c5 11 dxc5 ♘xc5 (11...bxc5 12 ♘e5 ♘c7 13 ♘c4 ♘e6 14 ♗e5) 12 ♖c1 a6 13 a3 ♖e8 14 ♘d4 ♗d6 15 ♗xd6 ♕xd6 16 ♕d2 ♖ad8 17 ♖ed1 g6 18 ♕f4 ♕xf4 19 gxf4 and White is slightly better, Gelfand-Karpov, Vienna 1996.

9 e4 ♘xc3 10 bxc3 c5

Via the English move order this position would arise after 1 c4 c5 2 ♘f3 ♘f6 3 ♘c3 e6 4 g3 b6 5 ♗g2 ♗b7 6 0-0 ♗e7 7 ♖e1 d5 8 cxd5 ♘xd5 9 e4 ♘xc3 10 bxc3 0-0.

11 d4

An important decision point for Black.

11...♘d7

Or:

a) 11...♘c6 12 d5 ♘a5 13 ♗f4 exd5 14 exd5 and now:

a1) 14...♗f6 15 ♘e5 ♗xe5 16 ♗xe5 ♕d7 17 ♕h5 f6 18 ♗f4 g6 19 ♕h6 ♖fe8 20 h4 ♘c4 21 ♖e6! ♕g7 22 ♕xg7+ ♔xg7, Chuchelov-Lopez Martinez, Berlin 1998, and here 23 ♖d1 ♔f7 24 ♖xe8 ♔xe8 25 ♗f1 ♗a6 26 ♖e1+ ♔d7 27 ♖e4 is very strong for White according to Chuchelov.

a2) 14...♗d6 15 ♗xd6 ♕xd6 16 ♘d2! c4 (Tukmakov gives 16...♖ad8 17 c4 b5, when White is still somewhat better) 17 ♘f1 ♕f6 18 ♕d2 ♖ad8 19 ♖ad1 g6 20 ♘e3 h5 21 d6 ♗xg2 22 ♔xg2 ♔g7 23 d7, when White is much better – the passed d-pawn drives a wedge into Black's position, Tukmakov-Gheorghiu, Zurich 2000.

b) 11...cxd4 12 cxd4 ♘c6 13 ♗b2 (13 h4!? and if 13...♗f6 14 e5 is Langeweg's suggestion; this is similar to Akopian's plan in the main game) 13...♗f6 14 ♖b1 ♖c8 15 d5 exd5 16 exd5 ♘a5 17 ♗xf6 ♕xf6 18 ♘e5 ♖fd8 19 ♖b4 ♕d6 20 ♖h4 h6, Ftacnik-Yudasin, Biel 1993, and here Yudasin suggests 21 ♘g4 followed by ♘e3-f5.

12 h4!?

This initiates a clear-cut plan of kingside attack. Kramnik's approach is a little more sophisticated, but somewhat harder for White to play as it relies on 100% accurate calculation: 12 ♗f4 cxd4 13 cxd4 ♘f6 14 ♘e5 ♗b4?! (14...♖c8) 15 ♖e3 ♖c8 16 d5! (a classic central break) 16...exd5 17 exd5 ♗d6 18 ♘c6 ♗xc6 19 ♗xd6 ♗a4 and now in Kramnik-Anand, Las Palmas 1996, White chose the queen sacrifice 20 ♗xf8!? ♗xd1 21 ♗e7 ♕c7 22 ♖xd1 ♘d7 23 ♗h3 h6 24 ♗f5 b5? (24...♕b7) 25 ♗b4 with a winning

position – the d-pawn eventually queened.
12...♘f6 13 ♕d3

With tactical ideas of ♘f3-g5, followed by e4-e5, with a triple attack on h7, f6 and b7.

13...h6 14 e5 ♘d5?!

This allows the white queen to 'zigzag' its way over to the kingside. After the improvement 14...♘d7 Akopian analyses the possibility 15 ♘g5 (15 a4 is the steady move, when White has a slight advantage) 15...hxg5 16 ♗xb7 ♖b8 17 ♗g2 gxh4 18 gxh4 ♗xh4 19 ♕h3 with attacking chances in return for the pawn.

15 ♕e4

Threatening 16 c4.

15...♖b8 16 ♕g4

It is surprising how strong this kind of kingside configuration (which can occur in several openings) can be for White.

16...♘h7 17 ♗d2 cxd4 18 ♘xd4 f5

Otherwise White's attack becomes too strong, e.g. 18...♕c7 19 ♗e4+ ♔h8 20 ♗xh6 gxh6 21 ♕h5 ♔g7 22 ♘xe6+ fxe6 23 ♕g6+.

19 exf6 ♘xf6 20 ♕xe6 ♗xg2 21 ♔xg2

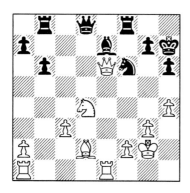

21...♕d5+?

21...♗c5 should be tried, though White has an extra pawn and a big plus after 22 ♗f4.

22 ♕xd5 ♘xd5 23 ♖e5 ♖fd8 24 ♘c6 ♗f6 25 ♖ee1

White wins the exchange, giving him a technically winning ending.

25...♘xc3 26 ♘xd8 ♖xd8 27 ♗xc3 ♗xc3 28 ♖ad1 ♖a8 29 ♖e3!

29 ♖e7 b5 gives Black some chances.

29...♗b4 30 ♖d7 a5 31 ♖e6 ♗b8 32 ♖c6 ♗f8 33 ♖dc7 ♗c5 34 ♖c8 ♖xc8 35 ♖xc8 ♔g6 36 a4 h5 37 ♖h8 ♗d4 38 f4 ♗e3 39 ♔f3 ♗g1 40 f5+ ♔xf5 41 ♖xh5+ ♔f6 42 g4 g6 43 ♖d5 ♔e6 44 ♔e4 ♗f2 45 h5 gxh5 46 ♖e5+ ♔d6 47 gxh5 1-0

Game 9
Tukmakov-Gheorghiu
Crans Montana 2000

---

1 ♘f3 c5 2 c4 ♘f6 3 ♘c3 e6 4 g3 b6 5 ♗g2 ♗b7 6 0-0 ♗e7 7 ♖e1 ♘e4

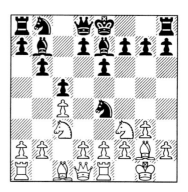

One of the main ways in which Black can avoid the 'Open' Hedgehog with e2-e4 and d2-d4. The other is 7...d5, which was covered in the previous game.

8 d4

The most complex and aggressive choice. Alternatively:

a) 8 ♘xe4 ♗xe4 9 d3 ♗b7 10 e4 leads to fairly level positions, for example:

a1) 10...0-0 11 d4 cxd4 12 ♘xd4 ♘c6 13 b3 (13 ♗f4 ♗c5 14 ♘xc6 ♗xc6 is similar) 13...♘xd4 14 ♕xd4 ♗c5 15 ♕c3 ½-½ Akopian-Adams, Dortmund 2000.

a2) 10...♘c6 11 d4 ♘xd4 12 ♘xd4 cxd4 13 ♕xd4 0-0 14 ♖d1 d6 (14...♗c6 is probably better as it frees the dark-squared bishop from defensive duties) 15 ♕e3 ♕c7 16 b3 ♕c5 17 ♕e2 ♗f6 18 ♗e3 ♕c7 19 ♗d4 ♗e7 20 ♗b2 and White is just slightly better due to his space advantage, Tukmakov-Gheorghiu, Crans Montana 2000.

b) 8 ♕c2 is less popular, but on current evidence White is slightly better: 8...♘xc3 9 dxc3 (9 ♕xc3 is harmless: 9...♗f6 10 ♕c2 ♘c6 11 a3 0-0 12 ♖b1 a5 13 d3 d5 Lobron-Adams, Brussels 1992)

White's short-term plan is to put one or both rooks on the d-file and the bishop on f4. The danger for Black is that he will be tied to the defence of his d-pawn, with few active prospects. White can make progress by preparing the eventual advance of his kingside pawns. In the few games played so far (a number with Adams playing the Black side), Black has not demonstrated a clear route to equality.

b1) 9...d6 10 ♖d1 (10 ♗f4 followed by ♖a1-d1 transposes) 10...♕c7 11 ♗f4 ♘c6 12 ♖d2 h6 13 ♖ad1 ♖d8 14 g4 0-0 15 ♗g3 a6 16 h4 keeps the pressure on Black, Kurajica-Kutuzovic, Pula 1999.

b2) 9...♘c6 10 ♗f4 0-0 11 ♖ad1 is preferable for White according to Ftacnik.

b3) 9...♕c7 10 ♗f4 d6 11 ♖ad1 ♘c6 and now:

b31) 12 ♖d2 h6 (12...♖d8 13 ♖ed1 0-0 14 ♘g5 ♗xg5 15 ♗xg5 f6 16 ♗f4 e5 17 ♗e3 ♘a5 18 ♗xb7 ♘xb7 19 ♖d5 ♖de8 20 ♕f5 ♕c8 21 ♕xc8 ♖xc8 22 g4 and Black is passively placed, Vaganian-Adams, Oviedo {rapidplay} 1992) 13 ♖ed1 transposes to note 'b1' above.

b32) 12 ♘g5 ♗xg5 13 ♗xg5 h6 and now:

b321) 14 ♗f4 ♖d8 15 h4 e5 16 ♗c1 0-0 17 e4 ♘e7 18 g4 (Akopian-Adams, Leon 1995) was still a little better for White.

b322) 14 ♗c1 0-0 (Adams suggests 14...0-0-0, which would change the nature of the game – it is not easy so for White to attack on the queenside) 15 e4 ♖ad8 16 f4 with a kingside pawn storm in mind, and

White is clearly better, Vaganian-Adams, Yerevan Olympiad 1996.

8...♘xc3

8...0-0 is a provocative alternative: 9 d5 ♘xc3 10 bxc3 ♗f6 and now:

a) 11 ♕c2 exd5 12 cxd5 ♗xd5 13 e4 ♗c6 14 ♗f4 ♘a6 15 ♖ad1 ♖c8 16 h4, Zontakh-Vuckovic, Belgrade 2000, gives White some attacking chances in return for the pawn.

b) 11 ♕d3 exd5 12 cxd5 c4 13 ♕d2 (Tukmakov suggests the pawn sac 13 ♕c2!? ♗xd5 14 e4 – the difference from 'a' is that Black's pawn is on c4 instead of c5, which gives White use of the d4 square – 14...♗c6 15 ♗f4 ♘a6 16 ♘d4 with compensation) 13...♘a6 14 ♗a3 ♖e8 15 ♘d4 ♘c5 16 ♗xc5 bxc5 17 ♘f5 d6 18 e4 g6 19 ♘e3 ♗a6 20 ♖ac1 ♖b8 with sufficient counterplay for Black, Sakaev-M.Gurevich, Neum 2000.

9 bxc3 ♗e4

9...0-0 allows a structure which is a kind of Nimzo-Indian/Czech Benoni hybrid: 10 d5 d6 and now:

a) 11 dxe6 fxe6 12 ♗h3 e5 13 ♗e6+ ♔h8 with a roughly even position, Van Wely-Yermolinsky, Merrillville 1997.

b) 11 e4 e5 12 a4 (12 ♘d2 ♘d7 {12...♗g5!?} 13 ♘f1 is slightly better for White) 12 a4 ♘d7 13 ♕c2 a5 14 ♘d2 ♗a6 15 ♕d3 ♗g5 16 ♘f1 ♗xc1 17 ♖exc1 ♘f6 18 ♗h3 g6 19 ♖cb1 ♖b8 20 ♖b2 ♘h5 21 ♘e3 f5 22 exf5 ♗c8 23 ♗g4 won a pawn in Malaniuk-Gipslis, Koszalin 1998, but 21...♖e8 should be fine for Black.

10 ♗f1

White needs to find a way of dislodging the bishop from e4 without allowing the exchange of his own light-squared bishop. The alternative is 10 ♗h3 ♗xf3 11 exf3 cxd4 12 cxd4 0-0 13 f4 ♘c6 14 ♗e3 ♘a5 15 ♖c1 ♖c8 16 ♕a4 g6 17 ♗g2 ♕c7 18 c5 d5 19 cxd6 ♕xd6 with equal chances, Petursson-Akesson, Munkebo 1998.

10...♗xf3 11 exf3 ♘c6

Or 11...cxd4 12 cxd4 with the following:

a) The immediate 12...♘c6 is not so accurate. After 13 d5 ♘a5 14 ♗d2 0-0 (or 14...♖c8 15 ♕a4 0-0 16 ♖ab1) 15 ♖b1 White has not spent a tempo on an f3-f4, when compared to note 'b'.

b) 12...0-0

b1) 13 f4 ♘c6 14 d5 ♘a5 15 ♗d2 ♖c8 16 ♗xa5 bxa5 17 ♖b1 ♗c5 18 ♕d3 ½-½ Savchenko-V.Gurevich, Ubeda 1998.

b2) After 13 d5 V.Gurevich gives 13...♘a6 'with the idea of ...♘a6-c5'. However it strikes me that, although the knight is well placed on c5, it has no way of improving its position. White can continue in prophylactic style with 14 ♖b1 ♘c5 15 d6 ♗f6 16 ♖e3 (16 f4 ♗c3 17 ♖e3 ♕f6 lets Black in). If White is careful to cut off any entry squares for the Black pieces, it is hard to see how Black will develop further. Meanwhile White can play on both wings, with, for example f3-f4 and h2-h4-h5, and also ♗c1-a3, ♖b1-b5 etc., with the idea of trading on c5 and then playing ♕d1-a4.

12 d5 ♘a5 13 f4 0-0 14 h4!

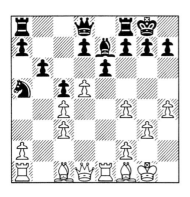

The quickest way of getting the kingside moving. 14 ♕f3 ♗f6 15 ♗d2 ♖b8 16 g4 g6 17 h4!? ♗g7 (it's not clear why Black did not try 17...♗xh4 18 g5 f6) 18 h5 ♘b7 19 hxg6 hxg6 20 ♕g3 favoured White in Ostojic-Colovic, Stara Pazova 2001.

14...♗f6 15 ♗d2

15 ♖e3 is also possible.

15...exd5 16 cxd5 c4 17 ♗g2 b5

After 17...♘b7 Tukmakov gives 18 d6 ♖b8 19 ♗xb7 ♖xb7 20 g4 ♕b8 (20...♗xh4 21 g5 f6 22 ♗e3) 21 g5 ♗d8 22 ♗e3 b5 23 ♕d5 and White has a huge space advantage. **18 ♖b1 a6 19 ♕c2 ♖b8 20 ♗e4 h6 21 ♔g2 ♘b7?!**

21...♖e8 was a better defence.

22 g4! ♗xh4

Otherwise Black will be overrun.

23 g5 f5

Or 23...hxg5 24 ♗h7+ ♔h8 25 ♖h1 and Black is on the precipice.

24 ♗xf5 ♘d6 25 ♗h7+ ♔h8 26 ♖h1 hxg5 27 ♗g6 ♕f6

Perhaps Black should try 27...♔g8.

28 ♗e3 ♔g8 29 ♗h7+ ♔f7 30 fxg5 ♗xg5

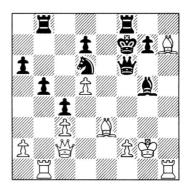

31 f4!

Opening lines that lead to the Black king!

31...♗xf4

31...♗h6 would be answered by 32 ♗d4.

32 ♗xf4 ♕xf4 33 ♖hf1 ♔e7 34 ♕e2+ ♔d8 35 ♖xf4 ♖xf4 36 ♕e5 ♖f6 37 ♖f1 ♔c7

Black's only hope lies in setting up a fortress on the queenside.

38 ♖xf6 gxf6 39 ♕xf6 ♖b6 40 ♕d4 ♘b7 41 ♔f2 ♖h6 42 ♕f4+ ♖d6 43 ♔e3 ♘c5 44 ♗f5 ♘a4 45 ♔d4 ♘b6 46 ♔c5 ♘a4+ 47 ♔b4 ♘b6 48 ♗e4 1-0

48 ♗e4 ♘a4 49 ♗c2 ♘b6 50 ♔c5 ♘c8 51 ♕e5 and Black is in zugzwang.

Summary

The Hedgehog continues to thrive, but is coming under more pressure these days as players of the White side have continually refined their attacking ideas. Black is doing fine after 7 d4, though he needs to know his way round White's various plans. 7 ♖e1 is currently the critical line, when 7...d5 and 7...♘e4 are not quite living up to expectations. This leaves the sharp main line. Marin's 12...♖e8 and 13...♗f8 stands up, but these lines are very sharp and no doubt further improvements are possible for both sides.

1 c4 c5 2 ♘f3 ♘f6 3 ♘c3 e6 4 g3 b6 5 ♗g2 ♗b7 6 0-0
6...♗e7 (D)

7 ♖e1
    7 b3 – *Game 3*
    7 d4 cxd4 8 ♕xd4 (D)
        8...d6
                9 e4 a6 10 ♕e3 – *Game 2*; 9 ♗g5 – *Game 5*; 9 b3 – *Game 4*
        8...♘c6 – *Game 1*
7...d6
    7...♘e4 – *Game 9*; 7...d5 – *Game 8*
8 e4 a6 9 d4 cxd4 10 ♘xd4 ♕c7 (D) 11 ♗e3 0-0 12 ♖c1 ♘bd7
    12...♖e8 13 f4 ♗f8 14 f5 – *Game 7*
13 f4 ♖fe8 14 g4 ♘c5 – *Game 6*

     6...♗e7

     8 ♕xd4

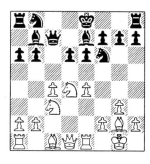
     10...♕c7

CHAPTER TWO

The Double Fianchetto Defence

1 c4 c5 2 ♘f3 ♘f6 3 g3

Here 3 d4 avoids the Double Fianchetto, and is covered in Chapter 3.

3...b6 4 ♗g2 ♗b7 5 0-0 g6

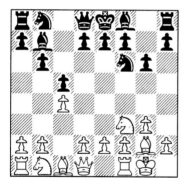

The Double Fianchetto Variation has been popular at a high level for many years, and indeed has featured in several World Championship matches, an accolade that the Hedgehog, for example, has yet to achieve. Some writers have suggested that it is hard for Black to win in this line, but I don't believe this is truer than of many other openings. It *is* true that there are spoilsports who will play 6 b3 (see Game 14 for the details) and dig in as White, but many openings feature drawing lines for White.

6 ♘c3 ♗g7 7 d4

7 ♖e1 (Game 13) is less effective here than in the previous chapter, so usually White goes for 7 d4.

7...cxd4 8 ♕xd4

8 ♘xd4 is covered in Game 12.

8...d6

For 8...♘c6 see Game 11.

9 ♖d1

This is the main line, covered in Game 10.

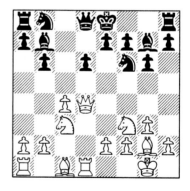

White's Ideas

These consist of the following:

1) White often swings his queen across to h4. This can be the prelude to kingside aggression or a more positional plan of first exchanging the dark-squared bishops with

♗h6 and then returning the queen to the centre.

2) White tries to put a 'bind' in place, based on control of the d5-square. It is hard for Black to contest this with ...e7-e6 as this leaves the d6-pawn very weak. If the light-squared bishops are exchanged, White's king's knight can manoeuvre, e.g. ♘f3-e1-g2-f4. With d5 under control, he can expand on the queenside, or move his forces over for a kingside attack.

3) Building a pawn centre with e2-e4 and pushing the kingside pawns is much less common than in the Hedgehog.

Black's Ideas

Black's ideas include:

1) The presence of the bishop on g7 introduces tactical possibilities along the a1-h8 diagonal. Examples are seen in Game 12 and Hartoch-*Genius* in the notes to Black's 8th move in Game 14.

2) The advance ...b6-b5 is Black's key break, and if Black can achieve it, will often undermine White's control of d5.

3) The move ...♘f6-e4 is an important simplifying idea in some positions.

4) Black's queen's rook usually moves to c8 to put pressure on the c4-pawn. Activating this rook on the 5th rank is a key idea. The rook harasses the white queen and can sometimes induce other weaknesses in White's position. Black implements this by ...♖c8-♖c5 and then the rook sometimes moves to f5 or h5 (see note 'a' to White's 10th move in Game 10).

Game 10
Kramnik-Karpov
Dos Hermanas 1999

---

1 ♘f3 ♘f6 2 c4 b6 3 g3 c5 4 ♗g2 ♗b7 5 0-0 g6 6 ♘c3 ♗g7 7 d4 cxd4 8 ♕xd4 d6

This is currently Black's main choice. 8...♘c6 and 8...0-0 are covered in the next

game.

9 ♖d1

Another plan is to fold the queen in on d2, behind the bishop on e3, e.g. 9 ♗e3 ♘bd7 10 ♖ac1 ♖c8 11 b3 0-0 12 ♕d2 and now:

a) 12...a6 13 ♗h3 ♖c7 14 ♘d4 ♘e4 15 ♘xe4 ♗xe4 16 f3 ♗b7 17 ♖fd1, Rogozenko-Ionescu, Bucharest 1999, and here Rogozenko recommends 17 ♘c2 b5 18 ♘a3 bxc4 19 ♘xc4 with an edge for White.

b) 12...♘e4 13 ♘xe4 ♗xe4 is the most straightforward, e.g. 14 ♗h3 ♕c7 15 ♘d4 a6 16 f3 ♗b7 17 ♘c2 ♖cd8 18 ♗xd7 ♖xd7 19 ♕b4 b5! 20 ♘d4 (20 cxb5 ♗b2) 20...♕c5 ½-½ Akopian-Lalic, Lucerne 1997.

9...♘bd7

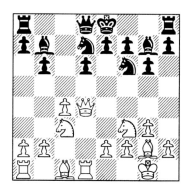

10 ♗e3

White waits for Black to castle before playing ♕d4-h4. Another approach is the queenside fianchetto, e.g. 10 b3 0-0 11 ♗b2 ♖c8 (11...♘e4 is also playable) and here:

a) 12 ♕e3 ♖e8 13 ♖ac1 a6 14 ♗a1 ♖c5 15 a4 ♕a8 16 ♘e1 ♖f5 (this game is an instructive example of the active 5th rank rook; Black's threat of ...♘f6-g4 causes some disruption in the White set-up) 17 ♗xb7 ♕xb7 18 f3 h5 19 ♘g2 ♖c5 20 ♗b2 ♖cc8 (mission accomplished, the rook returns home) 21 ♗a3 ♘c5 22 ♖b1 ♘e6 with a balanced position, Karpov-Kasparov, London/Leningrad (match game 23) 1986.

b) 12 ♖ac1 a6 13 ♕d2 ♖c7 14 ♘e1 and now:

b1) 14...♗xg2? (Black hastens the e1-knight to where it wants to go – ♘e1-g2-e3-d5; this would be less important if Black were ready for ...b7-b5, but White can clamp down on that intention as well) 15 ♘xg2 ♕a8 16 ♘e3 (White has a firm grip on d5) 16...♖e8 17 ♘cd5 ♖c6 18 a4 ♕b7 19 ♗d4 ♖cc8 20 ♘xf6+ ♗xf6? (20...♘xf6 is better; in order to play ♘e3-d5, White would then need to allow the exchange of both pairs of minor pieces – which in this specific position would lead to a drawish ending – or play ♗d4xf6, which leaves Black with the bishop as a long-term trump) 21 ♘d5 ♗xd4 22 ♕xd4 and White is much better, Kramnik-J.Polgar, Dos Hermanas 1999. These positions are often good for White if several minor pieces have been traded, since he can use his space advantage to swing his heavy pieces into action. Meanwhile the tension has gone out of Black's 'coiled spring'.

b2) Instead 14...♕a8 15 ♘d5 (15 ♗xb7 ♕xb7 16 ♘g2 and Black is ready for 16...b5) 15...♘xd5 16 cxd5 ♖fc8 gives equal chances according to Kramnik.

10...0-0 11 ♕h4 ♖c8 12 ♖ac1

White needs to bolster the c4-pawn before taking action such as ♗e3-h6 or ♗g2-h3. The reason for this can be seen from the blunder 12 ♗h3?? ♗xf3 13 exf3 ♘e5 14 ♔g2 ♖xc4, Topalov-Kasparov, Wijk aan Zee (rapid) 1999.

12...a6 13 b3

In the 14th game of the 2000 World Championship match, Kramnik, who only needed to draw out the match to beat Kasparov, chose the more cautious 13 ♘e1. The game continued 13...♗xg2 14 ♘xg2 ♖e8 15 b3 ♕c7 16 ♗g5 (16 ♗h6 should be preferred according to Kramnik's second Illescas) 16...♕b7 17 ♘e3 b5 18 ♘ed5?! (White should settle for equality with 18 ♘cd5 intending to recapture on c4 with the

c1-rook) 18...bxc4 19 bxc4 (when White picks up an isolated c-pawn – in either the Double Fianchetto or Hedgehog – it is usually a sign that something has gone wrong) 19...h5 20 ♕f4 ♕c6 and Black is slightly better, although of course Kramnik saved the game with resourceful play.

13...♖c7

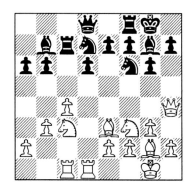

An alternative is the constructive waiting move 13...♖e8, which defends e7. 14 g4!? (White can of course continue with the normal 14 ♘e1, when 14...♗xg2 15 ♘xg2 ♕c7 transposes into Kramnik-Kasparov above, while 14 ♗h3 ♖c7 transposes to 13...♖c7 14 ♗h3 ♖e8 discussed in note 'c1' to White's next move) 14...b5! 15 cxb5 ♘xg4! 16 ♗d4 ♘gf6 17 a4 ♘c5 18 bxa6 ♗xa6 19 ♘d2 ♘e6 20 ♗e3 h5 21 h3 d5 with good play for Black, Filippov-Nikolic, Neum 2000.

14 g4!?

White has several important alternatives:

a) 14 ♘e1 ♗xg2 (The c7-rook provides a tempo-winning target for a later ♘d5; perhaps 14...♕a8 or 14...♕b8 is better) 15 ♘xg2 ♖e8 (Illescas questions this move, and instead suggests 15...♕b8; however, Black is faced with a similar outcome after 16 ♘f4 since 16...b5 is answered by 17 ♘cd5) 16 ♘f4 ♕b8 17 ♘fd5 ♖cc8 18 ♗g5 ♕b7 and Black is two tempi behind the Kramnik-Kasparov game above, as Illescas points out in his notes to the 2000 World

Championship match. At this point (White pieces in the same places), Kasparov had played ...b6-b5 and ...b5xc4. A big difference! Illescas Cordoba-Gelfand, Pamplona 1999 continued 19 a4 ♔h8 20 g4 ♘xd5 21 ♘xd5 e6 22 ♘f6 ♘xf6 23 ♗xf6 d5 and now 24 g5 would have kept White's initiative going.

b) 14 ♗h6 ♕a8 15 ♗xg7 ♔xg7 16 ♕d4 ♔g8 (16...b5! 17 cxb5 axb5 18 ♘xb5 ♖xc1 19 ♖xc1 ♕xa2 with equal chances according to Yermolinsky and Atalik) 17 ♕e3 ♖e8 18 ♗h3 ♖c5 19 ♘d4 ♖h5 20 g4! ♖e5 21 ♕d2 e6 (21...♘c5 22 f3) 22 f3 and White's structure is somewhat bizarre but nevertheless effective. 22...♖c5 23 ♘c2 ♘e5 24 ♘e1 ♖d8 25 g5 ♘e8 26 a4 was better for White in Yermolinsky-Ehlvest, Stratton Mountain 2000.

c) 14 ♗h3 and now:

c1) 14...♖e8 15 ♗h6 ♖c5 (the active rook again!) 16 ♘g5 b5 17 ♘d5 ♗xd5 18 cxd5 ♖xc1 19 ♖xc1 ♗xh6 20 ♕xh6 ♘f8 21 b4 ♕b6 22 ♖d1 a5 ½-½ Wojtkiewicz-Stohl, Suwalki 1999.

c2) The previous line is better than 14...♕b8 15 ♗h6 when Black is beginning to feel the heat: 15...♗xf3 (15...♖c5 is not possible because of 16 ♗xg7 ♔xg7 17 ♗xd7 ♘xd7 18 ♕xe7) 16 ♗xg7 ♔xg7 17 exf3 ♘e5 18 ♗g2 b5 19 cxb5 axb5 20 ♕b4 and White is a bit better, Topalov-Psakhis, FIDE World Championship, Las Vegas 1999.

14...h6!

Or perhaps 14...b5 (compare with Filippov-Nikolic, in the note to Black's 13th move above).

15 h3 g5 16 ♕g3 b5 17 h4!?

17 cxb5?? allows 17...♖xc3 18 ♖xc3 ♘e4 winning, while 17 ♘d4 ♗xg2 18 ♕xg2 bxc4 19 ♘c6 ♕e8 20 bxc4 offers chances for both sides.

17...bxc4

17...gxh4 18 ♘xh4 ♗xg2 19 ♔xg2 bxc4 20 ♘f5 gives White good attacking chances

on the kingside according to Kramnik.

18 hxg5 hxg5 19 b4

19 ♘xg5 can be answered by 19...cxb3 20 axb3 ♗xg2 21 ♕xg2 ♕a8.

19...♕a8 20 ♗xg5 ♖e8 21 ♗e3 ♘f8 22 a4 ♘e4 23 ♘xe4 ♗xe4 24 ♗d4 ♗xf3

Kramnik gives 24...e5 25 ♗c3 d5 26 e3 (or 26 b5) as unclear.

25 ♗xf3 ♕b8 26 ♗d5 ♕xb4 27 ♗xg7 ♔xg7 28 ♕f4 e6

At first sight, Black's king's position looks totally open, but this is classic Karpov defence. The f8-knight provides all the coverage he needs. In fact it is White who has to tread very carefully to avoid being worse.

29 ♗e4 c3 30 ♕xd6 ♖c4 31 f3 ♕xd6 32 ♖xd6 a5 33 ♗d3 ½-½

Game 11
Makarov-Mikhailov
Kemerovo 1995

1 ♘f3 ♘f6 2 c4 c5 3 ♘c3 b6 4 g3 ♗b7 5 ♗g2 g6 6 0-0 ♗g7 7 d4 cxd4 8 ♕xd4 ♘c6

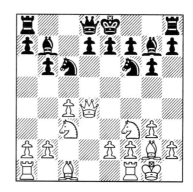

This move is less popular than the current main line 8...d6 (see the previous game), but can lead to double-edged positions based on Black making a quick grab for the c4-pawn.

8...0-0 can be answered by 9 ♕h4 and here:

a) 9...d6 and now White can play 10 ♗h6

---

without wasting a tempo on ♗c1-e3 first (which happens in Game 10 for example): 10...♘bd7 11 b3 ♖c8 12 ♗xg7 ♔xg7 13 ♕d4 ♔g8 14 ♖ac1 ♖c5 15 b4 ♖c8 16 a3, Kramnik-Adams, Biel 1993, is the kind of position White is hoping for in this line. The dark squared bishops are off, Black has no dangerous pawn breaks, and White can gradually increase the pressure using his space advantage.

b) 9...h5!? is a speciality of Bacrot, which has the benefit of stopping ♗c1-h6. Black bargains on the fact that White will not be able to exploit his unconventional kingside pawn structure. The evidence so far is:

b1) 10 ♗g5 d6 11 e4 ♘c6 12 ♘d5 ♖e8 13 ♖ad1 ♘h7 14 ♗c1 e6 15 ♕xd8 ♖axd8 16 ♘c7 ♖e7 17 ♘b5 ♖ed7 18 ♘fd4 ♘xd4 19 ♘xd4 d5 ½-½ Hübner-Bacrot, Berlin 1998.

b2) 10 ♖d1 ♘a6 11 e4 ♖c8 12 e5 ♘g4 13 ♗f4 ♖xc4 14 ♘d2 ♖c7 15 ♘b5 ♗xg2 16 ♘xc7 ♕xc7 17 ♔xg2 ♕c5 with fair compensation for the exchange, Summerscale-Bacrot, France 1998.

9 ♕f4

9 ♕h4 is met by 9...h6 10 ♘d4 g5 11 ♘xc6 dxc6, when White is reduced to 12 ♕h3.

9...♖c8

Or 9...0-0 10 ♕h4 (White doesn't mind losing a tempo to achieve the desirable ♗c1-h6; 10 ♖d1 ♖c8 11 ♖b1 transposes to the next note) and here:

a) 10...♖c8 11 ♗h6 ♘b8! 12 b3 d6 13 ♖ad1 ♖c5 (again activating the rook on the 5th rank via ...♖a8-c8-c5 is a typical theme in the Double Fianchetto) 14 ♗xg7 ♔xg7 15 ♕d4 ♘bd7 16 e4 a6 17 ♖fe1 ♕a8 18 ♘a4 ♖a5 19 ♘xb6 ♘xb6 20 ♕xb6 Speelman-Greenfeld, Beersheba 1987, and now 20...♖c5 21 ♕b4 ♗xe4 is unclear according to Speelman.

b) After 10...♘a5 NCO suggests 11 ♗h6!? (11 ♗g5 ♖c8 12 b3 ♖c5 is about equal) but doesn't analyse 11...♗xh6 12

♕xh6 ♘xc4 and Black gets a pawn for free. If he gets worried about ♘f3-g5, he can always chop the knight with ...♗b7xf3. An extreme example would be 13 ♖ad1 ♘xb2 14 ♖d4 ♖c8 15 ♘g5 ♗xg2 16 ♖h4 ♖c4.

10 ♖d1

10 ♖b1 pre-empts the idea used by Black in the main game: 10...0-0 (10...♘h5 11 ♕e3 ♘b4 does not threaten to win the exchange by ...♘b4-c2, so White can now play simply 12 a3) 11 ♖d1 ♕e8!? 12 ♘e1 ♘d8 13 ♗xb7 ♘xb7 14 b3 ♘c5 15 ♗b2, Drasko-Pavlovic, Subotica 2000, and here Drasko suggests 15 ♕h4 with a slight edge for White.

10...♘h5 11 ♕e3

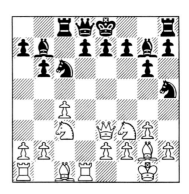

11 ♕d2 allows 11...♘a5 12 b3 b5.

11...♘b4 12 ♖b1 ♖xc4

A combative but risky idea.

13 ♘e5 ♗xe5

The forcing sequence 13...♘c2 14 ♕d3 ♖d4 15 ♕xc2 ♖xd1+ 16 ♕xd1 ♗xg2 17 ♘xf7 ♔xf7 18 ♕b3+ e6 19 ♔xg2 turns out to be favourable for White according to Makarov.

14 ♕xe5 f6 15 ♕b5 ♗a6 16 ♕a4 ♕c8 17 ♕b3 ♘g7 18 ♘d5 ♘c6

If 18...♘xd5 19 ♗xd5 ♘c2 20 ♗h6, followed later by ♖b1-c1, gives White good attacking chances.

19 ♕a3!

An improvement (whether prepared or not) over the much earlier game Panno-Ljubojevic, Petropolis 1973, which continued 19 e4 (this doesn't achieve much, and White can use the tempo for something more critical) 19...♘e6 20 ♗e3 ♔f7, and now 20...♘c5! is best according to Panno.

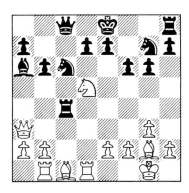

19...♘e6 20 ♗e3 ♔f7

If 20...♖c2 then 21 ♖dc1 is hard to meet.

21 ♖d2

White is weaving a net around the black rook.

21...♗b7 22 b3 ♖c5 23 b4

White could also just take the exchange immediately with 23 ♗xc5 bxc5 24 b4.

23...♖b5

Not 23...♖c4? because of 24 b5 winning a piece due to the threat of mate in two with ♕a3xe7+.

24 ♕d3 ♖xd5 25 ♕xd5 ♕a8 26 ♕b3 ♘e5 27 ♗xb7 ♕xb7 28 ♗f4 ♖c8 29 ♗xe5 fxe5 30 ♖bd1 d6 31 ♖c2 ♖xc2 32 ♕xc2

White has managed to effect multiple exchanges, leaving himself the technical task of exploiting his material advantage in the ending.

32...♘d4 33 ♕c4+ ♔f6 34 f3 b5 35 ♕d3 ♕d5 36 a3 ♕a2?!

Keeping the queen centralised with 36...♕c6 would put up more resistance.

37 ♔f2 a6 38 f4

Once the black king is exposed, it's all over.

38...♕f7 39 fxe5+ ♔xe5+ 40 ♔e1 ♘f5 41 ♕c3+ ♔e4 42 ♕f3+ ♔e5 43 g4 1-0

Game 12
Karpov-Kasparov
Moscow (13th match game) 1984

1 ♘f3 ♘f6 2 c4 b6 3 g3 c5 4 ♗g2 ♗b7 5 0-0 g6 6 ♘c3 ♗g7 7 d4 cxd4

The alternative 7...♘e4 went out of fashion after Black suffered a number of reverses. After 8 ♘xe4 ♗xe4 9 d5 Black can choose between:

a) 9...b5 by analogy with Summerscale-Adams (Game 13), may be better than its reputation, e.g. 10 ♘d2 ♗xg2 11 ♔xg2 and now:

a1) 11...♕b6 12 e4 0-0 13 h4 ♘a6 14 ♕e2 ♘c7 15 h5 is great for White, W.Schmidt-Ornstein, Yerevan 1976.

a2) But 11...bxc4 (11...d6!?) 12 ♘xc4 d6 13 ♕c2 0-0 14 ♗d2 ♘d7 is fairly comfortable for Black, Vovsha-Tsesarsky, Petah Tiqwa 1996.

b) 9...0-0 10 ♗h3 ♗xf3 11 exf3 and here:

b1) 11...e5 12 f4 exf4 13 ♗xf4 ♗xb2 14 ♖b1 ♗f6 15 ♕a4 d6 16 ♖b3 h5 17 ♖e1 and Black has difficulties developing his queen-side, Karpov-Timman, Amsterdam 1981.

b2) 11...e6 12 ♖e1 ♗d4 13 ♗h6 ♖e8 14 ♕a4 a6 15 f4 ♖a7 (Simic suggests 15...b5 but it doesn't change that much) 16 ♖ad1 b5 17 cxb5 ♕b6 18 dxe6 dxe6 19 bxa6 ♖d8 20 f5 with a strong attack, Korchnoi-Panno, Lucerne 1985.

c) 9...e5 10 ♕b3 0-0 11 ♗h3 ♗xf3 12 ♕xf3 f5 13 e4 f4 14 ♕d1 d6 15 ♗d2 a5 16 ♕a4 and White is better due to his domination of the light squares, Karpov-Timman, Brussels 1988.

8 ♘xd4 ♗xg2 9 ♔xg2 0-0

The original method of handling the 8 ♘xd4 line for Black was 9...♖c8 (9...♕c7 usually comes to the same thing) 10 b3 ♕b7+ 11 f3 d5 (or 11...♘c6 12 ♗b2 0-0 13 e4 a6 14 ♖c1 ♘xd4 15 ♕xd4 d6 16 ♘d5 ♖ab8 with an unclear position according to Kochiev, though White looks to be a little better after 17 ♖fd1) but White gets a slightly better game after 12 cxd5 ♘xd5 13 ♘xd5 ♕xd5 14 ♗e3 ♘c6 15 ♘xc6 ♕xc6 16 ♖c1 ♕e6 17 ♕d3 0-0 18 ♖fd1, as in Polugaevsky-Smyslov, Soviet Championship 1976.

10 e4 ♕c7

10...♘c6 11 ♘c2 is pleasant for White.

11 b3

White can avoid the forcing continuation that follows by 11 ♕e2, e.g. 11...♘c6 12 ♘c2 a6 13 ♗g5 e6 14 ♖ac1 ♖fc8 15 b3 ♘e8 16 ♗d2 ♕b7 17 f3 b5 18 ♘e3 f5!? 19 exf5 gxf5 with chances for both sides, Vukic-Psakhis, Bor 1985.

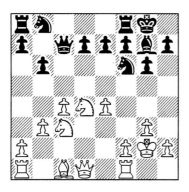

11...♘xe4

Exploiting the 'long diagonal tactics' to free the Black position. Suba calls this a 'beautiful but not very effective combination'. However the evidence suggests that Black is fine after this continuation. Alternatively 11...♘a6 12 f3 ♕b7 13 ♗e3 ♘c5 14 ♖c1 ♖ac8 15 ♘d5 ♖fe8, Morovic Fernandez-Psakhis, Novi Sad Olympiad 1990, and here Psakhis gives 16 b4 as slightly better for White.

12 ♘xe4 ♕e5 13 ♕f3 ♕xd4 14 ♗a3

14 ♖b1 is more critical as it practically forces Black to give up the exchange in order to free his queen. After 14...♕e5 15 ♗f4 (here a draw was agreed, just when it was getting interesting, in Kasparov-Karpov, {match game 20} Moscow 1984).

In this position we have:

a) 15...♕a5 16 ♘f6+ ♗xf6 17 ♕xa8 ♘c6 18 ♕b7 ♕f5 19 ♖bd1 ♗d4 20 ♖fe1 e5 21 ♗e3 ♗c3 22 ♖e2 ♕h5 23 ♖xd7 ♕xe2 24 ♕xc6 was good for White in Karoli-T.Horvath, Hungarian Championship 1985.

b) After 15...♕e6 16 ♘f6+ ♗xf6 17 ♕xa8 ♘c6 18 ♕b7, *Informator 38* quotes a prior game Shabalov-Kengis, USSR 1983, with an unclear position. Two more practical examples continued 18...g5 19 ♖be1 ♕f5 20 ♗e3 ♖b8 21 ♕a6 and here:

b1) 21...♘e5!? 22 f4? (22 ♕xa7) 22...♕e4+ 23 ♔g1 ♘f3+ 24 ♖xf3 ♕xf3 25 ♕xa7 ♖a8 26 ♕xb6 ♖xa2 27 ♗f2 gxf4 28 gxf4 ♕xf4 0-1 was Hernando Garcia-Estremera Panos, Zaragoza 1998.

b2) 21...♗c3 22 ♕b5 ♘e5 23 ♗d2 ♕f3+ 24 ♔g1 a6 25 ♕xa6 ♘c6 26 ♖xe5 ♗xe5 27 a4 ♖a8 28 ♕b5 ♕xb5 29 cxb5 f6 with an unclear ending, Vadasz-David, Zalaegerszeg 1992.

14...♘c6 15 ♖ad1 ♕e5 16 ♖xd7 ♕a5

Black also held the draw after 16...♖ad8 17 ♖fd1 ♖xd7 18 ♖xd7 ♖c8 19 ♕d3 h6 20 ♕d5 ♖c7 21 ♕xe5 ♗xe5 22 ♖xc7 ♗xc7 etc., Gritsak-Epishin, Koszalin 1999.

17 ♗xe7 ♘e5 18 ♕d1

Now it is White's turn to offer the exchange. Instead 18 ♖d5 ♘xf3 19 ♖xa5 ♖fe8 20 ♖d5 (20 ♔xf3?! bxa5 21 ♗g5 f5 was better for Black in the game Loginov-A.Ivanov, Borzomi 1984) 20...♘xh2 21 ♔xh2 ♖xe7 with an equal endgame according to Taimanov.

18...♘xd7 19 ♕xd7 ♕xa2

Returning the material to try and clarify the position. Taimanov gives 19...♖fb8 20 ♘f6+ (20 a4!?) 20...♗xf6 21 ♗xf6 and the dark-squared bishop is not inferior to the rook.

20 ♗xf8 ♖xf8 21 ♖e1

Trying to drum up an attack. Instead 21 ♕d3 is an attempt to 'grind' the ending. White has a slight initiative, but Black should hold reasonably comfortably with careful play.

a) Suba quotes the game Panchenko-Srokovsky from 1987, which continued 21...♕a5 22 ♖d1 ♕b4 23 h4 ♕e7 24 ♕d5 ♔h8 25 ♕c6 f5 26 ♘g5 ♕e2 27 ♖d7 and White is breaking through.

b) 21...a5 and here:

b1) 22 ♖e1 a4 23 bxa4 ♕xa4 24 ♕d5 ♕a5 25 ♖b1 ♕xd5 26 cxd5 f5 27 ♘g5 ♖b8 with equality, Brunner-Marinkovic, German Bundesliga 1991.

b2) 22 ♖d1 ♕a3 23 h4 h5 24 ♖d2 ♖e8 25 ♖e2 ♕f8 26 ♕f3 ♖e5 27 ♘c3 ♖xe2 28 ♘xe2 ♕e8 29 ♘f4 a4 30 bxa4 ♕xa4 ½-½ Olafsson-Sigurjonsson, Reykjavik 1985.

b3) Suba proposes 22 h4 a4 23 bxa4 ♕xa4 24 ♖b1, though Black should hold after 24...♕c6.

21...♕xb3 22 ♘d6 ♕c3 23 ♖e7 ♕f6

White has no way through.

24 ♘e4 ♕d4 25 ♕xd4 ♗xd4 26 ♖d7 ♗g7 27 ♖xa7 h6 28 ♖b7 ♗d4 29 ♖d7 ♗g7 30 h4 f5 31 ♘d2 ♖f6 32 ♖c7 ♖e6 33 ♘f3 ♗f6 ½-½

Game 13
Summerscale-Adams
British Championship 1997

---

1 ♘f3 ♘f6 2 c4 b6 3 g3 c5 4 ♗g2 ♗b7 5 0-0 g6 6 ♘c3 ♗g7 7 ♖e1

Since this move has become one of the main lines against the Hedgehog set-up, it has also been tried in the Double Fianchetto position.

7...♘e4

Or 7...d6 8 e4 and now:

a1) After 8...e5 White can play 9 d4! regardless, since 9...cxd4 (9...exd4 10 e5) 10 ♘xd4 exd4 11 e5 exploits the old '♗g2 v ♗b7' tactic in explosive fashion.

a2) 8...♘c6 is reasonable for Black: 9 d4 cxd4 10 ♘xd4 ♘xd4 11 ♕xd4 0-0 12 ♕d2 ♘d7, and now instead of 13 e5? ♗xg2 14 exd6 ♘e5, as in Malinin-Yevseev, Gatchina 2000, 13 b3 is given as equal by Yevseev,

though I think it looks fairly pleasant for White.

a3) 8...♘bd7 is also playable, e.g. 9 d4 cxd4 10 ♘xd4 ♖b8 11 b3 0-0 12 ♗b2 a6 13 ♕e2 e6 with chances for both sides, Rotstein-Grooten, Wijk aan Zee 1993.

b) 7...0-0 8 e4 ♘c6 is best answered by 9 e5!.

c) 7...d5 8 d4 leads to an early clash in the centre: 8...dxc4 9 ♕a4+ ♘bd7 10 dxc5 ♕c8 11 ♕xc4 ♕xc5 12 ♕h4 0-0 13 e4 ♖ac8 14 ♗e3 ♕h5 was played in Van der Sterren-Stohl, Prague 1992, and here Stohl prefers 14...♕a5 when Black should be able to equalise.

8 ♘xe4

8 ♕c2 has been tried a few times but Black is well placed because of his more flexible pawn-structure, e.g. 8...♘xc3 9 dxc3 d6 10 ♗g5 ♘d7 11 ♖ad1 ♕c7 12 e4 h6 13 ♗c1 g5! with ...0-0-0 to follow, Cummings-Speelman, British League 1998.

8...♗xe4 9 d4 0-0!

An improvement over the automatic recapture 9...cxd4, after which White gains an edge with the trick 10 ♗h6! ♗xh6 11 ♕xd4 0-0 12 ♕xe4 ♘c6 13 ♖ad1 ♖c8 14 h4 (this is not strictly necessary; 14 a3 followed by b2-b4 is possible, while Romanishin suggests 14 e3) 14...♖c7 (better is 14...e6 15 e3 ♕e7 16 ♖e2 ♖fd8 17 ♖ed2 ♗g7 18 ♕f4 h6 when Black should be okay, Romanishin-Psakhis, Jurmala 1987) 15 h5 e6 16 hxg6 hxg6 17 e3 ♕f6 18 ♖e2 ♖d8 19 ♖ed2 and White has an edge, Romanishin-Lau, Dresden 1998.

10 d5

10 ♗e3 d6 and Black completes his development while White can't yet play d4-d5.

10...b5

This Benko-style pawn sacrifice is Black's best approach. In *Simple Chess*, Michael Stean put forward the interesting idea that Benoni/Benko type positions are more comfortable for Black with one or two minor pieces exchanged. In addition, the active bishop on e4 takes a lot of the dynamism out of White's game.

11 cxb5

If 11 ♘d2 ♗xg2 12 ♔xg2 d6.

11...a6 12 bxa6

Or 12 ♗f1 d6 13 ♘h4 ♕a5 14 ♗d2 ♕xb5 15 ♗c3 ♕b7 16 ♗g2 ½-½ Romanishin-Conquest, Saint Vincent 2000.

12...♖xa6 13 ♘d2 ♗xg2 14 ♔xg2 d6 15 ♘c4 ♘d7 16 e4 ♕a8 17 a3 ♖a4

17...♘b6 is another way to dislodge (or exchange) the well placed knight on c4.

18 ♕c2 ♕a6 19 ♘e3 ♘e5 20 ♖d1 ♖d4 21 ♖a2 ♖b8

Black loses his momentum after this move. Instead Black can press his initiative with 21...f5! 22 exf5, when Adams gives 22...gxf5 23 f4 ♘d3 24 b3 ♘xc1 25 ♕xc1 ♖e4 with ...♗g7-d4 and ...♕a6-b7 in mind.

22 b4! ♖xd1 23 ♘xd1 ♖c8 24 bxc5 ♖xc5 25 ♕b1 ♘d3 26 ♗e3 ♖c8

It was time to considering baling out for a draw with 26...♘e1+ 27 ♔g1 ♘f3+.

27 f3 h5 28 a4 ♘b2?

28...♕c4 should be played.

29 ♖xb2

Not 29 ♘xb2 ♕e2+ 30 ♗f2 ♖c2 31 ♕f1 ♗d4.

29...♗xb2 ½-½

A draw was agreed here, even though White has a material advantage, with no risk, after 30 ♕xb2 ♕xa4 31 ♘f2; or 30...♕d3 31 ♕d4! ♕c2+ 32 ♘f2.

Game 14
Andersson-J.Polgar
Malmo 2000

---

1 ♘f3 ♘f6 2 c4 c5 3 g3 b6 4 ♗g2 ♗b7 5 0-0 g6 6 b3 ♗g7 7 ♗b2

Bagirov called this the 'Four Bishops Opening'. If Black is careful, he should equalise. However there are almost no winning chances for Black against a reasonable opponent. This is one of the downsides of the Double Fianchetto. While an easy draw

with Black is great for the world elite, it does not suit many Swiss warriors. On the other hand, if your opponent is playing for a win as well, you will likely get one of the more interesting lines (e.g. see Game 10) which gives chances for both sides.

7...0-0 8 ♘c3

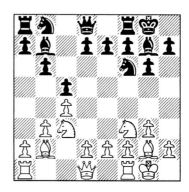

8...♘a6

This was discovered in the late 70s as the 'antidote' to this line. The idea is that Black can answer d2-d4 with an immediate ...d7-d5, since the a6-knight is handily placed to recapture on c5. The main thing to avoid as Black is a passive Maroczy Bind when White keeps a small but enduring edge. Actually, Black has a smorgasbord of equalising opportunities:

a) 8...♘c6 is also perfectly playable. After 9 d4 we have:

a1) 9...cxd4 10 ♘xd4 ♕b8 11 ♘c2 ♖d8 12 e4 a6 13 ♘d5 ♘xd5 14 ♗xg7 ♘e3 15 ♘xe3 ♗xg7 16 ♕d2 b5 17 ♖ac1 f6 18 h4 ♘e5 19 f4 ♘f7 20 c5 with an unclear position, Damljanovic-L.Hansen, Bled 1991.

a2) 9...♘xd4 10 ♘xd4 ♗xg2 11 ♔xg2 cxd4 12 ♕xd4 and now:

a21) 12...♕c7 13 ♘d5 ♕b7 14 e4 d6, Ribli-Dvoirys, Bayern 1992, when 15 ♖fd1 ♖ac8 16 a4 gives White a small advantage – this is the kind of thing to avoid as mentioned above.

a22) The 'computer move' 12...d5 simply equalises after 13 cxd5 (13 ♘xd5 ♘e8 14

♕d2 e6 is better for Black) 13...e6 (a draw was agreed here in Chernin-Psakhis, Kazan – played later in 1997) 14 ♖ad1 ♘xd5 15 ♕d2 ♘xc3 16 ♗xc3 ♕xd2 17 ♗xd2 ♖fc8 18 ♗e3 ♖c2 19 ♖d2 ♖xd2 20 ♗xd2 ♖c8 21 ♖c1 ♖xc1 22 ♗xc1, Hartoch-*Genius*, The Hague 1997. Hey – that WAS a computer playing Black!

Some other ways to equalise:

b) 8...d6 9 d4 cxd4 10 ♘xd4 ♗xg2 11 ♔xg2 d5.

c) 8...e6 9 d4 cxd4 10 ♘xd4 ♗xg2 11 ♔xg2 d5.

d) Just about the only line where Black needs to worry is 8...d5 9 ♘xd5 ♘xd5 10 ♗xg7 ♔xg7 11 cxd5 ♕xd5 12 d4 cxd4 (12...♘a6 is more interesting, e.g. 13 e4 ♕d6) 13 ♕xd4+ ♕xd4 14 ♘xd4 ♗xg2 15 ♔xg2 and White has a very slight edge in this endgame. It is somewhat unpleasant to defend this as Black, e.g. 15...a6 16 ♖ac1 ♖a7 17 ♖c2 ♖d8 18 e3 e5 19 ♘f3 f6 20 g4 ♖d6 21 ♖fc1 ♘d7 22 ♖c6 ♖xc6 23 ♖xc6 ♔f7 24 ♘d2 and Black is very passive, Andersson-Robatsch, Munich 1979.

9 d4

9 ♖c1 e6 10 d4 d5 11 e3 ♕e7 12 ♕e2 dxc4 13 bxc4 ♘e4 14 ♖fd1 ♖fd8 15 ♘e1 ♘xc3 16 ♗xc3 cxd4 17 exd4 (Andersson-Timman, Malmo 2000) is okay for Black.

9...d5

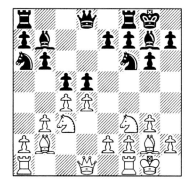

10 dxc5

Alternatively:

a) 10 ♘xd5 ♘xd5 11 cxd5 ♗xd5 12 e3 ♕c7 13 ♕e2 ♕b7 14 ♖fd1 ♖ad8 15 ♖d2 cxd4 16 ♗xd4 e5 17 ♗b2 ♗e4 18 ♖ad1 ♖xd2 19 ♖xd2 with equal chances, Gausel-Wojtkiewicz, Manila Olympiad 1992.

b) 10 ♘e5 e6 11 dxc5 with a choice:

b1) 11...♘xc5 (experience in this variation has shown the isolated d-pawn set-up to be more manageable for Black than the hanging pawn structure which occurs in 'b2' below) 12 cxd5 exd5 13 ♘f3 ♕d7 14 ♖c1 ♖fe8 15 ♖c2 ♖ad8 16 b4 (here White should play 16 ♘d4 ♘fe4 17 ♖e1 h5 18 f3 ♘d6 19 e3 with equality according to Ftacnik) 16...d4 17 bxc5 dxc3 18 ♕xd7 ♘xd7 19 ♗xc3, Ftacnik-Speelman, Thessaloniki 1984, and here Black could have seized the advantage with 19...♗xc3 20 ♖xc3 ♘xc5 21 e3 ♗xf3 22 ♗xf3 ♖d2 23 a3 ♖ed8.

b2) Not so good is 11...bxc5, for example 12 cxd5 exd5 13 ♘d3 ♕e7 14 ♘a4 ♖ac8 15 ♖c1 ♖fd8 16 ♗a3 ♘e4 17 ♕e1 d4 18 ♘dxc5 ♘axc5 19 ♘xc5 ♗d5 20 ♘xe4 and White is a pawn up and much better, Andersson-Miles, La Valetta 1980.

10...♘xc5 11 ♘xd5 ♘xd5 12 ♗xg7 ♔xg7 13 cxd5 ♕xd5 14 ♖c1 ♖fd8 15 ♕xd5 ♗xd5 16 ♖fd1 ♔f6 17 ♘d4

17 ♘d2 ♗xg2 18 ♔xg2 ♖ac8 19 ♔f3 ♔e6 20 ♔e3 f6 was also equal in Polugaevsky-Gipslis, Riga 1975.

17...♗xg2 18 ♔xg2 ♖ac8 19 ♘b5 ♖xd1 20 ♖xd1 ♘e4!

Using tactics to simplify the task of securing the draw.

21 ♘xa7 ♖c2 22 a4 ♘d6 23 ♖d4 ♖c7 24 ♘b5 ♘xb5 25 axb5 ♖c5 26 b4

26 ♖b4 would leave the rook about as passive as it is possible to be!

26...♖xb5 27 e4 ♔e5 28 ♖c4 f5 29 f3 g5 30 h3 h5

Black soon demonstrates that the position is a dead draw.

31 ♔f2 fxe4 32 fxe4 ♔d6 33 ♔e3 ♖e5 34 ♔d4 ♖b5 35 h4 gxh4 36 gxh4 ♔e6 37 ♔e3 ♔e5 ½-½

Summary

The Double Fianchetto has proved difficult to beat at the Super-GM level. Early deviations, such as 6 b3 or 7 ♖e1 seem to offer little, so White should go for the main line with 8 ♕xd4.

1 c4 c5 2 ♘f3 ♘f6 3 g3 b6 4 ♗g2 ♗b7 5 0-0 g6 6 ♘c3 (D)
> 6 b3 – *Game 14*

6...♗g7 7 d4
> 7 ♖e1 – *Game 13*

7...cxd4 8 ♕xd4
> 8 ♘xd4 (D) – *Game 12*

8...d6
> 8...♘c6 – *Game 11*

9 ♖d1 (D) – *Game 10*

6 ♘c3   8 ♘xd4   9 ♖d1

CHAPTER THREE

White Plays an Early d2-d4

1 c4 c5 2 ♘f3 ♘f6 3 d4 cxd4 4 ♘xd4

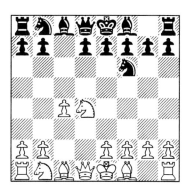

This position is often reached from the move order 1 d4 ♘f6 2 c4 c5 3 ♘f3 (1 d4 ♘f6 2 c4 e6 3 ♘f3 c5 4 ♘c3 leads into the same line), so the variation has often been called the Anti-Benoni. Certainly Benoni and Benko players need to have a reply prepared for this, even if they play something different against 1 c4. I would recommend such players look into 4...e6 or 4...e5.

The main moves given here lead to the old 'long' main line, but there are significant alternatives available on almost every half move, as noted below. I will cover the move order issues by illustrating the various branching points from the main line. I have not tried to hide the complexity of this, but

have pointed out short-cuts for pragmatists that want to limit the scope of their opponent's options.

There are also numerous transpositions possible out of the English and into, for example, the Nimzo-Indian or the Catalan.
4...e6

4...a6 was played by Kramnik against Kasparov, as a way of transposing to 5 ♘c3 e6 6 g3 ♕c7 (Game 18).

4...g6 is of course possible, when White has the option of an Accelerated Dragon after 5 ♘c3 ♗g7 6 e4, or can play 5 g3, with a likely transposition into Chapter 6.

4...b6 is for Hedgehog die-hards, and is dealt with in Game 16.

4...e5 is an aggressive response favoured by some Benoni players (see Game 15).

4...♘c6 usually transposes to the main line after 5 ♘c3 e6 (Game 22).

If White wants to avoid any of these, and indeed the options for Black on move 5 below, he can play 3 ♘c3, and if 3...♘c6 4 d4, though this of course gives Black the option of 3...d5, so you need a line against that also. This is the important kind of repertoire decision which you need to make.
5 ♘c3

White can also try 5 g3, when Black's main replies are 5...d5 which is a Catalan,

5...♗b4+ (Game 17) and 5...♕c7 (Game 18). White's only weakness in this position is his c4-pawn, and in several lines Black tries to exploit this. There are several gambit lines where Black can grab the pawn, e.g. 5 g3 ♕c7 6 ♘c3 a6 7 ♗g2 ♕xc4 (Game 18).

5...♘c6

Or 5...a6, when 6 e4 transposes to a Kan Sicilian, while 6 g3 ♕c7 is Game 18.

5...♗b4 is covered in Game 19, with the exception that 6 g3 would then lead to a Nimzo-Indian with g3, which is outside the scope of this book.

6 g3

White can also try to exploit the dark squares with 6 ♘bd5 (see Games 21 and 22), or Speelman's line 6 a3 (see Game 20).

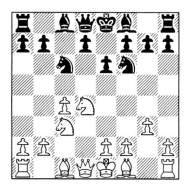

6...♕b6

If there is a theme that runs through these lines with ...e6, it is that Black develops his pieces very actively to avoid a positionally inferior outcome. His c8-bishop is potentially a problem piece, given that it cannot easily take up a post on b7 and is blocked by the d7- and e6-pawns. Routine development by Black would often lead to a 'bad Hedgehog' or, if he tries a belated ...d7-d5 thrust, to a 'bad IQP' position.

6...♗c5 (Game 23) and 6...♗b4 (note to Black's sixth move in Game 23) are alternatives.

7 ♘b3

7 ♘bd5 is also possible (Game 24).

7...♘e5

Continuing the active approach, Black's play is somewhat reminiscent of the Taimanov Sicilian. White has to develop somewhat unnaturally to cope with the pressure on the c4-pawn.

8 e4 ♗b4 9 ♕e2 d6

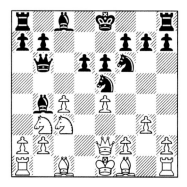

Now the traditional main line starts with 10 ♗e3 ♗xc3+ (Game 25) when the doubled c-pawns compensate for White's space and development advantage. White can choose a gung-ho kingside attack, or liquidate the forward c-pawn with c4-c5.

10 ♗d2 is an interesting alternative – see Game 26.

Game 15
Mikhalchishin-Kasparov
Soviet Championship 1981

---

1 d4 ♘f6 2 c4 c5 3 ♘f3

The 'English' move order to reach this position would be 1 c4 c5 2 ♘f3 ♘f6 3 d4.

3...cxd4 4 ♘xd4 e5

This line should be of great interest to Benoni and Benko players, and in fact is reached in the vast majority of cases by the move order 1 d4 ♘f6 2 c4 c5 3 ♘f3. It gives Black a chance to mix it in the combative spirit of those openings.

5 ♘b5

5 ♘c2 is an alternative. Although it would perhaps be unfair to label 3 ♘f3 as a

bit wimpish, this is taking things too far. Black can choose between:

a) A dull but equal position with 5...d5 6 cxd5 ♕xd5 7 ♕xd5 ♘xd5 8 e4 ♘b4 etc.

b) Or the adventurous 5...b5!?, e.g. 6 cxb5 ♗b7 7 e3 d5 8 ♗e2 ♗d6 9 0-0 0-0 10 ♘c3 ♘bd7 11 b3 ♖c8 12 ♗b2 ♕e7 13 ♖c1 ♖fd8 (Terzic-Bareev, Bihac 1999) with solid compensation for the pawn.

5...d5

This pawn sacrifice is the main line here. Black can also try 5...♗c5, when:

a) In practice, 6 ♘d6+ is usually played, when after 6...♔e7 7 ♘xc8+ ♕xc8 8 ♘c3 Black should play 8...d6. Konstantinopolsky-Taimanov, Soviet Championship 1948 continued 9 e3 (not 9 ♗g5? ♗xf2+ 10 ♔xf2 ♕f5+) 9...♖d8 10 ♗e2 ♘c6 11 0-0 ♔f8 12 a3 a6 13 ♕c2 ♘e7 14 ♗d2 ♕e6 with equality.

b) 6 ♗e3 ♗xe3 7 ♘d6+ ♔f8 8 fxe3 and now 8...♘c6 9 ♘c3 transposes to the position analysed in Game 22, notes to White's 8th move. Since that analysis indicates improvements over published theory that give Black fair chances, perhaps 5...♗c5 should be reconsidered.

6 cxd5 ♗c5 7 ♘5c3 0-0

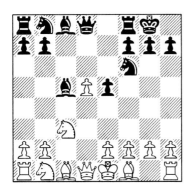

8 e3

8 h3 is a speciality of Raetsky, when Black has ventured:

a) 8...e4 9 g4 ♖e8 10 ♗g2 h6 11 ♘d2 e3 12 fxe3 ♗xe3 13 ♘c4 ♗c5 14 ♗f4 and:

a1) 14...♘h5 and now 15 ♕d2 ♕h4+ 16 ♔d1 ♘xf4 17 ♕xf4 ♘a6 would lead to an unclear position according to Raetsky and Sotnikov.

a2) 14...a6 15 a4 ♘bd7, Raetsky-Miezis, Bern 1995, and here 16 ♕d3 is a little better for White.

b) 8...♗f5 and now:

b1) 9 e3 ♗g6 10 g4 e4 11 ♗g2 ♘a6 12 g5 ♘b4! 13 gxf6?! (13 0-0) 13...♘d3+ 14 ♔d2 ♕xf6 15 ♖f1 ♖fe8 16 a3 b5 17 ♖a2 h5 with a big attack for Black, Aseev-Smirin, USSR 1988.

b2) The natural follow-up 9 g4 is taboo because of 9...♗e4 10 f3 (the alternative 10 ♖h2 is a bit sad) 10...♘xd5! and Black gets a big attack in return for the piece. Raetsky and Sotnikov give the following lines:

b21) 11 fxe4 ♕h4+ 12 ♔d2 ♘e3 13 ♕b3 ♖d8+ 14 ♘d5 ♘c6.

b22) 11 ♘xe4 ♕h4+ 12 ♔d2 ♖d8 13 ♘xc5 ♘e3+ 14 ♘d3 ♘xd1 15 ♔xd1 ♘c6.

b3) 9 a3 ♘bd7 10 e3 e4 11 b4 ♗d6 12 ♗b2 ♘e5 13 ♘d2 ♖c8 14 ♗e2 ♘d3+ 15 ♗xd3 exd3, Raetsky-Tyomkin, Biel 1999, and here Tyomkin recommends 16 ♕f3 (instead of 16 ♖c1 ♗e5 as played, and Black wins the d5-pawn back) e.g. 16...♗e5 17 ♕xf5 ♗xc3 18 ♗xc3 ♖xc3 19 e4 ♖c2 20 ♖d1 ♕c7 21 0-0 ♕c3 with compensation.

8...e4

The starting point for a popular variation. In return for the pawn, Black has a lead in development and a space advantage. Although White is not in immediate danger, unravelling his pieces without allowing a trivial recapture of the d5-pawn is not so easy, and castling too early can be dangerous. Overall, Black's results have been good, and White has struggled somewhat in a number of high-level games. Nevertheless, if White is well-prepared, he has chances of emerging with a slight plus. Black can also play 8...♕e7 but will usually follow up with ...e5-e4 in any case.

9 ♗e2

Delaying ♗f1-e2 is another idea, e.g. 9 ♘d2 and now:

a) 9...♖e8 10 a3 (10 ♗e2 transposes to the note to Black's 9th move below) 10...a5 11 ♗e2 ♘a6 12 b3 ♘c7 13 ♗b2 ♘cxd5 with equality, Lesiege-Bellon Lopez, Cienfuegos 1997.

b) 9...♕e7 10 a3 a5 and here:

b1) 11 d6 ♗xd6 12 ♘dxe4 ♘xe4 13 ♘xe4 ♖d8 14 ♘xd6 ♖xd6 15 ♕c2 ♘c6 was Palatnik-Kasparov, Moscow 1982. After 16 ♗e2 ♕g5 17 g3 ♗h3 Black has compensation for the pawn deficit.

b2) 11 b3 ♗f5 12 ♗b2 ♖d8 13 ♘c4 ♘bd7? (either 13...♗e6 or 13...♘c6 was essential; both look okay for Black) 14 d6 ♕f8 15 ♘b5 and White is well on top, Lesiege-Gomez, Havana 1999.

9...♕e7

Or 9...♖e8 10 ♘d2 and now:

a) 10...♘bd7 11 ♕c2 ♕e7 12 0-0 a6 13 a4 b6 14 ♘c4 ♗b7 15 ♖d1 ♖ad8 16 b3 and White is better, Lautier-Adams, Las Palmas 1994.

b) Both ECO and NCO give 10...♗b4 as leading to equality on the basis of the reference 11 ♕b3 ♗xc3 12 bxc3 ♕xd5 13 ♕xd5 ♘xd5 14 ♗b2 ♘c6 Perkovic-Barczay, Subotica 1981. However, the position looks slightly preferable for White after 15 ♖d1. Some sample lines:

b1) 15...♘b6 16 c4 frees the b2-bishop.

b2) 15...♗f5 16 g4 ♗g6 17 h4 h6 18 ♖g1 ♖ad8 19 h5 ♗h7 20 g5 hxg5 21 ♖xg5 f6 22 ♖xd5 ♖xd5 23 ♗c4 ♖ee5 (or 23...♖ed8 24 ♘f1 ♘e7 25 ♗a3) 24 ♘f3 winning material.

b3) 15...♘f6 16 ♘c4 ♗g4 17 ♘d6 ♖e7 18 c4 ♗xe2 19 ♔xe2 with good centralisation.

10 ♘d2

White decides to return the pawn. Alternatively, 10 a3 ♖d8 and now:

a) Normally White avoids castling 'into it' but 11 0-0 is certainly playable, e.g. 11...a5 12 ♘d2 ♗f5 13 ♕b3 h5 14 ♘c4 ♖a6 15 ♖d1 (15 ♘a4 maybe slightly better for

White) 15...♘g4 16 h3 ♘xf2 17 ♔xf2 ♗xh3 18 ♗f1 ♕h4+ 19 ♔g1 ♖f6 20 ♕c2 ♗g4 21 ♘xe4 ♖f4 with a wild position, Shabalov-D.Gurevich, New York 1998.

b) 11 b4 ♗d6 12 ♗b2 and:

b1) 12...♗e5 13 ♕b3 ♘bd7 14 ♘d2 ♘b6 15 ♖d1 ♗f5 16 ♘c4 ♘xc4 17 ♕xc4 ♖ac8 18 ♕b3 a6 (18...♘g4!?) 19 ♘a4 ♗xb2 20 ♕xb2 ♖xd5 21 ♖xd5 ♘xd5 22 0-0 ♕f6 with equality, Lautier-Illescas Cordoba, Linares 1995.

b2) 12...a5 13 bxa5 ♗e5 14 ♕a4? (Topalov's suggested improvements are 14 ♕c2 ♖xa5 15 ♘d2 and 14 ♘d2 ♗xc3 15 ♗xc3 ♘xd5 though Black should be no worse in either case) 14...♘a6 15 ♘d2 ♘c5 16 ♕b4 ♗g4, Timman-Topalov, Wijk aan Zee 1996, and Black is better.

10...♖d8 11 a3

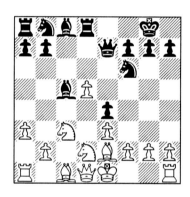

11...♘xd5

If Black does not take the pawn immediately, he will probably live to regret it, e.g. 11...♗f5 12 b4 (12 g4!?) 12...♗d6 13 ♘c4 ♗e5 14 ♘xe5 ♕xe5 15 ♗b2 ♘bd7 16 ♕b3 ♗g6 17 h4 and White retains the extra pawn with an initiative to boot, Lesiege-Goldenberg, Montreal 1998.

12 ♘xd5

12 ♘cxe4 didn't work out well after 12...♗b6 (12...♘xe3 is a more speculative piece sacrifice) 13 ♘c3 ♘xe3 14 fxe3 ♕xe3 15 ♖f1 ♘c6 16 ♕a4 ♘e5 17 ♔d1 ♗e6 18 ♖e1 ♖d4 19 ♗f3 ♕f4 20 ♕c2 ♘xf3 21 ♖e4

♕f6 22 ♖xe6 fxe6 23 gxf3 ♕xf3+ 24 ♔e1 ♕f2+ 0-1 Postny-Smirin, Israel 1999.

12...♖xd5 13 ♕c2

Two subsequent games showed new ideas for White, but were not picked up by any theory books. Both involve delayed castling for White, in order to annoy the Black pieces and retain the option of launching a kingside attack. It is true that it was not Kasparov sitting behind the Black pieces in either case, but there is certainly scope here for White to play for a win.

a) 13 ♕a4 ♗f5 14 b4 ♗b6 15 ♕b3 ♖d6 16 ♘c4 ♗g6 17 ♘xb6 axb6 18 ♕d5 ♗c8 19 ♗b2 ♘c6 20 ♖d1 ♖xg2 21 b5 ♕h4 22 ♖f1 ♗e6 23 ♕d6 ♘a5 24 ♕xb6 with chances for both sides, Vakhidov-Nesterov, Bishkek 1993.

b) 13 b4 ♗b6 14 ♗b2 ♘c6 15 ♕b3 ♖g5 16 ♕c2 ♗f5 when compared to Mikhalchishin-Kasparov, Black's rook is on g5 instead of d5, and White now tries to exploit this awkward placement: 17 g4 ♗xg4 18 h4 ♗xe2 19 hxg5 ♗d3 20 ♕c3 ♕xg5 21 ♘f3! exf3 22 ♕xd3 h5 23 0-0-0 ♘e5 24 ♕d5 ♖c8+ 25 ♔b1 and with White's king safe, he has a large plus, Panno-Glavina Rossi, Argentina 1989.

13...♗f5 14 b4 ♗b6 15 ♗b2 ♘c6 16 0-0 ♕g5

If Black plays routinely, he can easily end up worse, e.g. 16...♖ad8 17 ♘c4 ♕g5 18 ♖fd1 and if now 18...♗g4? 19 ♖xd5 ♖xd5 20 ♕xe4.

17 ♔h1!

17 ♘c4 ♗g4 18 ♗xg4 ♕xg4 gives Black a significant presence on the kingside.

17...♖d6

Kasparov highlights the possible improvement 17...♖c8 18 ♖ac1 ♖dd8 with unclear play. Indeed this looks awkward for White; it is not easy to suggest a constructive way forward.

18 ♘xe4 ♗xe4 19 ♕xe4 ♖d2 20 b5?

After this the tide definitely turns in Black's favour. Instead Kasparov gives the imaginative 20 ♗a6! which gives White a slight edge after 20...bxa6 21 ♕xc6 ♖ad8 22 ♗d4 ♗xd4 23 exd4 ♕f6.

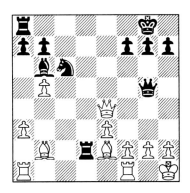

20...♖xe2

20...♘a5 is less clear because of 21 ♗c3 ♖xe2 22 ♕a4.

21 bxc6 ♖xb2 22 cxb7 ♖f8 23 ♖ac1

White was pinning his hopes on the b-pawn, but now we are treated to a display of precision calculation from Kasparov.

23...♗a5! 24 ♖c8 ♕b5! 25 ♖fc1 ♕xb7 26 ♕e8 ♕xc8! 27 ♕xc8 ♗d2!

A brilliant sequence of moves. Now White has to create a bolt-hole for his king, which gives Black a favourable two rooks v queen situation.

28 h3 h6 29 ♕c4 ♗xc1 30 ♕xc1 ♖xf2 31 ♕c7 a6 32 ♕a7 ♖f6

White essentially has no answer to the strategic threat of a double attack on the g2-pawn, followed by an exchange leading to a winning pawn ending.

33 a4 ♖d8 34 a5 ♖d1+ 35 ♔h2 ♖d2 36 ♕b8+ ♔h7 37 ♕b4 ♖ff2 38 ♕e4+ f5 0-1

Game 16
Ionov-Yudasin
Vilnius 1997

---

1 c4 c5 2 ♘f3 ♘f6 3 ♘c3

Another move order leading to the same thing is 3 d4 cxd4 4 ♘xd4 b6 5 ♘c3 ♗b7.

3...b6

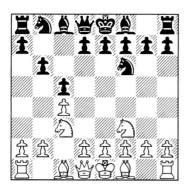

This move order will suit dedicated Hedgehog fans, who want to play their set-up no matter what.

4 e4

4 d4 cxd4 5 ᐅxd4 ᔑb7 6 ᔑg5 (6 f3 d6 7 e4 transposes to the main line) is another approach. Although ECO gives White an edge in this line, in practice Black has a healthy plus score. After 6 ᔑg5, Black has:

a) 6...d6 7 ᔑxf6 gxf6 8 e3 e6 9 ᙏh5 ᙏe7 10 ᔑe2 ᐅc6 11 ᔑf3 ᐅxd4 12 exd4 ᔑxf3 13 ᙏxf3 ᖦc8 14 0-0 ᔑg7 15 b3 f5 16 ᖦad1 0-0 17 ᖦfe1 and White is slightly better, Agzamov-Bönsch, Sochi 1984.

b) 6...a6 with the choice of:

b1) 7 e4!? is a rarely seen pawn sacrifice: 7...ᐅxe4 8 ᐅxe4 ᔑxe4 9 ᙏe2 ᔑg6 10 g4 f6 11 ᔑg2 ᖦa7 12 ᔑd2 e6 13 ᖦd1 (13 0-0 is also answered by 13...ᔑc5 followed by castling) 13...ᔑc5 14 ᔑc3 ᙏc7 15 0-0 0-0 16 ᖰh1 ᙏf4 and Black is better, Lerner-Psakhis, Frunze 1979.

b2) The tricky 7 ᐅf5 should be answered by 7...ᙏc7 8 ᙏd4 ᐅc6 9 ᐅd5 ᐅxd5 10 ᐅxg7+ ᔑxg7 11 ᙏxg7 ᙏe5 12 ᙏxe5 ᐅxe5 13 cxd5 ᔑxd5 with equality, Rashkovsky-Psakhis, Beltsy 1979.

b3) 7 ᔑxf6 gxf6 with a further branch:

b31) 8 ᐅf5 ᙏc7 9 ᙏd4 (Watson gives 9 ᐅd5 ᔑxd5 10 ᙏxd5 ᐅc6 11 ᖦd1 e6 12 ᐅd6+ ᔑxd6 as slightly better for Black) and here Black should try 9...ᖦg8 followed by

...e7-e6, instead of the 9...e6 10 ᙏxf6 ᖦg8 11 ᐅe3 ᐅc6 12 ᙏh4 of Enneper-Zierke, Germany 1995, which was good for White.

b32) 8 e3 e6 9 ᙏh5 ᙏc7 (note how the inclusion of 6...a6 instead of 6...d6 gives Black much more flexibility, for example his f8-bishop is not blocked in, and his queen can in some situations jump into e5) 10 ᐅf3 ᙏc5 11 ᙏh4 f5 12 ᔑe2 ᔑg7 13 0-0 ᐅc6 14 ᖦac1 ᐅe5 15 ᙏg3 ᐅg6 16 ᖦfd1 ᖦc8 17 a3 ᙏc7 18 ᙏxc7 ᖦxc7 19 ᐅd4 (19 g3) 19...f4 and Black is at least equal, Lerner-Psakhis, Riga 1985.

4...d6 5 d4 cxd4 6 ᐅxd4 ᔑb7 7 f3

With this move order White can also play 7 ᙏe2 or 7 ᔑd3 (see Game 63).

7...e6 8 ᔑe3 ᔑe7 9 ᔑe2 0-0

Black has to be very careful not to fall into a positional trap in this line. If Black plays ...ᐅb8-d7 too early, White can go for a quick a4-a5, which breaks the harmony of Black's set-up and gives White a lot of potential play on the queenside. After 9...a6 10 0-0 ᐅbd7 11 a4 0-0 12 a5 bxa5 13 ᐅb3 White is slightly better. One example: 13...ᖦb8 14 ᐅxa5 ᔑa8 15 ᙏd2 ᙏc7 16 ᖦfc1 ᐅe5 17 ᐅa4 ᔑc6 18 b4 ᔑxa4 19 ᖦxa4 ᐅfd7 20 ᖦaa1 when White has a clear plus due to his powerful queenside pawns, Ivanchuk-Adams, Dortmund 1992.

10 0-0 a6

Note that Black is delaying ...ᐅb8-d7 until he has played his other preparatory moves ...0-0 and ...a7-a6.

11 ᙏd2

With the knight still on b8, 11 a4 can be answered by 11...ᐅc6 12 ᐅxc6 ᔑxc6 13 ᙏb3 ᖦb8 14 ᖦfd1 ᙏc7 15 ᖦac1 ᔑa8 16 ᖦd2 ᖦfd8 17 ᙏd1 ᐅd7 with an equal game, Z.Polgar-Kudrin, Salamanca 1989.

11...ᐅbd7

This position is the starting point for a complex Hedgehog-based system with many positional nuances. The move order here is extremely subject to transpositions and permutations. My intention with the various game references is to give a number of instructive examples, so I suggest you approach the notes from the viewpoint of grasping the ideas and typical 'mini-plans', not in order to memorise all the possible sequences.

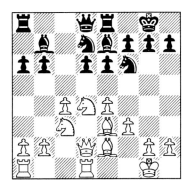

Some of Black's important ideas are:

1) The classic pawn breaks ...d6-d5 and ...b7-b5, though the latter occurs less often in this line.

2) Re-routing the dark-squared bishop via ...♗e7-d8-c7 to potentially target White's kingside after ...d6-d5.

3) The ambitious 'Fischer plan' ...♔g8-h8, ..♖f8-g8, ...g7-g5, with a view to a kingside attack. If you are not familiar with this idea, it is well worth studying the following game where Fischer (with reverse colours) introduced this new concept. Fischer-Andersson, Siegen Olympiad 1970 went 1 b3 e5 2 ♗b2 ♘c6 3 c4 ♘f6 4 e3 ♗e7 5 a3 0-0 6 ♕c2 ♖e8 7 d3 ♗f8 8 ♘f3 a5 9 ♗e2 d5 10 cxd5 ♘xd5 11 ♘bd2 f6 12 0-0 ♗e6 13 ♔h1 ♕d7 14 ♖g1 ♖ad8 15 ♘e4 ♕f7 16 g4 g6 17 ♖g3 ♗g7 18 ♖ag1 ♘b6 19 ♘c5 ♗c8 20 ♘h4 ♘d7 21 ♘e4 ♘f8 22 ♘f5 ♗e6 23 ♘c5 ♘e7 24 ♘xg7 ♔xg7 25 g5 ♘f5 26 ♖f3 b6 27 gxf6+ ♔h8 28 ♘xe6 ♖xe6 29 d4 exd4 30 ♗c4 d3 31 ♗xd3 ♖xd3 32 ♕xd3 ♖d6 33 ♕c4 ♘e6 34 ♗e5 ♖d8 35 h4 ♘d6 36 ♕g4 ♘f8 37 h5 ♘e8 38 e4 ♖d2 39 ♖h3 ♔g8 40 hxg6 ♘xg6 41 f4 ♔f8 42 ♕g5 ♘d6 43 ♗xd6+ 1-0

Meanwhile the key ideas for White are:

1) Achieving a queenside clamp with b2-b4.

2) Restraining the ...d7-d5 and ...b7-b5 breaks.

3) Generating a kingside pawn-storm, though this happens less often than you would think.

4) Combating the ...♗e7-d8-c7 manoeuvre. If White has played b2-b4 and can answer ...♗e7-d8 with ♘d4-b3 followed by ♗e3-f4 he is usually better, since the sequence ...♘d7-e5 ♗f4xe5 gives White a better structure, with Black's bishop boxed in on c7. If Black has already played ...♗e7-d8 then a subsequent b2-b4 can often be answered by ...♘d7-e5 and ...d5.

All the above points are illustrated by the numerous examples that follow.

12 ♖fd1

Black is better prepared than in the note to Black's 9th above for 12 a4 ♖c8 (or 12...♖e8 13 a5 d5!?) 13 a5 ♘e5 14 axb6 ♘xc4 15 ♗xc4 ♖xc4 16 ♘b3 ♖b4 17 ♘a5 ♗a8 18 ♘a4 ♖b5 19 ♘c3 ♖b4 20 ♘a4 ♖b5 21 ♘c3 ½-½ Adams-Van Wely, Tilburg 1997.

12...♖e8

Black's next three moves will typically be ...♕d8-c7, ...♖a8-c8 and ...♖f8-e8, the sequence being somewhat arbitrary. After 12...♕c7 13 ♖ac1 ♖ac8 White can continue to smooth out his piece placement, with for example, ♗e2-f1, ♔g1-h1 and ♕d2-f2 (see the main game) or can go for an earlier queenside clamp, e.g. 14 a3 ♕b8 15 b4 and now:

a) 15...♖fe8 16 ♗f1 (Perhaps more promising is 16 ♘b3 with the follow-up a3-a4-a5 in mind; 16...♗d8?! is answered by 17 ♗f4) 16...♗d8 17 ♖c2 ♘e5 18 ♘a4 d5! 19 exd5 exd5 20 c5 b5 21 ♘b6 ♗xb6 22 cxb6 ♖xc2 23 ♘xc2 ♘c4 24 ♗xc4 dxc4 25 ♕d6 ♕xd6?! (25...♕a8 with the idea of ...♘d5 and ...♖e6) 26 ♖xd6 ♖e6 27 ♖d8+ ♖e8 28 ♖xe8+ ♘xe8 29 ♗c5 (Seirawan-Kudrin,

Chandler 1997) and White has a slightly better ending.

b) 15...♗d8 16 ♘b3 transposes to Leko-Zapata, Yopal 1997, which continued 16...♗c7 17 ♗f4 ♘e5 18 ♗xe5 dxe5 19 ♔h1 ♖fd8 20 ♕e3 ♖xd1+ 21 ♖xd1 ♖d8 22 ♖xd8+ ♕xd8 23 c5 ♘d7 24 c6, when White gets a better ending due to his queenside majority.

13 ♖ac1 ♖c8 14 ♗f1

14 a3 ♕c7 15 b4 ♕b8 16 ♘b3! is (by transposition) the plan mentioned in the previous note.

14...♕c7 15 ♔h1

a) In the event of 15 b4 Yusupov gives 15...d5 16 cxd5 ♗xb4. Notice that this works for Black when his queen is still on c7 attacking the knight on c3.

b) 15 ♕f2 ♕b8 16 a3 ♗f8 17 b4 and now:

b1) 17...d5?! is premature. Beliavsky-A.Sokolov, Igalo 1994 continued 18 cxd5 exd5 19 ♘xd5 ♘xd5 20 exd5 ♖xc1 21 ♗xc1 b5 22 ♗b2 ♘f6 23 ♘c6 ♕d6 24 ♕b6, which is very good for White.

b2) 17...♘e5 18 ♘a4 ♘fd7 19 h3 ♗a8 20 ♘b3 ♖c6 with play for both sides, Seirawan-Ljubojevic, Mar del Plata 1981.

c) 15 a3!? is Yusupov's suggestion

15...♕b8

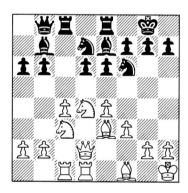

16 ♕f2

a) If White tries 16 b4 then:

a1) Black should not play 16...♗d8?!,

which allows the standard manoeuvre 17 ♘b3 ♗c7 (17...♘e5 18 ♘a4 d5 19 ♘xb6 ♗xb6 20 ♗xb6 dxe4 21 f4 is given by NCO as slightly better for White) 18 ♗f4 ♘e5 19 ♗xe5 dxe5 20 c5 b5 21 a4 and White is much better, Stohl-Ward, Isle of Man 1994.

a2) 16...♘e5 17 ♘a4 ♘fd7 is okay for Black, and is similar to Seirawan-Ljubojevic in the previous note, and the two Tseshkovsky games below.

b) 16 ♗g1

b1) 16...♘e5 17 ♘a4 ♘fd7 18 b4 h6 19 a3 ♗a8 20 ♖c2 ♗d8 21 ♖dc1 ♗c7 with chances for both sides, Sveshnikov-Tseshkovsky, Yerevan 1982.

b2) 16...♗f8 17 b4 ♘e5 18 ♘a4 ♘fd7 19 a3 ♗a8 20 ♘b3 b5?! (20...♘xc4 21 ♗xc4 b5 with an unclear position) 21 cxb5 axb5 22 ♘c3 ♘c4 23 ♕a2. White, who threatens ♘c3xb5, is clearly better, Yusupov-Tseshkovsky, Frunze 1981.

16...♗d8

This is the correct timing for the ...♗e7-d8 manoeuvre. Since ♕d2-f2 has taken pressure off the d6-pawn and he has not yet advanced his pawn to b4, White is not ready for the ♘d4-b3 and ♗e3-f4 plan, which we have seen to be so effective against ...♗e7-d8.

17 b3

a) The passive move 17 ♘b3 was played in Taimanov-Yusupov, USSR 1982, and allowed Black to implement the Fischer plan in a pure form. 17...♗c7 18 ♕g1 ♔h8 19 ♖c2 ♖g8 20 ♖cd2 g5 21 ♗d4 ♖g6 22 ♘c1 ♖cg8 23 ♘d3 ♕f8 24 ♖e1 g4 with strong kingside pressure.

b) The kingside pawn-storm with 17 ♘c2 ♗c7 18 g4 h6 19 h4 d5 20 g5 ♗g3 21 ♕g2 dxe4, as played in Ki.Georgiev-Rajkovic, Vrsac 1987, led to a wild position.

c) After 17 b4 Yusupov gives 17...♘e5 18 ♘a4 d5, which is okay for Black.

17...♘e5

Ionov suggests 17...♗c7, after which he was planning 18 g4 with a complex fight.

18 ♕d2 ♗c7 19 ♗g1

19 b4 is also possible.

19...♔h8 20 ♕f2 ♖g8 21 ♘de2 g5

The Fischer plan.

22 ♘g3 ♖g6 23 ♘a4 ♘fd7 24 ♕b2 ♗c6 25 ♘c3 ♖cg8 26 b4

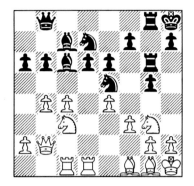

Compared to the Taimanov-Yusupov game above, Black has played a similar build-up, but White is much better placed than in the other game. His kingside is better defended with the knight on g3 instead of b3; he has gained space on the queenside and maintained piece co-ordination.

26...♗a8 27 ♘ce2 ♖h6 28 ♘d4 ♖g7 29 ♘b3 ♘g6 30 ♗d4 f6 31 ♔g1

31 ♗xf6 ♘xf6 32 ♕xf6 d5 is the kind of thing Black is hoping for.

31...♘de5 32 ♗e3 ♗b7 33 ♘d4 ♗c8 34 ♕d2 ♗d7 35 ♖c3 ♘e7 36 ♖dc1 ♕e8 37 ♗f2 f5

As happens in many Hedgehog games, a protracted series of manoeuvres is eventually broken by a pawn thrust and sharp play.

38 exf5 exf5 39 ♖e1 f4 40 ♘e4 ♕h5

In the case of 40...d5, Ionov gives 41 cxd5 ♘xd5 42 ♘f5 ♘xc3 43 ♘xh6 ♘xe4 44 ♖xe4 with an ongoing initiative for White.

41 h3 g4 42 fxg4 ♖xg4

Better was 42...♘xg4 43 ♕xf4 ♘g6.

43 ♘f6 ♖xf6

43...♖xg2+ was a better try, though White is still clearly on top after 44 ♗xg2 ♖xf6 45

♕e2.

44 hxg4 ♗xg4 45 ♗e2 f3 46 ♘xf3 ♖h6 47 ♘h4 ♘f5 48 ♖h3

Exploiting the pin on the g4-bishop, this removes any threats along the h-file.

48...♖f6 49 ♘xf5 ♕xf5 50 ♗xg4 ♕xg4 51 ♕e2 ♕e6 52 ♕e4 ♖g6 53 ♖g3 1-0

Game 17
Beliavsky-Adams
Dortmund 1998

---

1 d4 ♘f6 2 c4 e6 3 g3 c5 4 ♘f3 cxd4 5 ♘xd4

1 c4 c5 2 ♘f3 ♘f6 3 d4 cxd4 4 ♘xd4 e6 5 g3 is the standard English Opening order to reach this position.

5...♗b4+

5...♕c7 6 ♘c3 a6 is covered in Game 18.

6 ♗d2

6 ♘c3 transposes to the Nimzo-Indian.

6...♕b6

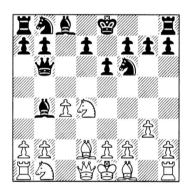

Black also has:

a) 6...♗e7 7 ♗g2 ♘c6 8 ♗f4 0-0 9 ♘c3 a6 10 0-0 ♘xd4 11 ♕xd4 d6 12 ♕d3 ♕c7 13 ♖fd1 ♖d8 14 ♖ac1 ♘h5 15 ♗d2 ♖b8 16 ♘e4 ♘f6 17 ♘xf6+ ♗xf6 18 ♗f4 e5 19 ♗e3 ♗e6 20 b3, when White has a slightly better game, Topalov-Kramnik, FIDE World Championship, Las Vegas 1999.

b) Alternatively, Black can adopt a policy of simplification with 6...♗xd2+ and now:

b1) 7 ♕xd2 ♘e4 8 ♕e3 ♕a5+ 9 ♘d2

♕xd2+ 10 ♕xd2 ♘xd2 11 ♔xd2 ♔e7 12 ♗g2 ♘c6 13 e3, which may be a fraction better for White.

b2) 7 ♘xd2 ♕b6 8 ♘2b3 ♕b4+ 9 ♕d2 ♕xd2+ 10 ♔xd2 ♘c6 11 ♗g2 ♘xd4 12 ♘xd4 d6 13 ♖ac1 ♔e7 14 ♖hd1 ♗d7 15 ♔e1 (Taimanov-Bronstein, Tbilisi 1959) and White can claim to be slightly better, but only slightly.

7 ♗xb4

Other options at this point:

a) 7 e3 looks tame against Timman's approach: 7...♘c6 8 ♗g2 0-0 9 0-0 ♖d8 (Previously 9...d5 10 cxd5 ♘xd4 11 ♗xb4 ♕xb4 12 ♕xd4 had worked out to be a little better for White) 10 ♗xb4 ♕xb4 11 ♗xc6 (11 ♕b3 is equal according to Timman) 11...bxc6 12 ♘xc6 ♕xb2 13 ♘xd8 ♕xa1 14 ♕d6 h6! 15 ♘a3 ♕xa2 16 ♕e7 ♗a6 17 ♘xf7 ♖f8 and White is scrambling to stay in the game, Adianto-Timman, Bali 2000.

b) After the sharp 7 ♗g2 ♗c5 White gives up two pawns, and the position can be dangerous for Black if he is not careful. White gets some compensation for the material, but ultimately this should not be worth more than equality against accurate play. After 8 e3 (not 8 ♗c3 e5) 8...♗xd4 9 exd4 ♕xd4 10 0-0 Black has:

b1) 10...♕xc4 11 ♘a3 (11 ♗f4!?) 11...♕d3 12 ♗b4 ♕xd1 13 ♖fxd1 d5 14 ♘b5 ♔d7 15 ♘d6 ♘c6 16 ♗a3 ♖f8 (the danger inherent in the position for Black is illustrated by 16...♘d8 17 ♖ac1 ♘e8 18 ♗xd5! Faibisovich-Vaganian, Voronezh 1969, and suddenly Black is in trouble) 17 ♖ac1 ♖b8 18 ♗h3 a5 19 ♘e4 ♔e8 and here White should repeat moves with 20 ♘d6+. Instead after 20 ♗xf8 ♔xf8 21 ♘c5 ♔e7 Black has consolidated and has two strong central pawns, which are more than enough for the exchange.

b2) Alternatively, Black can settle for one pawn instead of two, which seems to promise an equal game, e.g. 10...♘c6 11 ♘a3 0-0 12 ♗c3 ♕c5 13 ♕d2 ♕e7 14 ♘b5 d5 15

♗xf6 ♕xf6 16 cxd5 ♖d8 17 ♕c3 ♕xc3 18 ♘xc3 exd5 19 ♘xd5 ♔f8 20 ♖fc1 ♗d7 21 ♘c7 ½-½ Stean-Adorjan, Vienna 1980.

7...♕xb4+ 8 ♘c3 0-0

This is a natural move, especially as grabbing one of the pawns on offer seems too dangerous. However Black has a range of alternatives:

a) The capture 8...♕xc4 cannot be recommended – White quickly gets an initiative: 9 e4 ♕c5 10 ♘b3 ♕e7 11 e5 ♘d5 12 ♘xd5 exd5 13 ♕xd5 ♘c6 14 0-0-0 0-0 15 f4 with a big space advantage; Black will have trouble developing his c8-bishop, Zilberstein-Alburt, Odessa 1972.

b) 8...♕xb2 is more double-edged, e.g. 9 ♘db5 ♕b4 10 ♘c7+ ♔d8 11 ♕d2 ♘e4 12 ♘xe6+ fxe6 13 ♘xe4 ♕xd2+ and in this ending White has tried:

b1) 14 ♔xd2 b6 15 ♗g2 ♗b7 16 ♖hd1 ♘a6 17 ♔e3 (the pin on the h1-a8 diagonal means that White has to spend time unravelling) 17...♔e7 18 ♗f3 ♗xe4 19 ♗xe4 ♖ab8 (Petursson-Forintos, Ljubljana 1981) and given the weak c4-pawn, Black is at least equal.

b2) 14 ♘xd2 is more accurate since White gets control of the long diagonal: 14...♔c7 15 ♗g2 ♘c6 16 0-0 b6 17 ♘e4 ♗a6 18 ♖ac1 ♖af8 19 ♖fd1 ♖f5 20 ♘d2 ♖a5 21 c5, when White liquidates her only weakness and meanwhile has a fair initiative going, Alexandria-Litinskaya, Vilnius 1980.

c) 8...a6 9 a3!? (9 ♕b3 is also possible) 9...♕xc4 (9...♕e7 10 ♗g2 gives White a slightly preferable position, since Black cannot easily develop his queenside without getting a 'bad IQP' or 'bad Hedgehog' position) 10 ♖c1 0-0 11 ♗g2 ♘c6 12 ♘xc6 dxc6 13 ♘a4 ♕g4 14 ♘b6 ♖a7 15 ♕d6 and Black is under a lot of pressure, Zilberstein-Mochalov, USSR 1974.

d) 8...♘c6 may well be Black's best, e.g. 9 ♘db5 0-0 10 e3 d5 11 a3 ♕a5 12 b4 ♕d8 13 cxd5 exd5 14 ♗g2 ♗g4 15 ♕d2 ♘e5 16 ♘d4 ♖c8 17 0-0 ♕d7 and the position is equal, although Black's position is now somewhat easier to play, Hausner-Pinter, Skara 1980.

9 ♕b3

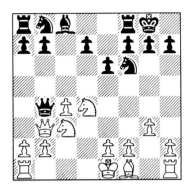

9...♕c5

9...♕xb3 10 axb3 ♘c6 11 e3 is slightly better for White according to Beliavsky. White gets the h1-a8 diagonal and open a-file, while Black has a cramped set-up.

10 ♖d1 a6

Adams gives 10...♘c6 11 ♕b5 ♕e7 12 ♗g2 as better for White.

11 ♗g2 ♘c6 12 ♘xc6 dxc6

After 12...bxc6 13 0-0 d5 14 ♘a4 ♕a5 15 ♕c2 ♖a7 16 a3 White has good play against Black's pawn structure and weakened dark-squares, Rashkovsky-Mikhalchishin, Cheliabinsk 1975.

13 0-0 e5 14 ♘a4 ♕e7 15 ♕b6

The natural 15 ♘b6 ♖b8 16 ♘xc8 ♖fxc8 17 ♖d2 is also quite good for White.

15...♗e6 16 b3 ♖ad8 17 h3

Adams prefers 17 ♕e3.

17...h5! 18 ♕e3

18 ♕a7 is also possible.

18...♗f5 19 ♘c5 a5 20 ♘a4! ♕c7

To prevent ♕e3-b6.

21 ♘b6

White has in mind c4-c5 and ♘c4-d6, as well as ♕c5.

21...♖fe8 22 c5

The immediate 22 ♕c5 allows the simplifying 22...♘d7 23 ♘xd7 ♖xd7 24 ♖xd7

♕xd7 hitting the h3-pawn.

22...♗e6 23 ♕g5 ♗d5 24 ♖fe1 ♗xg2 25 ♔xg2 ♕e7 26 ♖xd8 ♖xd8 27 ♖c1 ♖d4?!

Adams claims equality after 27...♕e6.

28 ♘c8 ♕e6 29 ♘d6 g6 30 ♖c4

Here 30 ♘xb7 can be answered by 30...h4 with some kingside play. However, the line 30 ♖c3! e4 31 ♖c4 ♖xc4 32 bxc4 b6 33 ♘b7 bxc5 34 ♘xa5 ♘d7 35 ♕d8+ ♔g7 36 ♕c8 leaves White on top in the endgame (Shirov).

30...b5 31 ♖xd4 exd4 32 ♕f4 ♘d5 33 ♕xd4 ♕xe2 34 a4 bxa4 35 bxa4 f5

Black tries a kingside rush, presumably in White's time trouble. 35...♕e1 is the steadier move.

36 ♘c4 h4 37 ♕xh4??

37 ♘xa5 ♕a6 (37...hxg3 is unsound because of 38 ♘xc6 gxf2 39 ♕xd5+ ♔g7 40 ♕e5+) 38 ♘b3 and White is a pawn up.

37...f4!

Out of the blue, White's knight is attacked, while Black also threatens ...f4-f3 with a quick mate to follow.

38 ♕d8+

38 ♕g4 is answered by 38...f3+.

38...♔h7 39 ♕d7+ ♔h6 40 gxf4 0-1

In this hopeless position, White lost on time.

Game 18
Dyachkov-Aseev
Russian Championship 1996

1 d4 ♘f6 2 c4 e6 3 g3 c5 4 ♘f3 cxd4 5 ♘xd4

1 c4 c5 2 ♘f3 ♘f6 3 d4 cxd4 4 ♘xd4 e6 5 g3 is the standard move order.

5...♕c7

Instead 5...♕b6 is perhaps an underestimated choice. After 6 ♗g2 ♗c5 7 e3 ♘c6 there is:

a) 8 ♕b3 ♗b4+ 9 ♗d2 ♘e5 10 ♕c2 d5 11 cxd5 and now:

a1) 11...♘xd5 12 0-0 ♗d7 13 ♘c3 ♘f6

14 ♘e4 ♖c8 15 ♕d1 ♘xe4 16 ♗xe4 ♗xd2 17 ♕xd2 ♘c4 18 ♕d4 ♕xd4 19 ♘xd4 is equal, Ellers-Suba, Bern 1995.

a2) 11...♕a6 12 ♗xb4 (12 ♗f1 ♘f3+ 13 ♔d1 ♕b6 and White's displaced king compensates Black for his sacrificed pawn) 12...♘d3+ 13 ♔d2 ♘xb4 14 ♕c3 ♘bxd5 15 ♕d3 ♕xd3+ 16 ♔xd3 b6 17 ♘c3 ♗a6+ and Black is on the attack, Sosonko-Suba, Tunis 1985.

b) White can try a pawn sacrifice with 8 0-0 ♘xd4 9 exd4 ♗xd4 10 ♘c3 e5 11 ♘b5 0-0 12 ♘xd4 exd4 13 b3 d5 14 ♗a3 ♖e8 15 c5 ♕a5 16 ♗b2 ♕xc5 17 ♗xd4 ♕d6 18 ♗xf6 ♕xf6 19 ♕xd5 with equality, Haba-Sax, German Bundesliga 1993.

6 ♘c3

6 ♘d2 is also possible. Given the theoretical status of the gambit played in the main game, this is perhaps White's best try at this juncture. Although it looks somewhat insipid at first sight, White has a fair chance of gaining a small edge from the opening.

a) 6...a6 7 ♗g2 ♘c6 and now:

a1) 8 ♘xc6 dxc6 9 0-0 ♗e7 10 ♕c2 0-0 11 b3 e5 12 ♗b2 ♗e6 13 a3 a5 14 c5 ♘d7 15 b4 f6 16 ♘c4 axb4 17 axb4, as in Stean-Cebalo, Smederevska Palanka 1980, gives White a typical, small but nagging edge.

a2) 8 ♘2b3 d6 9 0-0 ♗d7 10 e4 ♗e7 11 ♗e3 ♘xd4 12 ♕xd4 0-0 13 h3 e5 14 ♕d3 b5 15 ♖fc1 bxc4 16 ♖xc4 ♕b8 17 ♕d2 a5 18 ♖ac1 ♗d8 19 ♘a1 ♖a6 20 b3 h6 ½-½ Gelfand-Leko, Istanbul Olympiad 2000.

b) 6...♘c6 7 ♘b5 ♕b8 8 ♗g2 a6 9 ♘c3 b5 10 0-0 ♗e7 11 a3 0-0 12 b4 ♗b7 13 cxb5 axb5 14 ♘b3 ♘e5 15 ♗xb7 ♕xb7 16 ♘a5 ♕a6 17 ♗f4 and White has a slight advantage, Gaprindashvili-Alexandria, Tbilisi 1979.

c) 6...b6 looks like the pick of Black's alternatives, e.g. 7 ♗g2 ♗b7 8 ♘b5 ♕c8 and now:

c1) 9 ♗xb7 ♕xb7 10 ♘f3 ♘e4 11 0-0 a6 12 ♘c3 ♘xc3 13 bxc3 ♗c5 14 ♕d3 0-0 15 ♗e3 ♗xe3 16 ♕xe3 ½-½ Nogueiras-Van

der Wiel, Reggio Emilia 1986.

c2) 9 e4 a6 10 ♘c3 d6 11 0-0 ♘bd7 12 b3 ♗e7 13 ♗b2 0-0 14 ♖c1 ♖e8 15 ♕e2, Cifuentes Parada-Van der Wiel, Wijk aan Zee 1997, and now 15...♕c7 followed by ...♖a8-c8 and ...♕c7-b8 is a normal looking Hedgehog, naturally with chances for both sides.

6...a6 7 ♗g2

Alternatively:

a) 7 ♕d3 is fairly innocuous: 7...♘c6 8 ♘xc6 dxc6 9 ♗g2 e5 10 0-0 ♗e6 11 ♘a4 ½-½ Kasparov-Kramnik, London (7th match game) 2000.

Note the move order used by Kramnik in this game was 1 c4 c5 2 ♘f3 ♘f6 3 d4 cxd4 4 ♘xd4 a6!? 5 ♘c3 e6 6 g3 ♕c7. This is a clever move order which might find some followers. White could try 5 ♘c3 e6 6 ♗g5 which is similar to the line 1 c4 c5 2 ♘f3 ♘f6 3 ♘c3 ♘c6 4 d4 cxd4 5 ♘xd4 e6 6 ♗g5 (covered in the notes to Game 20) except that Black has committed himself to an early ...a7-a6. Having said that, Black has scored reasonably well from here.

Alternatively, if 5 g3, then Black can try 5...d5 6 ♗g2 and then either 6...dxc4!? or 6...e5!? with a theoretical position from the Catalan, where Black has the extra move ...a7-a6 (cf. 1 d4 ♘f6 2 c4 c5 3 ♘f3 cxd4 4 ♘xd4 e6 5 g3 d5 6 ♗g2 e5). Obviously 7 ♘b5 is prevented, but still, if White retreats with 7 ♘c2 (or 7 ♘f3 or 7 ♘b3), it is not entirely clear how much the move ...a7-a6 helps.

b) After the alternative 7 ♗g5 Black may as well grab the pawn, since this seems to leave him clearly better: 7...♕xc4 8 ♖c1 ♘c6 and here:

b1) 9 ♘b3 ♘e4 was very good for Black after 10 ♗g2 (10 ♘xe4 ♕xe4 11 f3 ♕g6) 10...♘xg5 11 h4 ♕g4 12 hxg5 ♕xg5 in Komarov-Aseev, St Petersburg 1997.

b2) 9 ♘cb5 ♕b4+ 10 ♗d2 axb5 11 ♗xb4 ♗xb4+ 12 ♖c3 ♖xa2 13 ♕b1 and Black is somewhat better according to Aseev – he has a decent amount of material in return for the queen.

7...♛xc4

Again, Black should probably take the pawn, unless he wants to avoid the drawish lines discussed later in this game. However, routine development will leave White with a nice position.

8 0-0

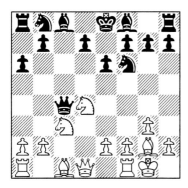

The alternative is to rush the a1-rook to the c-file 8 ♗f4 ♘c6 9 ♘xc6 bxc6 10 ♖c1 ♛b4 11 a3 and now:

a) 11...♛b7 12 ♗d6 ♗xd6 13 ♛xd6 with a further split:

a1) 13...♛b8 14 ♛c5 ♛a7 15 ♛d6 ♛b8, repeating moves (½-½ Sosonko-Kavalek, Wijk aan Zee 1978).

a2) 13...♛xb2 14 0-0 ♛b8 15 ♛c5 ♛c7 16 ♖b1 ♖b8 17 ♖xb8 ♛xb8 (Ca.Hansen) and now White should play actively with 18 e4 e.g.:

a21) 18...e5 (or 18...♘g4 19 f4) 19 f4 exf4 20 e5 fxg3 21 exf6 gxh2+ 22 ♔h1 gxf6 23 ♖e1+ ♔d8 24 ♛e7+ ♔c7 25 ♘d5+ winning.

a22) 18...d6 19 ♛xc6+ ♗d7 20 ♛xa6 0-0 is a way to return the material and equalise.

b) 11...♛xb2 (suggested by Ca.Hansen) can be met with 12 ♘a4 ♛xa3 13 0-0 when despite Black's 3-pawn advantage, he is struggling. White's immediate threat is ♘a4-b6, so Black needs to kick the f4-bishop: 13...♘h5 (or 13...♖a7 14 ♘b6 ♗b7 15 ♗b8 ♖a8 16 ♘xa8 ♗xa8 17 ♖a1 ♛c5 18 ♛b1

and the days of the bishop on a8 are numbered) 14 ♗e5 f6 15 ♘b6 fxe5 16 ♘xa8 ♗e7 17 ♘b6 and White will win back a couple of pawns, leaving him with a material edge.

8...♘c6

8...♛c7 continues the fight, e.g. 9 ♗g5 ♗e7 10 ♖c1 ♘c6 11 e4 0-0 12 ♗e3 ♛d8 13 ♛e2 and White has central pressure in return for the pawn, Flear-Renet, Paris 1986.

9 ♘xc6 bxc6 10 ♗f4 ♛b4

Instead after 10...d5:

a) 11 e4 ♗e7 12 a3 a5 13 ♖c1 ♛a6 14 exd5 exd5 (Ostojic-Petronic, Banja Vrucica 1991) leaves Black better – he has good chances to consolidate his pawn gain.

b) 11 ♖c1 ♛b4 12 a3 ♛a5 13 e4 ♗e7 14 exd5 exd5 15 ♘a4 ♛b5 16 ♛c2 ♗e6 17 ♖fe1 0-0 18 ♗f1 ♛a5 19 b4 ♛d8 20 ♛xc6 and White is on top, Wolf-Lau, German Bundesliga 1985.

11 e4 ♗e7 12 a3 ♛b7

Now both sides have to acquiesce to basically the same draw by repetition that we saw in Kavalek-Sosonko above.

13 ♗d6 ♗xd6 14 ♛xd6 ♛b8 15 ♛c5 ♛a7 16 ♛d6 ♛b8 17 ♛c5 ♛a7 18 ♛d6 ½-½

Game 19
Vaganian-Planinc
Hastings 1974/5

---

1 d4 ♘f6 2 c4 c5 3 ♘f3 cxd4 4 ♘xd4

Once again we've arrived at the normal position via an anti-Benoni move order.

4...e6 5 ♘c3 ♗b4 6 ♘db5

6 ♗d2 is not an awe-inspiring move, but is perfectly playable:

a) 6...♘c6 7 a3 ♗e7 8 ♗g5 h6 9 ♗h4 ♛b6 10 e3 0-0 11 b4 a5 12 c5?! (Instead Murey gives 12 b5 ♘e5 13 ♘a4 ♛d8 14 c5 d6 with an unclear position) 12...♛d8 13 ♖b1 axb4 14 axb4 b6 and White's pawn structure is collapsing, Cu.Hansen-Kindermann, Dortmund 1988.

b) 6...0-0 7 a3 ♗c5 8 ♘b3 ♗e7 9 g3 d5 10 cxd5 exd5 11 ♗e3 ♘c6 12 ♗g2 ♗e6 13 0-0 ♖c8 14 ♘b5 ♘e4 with a reasonable IQP position for Black, Salov-Lautier, Dos Hermanas 1995.

6 g3 transposes to the g3 variation of the Nimzo-Indian, which lies outside the scope of this book.

6...0-0

Alternatively 6...d5 7 cxd5 exd5 8 ♗g5 0-0 9 e3 a6 10 a3 ♗e7 11 ♘d4 ♘c6 12 ♗e2 h6 13 ♗h4 ♕b6 14 ♕b3 ♕xb3 15 ♘xb3 ♗e6 16 0-0 g5 17 ♗g3 ♘e4 18 ♖ac1 ♗f6 with equal chances, Murey-Brodsky, Helsinki 1992.

6...♘c6 transposes to Game 22, note to Black's 6th move.

7 a3 ♗xc3+ 8 ♘xc3 d5

And now White can grab the pawn, otherwise Black should get easy equality.

9 ♗g5 h6 10 ♗xf6 ♕xf6 11 cxd5 exd5

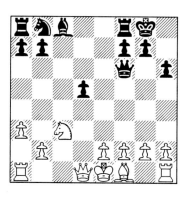

12 ♕xd5

Or 12 e3 and now:

a) 12...♖d8 13 ♕d4 ♕xd4 14 exd4 ♘c6, which Gipslis gives as slightly better for White, in fact looks okay for Black after 15 0-0-0 ♗f5 16 b4.

b) 12...♘c6 13 ♕xd5 ♖d8 14 ♕f3 ♕g6 15 ♖d1 is the move order quoted by ECO to reach Kaminsky-Kapengut (see note to Black's 13th), but this is bogus as here Black would have 15...♗g4 (instead of 15...♖xd1+) and if 16 ♖xd8+ ♖xd8 17 ♕g3 ♕b1+ 18

♘xb1 ♖d1 mate.

White needs to play something like 15 ♖c1, which in fact looks good for White.

12...♖d8 13 ♕f3

Or 13 ♕b3 ♘c6 14 e3 with an unclear position.

13...♕b6

Better than 13...♕g6, as played in Kaminsky-Kapengut, Orel 1974, even though after 14 ♖d1 ♖xd1+ 15 ♘xd1 ♘c6 Black still has compensation for the pawn.

14 ♖d1 ♖xd1+ 15 ♘xd1 ♘c6 16 ♕e3?

White must play 16 e3. Black now won in spectacular fashion.

16...♘d4 17 ♕e8+ ♔h7 18 e3 ♘c2+ 19 ♔d2

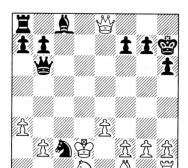

19...♗f5!! 20 ♕xa8 ♕d6+ 21 ♔c1 ♘a1 22 ♕xb7 ♕c7+!! 0-1

A dream finish – after 23 ♕xc7 ♘b3 is mate.

Game 20
Korchnoi-Ponomariov
Donetsk (8th match game) 2001

1 c4 c5 2 ♘f3 ♘f6 3 ♘c3 ♘c6 4 d4 cxd4 5 ♘xd4 e6 6 a3

An idea championed by Jonathan Speelman and also frequently adopted by Korchnoi. White aims to control the centre, usually with e2-e4, by first preventing the annoying ...♗f8-b4. Although perhaps initially adopted as a way of avoiding the highly theoretical 6 g3, rather ironically there is now a significant body of theory on the Speelman Variation.

6 ♗g5 is another attempt to avoid the main lines. After 6...♗e7 7 e3 0-0 8 ♗e2 b6 (or 8...♕a5 9 ♗h4 ♖d8 10 0-0 d5 11 cxd5 ♘xd4 12 ♕xd4 ♘xd5 13 ♗xe7 ♘xe7 14 b4 ♕c7 15 ♘b5 ♕d7 16 ♕b2 ♘c6 17 ♖fd1 and White is a little better, Gelfand-Kramnik, Amsterdam 1996) 9 ♘db5 d5 Black is in reasonable shape, e.g. 10 ♗xf6 ♗xf6 11 cxd5 exd5 12 ♕xd5 ♕xd5 13 ♘xd5 ♗xb2 14 ♖b1 ♗e5 15 ♖c1 ♘a5 16 f4 ♗b2 17 ♖c2 ♗f6 18 ♗f3 ♗f5 19 ♖c7 ♖ac8 20 ♘xa7 ♖xc7 21 ♘xc7 ♖d8 with good play for the pawn, Stangl-Alterman, Beijing 1995.

6...♗e7

Black has a number of alternative moves at this point, but his most common two plans are:

1) to play a quick ...d7-d5 or

2) a slower build up using the Hedgehog structure with ...b7-b6 and ...d7-d6. The c8-bishop can be developed on either b7 or a6, while the c6-knight is typically relocated via ...♘c6-e5-d7.

a) 6...♗c5 7 ♘b3 ♗e7 8 e4 0-0 9 ♗e2 b6 10 0-0 ♗a6 (10...♗b7 11 ♗e3 d6 12 f4 ♖c8 13 ♗f3 ♕c7 is also playable) 11 f4 ♖c8 12 ♗e3 d6 and now:

a1) 13 ♗f2 ♕c7 14 ♖c1 ♕b8 15 ♘d2 ♗b7 16 b4 ♕a8 17 ♖e1 ♘b8 18 ♗d3 ♘bd7 19 ♖e3 ♖fd8 with an unclear position, as in the game J.Horvath-Hracek, Budapest 2000.

a2) 13 ♖c1 ♘b8 14 ♘d2 ♗b7 15 ♗f3 ♘bd7 16 ♕e2 a6 17 ♗f2 ♕c7 18 ♖fe1 ♖fd8 with chances for both sides, Agdestein-Emms, Cappelle la Grande 1993.

b) Instead, a more ambitious idea is 6...♕c7 7 ♘db5 ♕b8 8 g3 a6 9 ♘d4 ♘xd4 10 ♕xd4 b5 11 e4 e5 12 ♕e3 ♕c7 13 cxb5 ♗c5 14 ♕f3 ♗d4 15 ♗g5 ♗xc3+ 16 bxc3 ♘xe4 17 ♕xe4 ♗b7 with complications which proved favourable for White in

Timman-J.Polgar, Hoogeveen 1999.

c) 6...d5 was played in some early Speelman games in this line, but has fallen out of favour. Still it is given as equal in ECO on the basis of 7 cxd5 exd5 8 ♗g5 ♗e7 9 e3 0-0 10 ♗b5 ♘e5 11 0-0 h6 and now:

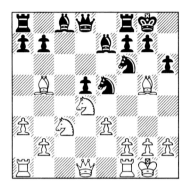

c1) 12 ♗xf6 ♗xf6 13 ♕b3 a6 14 ♗e2 ♘c6 15 ♖ad1 ♗xd4 16 exd4 ♗e6 17 ♗f3 ♘a5 18 ♕a2 ♘c4 with equality, L.Hansen-Petran, Budapest 1989.

c2) However, White can keep the tension with 12 ♗h4 (or 12 ♗f4!?) since 12...♘e4? 13 ♗xe7 ♘xc3? (13...♕xe7 14 ♘xd5) 14 ♗xd8 ♘xd1 15 ♗c7 wins for White.

d) 6...♘xd4 7 ♕xd4 b6 8 ♕f4 ♗b7 (8...♗c5 9 e4 d6 10 ♗e3 e5 11 ♕g3 0-0 12 ♗xc5 bxc5 13 ♕d3 ♖b8 14 0-0-0 is an unclear alternative given by Korchnoi) 9 e4 d6 10 ♗d3 ♗e7 11 ♕g3 0-0 (11...♖c8 12 ♕xg7 ♖g8 13 ♕h6 ♖c5 with compensation according to Korchnoi) 12 ♗h6 ♘e8 13 ♗d2 and White is better, Korchnoi-Sax, Wijk aan Zee 1991.

7 e4

Alternatively 7 g3 ♕b6 or 7 ♗f4!? d5 (7...0-0!?) 8 cxd5 ♘xd5 9 ♘xc6 bxc6 10 ♗d2 ♗f6 11 ♕c2 ♖b8 12 e3 0-0 13 ♗d3 h6 14 0-0, which is slightly preferable for White, Speelman-Lutz, Munich 1992.

7...0-0

7...d5 8 cxd5 exd5 9 ♗b5 is good for White, but after castling, Black is now ready for ...d7-d5.

8 ♘f3

a) 8 ♗e2 allows easy equality after 8...d5, for example 9 exd5 exd5 10 0-0 ♘xd4 11 ♕xd4 ♗e6 12 cxd5 ♘xd5 13 ♘xd5 ♗xd5 ½-½ Korchnoi-Kasparov, Horgen 1994.

b) After 8 ♘b3?! the knight is more awkwardly placed on b3 than f3 – it blocks the b-pawn and is further away from the kingside (see Korchnoi-Greenfeld below). Nevertheless, Korchnoi notes that no-one else has adopted his pet move 8 ♘f3, but that probably means that the majority is wrong!

8...b6 9 ♗e2 and now:

b1) 9...♗b7 10 ♗f4 d6 11 0-0 ♖c8 12 ♗g3!? ♘e5 13 ♘d2 g5!. An instructive idea. Black later built up kingside pressure with ...♘e5-g6, ...♔g8-g7, ...♖f8-h8 and ...h7-h5-h4 in Korchnoi-Greenfeld, Beersheba 1992.

b2) 9...♗a6 10 ♗e3 ♖c8 11 f4 d6 12 ♗d3? (12 ♖c1!?; 12 0-0 ♘b8 13 ♘d2 d5 14 cxd5 exd5 15 exd5 ♘xd5 16 ♘xd5 ♕xd5 17 ♗xa6 ♘xa6 18 ♘f3 ♕e4 is equal – analysis by Sax) 12...♘d7! 13 ♗e2? (13 0-0 ♘c5 14 ♘xc5 bxc5 is unclear) 13...♘c5 14 ♘d2 ♗h4+! 15 g3 ♗f6 16 ♖c1 ♘d4 17 ♗f1 e5 18 b4 ♘ce6 19 f5 ♗g5! and Black is more than OK!, Xu Jun-Adorjan, Shenzhen 1992.

8...♕c7

This was an improvement over an earlier game in the same match, which Korchnoi credits to Ponomariov's trainers (Kuzmin and Schneider). However, 8...♕c7 is on record as a recommendation from the early 90s, by... Korchnoi! In the earlier game, the young GM had a bad Hedgehog day after 8...d6 9 ♗e2 b6 10 0-0 ♗b7 11 ♗f4 ♖c8 12 ♖e1 a6 13 ♗f1 ♕c7 14 b4 ♖fd8 15 ♖c1 ♘e5 16 ♘d2 ♕b8 17 h3 ♗c6 18 ♕e2 ♘g6 19 ♗g3 ♕b7 20 ♘b3 h6 21 ♖b1 ♗f8 22 f3 ♖e8 23 ♗f2 ♕b8 24 ♕e3 ♘d7 25 ♖ed1 ♗b7 26 ♘a4 ♘ge5 27 ♘xb6 ♘xb6 28 ♕xb6 ♘xc4 29 ♗xc4 ♖xc4 30 ♘a5 ♖c7 31 b5. A model queenside attack by the master anti-Hedgehog protagonist. White is much

better, though he faltered and took 117 moves to win, Korchnoi-Ponomariov, Donetsk (2nd match game) 2001.

9 ♗g5 b6 10 ♗d3

10 ♗h4 with the idea of quickly targeting d6 is a possible improvement.

10...h6

Or 10...♗b7 with regular Hedgehog play.

11 ♗h4

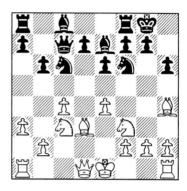

11...♘h5

An interesting and original treatment.

12 ♗xe7 ♘xe7 13 0-0 ♗a6 14 ♖c1 ♘f4 15 ♘b5 ♗xb5 16 cxb5 ♕d6 17 ♗b1 ♕xd1 18 ♖cxd1 d5 19 e5 g5!

Making it harder for White to defend his e5-pawn. Objectively, Black is doing fine, although Korchnoi is later able to make his greater endgame experience pay.

20 ♖fe1 ♖ac8 21 h4 g4 22 ♘h2 h5 23 f3 g3

23...gxf3 24 ♘xf3 ♖c4 leaves White with nothing special according to Korchnoi.

24 ♘f1 ♘eg6 25 ♖d4 ♖c4 26 ♖xc4 dxc4 27 ♗xg6 fxg6 28 ♘xg3

28 ♖e4 gives White better chances.

28...♘d3 29 ♖e2 ♖d8 30 ♘e4 ♘xe5 31 ♘g5 ♖d5 32 a4 ♔g7 33 ♘xe6+ ♔f6 34 ♘g5 ♔f5 35 ♘e4 ♖d3 36 ♘c3 ♖d4 37 ♘e4 ♖d3 38 ♔h2 ♖b3 39 ♘d6+ ♔f6 40 ♘e8+ ♔f5 41 ♘d6+ ♔f6 42 ♔g3 ♖b4 43 ♖e4 ♔e6 44 ♘c8 ♔f6 45 ♘xa7 ♖xa4 46 ♘c6 ♘d3 47 ♘e7 ♘xb2 48 ♘d5+ ♔f7

Korchnoi claims that this is the losing move. He gives 48...♔f5 49 ♘xb6 ♖b4 (but White wins after the alternative quoted: 49...c3 50 ♘xa4 c2 51 ♖f4+ ♔e5 52 ♘xb2). Now after 50 ♘c8 ♔f6 (Not 50...c3 51 ♘e7+ ♔f6 52 ♘d5+) 51 ♘d6 ♖b3 Black may be holding on. By winning this final game, the veteran tied the match.

49 ♖e7+ ♔f8 50 ♖b7 ♘d1 51 ♖xb6 c3 52 ♖c6 ♖a5 53 b6 ♖b5 54 ♖c7 ♖xd5 55 b7 ♖b5 56 ♖c8+ ♔f7 57 b8♕ ♖xb8 58 ♖xb8 c2 59 ♖c8 ♘e3 60 ♔f2 ♘f5 61 g3 ♘d4 62 g4 ♔e6 63 ♔e3 ♔d5 64 ♖c3 g5 65 hxg5 hxg4 66 fxg4 1-0

Game 21
Ki.Georgiev-Topalov
Sarajevo 2000

---

1 d4 ♘f6 2 c4 e6 3 ♘c3 c5 4 ♘f3 cxd4 5 ♘xd4 ♘c6 6 ♘db5

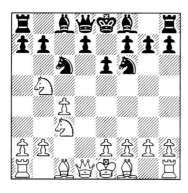

6...d5

For 6...♗c5 and 6...♗b4 see Game 22.
7 ♗f4

7 cxd5 is sometimes tried, and at least has the benefit of creating more unbalanced play than the main line with 7 ♗f4, e.g. 7...♘xd5 and now:

a) 8 ♘xd5 exd5 9 ♕xd5 ♗b4+ 10 ♗d2 ♕e7 11 a3 ♗xd2+ 12 ♕xd2 0-0 13 ♕f4 (If 13 ♕d6 Portisch gives 13...♕g5 with compensation) 13...♖d8 14 e3 a6 15 ♘c3 ♖d4 16 e4 f5 with play for the pawn, Burmakin-

Naumann, Budapest 1992.

b) 8 e4 ♘xc3 9 ♕xd8+ ♔xd8 10 ♘xc3 is pretty much equal, e.g. 10...♗c5 11 ♗g5+ f6 12 0-0-0+ ♗d7 13 ♗h4 a6 14 ♔b1 g5 15 ♗g3 ♔e7 16 h4 h6 17 ♖c1 ♗d4 18 ♘a4 ♘e5 19 ♘c5 ½-½ A.Petrosian-Sivokho, St Petersburg 1993.

7...e5 8 cxd5 exf4 9 dxc6 bxc6 10 ♕xd8+ ♔xd8

As happens in several lines of the Symmetrical English, an early clash in the centre quickly transposes to a queenless middlegame. This particular line was most popular in the early 1980s, and still occasionally pops up at GM level, but over the years, White has not been able to prove any path to an advantage. Black's two bishops and open lines for the rooks (the b- and e-files) compensate for his inferior pawn structure.
11 ♖d1+

Alternatively:

a) 11 ♘d4 ♗b7 (or 11...♗d7 12 g3 fxg3 13 hxg3 ♗b4 14 ♗g2 ♗xc3+ 15 bxc3 ♔c7 16 ♖b1 ♖ab8 17 0-0 ♖b6 18 ♖b4 ♖c8 with an equal ending, Oll-Emms, Copenhagen 1993) 12 g3 c5 13 ♘f3 ♗d6 14 ♗g2 ♖b8 15 0-0-0 ♔e7 16 ♘h4 ♗xg2 17 ♘xg2 fxg3 18 hxg3 ♗e5 19 ♘e3 ♔e6 and Black is not worse in this endgame, Salov-Karpov, Dos Hermanas 1997.

b) 11 0-0-0+ doesn't seem to gain White anything over 11 ♖d1+, e.g.: 11...♗d7 12 ♘d6 ♗xd6 13 ♖xd6 ♘g4 14 f3 ♘e3 15 ♖d4 g5 16 ♘e4 h6 17 ♘c5 ♘d5 18 g3 ♗f5 19 e4 ½-½ Wojtkiewicz-Mulyar, San Francisco 2001.

11...♗d7 12 ♘d6 ♗xd6

12...♔c7 is also possible, sacrificing the f7-pawn (usually only temporarily) in order to keep the dark-squared bishop: 13 ♘xf7 ♖g8 14 ♘e5 ♖b8 15 ♘xd7 ♘xd7 16 g3 ♖xb2 17 ♗h3 ♘c5 (or 17...♘f6) 18 0-0 ♖c2 19 ♖c1 ♖xc1 20 ♖xc1 fxg3 21 hxg3 ♗e7 22 ♗g2 ♖b8 with a level position, Korchnoi-Portisch, (5th match game) Bad Kissingen 1983.

13 ♖xd6 ♖b8 14 b3

14 ♖d2 ♖e8 15 g3 f3 16 ♔d1 fxe2+ 17 ♗xe2 ♔c7 18 ♗c4 ♖e7 19 ♔c1 ♗f5 20 b3 ♖be8 (Stohl-Xu Jun, Beijing 1996) and once again, Black is fine.

14...♖b4 15 g3 ♔e7

Or 15...♔c7 16 ♖d2 ♗f5 17 ♗g2 ♘e4 18 ♘xe4 ♗xe4 19 0-0 ♗xg2 20 ♔xg2 ♖d8 21 ♖xd8 ½-½ Hellers-Ernst, Sweden 1998.

16 ♖d2 h5

An improvement over 16...c5, Korchnoi-Portisch, (7th match game) Bad Kissingen 1983, after which White should try 17 gxf4 ♖xf4 18 ♖g1 g6 19 ♖g5 when the weakened light squares gives White some faint hope of maybe getting an edge.

17 ♗g2 h4

Black's energetic play aims to give White a weak pawn to counter-balance the isolated c-pawn.

18 0-0 hxg3 19 fxg3 fxg3 20 hxg3 ♖h5! 21 ♖f3 ♖e5 22 ♘d1 c5 23 ♖e3 ♖xe3 24 ♘xe3 ♗e6 25 ♔f2 a5

Now Black sets about a similar approach on the queenside!

26 ♘d5+ ♘xd5 27 ♗xd5 g6 28 ♗xe6 ♔xe6

The position is dead level.

29 ♔e3 a4 30 ♖d3 f5 31 ♔f2 ♔e5 32 ♖e3+ ♔d5 33 ♖d3+ ♔c6 34 ♔e1 axb3 35 axb3 ♖g4 36 ♔d2 ♔b5 37 ♖f3 ♖d4+ 38 ♖d3 ♖e4 39 ♖d8 ♖g4 40 ♖d3 ♔b4 41 ♖f3 ♖d4+ 42 ♔c2 ♖e4 43 ♖f4 ♖xf4 ½-½

Game 22
Sorokin-Rodriguez
Villa Gesell 1998

1 c4 c5 2 ♘f3 ♘c6 3 d4 cxd4 4 ♘xd4 ♘f6 5 ♘c3

More recently white players have started to experiment with the immediate 5 g3:

a) 5...♕a5+!? 6 ♘c3 ♘e4 7 ♘db5 a6 8 ♘c7+ ♕xc7 9 ♘xe4 ½-½ Nogueiras-Miles, Havana 1999, although of course there is still much to play for!

b) 5...e6 6 ♗g2!? (6 ♘c3 reaches the main lines) 6...♕b6 7 ♘b3 (7 ♘c2 d5 8 cxd5 exd5 9 0-0 ♗e6 10 ♘c3 ♖d8 11 ♗g5 ♗e7 was equal in Bischoff-Ftacnik, Hastings 2000/1) 7...♘e5 8 ♕c2 ♕a6 9 c5 d5 10 cxd6 ♗xd6 11 0-0 ♗d7 12 ♘c3 ♖c8 is unclear, Gelfand-Ivanchuk, Lviv 2000.

5...e6 6 ♘db5 ♗c5

Given the highly drawish nature of the main line 6...d5 (covered in the previous game), players trying to win with Black are in need of an alternative line. Well, here is your dynamic but risky option. It has also been played relatively infrequently, so there is more scope for original analysis.

Alternatively:

a) 6...♗b4 is also playable, e.g.

a1) 7 a3 ♗xc3+ 8 ♘xc3 d5 9 e3 (9 cxd5 exd5 10 ♗g5 0-0 11 e3 ♗e6 is also equal) 9...0-0 10 cxd5 exd5 11 ♗e2 ♗f5 12 0-0 d4 13 exd4 ♘xd4 14 ♗d3 ♗xd3 15 ♕xd3 ♘b3 and Black is at least equal, Z.Polgar-Agdestein, Groningen 1993.

a2) 7 ♗f4 0-0 and now

a21) 8 ♗d6 ♗xd6 9 ♘xd6 ♕b6 10 ♕d2 ♘d4 11 e3 ♘c2+ 12 ♕xc2 ♕xd6 13 ♗e2 a6 14 0-0 b6 15 ♖fd1 ♕c7 16 ♖d2 ♗b7 17 ♖ad1 ♖fd8 ½-½ Rustemov-Dvoirys, Skelleftea 2001.

a22) 8 ♗c7 ♕e7 9 ♗d6 ♗xd6 10 ♕xd6 ♕d8 11 e3 (11 0-0-0!? ♘e8 12 ♕g3 a6 13 ♘d6 ♘xd6 14 ♖xd6 b5 with decent play for Black) and here:

a221) 11...♕a5 12 ♕d2 d5 13 cxd5 ♘xd5 14 ♘xd5 ♕xd2+ 15 ♔xd2 exd5 16 ♗d3 ♗e6 17 ♖hc1 ♖ad8 and Black is close to equalising, though White retains a small initiative, Gulko-Kaidanov, Denver 1998.

a222) 11...a6 12 ♘d4 ♘e8 avoids too much simplification, e.g. 13 ♕c5 d6 14 ♘xc6 ♕c7 15 ♘e7+ ♕xe7 16 ♕d4 ♗d7 17 ♗e2 ♗c6 and Black has a reasonable position, McCambridge-De Firmian, USA 1989.

b) 6...d6 7 ♗f4 e5 8 ♗g5 a6 9 ♗xf6 gxf6 10 ♘a3 ♗e6 11 e3 f5 12 ♕d2 ♖c8 13 ♗e2

♗g7 14 0-0 e4 15 ♖ac1 h5 16 ♘d5 h4 17 f4 exf3 18 gxf3 and White is slightly better, Adamski-De Firmian, Roskilde 1998.

7 ♗f4

7 ♘d6+ should not worry Black, e.g. 7...♔e7 8 ♘xc8+ ♖xc8 9 e3 d5 10 cxd5 ♘xd5 11 ♘xd5+ ♕xd5 12 ♕xd5 exd5 13 ♗d3 ♘e5 14 ♔e2 ♘xd3 15 ♔xd3 ♗d6 16 ♗d2 ♗e5 17 ♖ac1 ♔e6 with equality, Timochenko-Zagorskis, Pula 1997.

7...e5!?

After 7...0-0 8 ♗d6 (8 ♗c7 ♕e7 9 ♗d6) Black has the additional option of 8...♕b6 (8...♗xd6) 9 ♗xc5 ♕xc5 10 e3 d5 with equal chances.

8 ♗g5

8 ♗e3 is the 'official' refutation, but read on. 8...♗xe3 9 ♘d6+ ♔f8 10 fxe3 ♘g4 11 ♕d2

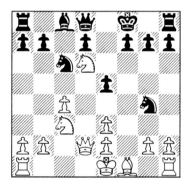

and now:

a) 11...h5 12 g3 ♕g5 13 e4 (13 ♘d1 is similar to the analysis below) 13...♕xd2+ 14 ♔xd2 h4 15 ♗g2 h3 16 ♗f3 ♘f6 17 e3 b6 18 ♖hd1 ♘a5 and Black has nothing to worry about, Anikaev-Yurtaev, Frunze 1979.

b) 11...♕g5 and now:

b1) 12 e4 ♕f6 13 e3 ♘xe3 14 ♕xe3 (14 ♘xc8? ♘d4 15 ♗d3 ♕h4+ 16 ♕f2 ♘xg2+ 17 ♔f1 ♕h3 wins for Black, Palatnik-Sideif Sade, Uzhgorod 1988, while 14 ♘xf7 is a suggestion of Rogulj) 14...♕xd6 15 ♗d3 h5 16 ♘d5 b6 17 ♖f1 ♘b4 18 ♕f3 ♘xd3+ 19

♕xd3 ♗b7 20 0-0-0 ♖c8 with an unclear position, Vadasz-Rogulj, Karlovac 1979.

b2) 12 ♘d1 is given as better for White in ECO and in a couple of monographs, on the basis of the obscure game Weise-Trapl, Oberhausen 1961, which continued 12...g6? 13 g3 ♔g7 14 h4 ♕e7 15 ♗h3 ♘h6 16 ♘c3 f5 17 0-0-0 b6 18 ♗g2 ♗a6 19 b4, with a crushing position for White.

However, this position definitely deserves further analysis. Not only is Black's play in this game very weak, but 12 ♘d1 and indeed 8 ♗e3 was rejected by several strong players. The Yurtaev game above should also not be ignored. There is nothing inherently better about White's set-up, and as always concrete factors come to the fore:

b21) 12...♘xh2!? is worth a look, but falls short, e.g. 13 ♕d5 ♘d8 14 ♘e4 ♕h6 15 ♘df2.

b22) 12...g6 is possible, when Black threatens ...♘g4xh2, e.g. 13 g3 (13 ♘xc8 ♖xc8 14 ♕xd7 is not possible because of 14...♖d8 15 ♕xb7 ♕c2) 13...♘d4!? (Black needs to act before White completes his development with ♗f1-g2 and 0-0) 14 exd4 ♕xd6 15 ♗h3 ♘f6 with an unclear position.

b23) 12...h5 to pre-empt g2-g3, and allow the rook lift ...♖h8-h6, is perhaps best of all. Black seems to have decent chances here.

8...♕b6

Black also has:

a) 8...h6 9 ♗xf6 ♕xf6 10 e3 0-0 11 ♗e2 ♕g6 12 0-0 d6 13 ♗h5 ♕f5 14 ♗f3 ♖d8 15 a3 ♗e6 16 ♗e4 ♕g5 17 ♗d5, Sorokin-Braga, Pico City 1996. White is slightly better because of his light-squared control.

b) 8...♗xf2+! 9 ♔xf2 ♘g4+ 10 ♔e1 ♕xg5 11 ♘c7+ ♔d8 12 ♘xa8 ♕f4! and here:

b1) 13 ♘d5 ♕f2+ 14 ♔d2 ♕d4+ 15 ♔e1 ♕f2+ ½-½ Grinshpun-Shabtai, Tel Aviv 1995.

b2) 13 ♕d6 ♕f2+ 14 ♔d2 and here:

b21) 14...♕e3+ 15 ♔d1 (or 15 ♔e1 ♕f2+ with a draw) 15...♘f2+ but here 16 ♔c2 (not

16 ♔e1 ♘b4 as given by Bagirov) 16...♘d4+ 17 ♔b1 is good for White after all!

b22) 14...♕f4+! (found by John Emms) 15 ♔c2 (15 ♔d1 ♘e3+ 16 ♔e1 ♘c2+ or 15 ♔e1 ♕f2+ draw, while 15 ♔d3? e4+ 16 ♘xe4 ♘f2+ wins for Black) 15...♘d4+ 16 ♔b1 ♕d2 and White cannot avoid a draw.

b3) White can play on with 13 ♕d2 but it might be asking for trouble: 13...♕f2+ 14 ♔d1 ♘e3+ 15 ♔c1 ♘xf1 with a wild position.

Okay, well Black only draws in this line too, but at least (compared to the previous game) you didn't have to suffer in a tedious ending! If the line given in the next note is indeed strong for White, then Black should probably bale with this draw.

9 e3

Bagirov gives the surprising 9 ♗xf6! ♗xf2+ (9...gxf6 10 e3 a6 11 ♘d5 ♕a5+ 12 ♘bc3 is good for White) 10 ♔d2 when Black is struggling to find a decent follow-up:

a) Bagirov suggests that Black's best may be 10...gxf6 11 ♘d5 ♕a5+ 12 ♔c1 0-0 13 e3, even though this still favours White.

b) 10...♗e3+ 11 ♔c2 ♘b4+ 12 ♔b3 is good for White.

c) 10...♘b4 is answered by 11 ♕b3.

d) 10...♕e3+ 11 ♔c2 gxf6 (11...0-0 12 ♘d5 ♕e4+ 13 ♔c3 a6 14 ♘bc7 ♖b8 15 ♗e7 ♗d4+ 16 ♔d2 wins) and now:

d1) 12 ♘d5 ♕e4+ 13 ♕d3 is given by Bagirov, but maybe here 13...♕xd3+ gives a playable position for Black.

d2) However, 12 ♘c7+ ♔d8 13 ♕d6! is decisive.

As mentioned above, Black should probably play 8...♗xf2+ to avoid all this.

9...a6 10 ♘a4

10 ♗xf6 is still critical. After 10...axb5 11 ♗xg7 ♖g8 12 ♗f6 bxc4 13 ♗xc4 ♖xg2?? (13...♕xb2 is unclear) met a swift end: 14 ♕d5 ♘d8 15 ♕xg2 ♕xf6 16 ♕g8+ ♗f8 17 0-0-0 b5 18 ♘e4 ♕f3 19 ♗d5 1-0 Berebora-Rade, Solin 1994.

10...♕a5+ 11 ♘bc3

11 ♕d2? loses to 11...♗b4 12 ♘bc3 ♘e4.

11...♘e4 12 ♘xc5 ♘xc3

Not 12...♘xg5 13 ♕d6, preventing Black from castling.

13 ♕d2 ♕xc5 14 ♕xc3 f6 15 ♗h4 d5

The dust has settled, and Black is fine. In return for the bishop pair, he has a lead in development and the h4-bishop is boxed in by Black's pawns.

16 cxd5 ♕xd5 17 f3 ♗e6

17...e4 could also be tried.

18 ♗d3 ♘b4 19 ♗e4 ♕b5

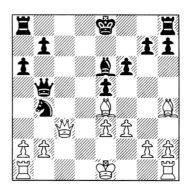

Black is slightly better according to Ribli, but he is unable to turn his initiative into anything substantive.

20 a4 ♕b6 21 0-0 ♖c8 22 ♕d2 0-0 23 a5 ♕b5 24 ♗e1 ♗c4 25 ♖f2 ♘d3 26 ♗xd3 ♗xd3 27 ♕b4 ♖fd8 ½-½

Game 23
Karpov-Topalov
Linares 1994

---

1 d4 ♘f6 2 c4 c5 3 ♘f3 cxd4 4 ♘xd4 e6 5 g3 ♘c6 6 ♗g2

Or 6 ♘c3 ♗c5 which usually comes to the same thing.

6...♗c5

6...♗b4+ is less flexible, e.g. 7 ♘c3 0-0 8 0-0 ♕e7 9 ♘a4 when White is able to complete his development unhindered and keep

Black under some pressure (compare this to the line 6...♕b6 7 ♘b3 ♘e5 8 e4 ♗b4 9 ♕e2 – Games 25-26 – when White has to go through some contortions before castling). Now after 9...d5 10 cxd5 exd5 11 ♗g5 h6 12 ♗xf6 ♕xf6 13 ♘c2 ♖d8 14 ♘xb4 ♘xb4 15 ♕d2 ♘c6 16 ♖ac1 and here:

a) 16...♗g4 and now instead of 17 h3 ♗f5 18 ♖fd1 ♗e4 with counterplay for Black (Akesson-Alterman, London 1994), Zviaginsev gives 17 ♖fe1!, so that if 17...♕e7?! White can win material with 18 ♗xd5 ♘b4 19 ♗xf7+ ♕xf7 (19...♔h8 20 ♕f4 or 19...♔xf7 20 ♕f4+) 20 ♕xb4 etc.

b) 16...♗f5 17 ♖fd1 ♗e4 18 ♗h3! d4! 19 ♘c5 ♗d5 20 ♘xb7, Ivanchuk – Zviaginsev, Elista Olympiad 1998, and now 20...♘e5 21 ♗g2 ♗xg2 22 ♔xg2 ♖d5 would have minimised White's advantage according to Zviaginsev.

7 ♘b3

7...♗e7

If Black plays 7...♗b4+ then 8 ♘c3 d5 9 cxd5 ♘xd5 10 0-0 is a promising pawn sacrifice: 10...♘xc3 (10...♗xc3 11 bxc3 ♘xc3 12 ♕xd8+ followed by ♗c1-b2 gives White good play for the material) and now White needs to decide whether the queen trade happens on d1 or d8:

a) 11 ♕xd8+ ♔xd8 12 bxc3 ♗xc3 13 ♖b1 a5 14 ♗e3 ♗b4 15 ♖fc1 ♔e7 16 ♘d4 with good play for the pawn, Lautier-Leko,

Cap d'Agde 1994.

b) 11 bxc3 ♕xd1 12 ♖xd1 ♗xc3 13 ♖b1 0-0 14 ♘c5 and now:

b1) 14...♖d8 (14...♘d4!? is Christiansen's suggestion) 15 ♖xd8+ (15 ♗b2!? can be answered by 15...♘a5) ♘xd8 16 ♘xb7 ♘xb7 17 ♗xb7 ♖b8 18 ♖b3 ♖xb7 19 ♖xc3 ♗d7 ½-½ Ftacnik-Smejkal, Marianske Lazne 1978.

b2) Black went quickly downhill after 14...e5 15 ♗a3 ♗f5 16 ♖xb7 ♘a5 17 ♖c7 ♖ac8 18 ♘a6 ♖fd8 19 ♖xd8+ ♖xd8 20 ♖xc3 1-0 Razuvaev-Polugaevsky, Moscow 1985.

8 ♘c3

1 c4 c5 2 ♘f3 ♘f6 3 d4 cxd4 4 ♘xd4 e6 5 ♘c3 ♘c6 6 g3 ♗c5 7 ♘b3 ♗e7 8 ♗g2 is another typical English move order to reach this position.

8...0-0

A more active alternative is 8...b6 9 ♗f4 0-0 10 0-0 ♗a6!? 11 ♘b5 d5 12 ♘c7 ♗xc4 and now White can play either:

a) 13 ♘xa8 ♕xa8 14 ♖c1 e5 15 ♗g5 ♖d8 16 ♖e1 h6 17 ♗xf6 ♗xf6 18 ♕c2 ♕b8 19 ♘d2 ♘d4 20 ♕d1 ♗a6 and Black has some compensation for the exchange, Korchnoi-Ftacnik, Ceska Trebova 1997.

b) 13 ♘d2 is less critical, e.g. 13...♖c8 14 ♘xc4 g5 15 ♗xg5 ♕xc7 16 ♘d2 ♕e5 17 ♗xf6 ♗xf6 18 ♖b1 ♖fd8 ½-½ Van Wely-Hracek, Batumi 1999.

9 0-0 d6 10 ♗f4 ♘h5

Black needs to oust the bishop before it becomes a pain. Instead 10...a6 11 ♖c1 ♘g4 12 ♘a4 ♖b8 13 h3 b5?! 14 cxb5 axb5 15 ♖xc6 bxa4 16 ♖xd6! ♗xd6 17 ♕xd6 e5 18 ♕xb8 exf4 19 ♘c5 ♕d4 20 ♘d3 gave White a decisive advantage, Vladimirov-Kunte, Kelamabakkam 2000.

11 e3

This is a clear-cut and instructive idea. 11 ♗e3 is also playable, and after 11...♗d7 12 ♘d4 ♕b8 13 ♖c1 ♘f6 14 h3 ♖d8 15 ♕d2 ♘e5 16 b3 a6 17 ♖fd1 White is slightly better, though Black's shell is hard to crack,

Spraggett-I.Ivanov, New York 1983.

11...♘xf4

If 11...g6 12 ♗h6.

12 exf4

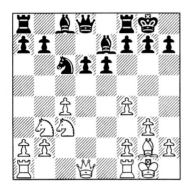

12...♗d7

Other moves that have been tried:

a) 12...♘a5 and now:

a1) 13 ♕d3 ♘xb3 14 axb3 ♕b6 15 ♕e3 ♕xe3 16 fxe3 a6 17 ♖fd1 ♖b8 with balanced chances, Pelletier-Larsen, Zurich 1998.

a2) 13 ♘d2 gives White a big plus according to Pelletier, e.g. 13...♗d7 14 b4 ♘c6 15 ♖b1 with a big space advantage.

b) 12...a6 13 ♖c1 and here:

b1) 13...♖b8 14 ♕e2 ♕b6, P.Nikolic-Feletar, Neum 1999, and now 15 c5 dxc5 16 ♘a4 ♕b5 17 ♕xb5 axb5 18 ♘axc5 is strong for White according to Feletar.

b2) 13...♘a5 14 ♘xa5 ♕xa5 is unclear according to Feletar, but White can just play 14 ♘d2 with advantage as in 'a2' above.

13 ♕d2 ♕b8 14 ♖fe1

With f4-f5 in mind.

14...g6

14...♖d8 allows White to carry out his plan and weaken Black's structure, e.g. 15 f5 ♘e5 16 fxe6 ♗xe6 17 ♘d5 ♗xd5 18 ♗xd5 ♕c7 19 ♖ac1 ♗f6 20 ♘d4 ♕d7 21 ♔g2 ♖ac8 22 b3 and White is in control thanks to his light-squared dominance, Teplitsky-G.Shahade, Bermuda 2001.

15 h4 a6 16 h5

White's 'crab' formation edges forward to nibble at Black's kingside.

16...b5

16...♖a7 17 h6 b5 18 ♘d4 with a big plus for White according to Karpov. Black could keep his disadvantage to a minimum by 16...♖d8 17 ♖ad1 ♗e8 but, quite typically, Topalov prefers active counterplay.

17 hxg6

One of the key ideas for the side with a kingside majority in such positions is to exchange off a pair of pawns and thereby loosen the opponent's defences. In this game, this pays off in spectacular fashion.

17...hxg6 18 ♘c5! dxc5 19 ♕xd7 ♖c8 20 ♖xe6!!

20 ♗xc6 ♖a7 21 ♕d3 ♖xc6 22 cxb5 axb5 23 ♘xb5 c4 is not so clear.

20...♖a7

If Black accepts the sacrifice immediately then 20...fxe6 21 ♕xe6+ ♔g7 22 ♗xc6 ♖a7 23 ♗e4 ♗f6 24 ♕g4 wins for White.

21 ♖xg6+! fxg6

If Black plays 21...♔f8 then 22 ♕h3 fxg6 23 ♕h8+ ♔f7 24 ♗d5 mate, while if 21...♔h7 22 ♕h3+ ♔xg6 23 ♗e4+ f5 24 ♕xf5+ ♔g7 25 ♕h7+ ♔f8 26 ♕h6+ ♔e8 27 ♗xc6+ is one way to win.

22 ♕e6+ ♔g7 23 ♗xc6 ♖d8 24 cxb5

One of the nice things about this game is that White first sacrifices material with great drama (18 ♘c5!, 20 ♖xe6!!, 21 ♖xg6+!), but then appears to play in slow motion. Black is so tied up that White can just take the queenside pawns.

24...&f6 25 &e4 &d4

If 25...&xb2 26 &b1 &d4 27 b6.

26 bxa6

Karpov points out two alternative winning lines: 26 &g4 axb5 27 f5 and 26 f5 gxf5 27 &xf5.

26...&b6 27 &d1 &xa6 28 &xd4

A 3rd rook sacrifice!

28...&xd4 29 &f6+ &g8 30 &xg6+ &f8 31 &e8+ &g7 32 &e5+

Or 32 &xc5.

32...&g8 33 &f6+ &f7 34 &e8+ &f8 35 &xc5+ &d6 36 &xa7 &xf6

Black could try for stalemate with 36...&d1+ 37 &g2 &g1+ but White escapes with 38 &h3 (38 &xg1 &d1+ 39 &g2 &h1+ 40 &xh1 is a draw) 38...&e6+ 39 &g4 winning.

37 &h5 &d2 38 b3 &b2 39 &g2 1-0

This game was awarded the prize for the Best Game of *Informator 60*.

Game 24
Timman-Alterman
European Team Ch., Pula 1997

---

1 c4 c5 2 &f3 &c6 3 &c3 &f6 4 d4 cxd4 5 &xd4 e6 6 g3 &b6 7 &db5

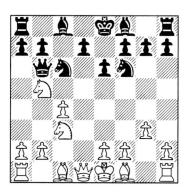

In order to avoid the extensive theory of the main line with 7 &b3 (covered in the next two games), White can try this move,

which probes at the dark squares c7 and d6.

7...&e5

This move is best, as it is against 7 &b3. Not only is c4 under attack, but ...&b6-c6 becomes possible in some positions, plus Black can sometimes attack f2 with ...&f6(or e5)-g4. Both sides needs to be alert to unusual tactics over the next few moves, before the game settles into a regular pattern. Alternatively:

a) After 7...&c5 White should continue with the bold 8 &g2! since Black does not appear to have a dangerous follow-up. Against non-forcing moves, White will simply castle, leaving Black with a silly piece formation – he would have to lose a lot of tempi just to develop his c8-bishop. Black has tried:

a1) 8...a6 9 &d6+ &e7 10 &de4 &xe4 11 &xe4 &b4+ 12 &f1! (This is better than the automatic 12 &d2 since it leaves the bishop hanging in the air on b4) 12...d6 13 &e3 &d8 14 &c2 &a5 15 a3 f5 16 &d1 fxe4 17 axb4 &xb4 18 &xe4 and White has an overwhelming advantage, Marin-Sion Castro, Benasque 1999.

a2) 8...&xf2+ 9 &f1 &g4 10 &d6 &d8 11 &g5+ f6 12 &a4 &a6 13 h3 &xa4 14 hxg4 &b6 (a better try is 14...&xg3 15 &xf6+ gxf6 16 &xg3 and White still has a large advantage according to Yemelin) 15 &xh7 &e8, Greenfeld-Yemelin, Beersheba 1998, and now 16 &h4 g5 17 &d1 &e7 18 b3 &a6 19 b4 wins according to Yemelin.

b) 7...d5 8 &g2 d4 9 &a4 &a5+ 10 &d2 &b4 11 &c5 0-0 12 &d3 &xd2+ 13 &xd2 &xd2+ 14 &xd2 &d8 15 c5 &e8 16 &a3 f6 17 f4 &d7, Kasparov-Vaganian, Skelleftea 1989; now 18 b4 is best and, according to Kasparov, White stands slightly better.

8 &g2

Instead after 8 &f4 &fg4 9 e3:

a) 9...&c6 does not work out because of 10 h3 &f3+ 11 &e2 &ge5 12 b3 g5 13 &g2 gxf4 14 exf4 and White wins his piece back but retains a strong grip on the position:

14...a6 15 fxe5 axb5 16 ♗xf3 ♛c5 17 ♘xb5 ♛xe5+ 18 ♔f1 ♗g7 19 a4! Greenfeld-Liss, Rishon Le Zion 1996.

b) 9...a6 and then:

b1) 10 ♘c7+? ♛xc7 11 ♛xg4 ♛xc4 12 ♛d1 ♛c6 13 e4 ♘g6 14 ♗d2 b5 15 ♗g2 ♗b7 (De la Villa Garcia-Rojo Huerta, Cala Galdana 1999) and White is fighting for equality.

b2) 10 h3 axb5 11 hxg4 ♘xc4 12 ♛b3 d5 13 ♗xc4 dxc4 14 ♛xb5+ ♛xb5 15 ♘xb5 ♗b4+ 16 ♔e2 and after a flurry of exchanges we have a fairly level position, for example:

b21) 16...0-0 (16...♔e7!?) 17 ♗d6 ♗xd6 18 ♘xd6 e5 19 g5 ♗e6 20 ♖h4 ½-½ Lalic-Emms, London 1997.

b22) 16...♖a5 17 a4 ♗d7 18 ♗d6 ♗xd6 19 ♘xd6+ ♔e7 20 ♘xc4 (White actually got into some trouble with 20 ♘xb7 ♖d5 21 b4 cxb3 22 ♖hb1 ♖c8 due to his errant knight, Delchev-Sax, Medulin 1997) 20...♖xa4 21 ♖xa4 ♗xa4 22 e4 ♖c8 23 ♔d3 ♗b5 ½-½ L.Hansen-Cu.Hansen, Aalborg 2000.

8...a6 9 ♛a4 ♖b8

Other tries for Black:

a) 9...♘eg4 10 0-0 ♖b8 11 b4!? axb5 12 ♘xb5 d5 (surprisingly, this is the only move, e.g. if 12...♗e7 13 c5 ♛d8 14 ♛a7) 13 ♘d6+ ♔e7 14 c5 ♛a6 15 ♛c2 ♘e8 16 b5 ♛a8 17 ♗f4 ♘xd6? (17...f5 – Seirawan) 18 ♗xd6+ ♔e8 19 ♗xb8 ♛xb8 20 a4 with a huge queenside pawn-roller, Kramnik-Anand, Monaco (rapid) 1994.

b) 9...♘fg4 10 0-0 ♖b8 11 ♘a3 h5!? 12 ♛b3 ♛c7 13 ♗f4 ♗e7 14 ♘e4 b6 15 ♛c3 f6 16 h3 ♘h6 17 b4 ♘hf7, Delchev-Hulak, Radenci 1998. Black has an unusual set-up but is doing okay.

10 ♗e3 ♗c5 11 ♗xc5 ♛xc5 12 ♛a3 b6

This is more popular than the original try 12...♛xa3, though Ponomariov used this move recently. 13 ♘xa3 and now:

a) 13...♔e7 14 f4 ♘c6 15 e4 d6 16 ♘c2 ♗d7 17 0-0 ♖hc8 18 ♖d3 ♘a5 19 b3 b5 20 cxb5 axb5 21 ♖hd1 b4 22 e5 ♘g4 23

♖xd6 and White is better, Pelletier-Ponomariov, Kharkov 2001.

b) 13...d6 14 f4 ♘c6 when:

b1) 15 0-0-0 ♔e7 16 ♖d2 ♘b4 17 ♗f3 ♗d7 18 ♖hd1 d5 19 g4 ♗c6 20 g5 ♘e4 21 ♖d4 ♖bc8, Speelman-Timman, London Candidates 1989, and now 22 c5 a5 23 ♗xe4 dxe4 24 ♘c4 ♗d5 is equal according to Timman.

b2) 15 ♘c2 looks better, preventing Timman's manoeuvre of ...♘c6-b4 to support ...d6-d5. Pelletier-Eljanov, Kharkov 2001 continued 15...♗d7 16 0-0-0 ♔e7 17 ♖d3 ♖hd8 18 e4 ♗e8 19 ♖e1 ♘d7 20 g4 with a more comfortable game for White.

13 ♘d6+ ♔e7 14 ♛xc5 bxc5 15 ♘xc8+ ♖hxc8 16 b3

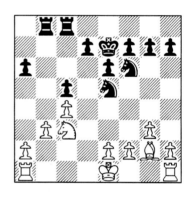

16...d5

a) 16...g5 is a more solid choice. It is less risky than 16...d5, but also doesn't give Black so many winning chances either. After 17 h3 h5:

a1) 18 f4 gxf4 19 gxf4 ♘g6 20 ♖f1 d6 21 ♗h1 ♖g8 22 e3 ♘h4 23 ♔f2 ♘f5 24 ♖g1 h4 and Black is at least equal, Agrest-Emms, Harplinge 1998.

a2) 18 0-0-0 d6 19 ♖d2 ♖d8 20 ♖hd1 ♖d7 21 ♗h1 g4 22 h4, and both sides have frustrated the other's pawn breaks – the position is equal, Agrest-Wedberg, Sweden 1999.

b) 16...d6 looks inferior, since White can play f2-f4 without creating any weaknesses in his own camp: 17 f4 ♘ed7 18 ♗f3 h5 19 h3 g6 20 ♔f2 ♘b6 21 ♖ad1 ♖d8 22 g4 was Bruzon-Herrera, Las Tunas 2001, with a slight plus for White.

17 cxd5 c4

Black plays energetically, trying to capitalise on his slight lead in development.

18 b4

This is a wiser choice than 18 bxc4 ♖xc4 19 ♖c1 ♖bc8 20 ♔d2 ♘eg4, and Black has pressure.

18...♖xb4

A critical point in the game.

19 h3?!

a) 19 dxe6 fxe6 20 h3 ♖d8?! (20...♘ed7 is satisfactory for Black) 21 ♖d1 (trading the rooks will dull Black's initiative and accentuate White's bishop v knight advantage, while if Black moves the rook again he has simply lost time) 21...♘ed7 22 ♖d2 ♘b6 23 ♖xd8 ♔xd8 24 ♔d2 ♘fd5 25 ♖b1 and White retains a slight advantage in the ending, Ehlvest-Rytshagov, Finland 1997.

b) 19 0-0-0 ♘ed7 20 ♔c2 ♘c5 21 ♖b1 a5 22 h3 ♖cb8 gives equal chances according to Alterman.

19...♘e8

19...♘ed7 may be better, with the idea of re-routing the d7-knight to the queenside via c5, for example 20 0-0-0 ♘c5 21 ♔c2 ♖cb8 22 ♖b1 a5.

20 f4

Or 20 0-0-0 ♘d6 21 f4 ♘d3+ 22 exd3 cxd3 23 ♖xd3 ♘b5 24 ♔c2 ♖bc4 and Black is slightly better – Alterman.

20...♘d7 21 dxe6 fxe6 22 ♗e4

22 0-0-0 can be answered by 22...♘d6 (or 22...♘b6); 22 f5 is more energetic.

22...♘ef6 23 ♗c2 ♘c5 24 ♖d1?

This allows Black to penetrate to the 7th rank. A better try would be 24 0-0-0, when 24...♘b3+ 25 ♔b2 ♘d4+ 26 ♔c1 ♘b3+ repeats moves.

24...♖b2 25 ♖d2?

25 ♗b1 put up tougher resistance.

25...♖d8 26 ♖f1 ♘d5 27 ♘xd5+ ♖xd5

28 a3 c3 29 ♖xd5 exd5 30 ♔d1 ♖a2 31 e3 ♘e4 32 ♖f3 h6 33 f5 ♘d2 0-1

34 ♖f2 ♘c4 wins material.

Game 25
Hjartarson-Arnason
Reykjavik 1995

---

1 ♘f3 c5 2 c4 ♘c6 3 d4 cxd4 4 ♘xd4 ♘f6 5 ♘c3 ♕b6 6 ♘b3 e6 7 g3 ♘e5

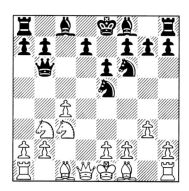

Black continues his 'active pieces' approach, probing the c4-pawn, which is White's chief weak point. Defending this pawn makes White's development a lot more problematic. The risk for Black is that his queen will be harassed by White's minor pieces, and his knights will be pushed back with gain of time, should White get his e- and f-pawns rolling.

a) 7...d5 is less popular. White can continue 8 cxd5 ♘xd5 9 ♘xd5 exd5 10 ♗g2 and here Black has tried:

a1) 10...♗b4+ 11 ♗d2 ♗g4 12 ♗xb4 ♕xb4+ 13 ♕d2 ♕xd2+ 14 ♔xd2 0-0-0 15 h3 ♗h5 16 ♖ac1 ♔b8 17 ♘c5 ♖d6 18 ♖hd1 f6 19 ♔e1 ♖hd8 20 ♖d2 with a slight edge in the endgame due to White's more active pieces, Smyslov-Olafsson, Copenhagen 1985.

a2) 10...♗e6 11 0-0 ♖d8 12 ♗g5 f6 13 ♗d2 ♗e7 14 ♘c3 0-0 15 ♘d4 ♘xd4 16 ♕xd4 ♗c5 17 ♕d2 ♕d6 18 b4 ♗b6 19 ♗d4 ♗f5 20 ♖ac1 ♗e4 21 ♗h3 and with

---

the d-pawn securely blockaded, White is a bit better, Karpov-Korchnoi, Brussels 1988.

b) 7...♗b4 is a less sophisticated approach. 8 ♗g2 and now:

b1) 8...♘e5 9 ♗e3 ♕a6 10 c5 ♘c4 11 ♕c1 ♘xe3 12 ♕xe3 d5 13 cxd6 ♗xd6 14 0-0 0-0 15 ♖fd1 ♗e7 16 ♘c5 (Tukmakov-Scavo, Lugano 1999), with 'Catalan style' pressure – White has a small edge.

b2) 8...d5 9 0-0 dxc4 10 ♗e3 ♕a6 11 ♘c5 ♕a5 12 ♕d6 ♘e7 13 ♗xb7 ♗xb7 14 ♘xb7 ♗xd6 15 ♘xa5 ♖c8 16 ♘b5 with an initiative for White, Tukmakov-Cherniaev, Geneva 1999.

8 e4 ♗b4 9 ♕e2 d6

This is better than the immediate 9...0-0 10 f4 ♘c6 11 e5 ♘e8 12 ♗e3 ♕c7 13 ♗g2 d6 14 exd6 ♘xd6 15 0-0 ♗xc3 16 bxc3 ♘f5 17 ♗f2 b6 18 c5 ♖b8 19 ♖ad1 ♗b7 20 g4 ♘fe7 21 f5 and the force is with White, Rotstein-Managadze, Halkida 2000.

10 f4 ♘c6 11 ♗e3 ♗xc3+ 12 bxc3 ♕c7 13 ♗g2 0-0

14 0-0

The other popular continuation is 14 c5, liquidating the weak front c-pawn. However, White has never proved more than equality with this approach, and in the latest word, even Kramnik had to tread carefully to secure the draw. 14...dxc5 15 ♗xc5 ♖d8 16 e5 ♘a5 17 ♗b4 ♘xb3 18 axb3 ♘d5 19 ♕c4 ♕d7 20 ♕d4 ♘xb4 21 ♕xd7 ♗xd7 22 cxb4 ♗b5 23 ♗xb7 ♖ab8 24 ♗a6 ½-½

Kramnik-Salov, Wijk aan Zee 1998.

14...b6 15 g4 ♗b7

This is an improvement over 15...♗a6. Black figures that the c4-pawn is doomed in the long run, so arranges his pieces to best counter White's kingside initiative. On b7, the bishop places pressure on e4, and helps to discourage f4-f5. In the event of the position opening up and the light-squared bishops being traded, this will reduce White's kingside forces and loosen his king's position. Also, when Black has completed his development, the bishop often jumps out to a6 after all, to finally snaffle the c4-pawn. 15...♗a6 16 g5 ♘d7 17 ♖f3 ♖fe8 18 ♖h3 and now:

a) 18...♘f8 with the further split:

a1) 19 ♕h5 ♗xc4 20 f5 ♘e5, Illescas Cordoba-Gelfand, Dos Hermanas 1994, and here White should play 21 f6 ♗xb3 22 axb3 ♕xc3 23 ♖f1 ♕b4 (Gelfand also gives 23...♕b2 as unclear, and if 24 ♖f2 ♕a1+ 25 ♖f1 ♕b2 repeating moves) 24 fxg7 ♔xg7 25 g6 ♘exg6 26 ♕f3 with good attacking chances for White.

a2) But not the premature 19 f5 ♘e5 20 ♕h5 ♕xc4 21 ♗d4 ♕e2 22 ♕h4 ♕g4 23 ♕xg4 ♘xg4 24 ♖g3 ♘e5 (Lobron-Hulak, Yerevan Olympiad 1996) and with the queens off, White has a hopeless position.

b) Another illustration of White's attacking potential in this position is 18...♘e7?! 19 f5 exf5 20 exf5 ♗xc4 21 ♕h5 ♘f8 22 ♘d4 ♗d5 23 f6 ♗xg2 24 ♔xg2 ♘d5 25 ♗d2 ♖e5 26 fxg7 ♔xg7 27 ♖f1 b5, Akesson-Cu.Hansen, Reykjavik 1995, and here White should go for 28 ♖hf3 f6 29 gxf6+ ♔h8 30 ♕h6 with a large advantage according to Hjartarson.

16 g5 ♘d7 17 ♖f3 ♖fe8

Another good prophylactic move. One of White's main ideas is to play f4-f5, usually after ♖f3-h3 and ♕e2-h5. On e8, the Black rook is ready for action on the e-file, after f4-f5, ...e6xf5 etc. In any case, Black needs to make room on f8 for the knight, in order to defend h7.

Also possible is 17...♘e7 18 ♖h3 ♖fc8 19 ♕h5 ♘f8 with chances for both sides, Lobron-Kramnik, Dortmund 1995. The game continued 20 ♘d2 d5!?.

18 ♖h3 ♖ac8

18...♘f8 19 ♖f1 ♗a6 20 ♘d2 ♘a5 is another good approach for Black. 21 ♕h5 ♘xc4 22 ♘xc4 ♗xc4 23 ♖f2 d5 24 f5 exf5 25 exf5 ♕e5 26 ♗d4 ♕e1+ was played in Akesson-Schandorff, Reykjavik 1997, when Black is doing very well. In fact this is the nightmare outcome for White, his kingside attack has been checked, and his major pieces adorn the h-file while Black powers through in the centre.

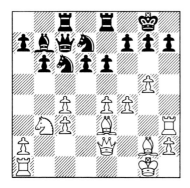

19 ♕h5

19 ♖f1!? was suggested by Leko.

19...♘f8

This position is the logical outcome of this whole variation, but unless White can find specific improvements, the line is looking good for Black.

20 ♖f1 ♘e7 21 ♘d2 ♗a6

The differences between this position and those arising after 15...♗a6 (see the notes to Black's 15th move) are quite subtle. It boils down to Black being ready for the f4-f5 thrust before allowing it. The danger in the position for Black, if he gets careless, was clearly seen in 21...d5 22 cxd5 exd5 23 ♗d4 dxe4 24 f5 ♘xf5 25 ♖xf5 e3 26 g6 fxg6 27 ♗d5+ ♗xd5 28 ♖xf8+ ♔xf8 29

♕xd5 ♖e7 30 ♖xh7 ♖f7 31 ♕e6 1-0 Lesiege-Sulypa, Gonfreville 1999.

22 f5

The attempted improvement 22 ♗d4 fared no better after 22...♗xc4 23 ♖f2 e5 24 fxe5 dxe5 25 ♘xc4 exd4 (25...♕xc4 gives more counter-chances after 26 ♗xe5 ♘eg6 27 ♗d4) 26 ♕xf7+ ♔h8 27 ♗f1 dxc3 28 e5 ♘eg6 29 ♕xc7 ♖xc7 30 ♖xc3 b5 31 ♘d6 ♖xc3 32 ♘xe8 ♘e6 with a slightly better ending for Black, Illescas Cordoba-Leko, Leon 1996.

22...♗xc4

Black has a big plus – the c4-pawn is back in the box and the rest of White's queenside is hanging. Meanwhile White does not have a breakthrough on the kingside.

23 ♖f2

Or 23 ♘xc4 ♕xc4 24 f6 ♘eg6 25 fxg7 ♔xg7 26 ♖hf3 ♖e7 and Black's kingside is solidly defended.

23...e5?

A slip, giving up most of Black's advantage. Black should open the e-file (similar to the Akesson-Schandorff example above) with 23...exf5!. Hjartarson analyses 24 ♗d4 (and 24 exf5 ♘xf5 25 ♖xf5 g6 26 ♕h6 gxf5 27 ♗d4 ♖e5) 24...f4 25 ♖xf4 ♘eg6 26 ♖f2 ♗e6 and in both cases Black is much better.

24 f6 ♘eg6 25 fxg7 ♔xg7 26 ♖hf3 ♖e7 27 ♗h3 ♖d8 28 ♗f5

Now White is back on track, with counterplay to compensate for the pawn minus.

28...d5 29 h4 ♖d6 30 ♕g4?

Another mistake. White should play 30 exd5 ♗xd5 31 ♗e4.

30...d4 31 cxd4 exd4 32 ♗f4 ♘xf4 33 ♕xf4 ♖c6 34 e5 ♕xe5?

Black would be on top after 34...♗d5 and if 35 ♗e4 ♘g6 36 ♕f6+ ♔g8 White's position is about to fall apart.

35 ♕xe5+ ♖xe5 36 ♗e4 ♖c7 37 ♘xc4 ♖xe4 38 ♘d6 ♖e6 39 ♘f5+ ♔g6 40 ♘xd4 ♖e4 41 ♖f6+ ♔h5 42 ♖h6+ ♔g4 43 ♖g2+ ♔f4 44 ♖f6+ ♔e3 45 ♘f5+

♔d3 46 ♖g3+ ♔c2 47 ♘e3+

47 ♖b3 was probably a more accurate way to play.

47...♔b1 48 ♖f1+ ♔c1 49 ♘d1 ♔a1

Made it!

50 ♖gf3

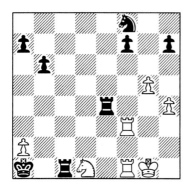

50...♖xh4

After this the game fizzles out as White liquidates almost all the pawns. Black's last hope was 50...♖g4+ 51 ♔h2 ♖xh4+ 52 ♔g3 ♘g6 53 ♖xf7 ♖d4 54 ♘e3 ♖xf1 55 ♘xf1 ♖a4 56 ♖xh7 ♖xa2 57 ♖g7 ♘e5 58 ♘h2 with some chances for Black according to Hjartarson.

51 ♘e3 ♖xf1+ 52 ♖xf1+ ♔xa2 53 ♖xf7 ♘e6 54 ♖xa7+ ♔b3 55 ♖b7 ♘xg5 56 ♖xb6+ ♔c3 57 ♔f2 ♖h2+ ½-½

Game 26
Ivanchuk-Khalifman
Elista (3rd match game) 1998

---

1 d4 ♘f6 2 c4 c5 3 ♘f3 cxd4 4 ♘xd4 ♘c6 5 ♘c3 e6 6 g3 ♕b6 7 ♘b3 ♘e5 8 e4 ♗b4 9 ♕e2 d6 10 ♗d2 0-0

In an attempt to improve on earlier games, Black accelerated his queenside play with 10...a5 11 f4 ♘c6 12 ♘a4 ♗xd2+ 13 ♕xd2 ♕b4 14 ♕xb4 ♘xb4 15 ♖d1, Huzman-Tsesarsky, Ramat Aviv 1999, and here Tsesarsky gives 15...♔e7 16 a3 ♘c6 17 ♘b6 (17 ♗d3!?) 17...♖a7 18 ♗g2 a4 19 ♘d4 ♘xd4 20 ♖xd4 e5 as equal.

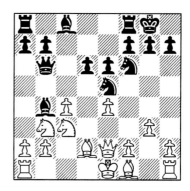

11 0-0-0

In the light of developments in the previous game, White has started looking elsewhere for a dynamic alternative. In this game, Ivanchuk tries a line which hitherto had only been tested rarely. Alternatively, 11 f4 ♘c6 12 0-0-0 e5 13 f5 ♘d4 14 ♘xd4 exd4 15 ♘d5 ♘xd5 16 cxd5 ♖e8 17 ♕d3 ♗d7 18 ♗xb4 ♕xb4 19 ♗g2 ♗a4 with chances for both sides, Tsesarsky-Gershon, Ramat Aviv 2000.

11...a5

Alternatives have not worked out that well:

a) 11...♘c6 12 ♗g2 a5 13 ♗e3 ♕c7 14 ♘b5 ♕e7 15 a3 a4 16 ♘3d4 ♗c5 17 ♘xc6 ♗xe3+ 18 ♕xe3 bxc6 19 ♘xd6 and White is a safe pawn up, Filippov-Notkin, Maikop 1998.

b) 11...♗d7 12 f4 ♘g6 13 ♗g2 ♗c6 14 ♔b1 a5 15 ♗e3 ♕c7 16 ♘b5 ♗xb5 17 cxb5 a4 18 ♘d4 a3 19 b6 with play against the loose bishop on b4, Korchnoi-Anand, Paris (rapid) 1991.

12 f4

In order to avoid the note to Black's 14th, perhaps White should try 12 ♗e3 ♕a6 (12...♕c6 13 ♘d4 ♕d7 14 ♗d2) 13 ♘b5 a4 (13...♕c6 14 a3 ♗c5 15 ♘xc5 dxc5 16 ♗g2 or 13...♗d7 14 ♘c7) 14 ♘3d4 a3 15 b3 and if 15...♘xe4 (or 15...♕a5 16 ♗g5 ♘ed7 17 ♗g2) 16 ♕c2 is very strong.

12...a4

Or 12...♘c6 13 ♗e3 ♕a6 14 ♘b5 a4 and now:

a) 15 ♘d2 a3 16 b3 ♕a5, Tukmakov-Berelovich, Donetsk 1998, with a complex and unclear position.

b) 15 ♘c7 axb3 16 ♘xa6 bxa2 17 ♔c2 ♖xa6 and with the a-pawn about to land, Black has a lot of play for his queen sacrifice:

b1) 18 ♗g2 e5 19 f5 ♗c5 20 b3 ♗d7 21 ♔b2 ♘d4 22 ♗xd4?? a1♕+ 23 ♖xa1 ♗xd4+ 24 ♔c2 ♗xa1 0-1 Gleizerov-Dvoirys, Cheliabinsk 1989.

b2) 18 e5 dxe5 19 fxe5 ♘xe5 20 ♔b3 a1♕ 21 ♖xa1 ♖xa1 22 ♔xb4 ♗d7 is unclear according to Dvoirys.

13 fxe5 axb3 14 a3

14 exf6 can be answered by 14...bxa2 15 ♘xa2 ♖xa2 and if 16 ♕g4 g6 17 ♕g5 ♕d4 wins for Black.

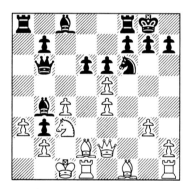

14...♗xc3

Ivanchuk gives 14...dxe5! 15 axb4 ♖a1+ 16 ♘b1 ♕a6 17 ♕d3 (17 ♗c3 ♕a2 18 ♕d3 ♘xe4 19 ♕xe4 f5 20 ♕d3 e4 wins for Black) 17...♕a2 18 ♗g2 ♖e8!! (with the brilliant idea of ...♖e7-d7) 19 ♗g5 (19 ♗c3 ♖e7 20 ♕d8+ ♖e8 also repeats the position):

a) 19...♖e7 20 ♕d8+ ♖e8 21 ♕d3 ♖e7 with a draw by repetition.

b) Black cannot afford a spare move to free his king from the back rank threats, e.g. 19...h6 20 ♗xf6 gxf6 21 ♗f3 ♖e7 22 ♕d8+

♔g7 23 ♕xe7 ♕xb1+ 24 ♔d2 ♕xb2+ 25 ♔e3 ♖a2 26 ♖hf1 and Black has run out of threats, for example 26...♕c3+ 27 ♖d3.

15 ♗xc3 dxe5 16 ♗xe5 ♕c6

Instead:

a) after 16...♖d8 17 ♗g2 ♘d7 18 ♗c3 e5 19 ♖d5 White has an edge, Nikcevic-Lesiege, Gonfreville 1999.

b) Ivanchuk gives 16...♖a4 17 ♕f3 ♘d7 18 ♗d6 ♖d8 19 ♗e7 ♖e8 20 ♗b4 ♖xb4 21 axb4 ♕xb4 as unclear.

17 ♗xf6 gxf6 18 ♕g4+ ♔h8 19 ♕f3

19 ♕h4 ♔g7 20 ♗d3 is a more efficient way to pursue a kingside attack.

19...e5 20 ♖d5 f5 21 ♖xe5 ♗e6

Black has generated some reasonable counterplay.

22 ♖b5 f6 23 ♖xb3 fxe4 24 ♕e3 ♗xc4 25 ♗xc4 ♕xc4+ 26 ♔b1 ♕d5 27 ♖b4 ♖ae8 28 ♖c1 ♖f7 29 ♖c5 ♕d1+ 30 ♔a2

30...♕d6?

30...♕d3 31 ♕xd3 exd3 32 ♖d4 ♖e2 33 ♖xd3 ♖xh2 was sufficient to hold.

31 ♖xe4 ♖xe4 32 ♖c8+ ♔g7 33 ♕xe4

White is a pawn up with his opponent's king exposed to boot.

33...f5 34 ♕c4 h5 35 ♖h8 ♕g6 36 ♕d4+ ♖f6 37 ♖d8 ♕f7+ 38 b3 ♕e6 39 ♖d7+ ♔g6 40 ♖xb7

The situation is hopeless for Black.

40...h4 41 a4 ♕c6 42 ♖b8 h3 43 ♖g8+ ♔f7 44 ♖h8 ♔g7 45 ♖h4 ♔g6 46 ♕e3 ♔f7 47 ♕a7+ ♔g8 48 ♕h7+ 1-0

Summary

The games in this chapter cover a wide range of strategic and tactical issues. Black's 4...e5 and 4...b6 systems are standing up well. Generally Black is fine in all the lines with an early ...♝b4 if White does not want to transpose to a Nimzo-Indian. Korchnoi's favourite 6 a3 line really deserves more widespread use as it looks fairly powerful. In the long main line, Ivanchuk's 10 ♝d2 could revitalise White's chances.

1 c4 c5 2 ♘f3 ♘f6 3 d4 cxd4 4 ♘xd4 e6

  4...e5 – *Game 15*; 4...b6 – *Game 16*

5 ♘c3 (D)

  5 g3

    5...♝b4+ – *Game 17*; 5...♕c7 – *Game 18*

5...♘c6

  5...♝b4 – *Game 19*

6 g3

  6 ♘db5

    6...♝c5 – *Game 22*; 6...d5 – *Game 21*

  6 a3 – *Game 20*

6...♕b6 (D)

  6...♝c5 – *Game 23*

7 ♘b3

  7 ♘bd5– *Game 24*

7...♘e5 8 e4 ♝b4 9 ♕e2 d6 10 ♝d2 (D) – *Game 26*

  10 f4 – *Game 25*

   5 ♘c3   *6...♕b6*   *10 ♝d2*

CHAPTER FOUR

Black plays an Early ...d7-d5

1 c4 c5 2 ♘c3

Of course White can also play 2 ♘f3 or 2 g3. After 2 ♘f3 ♘f6 3 g3 d5 and now 4 cxd5 will transpose to other lines while Kramnik has also tried 4 d4 (see Game 36).

2...♘f6 3 ♘f3

3 g3 limits the options (for both sides) and is the 'official' move order of the Rubinstein: 3...d5 4 cxd5 ♘xd5 5 ♗g2 ♘c7. This order also gives White the additional option of 6 ♕b3 and trading the g2-bishop for the c6-knight before developing with ♘g1-f3 (see Game 27).

3...d5 4 cxd5 ♘xd5

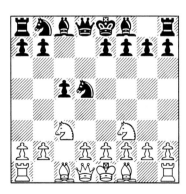

This chapter covers a number of systems, and the move order can be particularly opaque to the uninitiated, but is also crucial.

Both sides need to be aware of which kinds of set-up they are (and are not) happy with.

There are a number of different systems with ...d5, depending largely on Black's subsequent development. I have decided to cover them in one chapter, however, for clarity and because of the inter-related move orders etc. The systems are not independent of each other, for example if White plays 5 d4 or 5 e4, Black does not get to play the Rubinstein, so he needs to have a wider spread of knowledge.

White has two basic approaches:

a) Accept that Black will get a space advantage (by playing 5 g3), with a view to chipping away at it later. Fundamentally, Black then has a choice between three main development schemes:

1) Setting up a Maroczy bind structure with ...e7-e5. This necessitates the early ...♘d5-c7 to avoid tactics involving the d5-knight. This is the Rubinstein system (Games 27-29).

2) Solid development by ...e7-e6 and ...♗f8-e7. This is the Keres-Parma set-up (Games 32-34).

3) The Kingside fianchetto ...g7-g6. This is covered in Chapter 6, where it is approached from the Symmetrical move order (I had to cover it in one place or the other).

b) Challenge immediately in the centre, for example with 5 d4 or 5 e4.

Kramnik, for example has shown a marked preference for plan B, while a number of other GMs are happy with 'A'. Note that these dynamic early clashes quite often lead to endgames or queenless middle-games, several of which have become 'tabi-yas' for GM games.

5 e4 allowing 5...♘b4 is a provocative system which was popular in the 1980s. White's main options are 6 ♗c4 and 6 ♗b5+. The current state of theory is covered in Games 37 and 38, while the tricky 5 e3 is covered in Game 31.

After 5 d4 Black needs to decide what he wants. Happy with a Grünfeld? Then play 5...g6. Otherwise 5...cxd4 can be chosen – this line can also be reached from the QGD Semi-Tarrasch move order (see Game 30).

To avoid both 5 e4 and 5 d4, Black often plays 3...♘c6, waiting for 4 g3 before playing 4...d5. This in turn gives White the option of Tal's 5 d4 if he wants to continue with 'Plan B' – see Game 35.

5 g3 ♘c6 6 ♗g2

6...e6 is the so-called Keres-Parma, which is actually classified under the QGD Semi-Tarrasch (see Games 32-34), while 6...g6 often transposes into the lines covered in Chapter 6.

6...♘c7

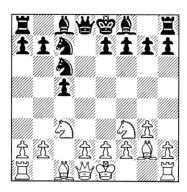

This is the Rubinstein variation. Here

Black is aiming for a 'Maroczy bind' space advantage with ...e7-e5 and gradually building up the position. In return, White gets rapid development, and can exert pressure on Black's centre by ♘f3-d2-c4, f2-f4, a2-a4 etc. The position after 6...♘c7 is covered in Games 28-29.

Game 27
Cu.Hansen-Schandorff
Stockholm 1996

1 c4 ♘f6

1...c5 2 ♘c3 ♘c6 3 ♘f3 g6 4 d4 cxd4 5 ♘xd4 ♗g7 6 ♘c2 ♗xc3+ 7 bxc3 ♕a5 often transposes into the same position (with reversed colours), since in the main game White takes two tempi over ♕d1-b3-a4. For example, Bönsch-Stohl, Stara Zagora 1990 continued: 8 ♗d2 ♘f6 9 f3 d6 10 e4 0-0 11 ♘e3 b6 12 ♗e2 ♗a6 13 ♖b1 ♕c5 14 0-0 ♖ac8 15 ♔h1 ♖fe8 16 ♕e1 ♘a5 17 ♖b4 ♕e5 18 ♗d3 ♕e6 19 f4 etc.

2 ♘c3 c5 3 g3 d5 4 cxd5 ♘xd5 5 ♗g2 ♘c7

5...e6? is a blunder which became well known when Kramnik slipped up in a 1994 Candidates match. However, the future world champion is in respectable company – GMs Lputian, Farago and Rustemov have also made the same mistake. Of the 43 games in my database with the position after 5...e6, it is surprising that only 12 players of the white side played 6 ♘xd5 and 7 ♕b3. GMs Portisch, Eingorn and Kinder-mann were among those that either missed the fact they could win a pawn or decided that it was too dangerous to do so. This is a good reminder that 'the tactics are out there'. 6 ♘xd5 (The routine 6 ♘f3 transposes into the Keres-Parma variation.) 6...exd5 7 ♕b3 and White wins a pawn for no real compensation after either:

a) 7...♗e6 8 ♕xb7 ♘d7 9 ♘h3 ♘b6 10 ♕a6 ♗d6 11 d3 0-0 12 ♘f4 ♗c8 13 ♕a5 Garcia Martinez-Farago, Polanica Zroj

1978.

b) 7...♞c6 8 ♕xd5 ♕xd5 9 ♗xd5 ♞b4 10 ♗e4 f5 11 ♗b1 g6 12 ♞f3 Gelfand-Kramnik, Sanghi Nagar (8th match game) 1994.

6 ♕b3

A very direct plan, aiming to give Black doubled isolated c-pawns. Of course there are a number of other openings where White trades his light-squared bishop for the c6-knight (for example the ♗b5 Sicilian), but the difference here is that White has loosened his kingside with g2-g3. Studying the games in this line, it is rare for Black to be able to mount a direct attack to exploit this; in fact White's kingside is more of a long-term factor, giving Black dynamic equality provided he can first contain White's initiative and defend his weak pawns.

6...♞c6

6...♞d7 avoids the doubled-pawns, but presents less of a challenge in the centre. After 7 ♞f3 (In the event of 7 ♗xb7?? Black does not need to calculate the consequences of 7...♜b8 8 ♗xc8 ♜xb3 9 ♗xd7+ ♕xd7 10 axb3, since 7...c4 wins on the spot) 7...e5 8 0-0 ♗e7 9 e3 ♞e6 10 ♜d1 ♗f6 (10...0-0 11 d4 is much better for White according to Saharov) 11 ♞e4 0-0 12 d3 b6 13 ♞d6 ♜b8 14 ♞xc8 ♜xc8 15 ♗d2 and White is slightly better, since the two bishops gives his position better long-term potential, M.Gurevich-Ponomariov, Shenyang 2000.

7 ♗xc6+ bxc6 8 ♞f3

8 ♕a4 cuts down Black's options somewhat (see notes to the next move), and 8...♗d7 9 ♞f3 f6 10 d3 e5 will transpose to the main game.

8...f6

8...♞e6 9 ♕a4 ♞d4 10 ♞e5 ♕c7 11 f4 f6 12 ♞c4 h5 was played in Contin-Tukmakov, Bern 1992, and now 13 e3 ♞b5 14 ♞e4 h4 15 ♕c2 hxg3 16 ♞xg3 ♗e6 leads to an unclear position.

9 ♕a4

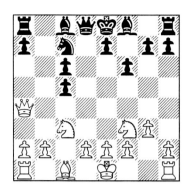

9...♗d7

9...♕d7 is also playable, but makes it slightly harder for Black to co-ordinate his defence. 10 d3 e5 11 ♗e3 and now:

a) 11...♞e6 12 0-0 (White now has a natural plan of piling up on the c5-pawn with ♞c3-e4 and ♜f1-c1) 12...♜b8 13 ♜ab1 h5 14 ♞e4 ♞d4 15 ♗xd4 cxd4 16 ♜fc1 ♜b5 17 ♜c2 a5 18 ♜bc1 ♗b7 19 ♞h4 ♜h6 20 b3 ♕d5 21 ♕c4 with a plus for White – the knights are better than the bishops as in the game Psakhis-Tukmakov, Rostov on Don 1993.

b) 11...♞d5 aims to cut across White's typical build-up:

b1) Indeed after 12 ♜c1 ♜b8 Black has counterplay, and in fact the game Sher-Brglez, Ptuj 1991, did not last much longer: 13 b3 c4 14 ♕xc4?? ♜b4 0-1

b2) Instead, Watson gives 12 ♞e4 ♞xe3 13 fxe3 ♜b8 14 ♕c2 with an advantage for White, quoting the game Nilssen-Trifunovic, Amsterdam 1954.

10 d3 e5 11 0-0

After the alternative 11 ♗e3:

a) Quinteros-A.Sokolov, Biel 1985 continued 11...♜b8 12 0-0 ♞d5 13 ♜fc1 a5 14 ♗d2 ♜xb2 15 ♞e4 ♕b6 16 ♕xa5 ♕xa5 17 ♗xa5 ♜xe2 18 ♞fd2 ♗h3 and now A.Sokolov gives 19 ♞b3 (instead of 19 a4 ♗e7 20 ♞c4 0-0 21 ♞c3 ♞xc3 22 ♜xc3 f5) 19...♔f7 20 ♞bxc5 ♗e7 as unclear.

b) 11...♘e6 12 ♖c1 ♕b6 13 b3 ♘d4 14 ♘d2 ♗e7 15 ♘c4 ♕b8 16 ♘a5 f5 (Poldauf-Götz, German Bundesliga 1992) and Black has everything defended.

11...♘e6 12 ♗e3

Two alternative approaches are:

a) 12 ♘e4 ♗e7 13 ♗e3 ♘d4 14 ♗xd4 cxd4 15 ♕c4 ♖b8 16 ♘c5 ♗xc5 17 ♕xc5 ♕b6 and Black has equalised, Romanishin-Mikhalchishin, Lvov 1987.

b) Perhaps White should investigate 12 b3 ♗e7 13 ♗a3 ♖b8 14 ♕c4 0-0 15 ♖ac1 ♔h8 16 ♖fe1 ♕e8 17 ♘a4 ♖b5 18 ♕e4 with pressure, as in Bönsch-Stohl, Stara Zagora 1990 (this game was played with colours reversed using the move order mentioned in the note at the start of the main game).

12...♘d4 13 ♖fc1

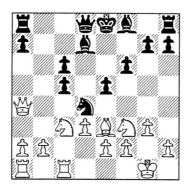

White's plan is to leave the c3-knight in place while re-arranging his major pieces. Placing the f1-rook on the c-file means that a later ...♗d7-h3 has less bite. Meanwhile, the queen drops back to d1 to defend e2.

13...♗e7

13...♘xf3+ 14 exf3 would make it impossible to defend the c5-pawn, while there is no quick way for Black to exploit White's kingside.

14 ♕d1 ♖b8 15 ♘a4 0-0

15...♘xf3+ 16 exf3 ♗f5 17 ♗xc5.

16 b3

Black now has time to shore up his de-

fence of c5.

a) 16 ♘xc5 doesn't work because of 16...♘xf3+ 17 exf3 ♖xb2 18 ♘b3 ♗f5.

b) 16 ♘d2 is a possible improvement, e.g.:

b1) 16...♗h3 17 ♘e4 f5 18 ♘exc5 ♕d5 (18...f4 19 ♗xd4 exd4 20 ♘e4) 19 f3 g5 20 ♖c4 g4 21 ♘c3.

b2) 16...f5 17 ♘xc5 ♖xb2 18 ♘cb3 ♗b4 19 ♗xd4 exd4 20 ♘c4 ♗c3 21 ♘xb2 ♗xb2 22 ♖c5 ♗xa1 (22...f4 23 ♖b1 ♗c3 24 ♘d2) 23 ♕xa1 f4 24 ♕xd4.

In both lines, White can probably hold his extra pawn and weather the counterattack.

16...♖b5 17 ♖c3 ♖f7 18 ♖ac1 ♕f8 19 ♘d2

White now has almost every piece aimed at c5, but Black is able to combine defence with (potential) attack effectively.

19...f5 20 f3 g5 21 ♘c4 ♕g7 22 ♘a3

With his kingside now starting to feel rather draughty, White decides to bale out for a draw.

22...♖a5 23 ♘c4 ½-½

Game 28
Piket-Kasparov
Internet 2000

---

1 ♘f3 ♘f6 2 c4 c5 3 ♘c3

An alternative move order to reach the Rubinstein system is 3 g3 d5 4 cxd5 ♘xd5 5 ♗g2 ♘c6 6 0-0 e5 7 ♘c3 ♘c7. Now 8 ♘e1 is Kosten's recommendation for White against the Rubinstein. However, Black should play 8...♗g4! 9 ♕a4 (not 9 ♘d3 ♕xd3) ♕d7 10 ♗xc6 bxc6 11 ♘d3 f6 12 f4 ♕d4+ (12...♘d5) and now:

a) Kosten gives 13 ♖f2 ♕xa4 14 ♘xa4 c4 15 ♘dc5 but Black is fine here after 15...♘e6 16 ♘xe6 ♗xe6 17 fxe5 fxe5. White is going to have difficulty developing his bishop and a1-rook, and Black has lots of open lines, e.g. 18 ♘c3 ♗c5 19 e3 and now 19...♔d7 or 19...♗e7.

b) 13 ♘f2 ♕xa4 14 ♘xa4 ♗xe2 15 ♖e1 ♗b5 16 ♘c3 0-0-0 was played in Friedgood-R.Webb, British League 1997, and Black is at least equal.

3...d5 4 cxd5 ♘xd5 5 g3 ♘c6 6 ♗g2 ♘c7

This is a necessary precaution, because the immediate 6...e5 fails to 7 ♘xe5 ♘xc3 8 ♘xc6 ♘xd1 9 ♘xd8 ♘xf2 10 ♘xf7 winning a pawn.

7 d3

7 ♕a4 aims to prevent Black from establishing a Maroczy bind with ...e5, e.g. 7...♗d7 (7...♕d7 is also playable) 8 ♕e4 g6 9 ♘e5. This is the point of White's play, gaining the two bishops and discouraging a typical Maroczy bind set-up. (Of course White needs to get ♘f3-e5 in before Black completes his development with 9...♗g7, or else the White queen will start to look silly on e4.) Nevertheless, Black's position is perfectly acceptable, and in fact the move 7 ♕a4 has waned in popularity. 9...♗g7 10 ♘xd7 ♕xd7 11 0-0 0-0

and now:

a) 12 d3 ♖c8 13 ♖b1 ♘e6 14 ♖d1 b6 15 ♗d2 ♖fd8 16 ♘d5 ♘ed4 17 e3 e6 with at least equality, Sherbakov-A.Sokolov, St Petersburg 1993.

b) 12 a3 ♖ac8 13 ♖b1 ♘e6 14 b4 b6.

One of the keys to this position for Black is to keep the knights flexibly placed. The e6-knight should aim for d4, while the c6-knight should be routed via e5.

b1) After 15 b5:

b11) In the game Pigusov-Estremera Panos, Las Palmas 1996, Black instead played 15...♘cd4 but after 16 e3 ♘f5 17 ♕a4 ♘d8 18 ♗b2 Black is passively placed – suddenly the knights have nowhere to go.

b12) 15...♘e5 is better, and if 16 f4 ♘g4 17 f5 ♕d4+ 18 e3 ♕xe4 19 ♘xe4 (19 ♗xe4 gxf5 20 ♖xf5 ♘xe3) 19...gxf5 looks okay for Black.

b2) 15 ♘d5 ♘ed4 and now:

b21) 16 bxc5 bxc5 17 e3 ♘e2+ 18 ♔h1 e6 19 ♕d3 exd5 20 ♕xe2 ♖b8 21 ♖xb8 ♖xb8 22 d3 ♖b3 and Black has an edge, Smejkal-A.Sokolov, Novi Sad 1984.

b22) White got into even worse trouble in Cu.Hansen-Korchnoi, Antwerp 1993, after 16 b5?! ♘e5 17 f4 f5 18 ♕e3 ♘g4 19 ♕xe7 ♖c7 20 ♕h4 ♘xe2+ 21 ♔h1 ♘xc1 22 ♖bxc1 ♗f6 23 ♕h3 ♖cc8; White's structure is shattered and his queen badly placed.

Note that 7 0-0 e5 8 ♘e1 transposes to the line analysed in the note to move 3 (Friedgood-Webb).

7...e5 8 0-0 ♗e7 9 ♘d2 ♗d7

A wise precaution. Allowing White to double the c-pawns gives Black a more difficult position, e.g. 9...0-0 10 ♗xc6 bxc6 11 ♘c4 f6 and now:

a) 12 ♗e3 ♗h3 13 ♖e1 ♘d5 14 ♖c1 ♖b8 15 ♕d2 ♗e6 16 b3 ♘xe3 17 ♕xe3 ♕d4 18 ♘a4 when White is somewhat better because of Black's fixed c-pawns, Van Wely-Salov, Wijk aan Zee 1997.

b) 12 b3 ♗h3 13 ♖e1 ♘e6 14 ♗b2 is also a little better for White, Dzindzichashvili-Timman, Tilburg 1985.

10 ♘c4 0-0!?

An interesting pawn sacrifice that has been around for many years, without being refuted. In return for the pawn, Black has long-term chances based on his control of central squares, the bishop pair and White's weakened kingside. 10...f6 is the solid main line, covered in the next game.

11 ♗xc6 ♗xc6 12 ♘xe5 ♗e8

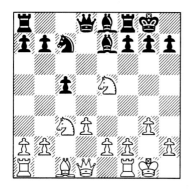

13 ♕b3!?

A relatively fresh approach. Other moves are:

a) 13 ♗e3 is quite popular.

a1) 13...♘e6 is then Black's main move. And now:

a11) After 14 ♖c1 Black can generate sufficient counterplay, e.g. 14...♗f6 15 ♘f3 (15 ♘c4 ♗c6 16 ♘e4 ♗d4 17 ♗xd4 cxd4 18 ♘e5 ♗d5 19 ♕a4 ♖e8 with some compensation for the pawn, Govbinder-Kapengut, USSR 1979) 15...♗c6 16 ♕b3 ♗d4 17 ♗xd4 ♘xd4 18 ♘xd4 cxd4 19 ♘e4, Hjartarson-Vaganian, Rotterdam 1989, and now Vaganian gives 19...♕d7 20 ♖c5 ♖ac8 21 ♖fc1 ♔h8 as slightly better for Black.

a12) 14 ♕b3 ♗f6 (ECO recommends the move order 14...♗d6 in order to avoid 14...♗f6 15 ♘g4, while 15 f4 transposes to 'a121', but now White has other options, e.g. 15 ♘c4), and now:

a121) 15 f4 ♗xe5 16 fxe5 ♗c6 17 ♘b5 (17 ♕c4!?) 17...♗xb5 18 ♕xb5 ½-½ Psakhis-Ehlvest, Tilburg 1992.

a122) 15 ♘g4 ♗d4 16 ♗xd4 cxd4 17 ♘e4 ♗c6 18 ♖ac1 ♔h8 19 ♘e5 ♗d5 20 ♕a4 f6 21 ♘f3 ♗c6 22 ♕a3 ♕d5 23 ♕d6! and White is well on top, Illescas Cordoba-Izeta Txabarri, Lleida 1991.

a2) Other tries are less good, e.g. 13...♘d5 14 ♕b3 ♘xe3 15 fxe3 b5 16 ♕d5

♕xd5 17 ♘xd5 ♗d6 18 ♘f3 ♗c6 19 ♘f4 ♖fe8 20 ♔f2 ♖ac8 21 ♖ac1 a5 22 e4 and White has a large advantage, Tukmakov-Berelovich, Koszalin 1998.

b) The rarer 13 e4 may be worth a try, e.g. 13...♗f6 (13...b5 14 ♗e3 f6 15 ♘f3 ♗h5 16 h3 ♕d7 17 ♔g2 ♖ad8 can be tried) 14 ♘g4 ♗d4 15 ♘e3 ♗c6 16 ♘f5 ♘e6 17 ♗e3 g6 18 ♘h6+ ♔h8 19 ♕b3 ♗xe3 20 fxe3 ♕xd3 21 ♘g4 ♕d8 22 ♘d5 when White is a bit better, Granda Zuniga-De la Villa Garcia, Leon 1997.

13...♗f6

13...b6 (13...♖b8!? and 13...♕c8!? are also possible) and now:

a) 14 ♕c4 ♖c8 (14...♗d6 15 ♕e4 or 14...♔h8 15 ♕e4) 15 ♗e3 ♘e6 16 ♕d5 ♕c7 17 f4 ♖d8 18 ♕g2 ♗d6 19 ♘f3 f5 20 ♖ad1 ♗c6 21 ♗c1 ♕b7, Sarno-Milloni, Porto Girgio 1993, and now 22 b3 ♖fe8 23 e4 fxe4 24 dxe4 ♗xe4 25 ♘xe4 ♕xe4 26 ♖fe1 ♕f5 27 ♗b2 is slightly better for White according to Sarno.

b) 14 ♗e3 with a further choice:

b1) 14...♔h8 15 ♖fd1 (15 a4 f6 16 ♘c4) 15...f6 16 ♘f3 ♗f7 17 ♕a4 ♘d5 18 ♘xd5 (18 ♗d2) 18...♗xd5 19 a3 a6 20 ♘d2 ♕c8 and Black is fine, Commons-Gheorghiu, Lone Pine 1975.

b2) 14...♗f6 15 f4 ♕e7 16 d4 cxd4 17 ♗xd4 ♕e6 18 e3 ♗e7 19 ♕xe6 fxe6 20 ♖ac1 ♘b5 21 ♘xb5 ♗xb5 22 ♖f2 with an extra pawn and c-file control, Pribyl-Meyer, Schwabisch Gmund 1996.

14 ♘g4 ♗d4

A novelty, improving over the earlier move 14...♗c6 15 ♘xf6+ ♕xf6 when White has:

a) 16 ♕c4 ♘e6 17 ♗e3 ♖fe8 18 ♖ac1 ♘d4 19 ♗xd4 cxd4 20 ♘e4 ♗xe4 21 dxe4 ♖xe4 with equality, Ribli-Chandler, Lugano 1985.

b) 16 ♗e3 ♘e6 17 ♘e4 ♕f5 18 f3 ♖fd8 19 ♖ac1 can be tried.

c) Bagirov suggests 16 e4 ♖ad8 17 ♗e3 ♖xd3 18 ♗xc5 ♕f3 19 ♖ae1 ♘e6 20 ♖e3 with a small plus for White.

15 e3

It would be dangerous to grab the second pawn, as Black gets a strong initiative after 15 ♕xb7 ♖b8 16 ♕g2 f5 17 ♘e3 f4.

15...♗xc3 16 ♕xc3 b6 17 f3

Piket suggests 17 b3!?.

17...♗b5 18 ♘f2 ♕d7

If 18...♗c6 19 e4 (or 19 ♘g4 ♗b5 20 ♖d1) 19...♘b5 20 ♕b3 ♘d4 21 ♕d1 f5 22 ♗e3 fxe4 23 fxe4 ♘f3+ 24 ♔g2 ♘e5 and Black has good compensation for the pawn.

19 e4 ♘e6 20 ♗e3 a5 21 ♖ad1 ♖ad8 22 ♖d2 ♕c6

Black can save a whole tempo here with 22...♕b7, though White can retain a slight advantage (albeit less than in the game) with 23 ♖c1 ♘d4 24 ♔g2 ♖d7 25 a3 a4 26 ♗xd4 ♖xd4 27 b4 according to Piket.

23 ♖c1 ♕b7 24 a3 ♘d4 25 ♔g2 ♖c8

25...h6 maintains the pressure.

26 ♖b1 ♖fd8 27 ♗xd4 ♖xd4 28 b4

White finally manages to open up the position, and he now achieves a better endgame.

28...axb4 29 axb4 ♕d7 30 bxc5 bxc5 31 ♖bb2 h6 32 ♖a2 ♔h7 33 ♖a5 ♖d8 34 ♕xc5 ♗xd3 35 ♖xd3

White gets better winning chances by keeping the minor pieces on, e.g. 35 ♖a7 ♕e6 36 ♖b2 ♖c4 37 ♕e7.

35...♖xd3 36 ♘xd3 ♕xd3 37 ♖a2 ♕b3 38 ♕c2 ♕xc2+ 39 ♖xc2

This position is a book draw, but Kasparov was running out of time, and does not play the correct defence.

39...h5 40 f4 g6 41 e5 ♖d3

The key is to defend from the side, e.g. 41...♖d7.

42 ♔h3 ♖e3 43 ♔h4 ♔g7 44 ♔g5 ♖e1 45 ♖c7 ♖e2 46 ♖e7 ♖a2 47 f5 gxf5 48 e6 h4 49 ♖xf7+ ♔g8 50 ♔f6 1-0

Game 29
Lputian-Leko
Wijk aan Zee 2000

---

1 ♘f3 ♘f6 2 c4 c5 3 g3 d5 4 cxd5 ♘xd5 5 ♗g2 ♘c6 6 ♘c3 ♘c7 7 d3 e5 8 ♘d2 ♗d7 9 0-0 ♗e7 10 ♘c4 f6 11 f4

White needs to take a swipe at Black's structure, else he will have little chance of an opening advantage once Black has completed his development. The alternative approach is to prevent ...b7-b5 before playing f2-f4. This leads to a somewhat quieter game.

After 11 a4, Black has:

a) 11...0-0 12 f4 exf4 13 ♗xf4 ♘e6 14 ♗d2 ♔h8 15 ♘d5 and now:

a1) 15...♖b8 16 ♗c3 ♘g5 17 h4 ♘f7 18 e3 ♘h6 19 ♖f4 ♗e6 20 ♕f3 ♕d7 21 ♖f1 ♖bd8 with balanced chances, Gulko-Yudasin, Seville 1992.

a2) Alternatively 15...♖e8 16 ♗c3 ♘g5 17 ♘f4 ♖b8 18 e3 ♖f8 (worried about a possible ♕d1-h5, Black has lost time with ...♖f8-e8-f8) 19 h4 ♘e6 20 ♘d5 ♘c7 21 ♘f4 ♘e6 22 h5, with pressure on the a1-h8 diagonal, Nogueiras-Rodriguez, Terrassa 1996.

b) Black can also try 11...♘e6 to discourage f2-f4, e.g. 12 ♗e3 (Mikhalchishin recommends that White plays 12 f4 in any case, recapturing after 12...exf4 with 13 gxf4) 12...0-0 13 a5 ♖b8 14 ♘d5 ♘ed4 15 ♗xd4 exd4 16 ♘f4 ♘b4 17 ♖e1 ♖e8 and Black is at least equal, Damljanovic-Mikhalchishin, Palma de Mallorca 1989.

11...b5

Black has to respond energetically. If 11...0-0 12 fxe5 fxe5 13 ♖xf8+ ♗xf8 14 ♗e3 Black has static weaknesses to defend.

12 ♘e3 ♖c8

An important alternative is 12...exf4 when White has tried:

a) 13 ♘f5 b4 14 ♘xe7 ♕xe7 and here:

a1) 15 ♗xf4 bxc3 16 ♗xc7 ♖c8 17 ♗f4 cxb2 18 ♖b1 0-0 19 ♖xb2 ♘d4 with chances for both sides, Akopian-Leko, Ubeda 1997.

a2) 15 ♘e4 fxg3 16 ♗f4 ♘e5 17 ♖c1 ♘e6 18 ♗xe5 fxe5 19 e3 gxh2+ 20 ♔h1 h5 when White does not have enough to justify his material investment, Nikolaidis-Lautier, Yerevan Olympiad 1996.

b) 13 gxf4 ♖c8!? (a relatively new move which seems at least as good as the alternative 13...♖b8) 14 f5 ♘d4 15 ♘e4 0-0 16 ♗d2 ♘a8 17 ♔h1 ♘b6 18 ♖c1 ♕e8 19 ♖f2 ♕h5 20 ♕f1 ♖fd8 with equal chances, Pelletier-Karr, Mulhouse 2001.

13 a4 b4

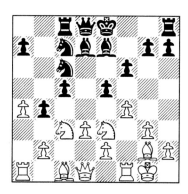

14 ♘b5

14 ♘cd5 is equally valid and complex, e.g. 14...0-0 15 ♘c4 exf4 16 ♘xc7 (16 ♘xe7+ ♕xe7 17 ♗xf4 may yield White a slight edge) and here Black has played:

a) 16...♕xc7 17 ♗xf4 ♘e5 (Black should go for 17...♕d8 18 ♘d6 ♗xd6 19 ♗xd6 ♖e8 20 ♗xc5 ♗g4 with sufficient play for the pawn, according to Sherzer) 18 ♗xe5

fxe5 19 ♗d5+ ♔h8 20 ♖xf8+ ♖xf8 21 ♕d2 ♗h3 22 ♕e3 when White has an unpleasant bind, Granda Zuniga-Estremera Panos, Leon 1997.

b) 16...f3!? 17 ♗xf3 ♕xc7 18 ♗f4 ♕d8 19 ♘d6 ♗xd6 20 ♗xd6 ♘e7 with an unclear position, Fridman-Van der Sterren, Hamburg 1997.

14...exf4 15 gxf4

a) After 15 ♘c4, in an earlier game, Leko got slightly the worse of the opening. Lputian varies, but Leko indicates that he had an improvement ready. 15...♘xb5 16 axb5 ♘d4 17 ♖xa7 ♗g4?! (Lautier pinpoints this move as dubious, and instead suggests 17...♘xb5 18 ♖b7 fxg3 19 ♗f4 gxh2+ 20 ♗xh2 ♘d4 with a messy position) 18 ♖f2 0-0 19 b6 fxg3 20 hxg3 g5 21 ♕f1 when White is a little better, Lautier-Leko, European Team Championship, Batumi 1999.

b) 15 ♘f5 ♗xf5 16 ♗xc6+ ♗d7 17 ♗xd7+ ♕xd7 18 ♘xc7+ ♖xc7 19 ♗xf4 ♖c6 20 ♖c1 h5 21 d4 g5 22 d5 ♖c8 23 ♗e3 h4 (Szilagyi-Pinter, Hungary 1992) with a rather wild position where Black should be no worse.

15...♘xb5 16 axb5 ♘d4 17 ♖xa7 ♘xb5 18 ♖a6 0-0 19 f5 ♘d4 20 ♖f4

Black's position is on a knife-edge, as he is in severe danger of being mated!

20...♔h8 21 ♕f1 ♗b5

Played after an hour's thought – Leko accurately checked the tactics in the position.

22 ♖a7?!

White should not back down. 22 ♗d5 ♗xa6 23 ♖h4 (threatening mate in 2) 23...h6 24 ♕h3 ♔h7 (24...♖g8 25 ♘g2!! with unstoppable threats) and now White can bale out by playing 25 ♘g4 ♕xd5 26 ♖xh6+ gxh6 27 ♕xh6+ ♔g8 28 ♕g6+ with a perpetual check.

22...c4 23 dxc4 ♗xc4

23...♗c5 24 ♖b7 ♗a6 25 ♖h4 ♗xb7 26 ♗xb7 gives White some compensation.

24 ♘xc4 ♖xc4 25 ♗e3

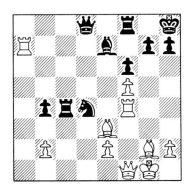

25...♘c2!!

An elegant tactic!

26 ♖a8

After 26 ♖xc4 ♘xe3 27 ♕c1 ♘xc4 28 ♕xc4 ♕b6+ the a7-rook drops.

26...♖xf4

Leko gives the following line as more accurate: 26...♕xa8 27 ♗xa8 ♘xe3 28 ♕f3 ♖c1+ 29 ♔f2 ♗c5 30 ♔g3 ♖g1+ 31 ♔h3 ♖f1 32 ♕c6 ♖xf4 33 ♕xc5 ♖xa8 34 ♕xe3 ♖xf5 35 ♕e4 ♖h5+ 36 ♔g3 ♖b8 winning.

27 ♗xf4 ♕d4+ 28 ♔h1 ♖xa8 29 ♗xa8 ♕xb2 30 ♕d1 b3 31 ♗e4

If 31 ♕d7 ♕a1+.

31...♕d4 32 ♕xd4 ♘xd4 33 ♗c1 ♘xe2 34 ♗b2 ♗c5 35 ♗d3 ♘d4 36 h3 ♘f3 37 ♗c4 ♗d4 0-1

In this hopeless position, White lost on time.

Game 30
Anand-Adams
FIDE World Ch., Groningen 1997

---

1 ♘f3

This game covers the line reached via the normal English Opening move order 1 c4 c5 2 ♘f3 ♘f6 3 ♘c3 d5 4 cxd5 ♘xd5 5 d4 This can be a good choice against a player who does not play the Grünfeld as Black. The line with 5...cxd4, while given as equal in most theoretical works, is in fact tough going for Black, and is not to everyone's

taste. Although Adams secured draws against Anand and Kramnik, this was through his world class technique. Against lesser mortals, White has good chances of securing a small edge in this line. After 5 d4, Black has:

a) A Grünfeld player would happily choose 5...♘xc3 6 bxc3 g6, not fearing the transposition into the main line Exchange variation after 7 e4 (7 e3 stays within 'English' territory and will be examined in the next game.) 7...♗g7 8 ♖b1 – in fact, Kramnik has used this move order to reach the 8 ♖b1 line several times.

b) 5...cxd4 6 ♕xd4 ♘xc3 7 ♕xc3 ♘c6 8 e4 and now Black has the additional option of 8...♗g4 (8...e6 transposes to the main game) 9 ♗b5 ♖c8 10 ♗e3 a6 11 ♖d1 ♕c7 12 ♗a4 b5 13 ♗b3 e6 14 0-0 ♗xf3 15 gxf3 ♗d6 16 ♕xg7 ♗xh2+ 17 ♔h1 ♗e5 18 ♕h6 and White is much better, since Black's king has nowhere to go, Topalov-Beliavsky, Linares 1994.

1...♘f6 2 c4 e6 3 ♘c3 d5 4 d4 c5 5 cxd5 cxd4

This QGD move order is an important one for reaching this Symmetrical English position, instead 5...exd5 is a QGD Tarrasch and 5...♘xd5 is a semi-Tarrasch.

6 ♕xd4 ♘xd5 7 e4 ♘xc3

7...♘c6 8 ♗b5 can transpose.

8 ♕xc3 ♘c6

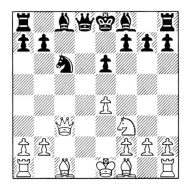

If Black can complete his development,

---

he should be fine as he has no significant weaknesses. Over the next few moves Black needs to figure out how to develop his f8-bishop without dropping the g7-pawn.

9 ♗b5

9 a3 has also been tried. 9...♗d7 10 ♗e2 ♖c8 11 0-0 ♘a5 12 ♕d3 (12 ♕e5 and 12 ♕e3 are also possible) and here:

a) Belov gives 12...♗e7, which is a logical move, now that Black has shifted the white queen from the a1-h8 diagonal. If now 13 ♖d1 then 13...♗a4 is equal.

b) 12...♗a4 13 ♕xd8+ ♖xd8 14 ♗e3 ♘b3 15 ♗d1 and here:

b1) 15...b5 met a swift demise after 16 ♗xb3 ♗xb3 17 ♖fc1 e5 18 ♘xe5 a6 19 ♘c6, Anand-Korchnoi, Tilburg 1998.

b2) 15...a6 16 ♗xb3 ♗xb3 17 ♖ac1 ♗d6 18 ♗b6 with a small edge for White, Kramnik-Van Wely, Monaco 1998.

9...♗d7 10 0-0 ♕b6 11 a4

11 ♗a4 has been superseded by 11 a4. Although it avoids creating a weakness on b4, the undefended bishop can in some lines give Black an important extra tempo to enable him to complete development. Nevertheless 'b2' looks quite good for White.

a) 11...♕b4 12 ♕c2 (12 ♕xb4 is harmless) 12...♕c5 13 ♕e2 (13 ♕d3 is line b2) 13...♕a5 (13...a6 transposes to the next line) 14 ♗b3 ♗e7 15 ♖d1 ♕c7 16 e5 0-0-0 17 ♗f4 h6 18 ♖ac1 ♔b8 19 a3 is too dangerous for Black, Kristiansen-L.Hansen, Danish Championship 1988.

b) 11...♕c5 and here:

b1) 12 ♕b3 ♕b4 13 ♕c2 ♕c5 14 ♕e2 a6 (or 14...♗e7 15 ♗f4 ♕a5 16 ♗b3 0-0 is also equal) 15 a3 b5 16 b4 ♕h5 17 ♗b3 ♗e7 18 ♖d1 ♘e5 19 ♗f4 ♘xf3+ 20 ♕xf3 ♕xf3 21 gxf3 ♖c8) with equality, L.Hansen-Stein, Copenhagen 1989.

b2) 12 ♕d3 ♕d6 13 ♕e2 a6 14 ♖d1 ♕c7 15 ♗xc6 (White can also try 15 ♗e3) 15...♗xc6 16 ♘d4 ♗d6 ½-½ Ribli-Miles, Baden-Baden 1981, though White should play on with 17 ♘xc6 bxc6 (presumably

White was concerned about 17...♗xh2+ 18 ♔h1 bxc6 19 g3 ♗xg3 20 fxg3 ♕xg3 21 ♖d3 ♕e5, but White can go on the attack, e.g. starting with 22 ♗d2!?) 18 h3 and White has a better pawn structure.

11...♕c5

In order to complete his kingside development, Black needs to pursue a 'queen chase', first to take the White queen's attention away from g7...

12 ♕d3

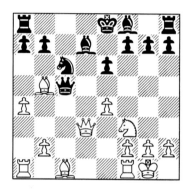

12 ♕e1!? is a novel method of escaping the attentions of the opposing queen. 12...a6 13 ♗e3 ♕b4 (Tukmakov recommends 13...♕d6 14 ♖d1 ♕c7 15 ♕c3 ♖c8 with an unclear position) 14 ♗d2 ♕d6 15 ♗e2 ♗e7 16 ♖d1 ♕c7 17 b4 (White's plan of advancing the b-pawn is instructive) 17...0-0 18 b5 axb5 19 axb5 ♘b8 20 ♗c3 f6 21 ♖c1 ♕d8 22 ♗c4 and Black is tied down, Tukmakov-Suetin, Lenk 2000.

12...♕d6

And now Black must avoid embarrassment after 12...♗e7 13 ♖d1 ♖d8 14 ♗e3 followed by ♗e3xa7.

13 ♕e2 ♕c7

This is an intended refinement over the older main line 13...a6 14 e5! ♕c7 15 ♗d3 ♘b4 16 ♗e4 ♗c6 17 ♗d2 ♗xe4 18 ♕xe4 and now:

a) 18...♘d5 19 ♖fc1 ♕d7 20 ♖c4 ♗e7 21 ♕g4 ♗f8 22 ♖ac1 White has the initiative, Kramnik-Adams, German Bundesliga 1997.

b) 18...♕c6 19 ♕h4 ♘d3 20 ♗e3 ♗e7 21 ♕g4 ♔f8 22 ♘d4 ♘xe5 23 ♕f4 ♕d5 24 ♖ad1 with compensation for the pawn, M.Gurevich-Barsov, Cappelle la Grande 1998. White has an ongoing initiative because it is difficult for Black to resolve his king's situation.

If 13...♗e7 then 14 b3, or 14 ♗d2 a6 15 e5 ♕c7 16 ♗d3 with good play for White.

14 e5 ♗c5!? 15 ♖d1

Instead 15 ♗e3 ♗xe3 16 ♕xe3 ♕b6 17 ♕g5 0-0 18 ♖fd1 is slightly better for White according to Adams.

15...a6 16 ♗d3 h6

16...0-0 would fall for the standard Greek gift 17 ♗xh7+.

17 ♗f4 ♘b4 18 ♗e4 ♗c6 19 ♘d2

According to Adams, 19 ♖ac1 allows 19...♗xa4 though White could then win material with 20 ♗e3 (Adams gives 20 ♖d2 ♕b6) 20...♗xd1 21 ♕xd1 ♖d8 22 ♕a4+ ♕d7 23 ♕xd7+ ♖xd7 24 ♗xc5 etc.

19...♖d8 20 ♗xc6+ ♕xc6 21 ♘e4

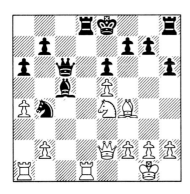

21 ♖ac1 ♘d3 is good for Black.

21...♖xd1+

After 21...0-0 White has 22 ♗xh6 gxh6 and now:

a) Ribli gives 23 ♘f6+ 23...♔h8 24 ♕h5 ♗xf2+ 25 ♔xf2 ♕c2+ as leading to an unclear position.

b) But instead 23 ♕g4+ wins for White: 23...♔h8 (or 23...♔h7 24 ♘f6+ ♔h8 25 ♕f4 ♔g7 26 ♘h5+ ♔h7 27 ♖xd8) 24 ♖xd8

♖xd8 25 ♕h4 ♗xf2+ 26 ♘xf2 and White's queen is hitting h6, d8 and b4!

22 ♖xd1 ♗e7

With Black now ready (at last) to castle, and with ...♘b4-d5 and ...♕c6xa4 in the air, White needs to create a passed d-pawn to keep the Black king in the centre and stir up some play. Adams also mentions 22...♘d5 as a possibility.

23 ♘d6+ ♗xd6 24 exd6 ♘d5

24...♔d7? 25 ♖c1.

25 ♗e5

Ribli questions this move and suggests 25 ♕g4 g6 as unclear.

a) Now 26 ♗e5 0-0 gives White good attacking chances. This position is also reached in the note to the next move.

b) But not 26 ♖c1, which was suggested by Hoeksema, because of 26...♕xa4 (26...♕d7 27 ♗e5) and if 27 ♖c8+ ♔d7 28 ♖xh8 ♕a1+.

25...f6

Still Black should not play 25...0-0 now because of 26 ♕g4 with a strong attack. But after the text, Black is able to hold a solid position, and Anand is unable to break through.

26 ♕h5+ ♔f8 27 ♗g3 ♕e8 28 ♕g4 h5 29 ♕e4 ♕d7 30 h4 ♔f7 31 ♖c1 g6

Black seals off all possible entry points.

32 ♕c2 ♖d8 33 ♕c4 ♔g7 34 a5 ♔f7 35 b3 ♔g7

Black is content to shuffle his king back and for. Now, in an attempt to put his rook in front of the queen, White allows the rooks to be exchanged.

36 ♕d3 ♖c8 37 ♖c4 ♖xc4 38 bxc4 ♘b4 39 ♕d2 ♘c6 40 ♗f4 ♘b8 41 ♗e3

Perhaps White could try 41 f3, though opening up the kingside with g2-g4 looks very double-edged.

41...♕c6 42 ♕b4 ♘d7 43 c5 ♕d5 44 ♕a4 ♕c6 45 ♕f4 ♔g8 46 ♕c4 ♔f7 47 ♕f4 ♔g8

There is no way through.

48 ♕c4 ½-½

Game 31
Korchnoi-Grosar
Ptuj 1995

1 c4 ♘f6 2 ♘c3 c5 3 ♘f3 d5 4 cxd5 ♘xd5 5 e3

Korchnoi's move order creates some differences from 5 d4 ♘xc3 6 bxc3 g6 7 e3 (7 e4 is of course the mainline Exchange Grünfeld) 7...♗g7 8 ♗b5+.

5...♘xc3

5...♘c6 6 d4 (6 ♗b5 ♘db4 7 d4 is also promising for White) 6...cxd4 (6...e6 gives the Semi-Tarrasch) 7 exd4 g6 (7...e6 and 7...♗g4 transpose to well-known lines) 8 ♗g5 transposes into Game 59, which is favourable for White.

6 bxc3 g6 7 ♗b5+

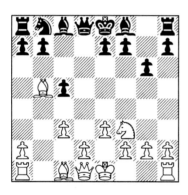

This is Korchnoi's speciality. After 7 d4 ♗g7, White has three main moves:

a) In the event of 8 ♗b5+ then 8...♗d7 may be a more reliable equalising attempt than interposing with the knight, e.g. 9 a4 and now:

a1) 9...♕a5 10 ♕b3 cxd4 11 exd4 0-0 12 0-0 ♕c7 13 ♖e1 e6 14 ♘g5 ♘c6 15 ♗a3 ♖fe8 16 ♘e4 ♘a5 17 ♕a2 ♗c6 with a level position, Anand-Leko, Linares 1999.

a2) 9...0-0 10 ♗a3 b6 11 0-0 a6 12 ♗e2 ♘c6 13 ♕c2 ♕c7 14 dxc5 bxc5 15 ♗xc5 ♕a5 16 ♗a3 ♕xc3 17 ♕xc3 ♗xc3 with a completely equal position, Bareev-Kaspa-

rov, Cannes (rapid) 2001.

b) 8 ♗d3 0-0 9 0-0 ♕c7 10 ♕e2 ♖d8 with:

b1) 11 ♖b1 b6 and the further choice:

b11) 12 ♖d1 ♘c6 13 ♗a3 ♗b7 14 dxc5 bxc5 15 ♗a6 ♗xa6 16 ♕xa6 ♘e5 17 ♘xe5 ♗xe5 18 g3 ♖xd1+ ½-½ Bagirov-Tal, Tbilisi 1978.

b12) 12 ♗e4 ♗a6! 13 c4 ♘c6 14 d5 f5 15 ♗d3 e5 16 e4 ♘d4, with unclear complications, Karpov-Kasparov, Seville (23rd match game) 1987.

b2) 11 ♖d1 b6 12 ♗b2 ♘c6 13 ♖ac1 ♗b7 14 e4 e6 15 h4 ♖ac8 16 h5 ♕f4 17 hxg6 hxg6 18 ♗b1 ♘a5 with equality, Kramnik-Topalov, Wijk aan Zee 1998.

c) 8 ♗e2 0-0 9 0-0 b6 10 a4 and here:

c1) 10...♘c6 11 ♗a3 ♗f5 12 ♘d2 ♕c7 13 e4 ♗d7 14 ♘b3 ♖ad8 15 ♕c2 ♘b8 16 dxc5 ♗xa4 17 cxb6 ♕xb6 18 ♗b4 ♗xb3 19 ♕xb3 ♘c6 with equality, Bareev-Lautier, Ubeda 1997.

c2) 10...♗b7 11 a5 ♕c7 12 ♕b3 e6 13 ♗b2 ♘d7 14 a6 ♗c6 15 c4 cxd4 16 exd4 ♖ac8 17 ♖fd1 ♖fd8 and Black restrains White's central pawns, Beliavsky-Sakaev, Herceg Novi 2000.

7...♘d7

After 7...♗d7 White can transpose into the ...♗d7 lines analysed above by 8 a4 followed by d2-d4. However this move order gives him an additional option: 8 ♕b3 and now 8...♕c7 9 ♖b1 b6 10 ♘g5 e6 11 c4 ♗g7 12 ♗b2 0-0 13 ♗xg7 ♔xg7 14 0-0 is given as slightly better for White in ECO, though I believe Black can equalise fairly easily. Smejkal-W.Schmidt, Warsaw 1979 continued 14...♘c6 15 ♕b2+ f6 16 ♘e4 ♖ad8 17 ♖fd1 e5 18 ♘c3 ♗e6 19 ♗xc6 ♕xc6 20 d3 ♖f7 21 e4 ♖d4 22 ♘b5 ♖d8 23 ♘c3 ♖d4 24 ♘e2 ♖d8 ½-½.

8 d4 ♗g7 9 a4 0-0 10 0-0 ♕c7

Black has several other moves:

a) After 10...♘f6, White can play 11 ♗a3 which is similar to many of the other lines discussed here. 11 ♗d3 ♗f5!? was played in

Spraggett-Shamkovich, New York 1983.

b) 10...a6?! illustrates one of the main points of ♗b5+. If Black is provoked into playing ...a7-a6, then b6 is weakened. After 11 ♗d3 b6 12 ♖b1 ♗b7 13 e4 ♕c7 14 ♖e1 e6 15 e5! h6 16 h4 ♖fd8, Karpov-Korchnoi, Merano (12th match game) 1981, and now 17 h5 gxh5 18 ♗e3 is much better for White according to Tal.

c) 10...b6 11 ♗a3 ♗b7 12 ♖e1 ♘f6 13 ♗d3 ♕c7 14 e4 ♖fd8 15 a5 ♘h5 (15...e6) 16 ♖c1, Korchnoi-Gavrikov, Horgen 1994, and now Gavrikov recommends (either on this move or the previous one) 16...e6. Instead he played 16...e5?!, when White's best is 17 ♗c4 with the initiative.

11 e4

11 ♗a3 b6 12 e4 ♘f6 13 ♖e1 ♖d8 14 ♗d3 ♗b7 would transpose to Korchnoi-Gavrikov in the previous note.

11...♖d8

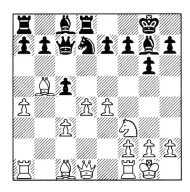

12 ♕e2

An improvement over 12 ♗a3 ♘f6 13 ♕e1 b6 14 ♖d1 a6 15 ♗d3 ♗g4 16 e5 ♗xf3 17 gxf3 ♘d5 18 ♗e4 c4 and Black is fine, Korchnoi-Sax, Wijk aan Zee 1992.

12...♘f8

Black would have to be very brave (or foolish) to grab the pawn with 12...a6 13 ♗c4 cxd4 14 cxd4 ♘b6 15 ♗b3 ♗xd4 16 ♘xd4 ♖xd4 17 ♗b2 etc.

13 ♗e3 ♗g4 14 ♖fd1 ♘e6?

This move doesn't fit with this structure.

Black usually wants to play ...e7-e6 and indeed a few moves later, the knight retreats again. 14...♖ac8 was better, with typical Grünfeld-style play.

15 e5 a6 16 ♗c4 cxd4 17 cxd4 ♗xf3 18 gxf3 ♘f8 19 ♖ab1 ♖ab8 20 f4

Using the doubled pawns to bolster the centre.

20...e6 21 d5 b5?

After 21...exd5 22 ♗xd5 White still has a strong initiative and active play for his two bishops. White need not be tempted by the win of the exchange with 22 ♗b6 ♕c6 23 ♗xd8 dxc4, when Black has good compensation according to Ribli.

22 axb5 axb5 23 ♖xb5 exd5 24 ♖bxd5 ♖xd5 25 ♗xd5 ♕e7 26 ♕c4

Despite all the pawns being on one side, White retains strong pressure and excellent winning chances.

26...♘e6 27 ♖a1 ♗f8 28 ♖a7 ♕e8 29 h3 ♕c8 30 ♕a2 ♕e8 31 ♔g2 ♕c8

Black is reduced to moving aimlessly back and forth, while White optimises his position.

32 ♖a6 ♕c3 33 ♗xe6 ♖b2 34 ♗xf7+ ♔g7 35 ♕e6 ♕xe3

Unfortunately for Black, Korchnoi had calculated a neat finish.

36 ♕f6+ ♔h6 37 ♕g5+ ♔g7 38 ♖xg6+ ♔xf7 39 ♕f5+ ♔e7 40 ♖e6+ 1-0

Game 32
Hauchard-Kinsman
French League 1998

1 c4 e6 2 ♘c3 c5 3 ♘f3 ♘f6 4 g3 ♘c6 5 ♗g2 ♗e7 6 0-0 0-0 7 d4 d5 8 cxd5 ♘xd5

This is the starting point of the Keres-Parma variation. Another English move order to reach this position is 1 c4 c5 2 ♘f3 ♘f6 3 ♘c3 e6 4 g3 d5 5 cxd5 ♘xd5 6 ♗g2 ♘c6 7 0-0 ♗e7 8 d4 0-0.

Note that 8...exd5 is a Tarrasch Queen's Gambit Declined.

9 ♘xd5 exd5 10 dxc5 ♗xc5

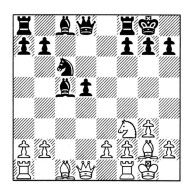

11 ♗g5

This is by a large margin the most popular move. Perhaps White should experiment more with some of the alternatives, though it has to be said that Black is looking comfortable in all but 'a', which is a little controversial, and 'e' which is rare.

a) 11 ♕c2 ♗b6 12 ♘g5 g6 13 ♕d1 and now:

a1) 13...♗e6 is the most reliable: 14 ♘xe6 (14 ♘h3 ♗xh3 15 ♗xh3 ♖e8 16 ♗g2 ♕e7 ½-½ Adorjan-Dlugy, New York 1985) 14...fxe6 15 ♗h6 ♖f7 and now 16 e3 ♕f6 or 16 e4 dxe4 17 ♗xe4 (17 ♕xd8+ ♖xd8 18 ♗xe4 ♗d4) 17...♕f6, when despite the fact that White has the two bishops and the more compact pawn structure, other concrete factors ensure that Black is okay – pressure against f2, good central control and the offside h6-bishop.

a2) 13...♗d4 leads to a long forcing line 14 ♕b3 ♗f6 15 ♕xd5 ♘d4 16 ♕xd8 ♘xe2+ 17 ♔h1 ♖xd8 18 ♘e4 ♗e7 19 ♗e3 ♗e6 20 ♖fd1 ♖ac8 21 ♗f3 ♖c2 22 ♖xd8+ ♗xd8 23 ♖e1 ♗c4 and here:

a21) 24 ♘d2 ♗a5! (getting out of trouble) was Benko-Peters, US Championship 1975, but White has several other tries, including the complex 24 ♗h6 analysed by Watson.

a22) Another attempt is 24 a3 which leaves Black with a difficult problem – his

knight is trapped, and White threatens 25 ♘d2 ♗a5 26 b4. After 24 a3 ♗b6 (24...♖xb2 25 ♘d2 ♗a5 26 ♘xc4 wins or 24...♗b5 25 ♘d6 ♗c6 26 ♔g2 ♖xb2 27 ♗xc6 bxc6 28 ♘c4 ♖c2 29 ♘d2 ♘c3 30 ♗h6 winning) White can proceed with 25 ♗xb6 axb6 26 ♘d6 ♗a6 27 b4 ♘d4 28 ♔g2 ♘xf3 29 ♔xf3 with a better ending for White.

b) 11 b3 ♕f6 cuts across White's queenside fianchetto plan: 12 ♗g5 ♕f5 13 ♖c1 ♗b6 14 ♗f4 ♖d8 15 e3 h6 16 h3 ♕f6 17 g4 d4 and White could hardly have been pleased with the outcome of the opening, Uhlmann-Agzamov, Potsdam 1985.

c) 11 a3 ♗f5 12 b4 ♗b6 13 ♗b2 ♗e4 14 ♖c1 ♕e7 15 ♕d2 ♖fe8 16 ♖fd1 ♖ad8 17 e3 d4 secures equality, Vilela-Rodriguez, Bayamo 1984.

d) 11 ♘g5 h6 12 ♘h3 (12 ♕c2 ♗xf2+ 13 ♖xf2 hxg5) 12...♗f5 (12...♗xh3!? is also playable) 13 ♘f4 d4 14 ♗d2 ♖e8 15 ♖c1 ♗b6 16 ♖e1 ♗e4 17 ♗xe4 ♖xe4 18 b4 ♕d7 19 b5 ♘e5 is satisfactory for Black, Rechlis-Greenfeld, Tel Aviv 1996.

e) 11 ♕d3 has only been played a few times, but it is worth a look. After 11...h6 we have:

e1) 12 ♗f4 ♖e8 13 ♖ac1 ♗b6 14 a3 ♕f6 15 b4 ♗f5 (Black's last 5 moves look like a good recipe to counter this line, i.e. ...♖fe8 to attack the e2-pawn, ...♕d8-f6 and ...♗c8-f5 to develop and hassle the queen on d3; if White does not now take on d5, he has lost a tempo and Black can continue ...♗f5-e4) 16 ♕xd5 ♖xe2 17 b5 ♖d8 18 ♕b3 ♘a5 and Black has a very nice position, Butnorius-Gogichaishvili, Brno 1991.

e2) 12 a3 a5 13 ♗d2 b6 (½-½ Petrosian-Keres, San Antonio 1972) with the possibility of ...♗c8-a6, is another way of exploiting the queen's position on d3.

e3) 12 ♗d2 looks to be the most challenging, when:

e31) 12...d4 (to prevent White from playing e2-e3) 13 ♖ac1 ♕e7 (or 13...♗b6 14 b4

♕f6 15 b5 ♗f5 16 ♕a3 ♘e7 17 ♘h4) 14 ♖fe1 ♖d8 15 ♘h4 is a little awkward for Black; his pieces are not ideally co-ordinated, Piasetski-Vaganian, Buenos Aires Olympiad 1978.

e32) 12...a5!? is a possible improvement, e.g. 13 ♖ac1 b6 14 ♖fe1 ♗a6 15 ♕f5 ♖c8 with chances for both sides.

11...♕d7

This is currently looking like Black's healthiest choice. The other options are:

a) 11...♕b6 12 ♖c1 d4 (12...♗e6 13 ♕c2 ♗e7 14 ♗xe7 ♘xe7 15 ♕c7 gives White a small edge) 13 ♕c2 ♗d6 14 ♘d2 ♗e6 15 ♘e4 ♗e7 16 ♗xe7 ♘xe7 17 ♘g5 ♗f5 18 ♕c5 and White has a small advantage, Illescas-Lautier, Dos Hermanas 1994.

b) 11...♗e7 is a positional error. White proceeds 12 ♗xe7 ♕xe7 13 ♕d2 with good play against the IQP.

c) 11...f6 is playable, but creates light-squared weaknesses. Given that there are good alternatives, this seems somewhat needless. 12 ♗d2 and now:

c1) 12...♗f5 13 ♕b3 ♗b6 14 ♗e3 ♘a5 15 ♕c3 ♗xe3 16 ♕xe3 ♖e8 17 ♕c5 b6 18 ♕b5 a6 19 ♕a4 b5 20 ♕f4 and White is better, Kramnik-Kengis, Riga 1995.

c2) 12...♗b6 13 e3 ♗f5 14 ♗c3 ♗e4 (Bern-Butnorius, Oslo 1992) and now Kosten recommends the manoeuvre invented by Larsen, namely 15 ♕b3 followed by ♖f1-d1 and ♗c3-d4.

c3) 12...♗e6 13 e3 ♕d7 14 ♗c3 ♖ad8 15 ♗d4. If Black only exchanges one pair of minor pieces, White wants to make sure that he ends up with a knight on d4. 15...♗d6 16 ♖c1 ♖fe8 17 ♕b3 ♘a5 18 ♕c3 b6 19 ♕d2 ♘c4 20 ♕d1 ♗b4 21 b3 ♘a5 22 ♗c3 ♗a3 23 ♖c2 ♗f5 24 ♖d2 ♗e4 25 ♘d4 ♗xg2 26 ♔xg2 and once again Black has not quite equalised, Korchnoi-Sturua, Basle 2001.

12 ♘e1

Instead after 12 a3 h6 13 b4 ♗b6 14 ♗f4 ♖d8 15 ♖c1 ♕e7 16 h3 (16 ♕d3 can be

answered by 16...♗g4) 16...♗f5 17 ♖e1 ♗e4 18 ♕a4 ♖e8 19 ♔f1 ♖ad8 Black has a well co-ordinated set-up, Rustemov-Smetankin, Minsk 1997.

12...h6

12...d4 gives White more chances of achieving a slight advantage. Quite often, after an early ...d5-d4, Black's position seems to lose its flexibility, for example 13 ♘d3 ♗b6 and now:

a) 14 ♗d2 ♕e7 15 ♘f4 ♗e6 16 ♕a4 ♖ac8 17 ♖ac1 ♖fd8 18 ♖fe1 h6 19 a3 ♕d7 20 ♘xe6 ♕xe6 21 ♕c4 (Kramnik-Anand, Monaco {rapid} 1995) when White is a little better.

b) 14 a4 ♕f5 15 ♗d2 ♗d7 16 b4 a6 17 ♘f4 ♕e5 18 ♘d5 ♗d8 19 ♗f4 and White has a small initiative, Topalov-Cu.Hansen, Istanbul Olympiad 2000.

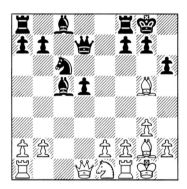

13 ♗f4

After 13 ♗d2 ♗b6 14 ♘d3 ♕d6! 15 ♗f4 ♕f6 16 ♗xd5 ♗g4 Black has good compensation for the pawn, and in fact soon regains the pawn, while keeping the initiative: 17 ♔h1 ♖ad8 18 ♗g2 ♘b4 19 ♕b3 ♘xd3 20 exd3 ♗e2 21 ♖fe1 ♗xd3 etc., W.Schmidt-Greenfeld, Moscow Olympiad 1994.

13...♖d8 14 ♘d3 ♗b6 15 ♗d2

This clears the way for ♘d3-f4, but White has lost a tempo with ♗g5-f4-d2. Instead 15 ♖c1 'with a typical edge for White' according to Kosten, though it is not clear this is the case after 15...♕e7. In fact, Black seems to have typical (good) counterplay. Black can follow up with ...♗c8-g4 or ...♗c8-f5-e4. Compare this with the several examples given in notes to the earlier moves above. Black has made none of the concessions which enabled White to get an edge, e.g. an early ...f7-f6 or ...d5-d4 allowing play on the light squares, or a queenside pawn advance with penetration on c5 or c7.

15...♕e7 16 ♘f4 ♗e6 17 ♕a4 ♖d7 18 ♖fd1 ♖ad8 19 ♗e1

Whenever White has to play ♗d2-e1 in this kind of position, it is often a hint that his initiative has run its course.

19...♕f6 20 ♗c3 d4 21 ♗e1

See the note to White's 19th!

21...♗g4 22 h3 g5 23 ♘d5 ♖xd5 24 hxg4 ♖e5 25 ♕c4 ♖de8 26 ♗f3 ♖c5 27 ♕b3 ♘e5

Black is pressing but doesn't have enough to get a clear plus, for example 27...♖e7 28 ♖ac1 ♖xc1 29 ♖xc1 ♘e5 30 ♖c8+ ♔g7 31 ♗b4 ♘xf3+ 32 exf3 etc.

28 ♗xb7 d3

28...♘xg4 was perhaps preferable.

29 e3 ♖c2 30 ♖xd3 ♖xb2 31 ♖d6 ♕xd6 32 ♕xb2 ♘xg4 33 ♗f3? ♘e5?

A double oversight. 33...♘xe3! 34 fxe3 ♖xe3 35 ♔g2 ♖xf3 36 ♔xf3 ♗d4 37 ♗c3 ♕c6+ 38 ♔e2 ♗xc3 is very good for Black.

34 ♗g2 ½-½

Game 33
Korchnoi-Brunner
Bern 1996

---

1 c4 c5 2 ♘f3 ♘f6 3 ♘c3 e6 4 g3 d5 5 cxd5 ♘xd5 6 ♗g2 ♘c6 7 0-0

7 d4 transposes to the game after 7...♗e7, but this move order allows Black several alternatives (see Game 34). While White has nothing to fear in those lines, it does mean that Black needs to be ready for the Keres-Parma 'main line,' as in this and the previous game.

7...♗e7

Occasionally Black has tried to exploit the delay in d2-d4, but in general has not fared that well, e.g. 7...♘f6 8 e3 ♗e7 9 d4 cxd4 10 ♘xd4 ♘xd4 11 exd4 0-0 12 ♗f4 ♕b6 13 ♕e2 ♗d7 14 d5 ♖fe8 15 dxe6 ♗xe6 16 ♕b5 and White is much better, Korchnoi-Wirthensohn, Bad Kissingen 1981.

8 d4 0-0 9 e4

Suba's move 9 ♖b1 is a constructive waiting move which aims to place the rook in a useful position should the b-file open up after a later ...♘d5xc3. Black should have no problems, however:

a) 9...♘b6 10 dxc5 ♗xc5 11 ♗f4 ♕e7 12 ♘e4 e5 13 ♗g5 f6 14 ♘xc5 ♕xc5 15 ♗e3 ♕b5 16 ♕c2 ½-½ Lalic-Turner, British Championship 2000.

b) 9...h6 10 ♖e1 ♖e8 11 e4 ♘b6 12 dxc5 ♗xc5 13 ♕xd8 ♖xd8 14 e5 ♗b4 15 ♗f1 ♗d7 16 ♗d2 ♗e8 and Black is fine, Ivanchuk-Lautier, Monaco (rapid) 1997.

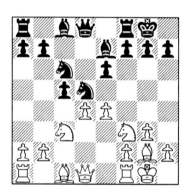

9...♘b6

Black has two major alternatives:
a) 9...♘db4 and White has now tried:
a1) 10 d5 is adequately met by 10...exd5 11 exd5 ♘d4! 12 ♘xd4 cxd4 13 a3 dxc3 14 axb4 ♗xb4 with equality 15 ♕d4 ♗d6 16 bxc3 b6 17 ♗f4 ♗b7 18 ♖fe1 ♗c5 and Black is active enough to contain the White d-pawn and hold the balance, Gulko-Kramnik, Riga 1995.

a2) 10 dxc5 is rare but worth considering, e.g. 10...♗xc5 11 a3 ♘d3 12 b4! (12 ♕e2 is usually played) 12...♘xc1 13 ♖xc1 ♗b6 14 e5 ♕e7 15 ♕e2 and White is slightly better. He has deceptively dangerous attacking chances on the kingside, as witnessed by the game Filippov-Volzhin, Gistrup 1996, which concluded quickly: 15...♗d7 16 ♘e4 ♖ad8 17 ♖c4 a6 18 ♖fc1 ♘a7 19 ♕c2 h6 20 ♘f6+ 1-0.

a3) 10 a3 cxd4 11 axb4 dxc3 12 bxc3 b6 13 ♗f4 ♗b7 and here:

a31) 14 ♕b3 ♕c8 15 ♘d2 ♖d8 16 ♖fd1 ♖d3 17 ♕c4 ♕d8 18 ♗f1 ♖d7 19 ♕e2 with a further split:

a311) 19...♗f6 20 e5 ♗g5 (20...♘xe5? 21 ♗xe5 ♗xe5 22 ♕xe5 ♖xd2 23 ♖xd2 ♕xd2 24 ♖xa7! wins) 21 ♗xg5 ♕xg5 22 ♘e4! ♖xd1 23 ♖xd1 ♕e7 (23...♕xe5? 24 ♘d6 ♕xe2 25 ♗xe2 ♖b8 26 ♘xb7 ♖xb7 27 ♗f3 wins) 24 ♘d6 and the knight has achieved its ideal post. White has the option of trading knight for bishop, giving him a superior endgame, Savchenko-Sturua, Helsinki 1992. As long as Black avoids this kind of outcome, he should be holding – see 'a312' below.

a312) Ftacnik gives 19...♗g5 which leads to equality after 20 ♗xg5. If White inserts 20 b5 to limit the options for Black's knight, then 20...♘a5 21 ♗xg5 ♕xg5 22 ♘f3 ♕e7 23 ♖xd7 ♕xd7 24 ♖d1 ♕c7 and Black is okay.

a32) 14 ♕e2 ♕c8 15 h4 a5 16 b5 ♘b8 17 ♘e5 and with ♘e5-c4 to follow, White is more comfortable position, Garcia-Chandler, Bochum 1981.

b) 9...♘xc3 10 bxc3 when Black has:

b1) 10...cxd4 11 cxd4 b6 12 d5 exd5 13 exd5 ♘b4 14 ♘e5 ♗f6 15 ♖e1 ♗b7 16 ♗a3 ♖e8 17 ♗xb4 ♖xe5 18 ♖c1 ♖xe1+ 19 ♕xe1 and White retains a small advantage due to his passed d-pawn which ties Black down to defence, Yusupov-Tukmakov, Frunze 1979.

b2) 10...b6 11 d5 ♘a5 (11...exd5 12 exd5

♘a5 13 ♘e5 ♗f6 14 ♖e1 transposes) 12 ♖e1 exd5 13 exd5 ♗f6 14 ♘e5 and now:

b21) 14...♖e8 15 ♗f4 ♗xe5 16 ♖xe5 ♖xe5 17 ♗xe5 and the two bishops give White an ongoing plus, Van Wely-Brunner, Garmisch 1994.

b22) 14...♗b7 15 ♗f4 ♖e8 16 ♕d3 ♗xe5 17 ♗xe5 ♘c6 18 ♗f4 ♕d7 (this loses a pawn, but White already has a dominating position) 19 ♗e4 ♘e7 20 ♗xh7+ ♔h8 21 ♗e4 and White is in charge, Gulko-Adamski, Copenhagen 2000.

10 dxc5!?

The older main line was 10 d5 exd5 11 exd5 ♘b4 and now:

a) 12 ♘e5 ♗d6 13 ♘d3 ♗g4 14 ♕xg4 ♘xd3 has scored well for Black, e.g. 15 ♗g5 f5 16 ♕h5 ♕d7 with chances for both sides, Dorfman-Tukmakov, Lvov 1984.

b) 12 ♘e1 is more circumspect. Black can choose:

b1) 12...c4 13 ♗f4!? ♗d6 14 ♗xd6 ♕xd6 15 ♘c2 ♗f5 16 ♘e3 ♗d3 17 ♖e1 f5 18 a3 ♘a6 19 b3 ♕f6 20 ♖c1 f4 21 ♘xc4 fxg3 22 fxg3 ♗xc4 23 bxc4 ♘xc4 24 ♔h1 and Black's initiative has run out of steam, leaving him with a difficult task of defending against the d-pawn and g2-bishop, Mohr-Farago, Bled 2000.

b2) 12...♗f6 13 ♗e3 ♗xc3 14 bxc3 ♘4xd5 15 ♗xc5 ♖e8 16 ♗d4 ♗e6 17 ♘d3 ♕d6 18 ♖c1 ♖ac8 19 ♖e1 ♖ed8 20 ♗e4 ♘d7 21 ♘e5 ♘7f6 22 ♗b1 with active play for the bishops, Chernin-Petursson, Skien 1979.

10...♕xd1

After 10...♗xc5 White should also play 11 ♗f4 (to prevent ...e6-e5 freeing Black's game) 11...♕xd1 and now 12 ♖axd1 is an attempted refinement over ♖fxd1, which transposes to the main game. Here Black should choose 12...f6 13 e5 f5 (but not 13...g5 14 ♘e4) according to Tukmakov. Instead 12...♘c4?! 13 b3 e5 (Black is determined to get in ...e6-e5, in order to develop his queenside) 14 bxc4 exf4 15 gxf4 ♘a5 16

♘e5 ♗e6 17 ♘d5 ♗d6 18 c5! ♗xc5, Tuk-makov-Cherniaev, Biel 2000, and now 19 ♘c7 ♖ac8 20 ♘xe6 fxe6 21 ♗h3 ♖fe8 22 ♖d7 is better for White – Tukmakov.

11 ♖xd1 ♗xc5 12 ♗f4

White's main chance of an advantage lies in stifling Black's development. After 12 e5, Ivanchuk-Xu Jun, FIDE World Cup, Shen-yang 2000 continued 12...♘c4 (12...♗b4! with equality is Korchnoi's recommenda-tion) 13 ♘a4 ♗e7 14 ♗f4 f6 15 ♖ac1 ♘4xe5 16 ♘xe5 ♘xe5 17 ♗xe5 fxe5 18 ♘c5 ♗g5 19 ♖c2 ♖b8 20 ♗h3 ♖d8 21 ♖xd8+ ♗xd8 22 ♗xe6+ ♗xe6 23 ♘xe6 ♗b6 and Black held on.

12...f6 13 ♖ac1

13 e5 is not possible because of the weakness on f2 – note how Tukmakov avoided this in the note to Black's 10th move.

13...e5 14 ♘b5

14 ♘d5 ♗d4 15 ♗e3 ♗g4 (Yermolinsky-Alburt, Philadelphia 1993) is inferior.

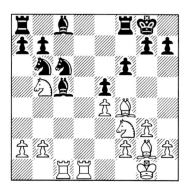

14...exf4

Korchnoi judges White as better in the event of any of the alternatives:

a) 14...♘a4 15 b3 exf4 16 bxa4.

b) 14...♗xf2+ 15 ♔xf2 exf4 16 gxf4.

c) 14...♗e7 15 ♗e3 ♗g4 16 h3 ♗h5 17 ♘d6.

15 ♖xc5 fxg3 16 hxg3 ♗g4 17 ♖d2

This is an improvement over 17 ♖d6 ♖ad8 18 ♘h2, Yermolinsky-Hellers, Phila-

delphia 1992, when Black should play 18...♗e2!.

17...♖ad8

Or 17...♖fd8 18 ♘d6 ♗xf3 19 ♗xf3 ♘e5 (19...♘c8 20 e5!) 20 ♗d1 ♘c8. Thus far this is Bareev-Sax, Bosnian Team Cham-pionship 1999, and now Korchnoi recom-mends 21 ♖cd5 ♖xd6 22 ♖xd6 ♘xd6 23 ♖xd6 ♔f8 24 f4 with the initiative.

18 ♘d6 ♗xf3

a) 18...♖d7 is answered by 19 ♘xb7.

b) In *Informant 66*, Korchnoi recom-mends 18...♘e5. However, the analysis as published is open to question:

b1) 19 ♘h2 ♗e6 20 b3 ♘f7 is given as equal, though it actually looks good for Black after 21 ♘c4 ♘xc4 22 ♖xd8 ♖xd8 23 bxc4 ♘d6.

b2) 19 ♘xe5 fxe5 and now (instead of the quoted 20 ♖cc2 ♖d7, which is equal) White can play 20 ♖xe5 with an extra pawn.

19 ♗xf3 ♖f7?!

Better is 19...♘c8 20 e5 ♘xe5 21 ♗d5+ ♔h8 22 ♖xc8 ♖xc8 23 ♘xc8 ♖xc8 24 ♗xb7, Sunye Neto-Bouaziz, Novi Sad Olympiad 1990, and now 24...♖b8 leaves White only slightly better.

20 ♗g4

White has pressure.

20...♖e7

Perhaps Black should try 20...♖c7!? or 20...♔f8.

21 f4 ♔f8

Black fared no better after 21...g6 22 ♗h3 ♘a8 23 ♗c8 ♘b6 24 ♗xb7 ♘b4 25 ♖b5 ♖xb7 26 ♖xb4 ♖bd7 27 ♖bd4 ♔f8 28 ♔f2 with a safe extra pawn for White, Ruck-Farago, Pula 2000.

22 a3 g6 23 ♗h3 ♖c7

Perhaps 23...f5!? or 23...h5.

24 ♖cc2!

24 e5 allows things to get slightly more messy after 24...♘xe5.

24...a6 25 ♔g2 ♔e7?!

Black should have played 25...♖e7 to hold up the e-pawn.

26 e5!

Now White is well on top.

26...fxe5 27 fxe5 ♞a8

27...♞d7 is answered by 28 ♞xb7!.

28 ♖f2 ♞xe5 29 ♖xc7+

Or 29 ♞c8+.

29...♞xc7 30 ♞c8+

Winning material by force.

30...♖xc8

30...♚e8 31 ♖e2 ♖d5 32 ♞b6 ♖c5 33 b4 or 33 ♞d7 wins.

31 ♗xc8 b6

Now White cleans up efficiently.

32 ♖d2 a5 33 b3 h5 34 ♚f2 g5 35 ♚e3 a4 36 ♚e4 ♞f7 37 ♖d7+ ♚e8 38 ♖xc7 1-0

38...♞d6+ 39 ♚d5 axb3 40 ♚xd6 b2 41 ♗e6 delivers mate as Black queens.

Game 34
Kramnik-Topalov
Linares 1999

---

1 ♞f3 c5 2 c4 ♞f6 3 ♞c3 ♞c6 4 g3 d5 5 d4 e6 6 cxd5 ♞xd5 7 ♗g2

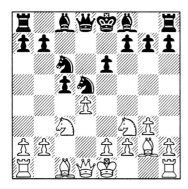

This position is formally part of the Semi-Tarrasch Variation of the Queen's Gambit Declined. However, since it is central to the theory of the Symmetrical English (especially the move order with 5 d4), and is very often reached by this route, I am covering it in some detail. Black has a very wide choice in this position.

7...♞db4

Black has many alternatives here:

a) 7...cxd4 8 ♞xd4 and now:

a1) 8...♞db4?! 9 ♞db5 a6 10 ♛xd8+ ♚xd8 11 ♞a3 e5 12 0-0 ♗e6 (Anand-Krasenkow, Madrid 1998) and now Krasenkow suggests 13 f4 threatening f4-f5, and if 13...f6 (or 13...♗c5+ 14 ♚h1 f6 15 fxe5 fxe5 16 ♞e4) 14 fxe5 fxe5 15 ♗e3 with good play for White along the open d- and f-files.

a2) 8...♞xc3 9 bxc3 ♞xd4 10 ♛xd4 ♛xd4 11 cxd4 ♗b4+ (11...♗d6 12 0-0 ♖b8 13 e4! is Kramnik's improvement over old theory, and gave White an edge in Kramnik-Lautier, Horgen 1995) 12 ♗d2 ♗xd2+ 13 ♚xd2 and we reach an ending which has been the subject of debate for some years. White is slightly better, with the factors in his favour being his control of the h1-a8 diagonal, his active rooks and central pawn majority. However in an ending being 'slightly' better means that the game is closer to a draw than a win, and indeed Black has held the majority of grandmaster games played from this position. Some practical examples of initial play from here:

a21) 13...♚d8 14 ♖ab1 ♖b8 15 ♖b3 b6 16 ♖a3 ♗b7 17 e4 ♖a8 18 g4 h6 19 h4 ♚e7 20 ♖c1 ♖hd8 21 ♚e3 ♖d7 22 ♗f1 ♖c8 23 ♖xc8 ♗xc8 24 ♖c3 ♚d8 25 f4 ♗b7 26 f5 and White is slightly better, Tukmakov-Sax, Pula 1999.

a22) 13...♚e7 14 ♖hc1 ♖d8 15 ♖c7+ ♖d7 16 ♖ac1 ♚d8 17 ♖xd7+ ♚xd7 and again White has a slight edge in the ending in the event of both:

a221) 18 g4 h6 19 f4 ♖b8 20 g5 (Kramnik-Lautier, Belgrade 1995).

a222) 18 f4 ♖b8 19 e4 b6 20 ♚e3 ♗b7 21 ♗h3 ♖c8 22 ♖xc8 ♗xc8 23 d5, Benko-Donner, Wijk aan Zee 1970.

b) 7...♞b6 8 ♗g5 f6 9 dxc5 ♗xc5 10 ♞e4 ♛xd1+ 11 ♖xd1 ♗b4+ 12 ♗d2 ♗xd2+ 13 ♞fxd2 ♚e7 14 f4 a5 15 ♞c5 a4 16 a3 ♖a5 17 ♖c1 ♖d8 18 ♞d3 ♗d7 19 ♚f2 ♗e8

20 ℤhd1 ♘c8 21 ♘c5 with a slight advantage for White, Agdestein-Chandler, Hastings 1991/2.

c) 7...♘xc3 8 bxc3 cxd4 9 cxd4 (9 ♘xd4 transposes to line 'a2' above) 9...♗b4+ 10 ♗d2 ♗e7 11 ♘c3 0-0 12 0-0 ♗d7! 13 ♕d2, Gulko-Vaganian, Yerevan Olympiad 1996, and now 13...ℤc8? allowed White to push his central pawns in classical style: 14 e4 ♗f6 15 ℤac1 ♕b6 16 d5 and White's d-pawn gives him a big advantage. Instead Gulko gives 13...b5! 14 ℤac1 (14 e4 b4 15 ♗b2 ♘a5) 14...b4 15 ♗a1 with chances for both sides.

d) 7...♘f6 8 e3 ♗e7 9 0-0 0-0 10 a3 cxd4 11 exd4 ♕b6 12 ♕d3 ℤd8 13 ♗e3 ♘g4 14 b4 a6 15 ℤad1 ♘xe3 16 fxe3 ♕a7 17 ♔h1 h6 18 ♘e4 ♗d7 19 g4 and White is better, Mikhalchishin-Lalic, Sarajevo 1985.

e) 7...♗e7 transposes into Games 32 and 33, i.e. the 'Keres-Parma' main line. Note that Black has more options when White plays an early d2-d4 – which is why Korchnoi played 0-0 before d2-d4 in the previous game.

8 e3

As with 7...♘f6 and 7...♘b6, White has do something about his d4-pawn, and this move, involving a pawn sacrifice, is the only way to play for an advantage:

a) After 8 a3?! cxd4 9 axb4 ♗xb4 10 ♘xd4 ♘xd4 Black wins a pawn for little compensation.

b) 8 dxc5 is only good for equality, e.g. 8...♕xd1+ 9 ♔xd1 ♗xc5 10 a3 ♘d5 11 ♘xd5 exd5 12 b4 ♗b6 13 ♗b2 0-0 14 e3 ♗f5 15 ♔e2 d4 16 ♘xd4 ♘xd4+ 17 ♗xd4 ♗xd4 18 exd4 ℤfe8+ 19 ♔d2 ℤad8 20 d5 ♗e4 21 ♗xe4 ℤxe4 (Filippov-Krasenkow, Shanghai 2000) with a level endgame.

8...cxd4 9 exd4 ♘xd4

9...♗e7 10 0-0 0-0 11 ♗e3 gives White a slight advantage according to Kramnik.

10 0-0!

An improvement over an earlier game which ran 10 ♘xd4 ♕xd4 11 0-0 ♕xd1 12 ℤxd1 ♗c5 13 ♗f4 0-0 14 ♘b5, Biriukov-Aseev, St Petersburg 1998, and now Tsesarsky gives 14...a6 15 ♘c7 ℤa7 16 a3 ♘c6 17 ℤac1 ♗b6 18 ♗xc6 bxc6 19 ℤxc6 ♗xc7 20 ♗xc7 ♗b7 21 ℤc3 ♗d5 with equality.

10...♘xf3+ 11 ♕xf3 ♗e7 12 ℤd1 ♕a5 13 a3

Or 13 ♗f4 0-0 14 ♕e2 ♘c6 15 a3 ♕f5 16 ♗e4 ♕h3 17 ♗g2 ♕f5 18 ♗e4 ♕h3 19 ♗g2 ½-½ Stefansson-Macieja, Bermuda 2001.

13...0-0 14 ♗f4 ♘c6

14...♘d5 15 ♘xd5 exd5 16 ℤxd5 ♕b6 17 ℤd2 gives White a big plus according to Kramnik.

15 b4 ♕f5 16 b5 ♘a5?

Kramnik prefers 16...♘e5 17 ♕e2 ♘g6 18 ♗e3 when White has play for the pawn, but Black is still well in the game, e.g. 18...♘f6 19 ℤac1 ♗xc3 20 ℤxc3 e5.

17 ♗c7! ♕xf3 18 ♗xf3

Now White has unpleasant pressure in the endgame. The absence of queens gives White more freedom of movement.

18...♘b3

18...♘c4 is possible.

19 ℤab1 ♘c5 20 a4

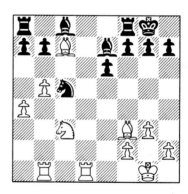

White is threatening to overrun Black's queenside with a4-a5-a6.

20...a5

If 20...♗f6 Kramnik gives the pretty 21 ♘e4 ♘xa4 22 ♘xf6+ gxf6 23 ℤb4 ♘c3 24 ℤg4+ ♔h8 25 ♗d8! winning.

21 b6 f6 22 ♗d6

22 ♘b5 ♘xa4 23 ♖dc1, followed by ♘b5-a7 is also possible.

22...♗xd6 23 ♖xd6 e5! 24 ♗d5+ ♔h8 25 ♖b5 ♘d3 26 ♗e4 ♘b4 27 ♘d5 ♘c6 28 ♘c7 ♖b8 29 ♔g2?

Black obtains counterplay based on the weak back-rank after 29 ♖c5 ♗h3. However, 29 h4! was the right way to deal with this worry, and maintains White's large advantage. The king is poorly placed on g2, as Black's follow-up makes clear.

29...f5 30 ♗xc6 bxc6 31 ♖xe5

Of course, White cannot capture 31 ♖xc6 because of ♗b7, which is why 29 h4 was required. Now White is only slightly better.

31...f4?!

31...♖xb6 was preferable.

32 gxf4 ♖xb6 33 ♘e6 ½-½

A mistake in time trouble. White can still play for a win with 33 ♖xa5 ♖b4 34 f5.

Following 33 ♘e6, play could continue 33...♗xe6 34 ♖dxe6 ♖b4 35 ♖e8 ♔g8 36 ♖xf8+ ♔xf8 37 ♖xa5 ♖xf4 etc, with a drawn position.

Game 35
Kramnik-Timman
Wijk aan Zee 1999

---

1 ♘f3 c5 2 c4 ♘f6 3 ♘c3 ♘c6

In this line, Black waits for White to commit himself to g2-g3 before playing ...d7-d5. This avoids lines such as 3...d5 4 cxd5 ♘xd5 5 d4 or 5 e4 – see Games 30, 37 and 38. This kind of choice is partly dependent on the current state of theory, but perhaps even more so on individual taste, and other elements of one's opening repertoire. For example, the immediate 3...d5 is fine if you are a Grünfeld player, since you will be comfortable in the line 4 cxd5 ♘xd5 5 d4 ♘xc3 6 bxc3 g6.

4 g3 d5 5 d4

This dynamic move was introduced by

Mikhail Tal in his 1988 match against Timman. The idea is to avoid lines where Black gets a space advantage, such as the well-respected Rubinstein variation 5 cxd5 ♘xd5 6 ♗g2 ♘c7 7 0-0 e5 – see Games 28 and 29.

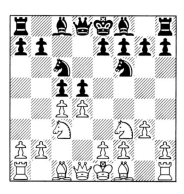

5...cxd4

This occurs with approximately equal frequency as 5...e6 (see Games 32-34). 5...♗g4 and 5...♗f5 could also be considered.

Instead 5...dxc4 was played in the stem game, but is too risky and has fallen out of favour, e.g. 6 d5 and now:

a) 6...♘a5 7 e4 b5 8 ♘xb5 ♘xe4 9 ♘e5 ♗d7 10 ♘xd7 ♕xd7 11 ♕a4 ♖b8 12 ♘c7+ ♔d8 13 ♘e6+ fxe6 14 ♕xa5+ is very strong, Tal-Timman, Hilversum 1988.

b) 6...♘b4 7 e4 e6 (or 7...♗g4 8 ♗xc4 ♗xf3 9 ♕xf3 ♘c2+ 10 ♔f1 ♘xa1 11 e5 a6 12 exf6 ♘c2 13 d6 e6 14 ♕xb7 ♕b8 15 ♕c6+ ♔d8 16 ♗xe6 ♖a7 17 fxg7 ♗xg7 18 ♗g5+ with a big attack, Wojtkiewicz-Yudasin, New York 1991) 8 ♗xc4 exd5 9 exd5 ♗d6 10 a3 ♘a6 11 ♕e2+ ♕e7 12 ♕xe7+ ♔xe7 13 0-0 ♖d8 14 ♘b5 ♗b8 15 ♘g5 and Black is being pushed back, Sorokin-Lesiege, Elista Olympiad 1998.

6 ♘xd4 dxc4

6...e5 is a reversed Grünfeld, which is too ambitious for Black: 7 ♘xc6 bxc6 8 ♗g2 ♗e6 9 ♗g5 etc.

7 ♘xc6

As with a number of lines where both d2-d4 and ...d7-d5 are played, the early release of tension in the centre results in a queen exchange. This particular variation proved to be very popular at the top level in the mid-late 1990s. Playing the black side of this line against an endgame expert is a dour defensive task which will not appeal to everyone. Interestingly, this whole line with 5 d4 has not yet taken off in the lower echelons of the chess world, even though Black scores well at all levels after 5 cxd5.

7...♕xd1+ 8 ♘xd1 bxc6 9 ♗g2 ♘d5 10 ♘e3 e6

Alternatively, 10...♗a6 11 ♘xd5 cxd5 12 ♗xd5 ♖c8 13 ♗d2 e6 14 ♗f3 ♗c5 15 ♗c3 0-0 16 0-0 ♗b5 17 ♖fd1 ♖fd8 18 ♖xd8+ ♖xd8 19 e3 and the weakness of Black's c-pawn gives White an edge in the endgame, Xu Jun-Alterman, Yerevan Olympiad 1996.

11 ♘xc4 ♗a6

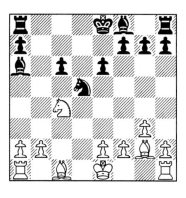

12 ♘a5

A new move in this game. The alternative 12 b3 had been played over 30 times at GM level (including several games involving Kramnik as both Black and White), but as Kramnik wrote 'it is surprising that this natural move is an innovation'. Some typical examples: 12 b3 ♗b4+ 13 ♗d2 and now:

a) 13...♗xd2+ 14 ♘xd2 (14 ♔xd2 0-0-0 15 ♔c2 has also been played) 14...♘b4 15 ♗e4 ♔e7 16 a3 ♘d5 17 ♖c1 ♖hc8 18 f4 c5 19 ♔f2 ♖ab8 20 ♖c2 ♘f6 21 ♗f3 ♖d8 22

♖hc1 with a level position, Gulko-Topalov, Novgorod 1995.

b) 13...♔e7 14 ♖c1 ♖hc8 15 ♗xb4+ ♘xb4 16 a3 ♘d5 17 ♘a5 c5 18 e4 ♘f6 19 e5 ♘d5 20 ♔d2 ♖ab8 21 b4 and here

b1) 21...♖b5 was played in Gelfand-Timman, Malmo 1999. Note that Timman was willing to repeat the line that Kramnik had played against him. The game continued 22 ♗xd5 exd5 23 ♘b3 cxb4 24 ♘d4 ♖bc5 25 ♘f5+ ♔e6 26 ♘xg7+ ♔xe5 27 ♖he1+ ♔f6 28 ♖xc5 ♖xc5 29 axb4 ♖c4 with equality.

b2) The previous line is an improvement over 21...f6? (Kramnik-Polgar, Tilburg 1997) when according to Kramnik, White should play 22 ♖he1 fxe5 23 ♖xe5 ♔f6 24 ♖ce1 ♖b6 25 ♗h3 ♘c7 26 ♖xc5 ♖d6+ 27 ♔c1 winning.

12...♗c5

Inevitably, others have started to follow Kramnik's example. Alternatives at this point are:

a) 12...♖c8 13 ♗d2 ♔e7 14 ♖c1 c5 15 b3 0-0 16 0-0 ♖c7 (Black could not play 16...♗xe2 because of 17 ♖fe1 followed by ♗xd5, but having guarded the e7-bishop, he is now threatening to take on e2) 17 ♘c4 ♘b6 18 ♗a5 (18 ♗f4 ♖cc8 19 ♘d6 is also quite good for White) 18...♗xc4 19 ♖xc4 ♘xc4 20 ♗xc7 ♖c8 21 ♗f4 g5 22 ♗c1 ♘b6, Kasimdzhanov-Berelovich, Wijk aan Zee 1999, and here Berelovich gives 23 ♗d2! c4 24 ♖c1 ♗f6 25 bxc4 ♖xc4 26 ♖xc4 ♘xc4 27 ♗b4 with a small plus for White thanks to the two bishops.

b) 12...♗b4+ 13 ♗d2 ♗xd2+ 14 ♔xd2 ♖d8? (White is slightly better in any case, but this just loses a pawn) 15 ♘xc6 ♖d6 16 ♗xd5 ♖xd5+ 17 ♔e3 ♖b5 18 b4, Grebionkin-Zakharov, Nizhnij Novgorod 1999.

Other untried suggestions are:

c) Ribli's 12...♔d7 13 ♗d2 ♖b8 and

d) Kramnik's 12...♘b4.

13 ♗d2 0-0 14 ♖c1 ♗d4 15 b4! ♗b5 16 ♘xc6 ♗b2

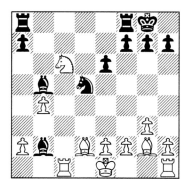

17 ♖c5

17 ♖c2 ♗a3 18 ♗xd5 exd5 19 ♘e7+ ♔h8 20 ♘xd5 ♖ac8 is better for White according to Kramnik.

17...♗xc6 18 ♖xc6 ♖ac8 19 ♖xc8 ♖xc8 20 ♗xd5 exd5 21 f4!!

Kramnik awards this move a double exclamation mark. It provides a remarkable route for the h1-rook to reach the queenside!

21...♗a3 22 ♖f1 ♖c4 23 ♖f3 ♗xb4 24 ♗xb4 ♖xb4 25 ♖a3 h5 26 ♖xa7 ♖b2 27 a4 ♖a2?

27...g6 28 a5 ♖a2 puts up much stiffer resistance.

28 f5!

Now it is much harder for Black's king to join the fray.

28...♖a1+ 29 ♔f2

29 ♔d2 makes White's life easier, since he can more easily approach the d-pawn if it advances to d4.

29...d4 30 a5 f6 31 ♔f3 ♔h7 32 a6 ♔h6 33 h4 g6 34 fxg6 ♔xg6 35 ♖a8 ♖a2 36 ♔f4 ♔f7

Black should play 36...♔g7 and shuffle between g7 and h7.

37 a7 ♔g7 38 ♔f5

Black is now in zugzwang. He has to take the rook away from attacking e2, which enables White to cross via e4 without losing the e2-pawn with check.

38...♖a5+ 39 ♔e4 ♖a4 40 ♔d5 ♖a1 41

♔xd4 1-0

The winning technique is to manoeuvre the king to the 6th rank. Then Black cannot avoid the rook exchange on the 7th, and the pawn ending is winning for White.

Game 36
Kramnik-Kasparov
Linares 2000

---

1 ♘f3 ♘f6 2 c4 c5 3 g3 d5 4 d4!?

4 cxd5 ♘xd5 5 ♗g2 ♘c6 6 d4 is a distinct line for the 2 ♘f3, 3 g3 move order (otherwise 6 0-0 or 6 ♘c3 would transpose into lines considered elsewhere in this chapter).

a) 6...♘b6 7 dxc5 ♕xd1+ 8 ♔xd1 ♘a4 9 ♘c3 ♘xc3+ 10 bxc3 ♗f5 (in a later game against the same opponent, Timman played 10...♗d7 and lost, so I suspect this position is not as easy as the short draw would suggest) 11 ♗e3 (perhaps White should try 11 ♘h4!?) 11...♗e4 12 ♖g1 e6 13 ♘d2 ♗xg2 14 ♖xg2 ♘e5 ½-½ Andersson-Timman, Tilburg 1981.

b) 6...♘f6 looks more reliable, e.g. 7 ♕a4 ♗d7 8 dxc5 e5 9 0-0 ♗xc5 10 ♘c3 h6 11 ♘d2 0-0 12 ♘de4 ♘xe4 13 ♕xe4 ♗e6 14 ♖d1 ♕e7, Antunes-Motwani, Yerevan Olympiad 1996, with a level position.

c) 6...cxd4 7 ♘xd4 ♘db4 8 ♘xc6 ♕xd1+ 9 ♔xd1 ♘xc6 10 ♘c3 ♗d7 11 ♗e3

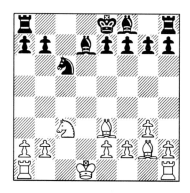

and here:

---

c1) 11...g6 12 ♖c1 ♗g7 13 f4 0-0 14 ♔e1 ♖ac8 15 ♔f2 e5 16 ♖hd1 ♗e6 17 ♘b5 ♗xa2 18 ♗c5 ♖fd8 19 ♗xc6 bxc6 20 ♘xa7 ♖xd1 21 ♖xd1 ♖a8 22 b4 exf4 23 gxf4 ♗b3 and White is pressing, though Black should hold the ending, Smirin-Alterman, Dresden 1998.

c2) 11...0-0-0 12 ♔e1 (12 ♔c1 and 12 ♔c2 have also been played) 12...e5 13 ♖c1 ♔b8 14 f4 (14 ♗d5 followed by f2-f3 and ♔f2 looks quite good for White) 14...f5 15 fxe5 ♘xe5 16 ♗f4 ♖e8 17 ♖d1 ♗c6 18 ♗xc6 bxc6 19 ♖d7 g5 and Black held the balance by active play in the endgame, Kramnik-Kasparov, Frankfurt (rapid) 2000.

4...dxc4

4...cxd4 is an important alternative. After 5 ♗g2 (5 cxd5 ♕xd5 6 ♕xd4 ♘c6 7 ♕xd5 ♘xd5 is equal), Black can choose:

a) 5...dxc4 6 ♕xd4 ♘c6 7 ♕xd8+ ♘xd8 8 ♘a3 ♗d7 9 ♘e5 ♖c8 10 ♘axc4 ♗e6 11 b3 ♗d5 12 0-0 e6 13 ♗e3 b5 14 ♘b2 ♗a3 15 ♘bd3 a5 16 ♗c1 ♗d6 17 ♗d2 ♗xg2 18 ♔xg2 ♘b7 19 a4 and White is a touch better, Sulava-Ruck, Charleville 2000.

b) 5...♕a5+ 6 ♘bd2 with a further split:

b1) 6...dxc4 7 ♘xd4 e5 8 ♕c2 ♗e7 9 0-0 0-0 10 ♘xc4 ♕c7 11 ♘2e3 ♗e6 12 ♗d2 ♘c6 13 ♖c1 ♖ad8 and Black is slightly better, Calotescu-Wang Yu, Yerevan 2000. This line looks useful – White needs an improvement.

b2) 6...♘c6 7 0-0 e5 8 ♘b3 ♕d8 9 cxd5 ♘xd5 10 ♘xe5! ♘db4 11 ♘xc6 ♘xc6 12 ♗xc6+ bxc6 13 ♕xd4 and White has won a pawn, Topalov-Shirov, Monaco (rapid) 1999.

5 ♕a4+ ♗d7

5...♘c6 6 dxc5 e6 7 ♗g2 ♗d7 8 ♕xc4 transposes into a Catalan, e.g. 8...♕a5+ 9 ♗d2 ♕xc5, Sulava-Jelen, Charleville 2000.

6 ♕xc4 ♗c6

6...e6 7 ♗g2 ♗c6 is another Catalan transposition, as in Cummings-Delchev, Istanbul Olympiad 2000. 6...cxd4 is also possible.

7 dxc5

Or:

a) 7 ♗g2 cxd4 8 0-0 ♕d5 9 ♘a3 a6 10 ♖d1 e6 (again play is similar to a Catalan once Black has played ...e7-e6) 11 ♖xd4 ♕xc4 12 ♘xc4 ♗c5 13 ♖d1 ♘bd7 14 ♗f4 0-0 15 ♖ac1 ♖ac8 16 ♗d6 ♗xd6 17 ♘xd6 ♖b8 18 ♘d4 was played in Kramnik-Leko, Frankfurt (rapid) 2000. White has a slight initiative, though Black's position is solid enough.

b) After the risky 7 ♕xc5 Dokhoian gives the sample line 7...♘a6 8 ♕c2 e5 9 dxe5 ♘b4 10 ♕b3 ♗e4 11 ♘a3 ♘d3+ 12 exd3 ♗xf3 13 exf6 ♕a5+ 14 ♗d2 ♕e5+ 15 ♗e3 ♕a5+ with a draw by repetition.

7...♗d5 8 ♕a4+ ♗c6 9 ♕c4 ♗d5 10 ♕c2

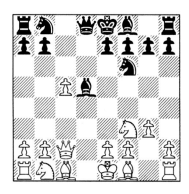

White shuns the repetition of moves.

10...e6

Instead, the more ambitious 10...e5 was played in Cvitan-Delchev, Istanbul Olympiad 2000. After 11 ♗g2 ♘bd7 12 ♘c3 ♗c6 13 b4 a5 14 b5 ♗xf3 15 ♗xf3 ♗xc5 16 0-0 ♕c7 17 e3 0-0 18 ♗b2 ♖ac8 19 ♖ac1 ♖fe8 20 ♖fd1 White has some advantage, not least because of his control of the light squares.

11 ♗g2 ♗e4 12 ♕c4 ♗d5 13 ♕h4 ♗xc5 14 ♘c3 ♗c6 15 0-0 ♗e7?!

Dokhoian denotes this as an inaccuracy, and instead suggests 15...♘bd7 16 ♗g5 (16 b4 is too loosening, e.g. 16...♗e7 17 ♗g5

Ic8 18 Iac1 0-0 19 b5 ♗xf3 20 ♗xf3 h6)
16...♗e7 17 Ifd1 ♕b6 with a comfortable
game for Black.

16 Id1 ♕a5

If 16...♘bd7 17 ♘e5.

17 ♗d2

Kramnik gives 17 Ib1 ♘e4 18 ♕g4
♘xc3 19 bxc3 0-0 20 ♘d4 with an initiative
for White.

17...♘bd7 18 g4

18 Iab1 is a simpler approach.

**18...h6 19 ♕g3 ♕a6 20 h4 ♕c4 21 ♗f4
♕b4**

21...g5!? looks interesting.

22 a3

White provokes even greater complications.

22...♕xb2 23 ♘d4 g5

With this thrust, Black gets his counterplay in, just in time.

**24 ♘xc6 gxf4 25 ♕d3 bxc6 26 ♗xc6
0-0 27 ♗xa8 ♘e5 28 ♕d4 Ixa8 29
♕xe5 Ic8 30 Iac1 ♘d5**

Kasparov correctly calculates that his
queen will be sufficiently active in the en-
emy camp to force a draw, despite his material deficit.

**31 ♘xd5 ♕xe5 32 ♘xe7+ ♔g7 33 Ixc8
♕xe2 34 Ig8+ ♔f6 35 Id7 ♕e1+ 36
♔g2 ♕e4+ 37 ♔h2 ♕c2 38 ♔g2 ♕e4+
39 ♔h2 ♕c2 40 g5+ hxg5 41 Ixg5
♕xf2+ ½-½**

Game 37
Ftacnik-Pinter
Prague 1985

**1 c4 ♘f6 2 ♘f3 c5 3 ♘c3 d5 4 cxd5
♘xd5 5 e4**

A bold move, staking a claim in the centre.

5...♘b4

5...♘xc3 6 dxc3 (or 6 bxc3 with a likely
transposition into the Grünfeld Defence)
6...♕xd1+ 7 ♔xd1 is a pleasant position for
White.

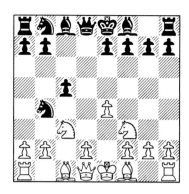

6 ♗c4

For the alternative 6 ♗b5+, see the next
game.

6...♘d3+

The older move is 6...♗e6 which was
supplanted by 6...♘d3+ in the early 1980s.
After 6...♗e6 7 ♗xe6 ♘d3+ 8 ♔f1 fxe6 9
♘g5 ♕b6 (if 9...♕d7 10 ♕f3 ♘e5 11 ♕h3
♕d3+ 12 ♕xd3 ♘xd3 13 g3 e5 with a slight
advantage for White according to Suba) 10
♕f3 c4 11 b3 Black has tried:

a) 11...♕a6 12 a4 ♔d7 13 ♘b5 and
White is much better, Gheorghiu-Chow,
New York 1984.

b) 11...h6 and now:

b1) White fumbled the move order with
12 ♘f7 ♔h7 13 bxc4 ♕d4 14 ♔e2 ♘c5 15
♗a3 ♕xc4+ 16 ♔d1 ♘bd7 17 Ib1 g6 18
♘b5 Ic8 19 Ib4 ♕xa2 0-1, Tsesarsky-
Tseitlin, Kiryat Shmuel 1997.

b2) 12 bxc4 is much better, e.g.
12...♘xc1 13 ♘f7 Ih7 (or 13...Ig8 14 ♘e5
♕b2 15 ♕f7+ with a winning attack, Tuk-
makov-Piesina, USSR 1980) 14 ♘e5 g5 15
Ixc1 and White has a material and positional advantage.

7 ♔e2 ♘f4+ 8 ♔f1 ♘e6 9 b4

This gambit was all the rage in the early
to mid 1980s, but since around the time of
this game, the theory has not developed
significantly. Other moves here include:

a) Suba's attempted improvement 9 h4
(pre-empting ...g7-g6) has not caught on:

9...♘c6 10 ♘g5 ♘xg5 11 hxg5 ♘e5 12 ♗b5+ ♗d7 13 d3 g6 14 f4 ♗xb5 15 ♘xb5 ♘c6 and Black is okay, Murey-Cserna, Copenhagen 1986.

b) 9 ♘e5 was popular for a while, until Timman discovered 9...g6!, which drew the sting from White's threats: 10 ♕a4+ ♗d7 11 ♘xd7 (11 ♗xe6 fxe6 12 ♕c4 ♗g7 13 ♘xd7 ♕xd7 14 d3 ♘c6 15 ♗e3 b6 16 ♖d1 0-0 17 h4 ♘e5 18 ♕a4 ♖ad8 and Black is better, Bauer-Leko, Bordeaux 1999) 11...♕xd7 12 ♗xe6 fxe6 13 ♕xd7+ ♔xd7 14 d3 ♘c6 15 ♗e3 b6 with equality, Larsen-Timman, Bugojno 1984.

c) 9 d3 ♘c6 (this is better than 9...g6 10 h4 h6 11 ♗e3 ♗g7 12 ♗xe6 ♗xe6 13 ♗xc5, Speelman-Timman, Dordrecht 2000) 10 ♗e3 ♘ed4 11 ♘b5 a6 12 ♘bxd4 cxd4 13 ♗f4 e6 14 ♖c1 ♗e7 15 h4 ♗d7 16 e5 ♕b6 17 ♗b3 ♘a5 when Black is a bit better, Suba-De la Villa Garcia, Palma de Mallorca 1992.

9...g6

This counter-gambit seems to give Black good chances. Accepting the pawn with 9...cxb4 is fully playable, but many players would prefer to have the initiative rather than defend, so interest generally shifted over to 9...g6. After 9...cxb4 White has:

a) 10 ♘d5 (this in turn was replaced by line 'b' as White found his piece placements were too artificial) 10...g6 (10...♘c6 11 d4 g6 12 ♗e3 ♗g7 13 ♕d2 0-0 14 ♖d1 a5 15 h4 h5 16 ♗h6 ♔h7 17 ♗xg7 ♘xg7 18 ♘g5+ ♔g8 19 ♕f4 and a draw was agreed in this unclear position, Piket-Van Wely, Escaldes 1998) 11 ♗b2 ♗g7 12 ♗xg7 ♘xg7 and now:

a1) 13 ♘xb4 0-0 14 h3 e5 15 g3 ♗e6 16 ♖c1 ♘d7 17 ♘d5, Seirawan-Sax, Linares 1983, and now Beliavsky and Mikhalchishin recommend 17...♘b6 with an edge for Black.

a2) 13 ♕c1 ♘c6 14 d4 ♗e6 15 h4 ♖c8 16 h5 is a wild alternative, e.g. 16...♘xh5 17 ♕h6 ♘xd4 18 ♘xd4 ♖xc4 19 ♘xe6 fxe6 20 ♖xh5 exd5 21 ♖xd5 ♕b6 22 ♖ad1 with enough play for the pawns, Seirawan-Peters, South Bend 1981.

b) 10 ♘e2 ♘c7 11 d4 e6 and here:

b1) 12 h4 ♗d6 (12...♗e7 can be met by 13 ♗f4 followed by ♖a1-c1) 13 h5 h6 14 ♖h4 ♘d7 15 ♗b2 ♗e7 16 ♖h3 ♘f6 17 ♗d3 ♗d7 18 ♘e5 ♗b5 19 ♔g1 0-0 20 ♘f4 ♖c8 21 ♖g3 with some attacking chances in return for the pawn, Hübner-Tukmakov, Wijk aan Zee 1984.

b2) 12 ♗f4 ♗d6 13 ♖c1 ♗xf4 14 ♘xf4 0-0? (castling into it; instead White has to prove his compensation is enough after 14...♗d7 or 14...♘d7) 15 h4 ♘d7 16 e5 h6 17 ♕d3 ♖e8 18 ♖h3 ♘f8 19 ♖g3 with a huge attack, Hutchings-Badea, Novi Sad Olympiad 1990.

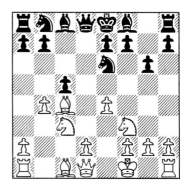

10 bxc5

10 ♖b1 is mentioned by Watson in *Secrets of Modern Chess Strategy* as being a yet further refinement in the genealogy of this variation. However, this line does not look very convincing, though it has not yet had any high-level tests. Following 10...♗g7 11 ♘e2 the scant material available is:

a) 11...0-0 12 h4 ♘c6 13 bxc5 ♘xc5 and now White blundered with 14 ♕c2 (though Black is doing fine after 14 ♗d5 ♗e6), allowing 14...♘xe4 winning a pawn since 15 ♕xe4 is answered by 15...♗f5, Babik-Laptos, Bielsko-Biala 1991.

b) 11...cxb4 12 ♖xb4 ♕c7?! (but the

natural 12...♘c6 looks okay) 13 d4 0-0 14 ♗b3 ♘a6 15 ♖c4 ♕d8 16 h4 ♘ac7 17 ♗e3 ♘b5 18 d5 ♘ec7 19 h5 is the kind of position White wants to see, Losos-Radola, correspondence 1992.

10...♗g7 11 ♗xe6 ♗xe6 12 d4 ♘c6 13 ♗e3 ♕a5 14 ♕d2

14 ♖c1 was given as an improvement by Stohl. Now Black has:

a) 14...♗c4+ 15 ♔g1 0-0-0 is the main thrust of the analysis by Stohl, leading to an assessment of 'unclear' after 16 h3 (though Carsten Hansen's 16 ♘b1 or 16 ♕a4 may improve for White) 16...f5 17 exf5 gxf5 etc.

b) The position after 14...0-0-0 15 d5 ♗xc3 16 ♕b3 ♗f6 (16...♕a6+ leads to the same thing) 17 dxe6 is given as much better for White by Stohl in *Informator 39*, and this assessment has been copied from book to book. However, this is simply not correct, e.g. 17...♕a6+ 18 ♔g1 ♖d3 19 ♕c2 fxe6 and Black has a great position. White has to try and develop his kingside with, for example, 20 h3 ♖hd8 21 ♔h2 but it doesn't look very promising for him.

14...0-0-0

14...♗c4+ 15 ♔g1 0-0-0 16 ♖c1 f5 (16...♘xd4 17 ♗xd4 ♗xd4 18 ♘xd4 e5 19 ♘b3 ♗xb3 20 ♕b2 is unclear – analysis by Stohl) 17 e5 ♖d7 18 h4 took place in Kasparov-Shirov, (simul) USSR 1987.

15 ♖c1

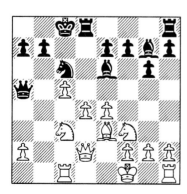

15...f5!

Sniping at White's central edifice.

16 exf5 gxf5

16...♗xf5 is also possible.

17 ♕e2 ♕b4

Black is clearly better according to Stohl. He uses the threat of the queen exchange, which would favour Black despite his current pawn deficit, to gain time and coordinate his pieces.

18 ♔g1 ♕c4 19 ♕e1

19 ♕xc4 ♗xc4 20 ♖d1 ♖hf8 21 g3 e5 22 d5 ♘b4 23 d6 f4 and Black has a firm grip on the initiative.

19...♖hg8 20 h4 ♗d5 21 ♘d2

21 ♖h3 was preferable.

21...♕a6 22 ♘xd5 ♖xd5 23 ♘f3

Again 23 ♖h3 would have minimised Black's advantage.

23...♕xa2 24 ♖h3 ♖dd8 25 ♖b1 ♗f6 26 ♗g5 ♕d5 27 ♕f1 ♖d7 28 ♗xf6 exf6 29 ♖g3 ♖e8

Black should pile up on the d-pawn with 29...♖gd8.

30 ♕c1 ♕e4 31 h5 ♖ed8 32 h6 ♘xd4?!

Allowing White too many counter-chances; instead 32...f4 33 ♖g7 ♖xg7 34 hxg7 ♖g8 35 ♕e1 ♕d5 and Black can pick off the g7-pawn when the time is right.

33 ♘xd4 ♖xd4 34 ♖g7 ♖4d7

34...♕e2 35 ♕e3 ♖d1+ 36 ♖xd1 ♖xd1+ 37 ♔h2 ♕xe3 38 fxe3 ♖d7 39 ♔g3 a5 40 ♖g8+ ♖d8 41 ♖g7 a4 42 c6 bxc6 43 ♖xh7 and White holds on.

35 ♖xd7 ♖xd7 36 ♕b2 ♖d2 37 ♕b5 ♖d7 38 ♕b3 f4 39 ♖a1 a6 40 ♖c1 ♕d5

Black is still a pawn up, but it is very difficult to exploit this in such an open position with queens and rooks on the board.

41 ♕c3 ♕c6 42 ♕c4 b5 43 ♕xf4 ♖d5 44 ♕g4+ ♔c7 45 ♕g3+ ♔b7 46 ♖e1 ♖d7 47 ♕f4 a5 48 ♕f5 ♖c7 49 ♖e6 ♕xc5 50 ♕e4+ ♔a7 51 ♖xf6 ♖e7 52 ♕f3 a4 53 g3 ♖c7 54 ♖f5 ♕b6 55 ♖f6 ♕d4 56 ♕f5 ♕d7 57 ♕e4 ♕e7 58 ♖e6 ♕c5 59 ♖e5 ♕b6 60 ♕e1 ♔a6 61 ♕e4 ♖c6

Black is trying everything to get his pawns moving while defending his own king.

62 ♖e7 a3 63 ♖e8 ♖c1+

63...♕b7 would keep the game alive from Black's perspective.

64 ♔g2 ♕b7

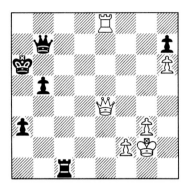

65 ♖e6+

Missing 65 ♖a8+, which leaves White on the better side of a draw after 65...♔b6 66 ♕xb7+ ♔xb7 67 ♖xa3.

65...♔a7 66 ♖e7 ♖c7 67 ♖xc7 ♕xc7 68 ♕e3+ ♔b7 69 ♕xa3 ♕c6+ 70 ♔g1 ♕xh6 71 ♕c5 ♕b6 72 ♕xb6+ ♔xb6 73 ♔f1 ♔a5 74 ♔e2 ♔a4 75 f4 ½-½

Both sides queen at the same time. A hard fought struggle!

Game 38
Lautier-Kasparov
Tilburg 1997

1 c4 c5 2 ♘f3 ♘f6 3 ♘c3 d5 4 cxd5 ♘xd5 5 e4 ♘b4 6 ♗b5+

Unlike the 'caveman' 6 ♗c4, this line usually soon results in a queenless middle-game. White sacrifices a pawn for quick development and tries to exploit the loose position of Black's king. While regaining his pawn is usually a trivial matter, Black usually has sufficient resources to equalise fairly comfortably.

6...♘8c6 7 d4 cxd4 8 a3 dxc3

8...♗d7 is also adequate, e.g. 9 axb4 dxc3 10 bxc3 g6 11 0-0 ♗g7 12 ♕b3 ♕c7 13 ♗e3 0-0 14 ♖ac1 ♘e5 15 ♗xd7 ♘xf3+ 16 gxf3 ♕xd7 17 ♔g2 with equality, Azmaiparashvili-Kamsky, Brussels 1992.

9 ♕xd8+ ♔xd8 10 axb4

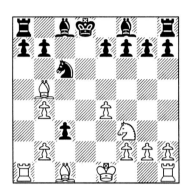

10...cxb2

Alternatively:

a) 10...♘xb4 and now:

a1) White does not need to explore the murky continuation 11 bxc3 ♘c2+ 12 ♔e2 ♘xa1 13 ♖d1+ ♔c7 14 ♗f4+ e5 15 ♗xe5+ ♔b6 (Hergott-London, New York 1994), but is best off answering with:

a2) 11 0-0, e.g. 11...c2 12 ♘g5 ♖g8 13 ♘xf7+ ♔c7 14 ♗f4+ ♔b6 15 ♗a4 ♗e6 16 ♘g5 ♗c4 17 ♖fc1 and White is better due to Black's exposed king, Leontiev-Monakhov, Moscow 1996.

b) 10...c2 11 ♗xc6 bxc6 12 ♘e5 ♔e8 13 ♗e3 f6 14 ♘d3 e5 15 ♔d2 a6, Salnev-Mikhalchishin, Struga 1991, and now 16 ♖hc1 (instead of 16 ♔xc2) would have given White a large advantage according to Mikhalchishin.

11 ♗xb2 e6

Instead:

a) 11...♗d7 12 ♗xc6 ♗xc6 13 ♘e5 ♔e8 14 ♘xc6 bxc6 15 ♔e2 f6 16 ♖a6 e5 17 ♗c3 ♔d7 18 ♖ha1 gives White a little something, Piket-Shirov, Wijk aan Zee 1999. The position is similar to the end of Lautier-Kasparov, except that White's king is in the centre instead of on the back rank. Having said that, Shirov managed to hold the draw.

b) 11...f6 is inferior, e.g. 12 e5 ♗g4 13 ♗xc6 bxc6 14 ♘d4 fxe5 15 ♘xc6+ ♔c7 16 ♘xe5 ♗h5 17 0-0 ♗e8 18 ♖fc1+ ♔b7 19 ♘c4, Kasparov-Korchnoi, Skelleftea 1989, and White is much better. Black is undeveloped and his king is feeling the heat.

12 0-0 ♗d7!?

Before this game, the theoretical main line was 12...f6 13 e5

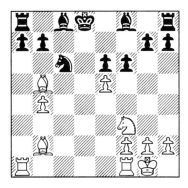

and now:

a) 13...f5 14 ♖fd1+ ♔c7 15 ♗xc6 bxc6 16 ♗c3 ♗e7 17 ♘d4 ♖d8 18 b5 ♗c5 19 ♗a5+ and White had a strong initiative in the game Pychkin-Srantinsh, correspondence 1983.

b) 13...♗e7 14 ♗xc6 bxc6 15 ♘d4 ♗d7 16 ♖fc1 fxe5 17 ♘xc6+ ♗xc6 18 ♖xc6 ♔d7 19 ♖ca6 when Black has to tread carefully:

b1) 19...♗f6 20 b5 ♖hb8? 21 b6 is strong, Ivanov-Jauernig, Regensburg 1997.

b2) 19...♗xb4 20 ♖xa7+ ♖xa7 21 ♖xa7+ ♔d6 22 ♖xg7 ♖c8 23 ♖g5 and White has a small endgame plus.

b3) 19...♖hb8 20 ♖xa7+ ♖xa7 21 ♖xa7+ ♔e8 22 g3 when White has a tiny edge.

Another line is 12...♗xb4 13 ♗xg7 ♖g8 14 ♗f6+ ♔c7 15 ♖fc1 ♔b6 (15...♗d7!?),

Kamp-Heinzel, Germany 1989, and here White has 16 ♗xc6 bxc6 17 ♖ab1 a5 18 ♗e7, regaining the pawn and keeping an edge in the endgame, e.g. 18...♗a6 19 ♗xb4 axb4 20 ♖xb4+ ♗b5 21 ♘e5.

13 ♗xc6 ♗xc6

Or 13...bxc6 14 ♘e5 ♗e8 15 ♖fc1 ♗xb4 16 ♖xc6, Kovalev-Efimenko, Sevastopol 2000, and now White should play 16 ♘xc6+ ♗xc6 17 ♖xc6 a5 18 ♖d1+ ♔e8 19 ♗xg7 ♖g8 20 ♗f6 with balanced chances.

14 ♘e5 ♔e8 15 ♘xc6 bxc6 16 ♖a4 f6 17 ♖fa1

17 ♖c1 is slightly more testing, for example 17...♔d7 (17...♗e7 18 ♖xc6 ♔f7 is preferable) 18 ♖ca1 ♗d6 19 e5!? ♗xe5 20 ♗xe5 fxe5 21 ♖xa7+ ♖xa7 22 ♖xa7+ ♔d6 23 ♖xg7 h5, Ivanov-Biriukov, St Petersburg 1999, and now 24 h4 gives White something to play for in the endgame, e.g. 24...♖b8 25 ♖g5 ♖xb4 26 ♖xh5 c5 27 ♖h8 c4 28 h5 with some winning chances.

17...♔f7 18 ♖xa7+ ♖xa7 19 ♖xa7+ ♗e7 20 ♖c7? ½-½

A draw was agreed here (a win would have enabled Kasparov to finish in sole first place), even though 20...c5 wins a pawn, e.g. 21 b5 ♖b8 or 21 bxc5 ♖b8. Instead 20 ♔f1 is equal.

Summary

The Rubinstein is doing well. Perhaps many players are being over-deferent to its gilt-edged reputation, or perhaps try to avoid the theory. 6 ♕b3 (Game 27) is worth a further look. The Keres-Parma is solid, though White can get a comfortable game, and perhaps a tiny edge with 9 e4 (Game 33).

Meanwhile 5 e4 looks fine for Black at the moment: 6 ♗b5+ leads to equality, while the once-critical 6 ♗c4 is under a cloud. 5 d4 is a common way to reach the Grünfeld, though either side can prevent this.

1 c4 c5 2 ♘c3
> 2 ♘f3 ♘f6 3 g3 d5 – *Game 36*

2...♘f6 3 ♘f3
> 3 g3 d5 4 cxd5 ♘xd5 5 ♗g2 ♘c7 *(D)* – Rubinstein Variation
>> 6 ♕b3 – *Game 27*
>> 6 ♘f3 ♘c6 7 d3 e5 8 0-0 ♗e7 9 ♘d2 ♗d7 10 ♘c4
>>> 10...0-0 – *Game 28*; 10...f6 – *Game 29*

3...d5
> 3...♘c6 4 g3 d5 5 d4
>> 5...cxd4 – *Game 35*; 5...e6 – Keres-Parma Variation

4 cxd5 ♘xd5 5 e4
> 5 e3 – *Game 31*
> 5 g3
>> 5...e6 – Keres-Parma Variation
>> 5...g6 6 ♗g2 ♘c6 – see Chapter 6
>> 5...♘c6 6 ♗g2 ♘c7 – Rubinstein Variation
> 5 d4
>> 5...cxd4 – *Game 30*
>> 5...e6 6 g3 ♘c6 7 ♗g2 (D)
>>> 7...♘db4 – *Game 34*
>>> 7...♗e7
>>>> 8 0-0 0-0 9 e4 – *Game 33*; 8 ♘xd5 exd5 – *Game 32*

5...♘b4 6 ♗b5+ (D) – *Game 38*
> 6 ♗c4 – *Game 37*

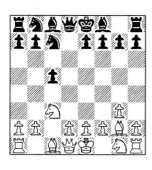
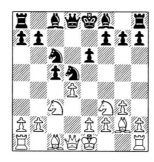
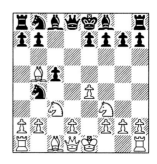

| *5...♘c7* | *7 ♗g2* | *6 ♗b5+* |

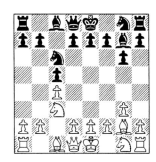

CHAPTER FIVE

Symmetrical English with g2-g3

1 c4 c5 2 ♘c3 ♘c6 3 g3 g6 4 ♗g2 ♗g7
This chapter covers symmetrical lines without 5 ♘f3 and also lines with an early ♘f3 but without ...♘f6. 5 a3 is dealt with in Games 39-40, for 5 e3 see Games 41-43, 5 e4 is covered in Games 44-46, while for 5 ♘f3 (with 5... e6 or 5... e5) see Games 47-49.

The next chapter covers the position after 5 ♘f3 ♘f6.

The very nature of the 'pure' Symmetrical English is that certain set-ups and ideas can be adopted by either (or both) sides. So bear in mind in the following discussion, that most of the concepts can be applied with either White or Black. For the sake of brevity I have not repeated the Black equivalent (e.g. b2-b4 and ...b7-b5 etc.) in each and every example.

Queenside expansion
5 a3
One of the most natural plans in this line is to expand on the queenside with b2-b4 (...b7-b5 for Black). In general terms this gains space, puts pressure on the c5-pawn and offers a potential open b-file for White's rook. Usually the b2-b4 thrust is prepared by a2-a3 and ♖a1-b1, but in the 'accelerated' form it can involve a pawn

sacrifice (e.g. by leaving the rook on a1).

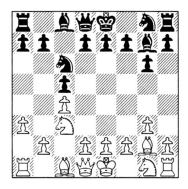

The course of the game is shaped by Black's response to this plan. There are four possible reactions:

Take it – in the event of a b2-b4 gambit, Black can of course grab the offered pawn. Usually White gets 'Benko Gambit style' compensation with pressure down the a- and b-files and often pressure on the dark squares with ♗c1-a3. See Game 39 and the notes to Game 47 for examples.

Block it – at least temporarily with ...a5. This weakens the b5-square but this is sometimes of lesser significance. Black can even later aim for ...♖b8-a8 and ...b7-b5.

Copy it – Black plays ...a7-a6, ...♖a8-b8, ...b7-b5 etc. After the queenside has been clarified, the battle switches to the centre. See Game 40 for an example of plagiarism in action.

Ignore it – Black says 'so what?' and simply gets on with his development. This is fine as long as Black gets a decent structure in place, and does not cede White too much play on the queenside.

Flexible formations

1 c4 c5 2 ♘c3 ♘c6 3 g3 g6 4 ♗g2 ♗g7 5 e4 e6 6 ♘ge2 ♘ge7 7 a3 b6 8 ♖b1 ♗b7 9 b4 d6 10 d3 ♕d7 11 0-0 0-0

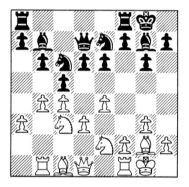

There are a number of characteristic set-ups which can be adopted by either colour. First of all there is the Botvinnik structure (pawns on e4 and c4), adopted by White in this example. In this case Black has adopted the ...e7-e6 and ...♘ge7 formation. This can be further supplemented by ...b7-b6 and ...♗b7, giving a structure which has some-times been called the 'Hippopotamus'. This is quite a good approach for combating the b2-b4 thrust, since c5 is securely defended.

In addition to knowing specific move or-ders, it is important to find a structure or structures you are happy with. As well as the objective state of theory in any one line, this choice is also related to your experience and other openings in your repertoire. For example, there are players who will always adopt the Botvinnik set-up, almost regard-less of his opponent's first 7-8 moves!

Other common set-ups include the straightforward c4, ♘c3, g3, ♗g2, ♘f3, d3 etc.

12 ♗e3 ♘d4

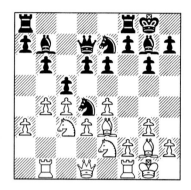

The d4 battleground

The previous diagram also illustrates an-other important factor – the fight for the d4- (or d5-) square. In the case of an ...e7-e6 approach, Black's ideal is to achieve ...d7-d5.

In the Botvinnik set-up, Black tries to exploit the hole on d4, while White combats this and would like to achieve d3-d4, with an (often favourable) Maroczy bind.

There is a rule of thumb in these types of position, which is important to understand if you haven't come across it before. Black usually does not play ...♘c6-d4 before White has played ♗c1-e3, since White then has the option of ♘e2xd4 followed by ♘c3-e2. However as soon as White does play ♗c1-e3, Black will often occupy d4 to prevent White from achieving the d3-d4 break.

Now, of course, capturing with the knight on d4 loses a piece, while White typi-cally avoids ♗e3xd4 because his dark squares are weakened. A thematic example of this is Game 45.

In order to resolve the situation in the centre, White can, for example, play f2-f4 and drop his bishop back to f2, with the idea of ♘e2xd4 and pressure against the black pawn which ends up on d4. Alternatively, White can play 'around' the d4-square and prepare action on the queenside and/or the kingside. Finally, Black sometimes voluntarily plays ...♘d4xe2 if there is some specific gain, e.g. ...a5-a4 to disrupt White's queenside after the c3-knight has recaptured on e2.

Of course (here is a disclaimer) every chess rule has its exceptions. Nevertheless, this is one of the building blocks of knowledge which prove useful in a variety of situations, and even in other openings such as the Closed Sicilian.

Tactical ideas

The Symmetrical English has a reputation as being a 'positional' opening, but the rapid expansion of opening theory, and the dynamic style of many modern GMs has left its mark. Many gambit lines and new tactical ideas have been discovered in the most sedate variations. For example, in addition to the b2-b4 sacrifice mentioned above, there is the d4-sacrifice after 1 c4 c5 2 ♘c3 ♘c6 3 g3 g6 4 ♗g2 ♗g7 5 ♘f3 e6 6 d4!? (see Game 48). In fact, after getting a basic understanding of the plans, I would recommend study of the critical sharp lines, since this is where specific opening knowledge is of most use.

Symmetry – does the extra move count?

How valuable is White's extra tempo in some of the symmetrical lines in this chapter? Personally, I think that at least part of the value is the ability for White to steer the game more than his opponent. In other words, White is more often able to play his own game.

On the subject of **reversed** (asymmetric) openings, Yermolinsky notes that White (with an extra tempo) often scores worse than Black in the same positions (which he puts down to a difference in opening philosophy when playing Black or White). He

quotes GM Malaniuk, a leading exponent of the Dutch Defence (for Black) who was once asked why he doesn't play 1 f4 as White. His response? 'That extra move's gonna hurt me'. Perhaps an extreme example is when the 'extra move' actually puts something en prise (e.g. the h3-pawn in Williams-Emms, Game 46).

| Game 39 |
| **Krasenkow-Brynell** |
| *Copenhagen 1996* |

1 c4 c5 2 ♘c3 ♘c6 3 g3 g6 4 ♗g2 ♗g7 5 a3 e6

5...a6 is covered in Game 40.

6 b4!?

White makes this thematic thrust immediately, without wasting time on 6 ♖b1. Whether this expedites White's queenside play, or is just a blunder, however, has been the subject of some controversy over the years. Of course 6 ♖b1 is perfectly sound, as is 6 e4, which transposes to Game 44.

6...♘xb4

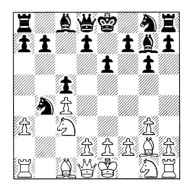

There is no doubt that this move came as a surprise in the early games in this line. Steve Giddins goes so far as to list this move in his book *101 Chess Opening Traps*. By contrast, Tony Kosten recommends 6 b4 as a good way for White to play for a win!

6...cxb4?! justifies White's play, and is

probably what many of the 'gambiteers' were expecting, e.g. 7 axb4 ♘xb4 8 ♗a3 ♗xc3 9 dxc3 ♘c6 10 h4 ♕f6 11 ♘f3 ♕xc3+ 12 ♘d2 with good compensation, Renet-Yudasin, Ostend 1988.

6...♘ge7 and 6...d6 are also possible.

7 axb4 cxb4 8 d4

8 ♘b5 is an enterprising alternative, and it comes as no surprise that this was Julian Hodgson's choice when faced with this position. It seems, however that Black can keep his extra material and survive. 8...♗xa1 9 ♕a4 ♗f6 (But not 9...♗e5?! 10 ♘f3 ♗b8 11 ♗b2 f6 12 h4 a5 13 h5 gxh5 14 ♖xh5 ♕e7 15 ♘g5 ♖a6 16 ♘e4 e5 17 c5 and White has managed to manufacture a strong attack, Hodgson-Gulko, Groningen 1994) 10 d4 a6 11 ♘d6+ ♔f8 12 ♘f3 ♗e7 13 ♕xb4 a5 14 ♕c5 f6 15 h4 h5 16 0-0 ♘h6 17 e4 ♘f7 18 e5 ♗xd6 19 exd6 b6 and Black has repulsed White's attack, remaining a clear pawn up, Lobron-Kavalek, Bochum 1981.

8...bxc3 9 e3 ♘e7

9...♘f6!? was played in Delchev-Stohl, Pula 2000. This soon transposes into the line with 9...♘e7 and ...d7-d5, but perhaps restricts Black's options somewhat, since White's bishop on a3 prevents Black from castling, without the need to prompt Black's knight to move from e7: 10 ♗a3 d5 11 ♘e2 ♗d7 12 0-0 ♖c8 13 cxd5 ♘xd5 14 ♕b3 ♗c6 15 ♖fc1 ♕b6 16 ♕d1 ♗f8 17 ♗xf8 ♔xf8 18 ♘xc3 ♘b4 (Black can play more solidly with 18...♘xc3 19 ♖xc3 ♔g7; or 18...♔g7 when White can win his pawn back, but this does not suffice for more than equality, e.g. 19 ♘xd5 ♗xd5 20 ♖cb1 ♕c6 21 ♗xd5 ♕xd5 22 ♖xa7 ♖c7) 19 ♘e4 ♖d8 (again 19...♔g7 and if 20 ♘d6 ♖a8 21 ♗xc6 bxc6) 20 ♕f3 ♖g8 (Black now finds himself in trouble – 20...f5 21 ♕f4 or 20...♗xe4 21 ♕xe4 ♘c6 22 ♕f4 leaves White on top) 21 ♕f4 ♗xe4 22 ♗xe4 ♘d5 23 ♗xd5 ♖xd5 24 ♖c7 1-0. If 24...♔g7 then 25 ♖ac1 is painful.

10 ♘e2 d5

This is the critical line, though it allows White to temporarily prevent Black from castling by posting his c1-bishop on a3. If Black does not challenge in the centre however, White gets good play on the queenside, e.g. 10...0-0 11 ♘xc3 ♕c7 (11...e5 is an interesting idea: 12 0-0 exd4 13 exd4 ♘f5 14 ♘e4 h6 15 ♗b2 d5 16 cxd5 b6 17 d6 ♗b7 18 ♘f6+ ½-½ Kozul-Lalic, Pula 2000) 12 ♕b3 a6 13 ♗a3 d6 14 0-0 ♖b8 15 ♖ab1 with fair compensation, Masculo-D.Gurevich, New York 1991.

11 cxd5

Alternatively 11 ♘xc3 dxc4 12 0-0 0-0 13 ♗a3 a6 14 ♕e2 and now Yudasin recommends 14...♖e8 15 ♕xc4 ♘f5 (or 15...b5) with an unclear position. Instead M.Gurevich-Yudasin, Haifa 1995 continued 14...♕c7 15 ♖fc1 ♖a7 16 ♕b2 ♖e8 17 ♗c5 ♖a8 18 ♕b4 ♘c6 19 ♕xc4 when White is clearly better according to Yudasin.

11...♘xd5 12 ♗a3

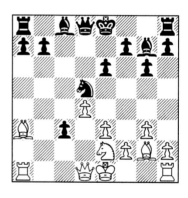

12...♗f8

12...♗d7 maybe the stiffest test of White's gambit. Since the Black king is not in immediate danger, Black develops his queenside before resorting to (if necessary) ...♗g7-f8. Play can continue:

a) 13 ♕b3 ♕b6 14 ♗xd5 exd5 15 ♕xb6 (15 ♕xd5 ♗c6 {15...♕c6} 16 ♕d6 ♕d8) 15...axb6 16 0-0 (16 ♘xc3 ♗f8 17 ♗b2 ♖xa1+ 18 ♗xa1 ♗b4 is slightly better for

Black, but the text is tantamount to surrender) 16...♗b5 17 ♖fe1 ♗xe2 18 ♖xe2 ♔d7 and Black is winning, Kaspret-Fabisch, Austrian League 1993.

b) 13 ♗xd5 exd5 14 ♘xc3 ♗c6. Note that White has fewer options here than after 15...♗d7 in the notes to Black's 15th move in the main game.

c) 13 0-0 and now:

c1) 13...♖c8 14 ♕b3 ♗c6 would transpose to Delchev-Stohl (see the note to Black's 9th move).

c2) 13...f5!? is risky, but perhaps Black can get away with it, e.g. 14 ♕b3 ♗c6 15 ♘xc3 ♔f7 16 ♘b5 ♗xb5 17 ♕xb5 ♖b8 is unclear, Polajzer-Schinzel, St Johan ID Haide 1981.

c3) 13...♗c6 14 ♕b3 (14 e4 ♘e7 15 ♕b3 0-0) 14...♕b6 (14...♖c8 is Delchev-Stohl) 15 ♗xd5 ♗xd5 16 ♕xc3 (16 ♕xb6 axb6 17 ♘xc3 ♗f3 18 ♖fb1 ♖a6) and now since 16...♗f8 17 ♗xf8 ♔xf8 18 e4 ♗xe4 19 d5 ♔g8 20 dxe6 gives White some compensation for the two pawns, perhaps Black can even try the daring 16...♔d7!? with the idea of a quick ...♖h8-c8, e.g. 17 ♗c5 (or 17 ♖ab1 ♕a6 or 17 ♖fb1 ♕c6 18 ♕b4 ♗f8 19 ♕b2 ♗xa3 20 ♖xa3 ♖hc8) 17...♕b5 and Black is set to consolidate.

13 ♗xf8

13 0-0 ♗xa3 14 ♖xa3 ♗d7 15 e4 ♘e7 16 ♘xc3 0-0 17 ♕a1 a5 18 ♖b1 ♘c6 ½-½ was Smyslov-Hartston, Hastings 1972/3.

13...♔xf8 14 ♕b3 ♔g7 15 0-0 b6

Krasenkow suggests 15...♗d7, giving an unclear verdict. After 16 ♗xd5 (16 ♕xb7 ♖b8 17 ♕xa7 ♗b5) 16...exd5 17 ♕xb7, Kosten gives 17...c2 18 ♕xd5 ♗f5 19 ♕xd8 ♖hxd8 20 f3 ♗d3 21 ♔f2 with the idea of rounding up the c-pawn, and indeed the ending looks slightly better for White.

So Black should probably dig in with 17...♗e6 18 ♘xc3 (18 ♖xa7 ♖xa7 19 ♕xa7 c2 followed by ...♗e6-f5) 18...a5 and if White takes his time in getting organised on the queenside, then ...h5-h4 is a possible

follow-up.

16 e4 ♘f6

16...♘c7!? is possible, e.g. 17 e5 (or 17 ♕xc3 ♗a6 18 d5+ f6 19 ♖fc1 ♖c8) 17...♗a6.

17 e5 ♘d5 18 ♘xc3 ♗b7 19 ♘b5 ♕b8

Black gets terribly boxed in after this. 19...♕d7 is better.

20 ♖fc1 a6 21 ♘d6 ♖d8 22 ♕a3

White doesn't want to allow an exchange sacrifice on d6 if Black can pick up a pawn as well.

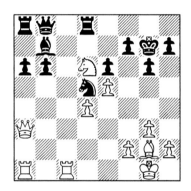

22...♖a7

Krasenkow prefers 22...♖d7.

23 ♖a2 ♗a8 24 ♗xd5

Removing Black's strong knight emphasises White's dominance of the dark squares. White finishes the game with a crisp attack.

24...♗xd5 25 ♖ac2 b5 26 ♖c8 ♕b6 27 ♖xd8 ♕xd8 28 ♖c8 ♕e7 29 ♕c1

Preventing the king from escaping via h6.

29...♖a8 30 ♖c7 ♕f8 31 ♕f4 ♔h8 32 ♖xf7 ♕d8 33 ♕h6

This wins easily, but 33 ♘e8 was mate in two.

33...♕g8 34 ♖c7 1-0

Game 40
Kasparov-Kramnik
New York (rapid) 1995

---

1 c4 c5 2 ♘c3 g6 3 g3 ♗g7 4 ♗g2 ♘c6

5 a3

5 ♘f3 a6 6 a3 ♖b8 7 ♖b1 b5 8 cxb5 axb5 9 b4 cxb4 10 axb4 is another way of reaching the same position after White's 10th move.

5...a6 6 ♖b1 ♖b8 7 b4

If White attempts to shepherd the queenside pawns forward with 7 ♕a4 then Black has the strong gambit reply 7...d6!, when play can continue:

a) 8 b4 ♗f5 9 ♗xc6+ bxc6 10 ♕xc6+ ♗d7 11 ♕xa6 ♗xc3 12 dxc3 ♘f6 with excellent compensation, Seirawan-Timman, Montpelier 1985.

b) 8 ♗xc6+ bxc6 9 ♕xc6+ ♔f8! and White's queen is embarrassed, e.g. 10 ♕a4 ♗b7 11 ♘f3 ♘h6 12 ♘d5 ♘f5 13 0-0 e6 14 ♘e3 ♗xf3 15 exf3 ♘d4 when White's position is a mess, G.Horvath-Plachetka, Austrian League 1995.

7...cxb4 8 axb4 b5 9 cxb5

If 9 c5?! a5! 10 ♗a3 axb4 11 ♗xb4 ♘h6 12 ♘f3 0-0 13 0-0 ♘f5 and White's bishop looks rather ridiculous on b4, Krasenkow-Kosten, Asti 1996.

9...axb5

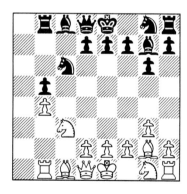

10 ♘f3

10 e4 e5 11 ♘ge2 ♘ge7 12 0-0 0-0 13 d3 d6 is dead equal.

10...d5

Black has some significant alternatives:
a) 10...♘f6 11 d4 d5 and now:
a1) 12 ♗f4 ♖b6 13 ♘e5 0-0 14 0-0 ♗b7

15 ♕d3 e6 16 ♖fc1 (16 ♘xb5? ♗a6 17 ♘xc6 ♖xc6 18 ♖a1 ♖b6 19 ♖a5 ♕d7 wins for Black) 16...♕e7 17 ♕d2 ♖c8 18 ♗g5 ♕e8 19 ♘xc6 ♗bxc6 20 ♗xf6 ♗xf6 21 e3 ♗e7 22 ♗f1 ♕f8 ½-½ Ki.Georgiev-Ehlvest, Manila 1990.

a2) 12 0-0 0-0 13 ♘e5 ♖b6 14 ♗g5 (14 ♘xc6 ♖xc6 15 ♘xb5 ♗f5 16 ♖b2 ♕b6 17 ♘a3 is suggested by Kosten, but Black looks fine after 17...♖fc8 18 ♗f4 ♖c3 and if 19 ♖b3 ♖xb3 20 ♕xb3 ♕xd4 21 b5 ♖c3 22 ♕b2 ♕c5 23 b6 ♕xa3 24 ♕xa3 ♖xa3 25 b7 ♘d7) 14...♗e6 and here:

a21) Kosten suggests grabbing the b5-pawn with 15 ♘xc6 ♖xc6 16 ♘xb5 which is certainly worth a try. Black may have some compensation due to the awkward placing of White's knight, but it looks insufficient, e.g. 16...♕b6 17 ♕a4 (17 ♘a3 ♖c3 18 ♗xf6 ♗xf6 19 ♘c2 ♗f5 20 ♘e3 ♗xb1 21 ♘xd5 ♗c2 22 ♘xb6 ♗xd1 23 ♖xd1 ♖b8 24 ♘d5 ♖c2 is okay for Black) 17...♖b8 18 ♘a3 ♗f5 19 ♗f4 ♖bc8 20 b5 ♖c3 21 ♖bc1 ♘e4 22 ♗xe4 dxe4 23 ♖xc3 ♖xc3 24 ♘c4 and White is in charge.

a22) Instead 15 e3 ♘e8 16 e4 ♘xe5 17 dxe5 d4 18 ♗f4 ♘c7 19 ♘d5 ♗xd5 20 exd5 ♘xd5 21 ♕xd4 ♘xf4 is equal, Renet-Ashley, St. Martin 1993.

b) 10...e5 gives White the option of an unclear pawn sacrifice: 11 d4!? and now:

b1) 11...♘xd4 12 ♘xd4 exd4 13 ♘e4 (13 ♘d5 ♗b7 14 ♕b3 with compensation for the pawn according to Taimanov) 13...d5 14 ♗g5 (14 ♗f4 dxe4 15 ♗xb8 ♗f5 gives Black good compensation) 14...♕b6 (14...f6 blocks the g7-bishop, allowing 15 ♗f4 dxe4 16 ♗xb8 ♗f5 17 ♗a7 – Kosten) 15 ♘c5 ♘e7 16 0-0 ♕d8 17 ♖a1 h6 18 ♗f4 ♖b6 19 ♖a7 ♖c6 20 ♕d3 0-0 21 ♕xb5 ♖b6 22 ♕a4 ♕e8 23 ♕a5 ♖b5 24 ♖xe7 winning, Hickl-Jansa, Eupen 1996.

b2) 11...exd4 12 ♘d5 with the further branch:

b21) 12...d6 13 ♗g5 (13 ♗b2!?) 13...♕d7 14 0-0 h6 15 ♗c1 ♘ge7 16 ♘xe7 ♕xe7 17

♗b2 0-0 18 ♘xd4 ♘xd4 19 ♗xd4 ♗xd4 20 ♕xd4 ♕xe2 21 ♖fe1 ♕g4 22 ♕xd6 ♗f5 and Black has (almost) equalised, Hickl-Lehner, Austrian League 2000.

b22) 12...♘f6 13 ♗g5 0-0 (13...h6 14 ♘xf6+ ♗xf6 15 ♗f4 d6 16 ♗xh6! ♗f5 17 ♖c1 ♗e4 18 ♗d2 ♘e5 19 0-0, Zaichik-Thorsteins, Moscow 1988, gave White a slight edge) 14 0-0 (14 ♘d2 h6 15 ♘xf6+ ♗xf6 16 ♗xh6 ♖e8 17 ♘e4 d5 18 ♘xf6+ ♕xf6 19 ♖c1 ♘xb4 20 ♕d2 ♗g4 21 0-0 ♗xe2 22 ♕xb4 ♗xf1 23 ♔xf1 g5 0-1 Matamoros Franco-Komljenovic, Coria del Rio 2001) 14...♗b7 (maybe 14...♖e8) 15 ♖c1 ♖e8 16 ♖e1 h6 17 ♘xf6+ ♗xf6 18 ♗xh6 is slightly better for White, Hickl-Ree, Lippstadt 1992.

11 d4 e6

Now 11...♘f6 transposes to note 'a' to Black's 10th.

11...♗f5 is an important alternative (11...♗g4 is also playable), and perhaps a better bid for equality. After 12 ♖b3 ♗e4 we have:

a) Kosten recommends 13 e3 as part of his repertoire for White, but doesn't analyse the natural 'a1'.

a1) 13...♘f6 14 0-0 0-0 15 ♘e5 ♕d6 16 ♘xe4 (if instead 16 f3 ♗f5 17 g4 ♗e6 18 ♘d3 ♘e8 19 ♘c5 ♗c8 20 ♗d2 e5 is fine for Black, T. Sorensen-J.Sorensen, Norresundby 1992) 16...♘xe4 17 f3 ♘f6 18 ♗b2 ♘d7 19 ♘xd7 ♕xd7 20 ♕d2 e6 with equality, Rasmussen-T.Sorensen, Aarhus 1985. The pawn structure does not allow the white bishops enough scope for an advantage.

a2) Instead 13...♗xf3 cedes the bishop pair under less favourable circumstances. Kosten-Syre, Slough 1997 continued 14 ♗xf3 e6 15 ♗e2 and now Kosten suggests 15 0-0 ♘ge7 16 ♕d3 ♘a7 17 e4 dxe4 18 ♘xe4 ♕xd4 19 ♕b1 0-0 20 ♗b2 ♕b6 21 ♘f6+ as an interesting pawn sacrifice.

b) 13 ♗f4 and then:

b1) According to Krasenkow, Black can force a draw by 13...♗xf3 14 ♗xf3 ♘xd4 15 ♗xb8 ♘xb3 16 ♕xb3 ♕xb8 17 ♗xd5 ♗xc3+ 18 ♕xc3 ♘f6 19 ♗c6+ ♔f8 20 ♕c5 ♔g7, as now 21 ♕xe7? ♖c8 22 ♗f3 ♖c1+ 23 ♔d2 ♖c7 24 ♕e3 ♖c4 is risky for White.

But what about 21 0-0 ♖c8 22 ♖a1, which gives White an annoying edge? The threat is ♖a1-a6 and I don't see a way for Black to save his b-pawn.

b2) 13...♖b6 14 e3 ♗xf3 15 ♗xf3 e6 with approximate equality. Now White hung a piece with 16 ♗e2?? (16 h4) 16...g5 in Van Wely-Lautier, Monaco (rapid) 1997, although White still won the game!

12 ♗f4 ♖b6 13 e4

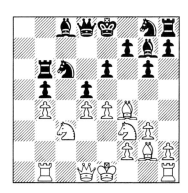

The earlier theory was 13 h4 ♘ge7 14 h5 ♘f5 15 e3 f6 16 hxg6 hxg6 17 ♖xh8+ ♗xh8 18 g4 ♘fe7 19 g5 e5 20 gxf6 exf4 21 fxe7 ♕d6 22 exf4 and a draw was agreed in this unclear position in Ribli-Ftacnik, Thessaloniki Olympiad 1988.

13...♘f6

If 13...dxe4 14 ♘xe4 White gets dangerous attacking chances after 14...♘xd4 15 ♖c1! (or 15 ♘xd4 ♗xd4 16 0-0 e5 17 ♖e1) 15...♘xf3+ 16 ♕xf3 e5 17 ♕c3. 13...♘ge7!? is also possible.

14 e5 ♘e4

Vaiser suggests 14...♘d7, keeping the centre closed. Opening up the position leads to complications which favour White.

15 ♘xe4 dxe4 16 ♘d2 0-0

16...♘xd4 17 ♘xe4 ♗b7 18 ♗g5 ♘c2+

19 ♕xc2 ♗xe4 20 ♖d1! wins for White.

17 ♗e3

If 17 ♘xe4 ♕xd4 18 ♗e3 ♕xd1+ 19 ♖xd1 ♖b8 20 f4 and White is much better.

17...f5

After 17...♘xd4? 18 ♘b3 ♗xe5 19 ♗xd4 ♖d6 20 ♗xe5 ♖xd1+ 21 ♖xd1 White has too many pieces for the queen.

18 exf6 ♗xf6 19 ♘xe4

If 19 d5 exd5 20 ♗xb6 ♕xb6 21 ♕b3 ♘e7 then Black is okay, since if 22 ♘xe4? ♕e6.

19...♗xd4 20 0-0 e5

White is only slightly better after 20...♗xe3 21 fxe3 ♖xf1+ 22 ♕xf1 ♕e7.

21 ♗g5

This lets White's advantage slip. Instead White is on top after 21 ♗h6, e.g. 21...♖e8 (21...♖f7 22 ♘g5; or 21...♖f5 22 ♕b3+ ♔h8 23 g4 winning material) 22 ♗g5 ♘e7 23 ♘f6+

21...♘e7

Now Black has f6 well defended.

22 ♖c1 ♗b7 23 ♕c2 ♖f7 24 ♕d2 ♕a8 25 ♕d3 ♘d5 26 ♕b3 ♘c3! 27 ♖xc3 ♗xc3 28 ♘f6+ ♖bxf6 29 ♗xb7 ♕xb7 30 ♗xf6 ♕f3 31 ♕e6 ♕xf6 ½-½

The position is equal after 32 ♕c8+ ♔g7 33 ♕xc3.

Game 41
Mednis-Ernst
Gausdal 1990

---

1 c4 c5 2 g3 ♘c6 3 ♗g2 g6 4 ♘c3 ♗g7 5 e3 e6 6 ♘ge2

In many ways, White's structure is a model of co-ordination. The only downside is that Black can simply copy the same moves!

6...♘ge7

This is notorious as a drawing variation, with many 'grandmaster' games not going beyond the 10th or 15th move. However, if you are going to play this line, there are a few subtleties that you need to be aware of.

There is little comfort in playing a drawing line, only to lose a long and painful ending!

7 d4

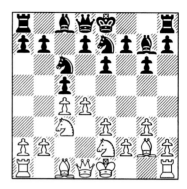

7 ♘f4 is covered in the next game. Castling before playing d2-d4 gives Black an additional option, which secures easy equality: 7 0-0 0-0 8 d4 cxd4 9 ♘xd4 d5 10 cxd5 ♘xd5 11 ♘xd5 ♘xd4 and a draw was agreed in Rasmussen-Adorjan, Esbjerg 1988 (and many similar games). If now 12 ♘c3 ♘c6 13 ♕xd8 Black can recapture with the rook – 13...♖xd8.

7...cxd4 8 ♘xd4

8 exd4 d5 leads to similar (and equal) play.

8...♘xd4

Alternatively:

a) If Black now tries the recipe outlined in the note to White's 7th move, White has 8...d5 9 cxd5 ♘xd5 10 ♘xd5 ♘xd4 11 ♘c3!, when after 11...♘c6 12 ♕xd8+ ♘xd8 13 ♗d2 0-0 14 ♖c1 White can play for a tiny edge: 14...♗d7 15 0-0 ♗c6 16 ♖c2 ♗xg2 17 ♔xg2 ♘c6 18 ♘e4 ♖fd8 19 ♗c3 ♖ac8 20 ♗xg7 ♔xg7 21 ♖fc1 ♖b8 22 a3 and White now has a discernible plus, Andersson-Miles, Tilburg 1981. In fact, White eventually won this game.

b) A recent attempt to inject some life into this variation is 8...0-0 9 0-0 ♕b6!? 10 ♘de2 ♕c5 11 b3 d5 12 ♗b2 (12 ♘a4 is suggested by Aseev) 12...dxc4 13 ♘e4 ♕b4 14 ♗xg7 ♔xg7 15 bxc4 ♕xc4 16 ♘d6 ♕c5

17 ♕d2 with compensation for the pawn, Aseev-Dvoirys, Samara 2000.

9 exd4 d5 10 cxd5 ♘xd5 11 0-0 0-0 12 ♕b3

Or 12 ♘xd5 exd5 13 ♕b3 ♗e6 14 ♕xb7 ♗xd4 15 ♗f4 ♕b6 16 ♗xd5 ♗xd5 17 ♕xd5 ♖fd8 18 ♕f3 ♗xb2 19 ♖ab1 ♕f6 20 ♔g2 ♗e5 with complete equality, Gufeld-Gipslis, Tallinn 1969.

12...♘e7

12...♗xd4 13 ♗h6 ♗g7 14 ♗xg7 ♔xg7 15 ♖fd1 ♕b6 16 ♘xd5 ♕xb3 17 axb3 exd5 18 ♖xd5 a6 19 b4 was played in Smyslov-Petrosian, Moscow 1974 and is quoted as slightly better for White in ECO and equal in NCO. White may have a microscopic advantage, but in those days Petrosian was not the opponent you could grind down in such an ending – a draw was agreed a few moves later.

13 ♖d1 ♘c6

13...♘f5!? 14 d5 (14 ♗e3 ♘xe3 {14...♘xd4 transposes to the main game} 15 fxe3 is solid) 14...♘d4 15 ♕c4 e5 16 ♗e3 ♗g4 with some initiative for Black, Naumann-Joachim, Germany 1996.

14 ♗e3 ♘xd4 15 ♗xd4 ♗xd4 16 ♘e2 e5 17 ♘xd4 exd4 18 ♕c4 ♗e6 19 ♕xd4 ♕xd4 20 ♖xd4 ♖fd8 21 ♗xb7

21 ♖ad1 ♖xd4 22 ♖xd4 ♖c8 led to an equally peaceful outcome in Pfleger-Matanovic, Hamburg 1965.

21...♖xd4 22 ♗xa8 ½-½

Game 42
Spraggett-Ivanisevic
Istanbul Olympiad 2000

---

1 c4 c5 2 g3 g6 3 ♗g2 ♗g7 4 ♘c3 ♘c6 5 e3 e6 6 ♘ge2 ♘ge7 7 ♘f4

This move not only defers the immediate d2-d4, but also prevents Black from breaking with ...d7-d5, and sets up an intricate manoeuvring game. If White is playing for a win and wants to avoid the well-trodden paths of the previous game, this is a good

choice – ideal against opponents who were expecting a 15-move draw! In fact White has a healthy plus score with this (albeit rare) move at GM level. Whether White gets a theoretical small advantage or just gets to play 'his' game is debatable. The player with a better understanding of the ideas will tend to score well.

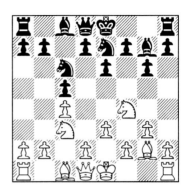

7...♘e5

Alternatively 7...0-0 8 0-0 (White can also delay castling with 8 h4, e.g. 8...h6 {8...h5!?} 9 a3 d6 10 ♖b1 a5 11 b3 ♖b8 12 ♗b2 b6 13 d3 ♗b7 14 g4 e5 15 ♘fe2 ♗c8 16 ♘g3 ♗e6 17 ♘d5 ♕d7 18 g5 and White is better, Mohr-Tratar, Ljubljana 1995). Since the move order is fairly interchangeable over the next few moves, I have summarised the material on the basis of the short-term development scheme which either side adopts.

a) 8...d6 and now both sides go for queenside expansion: 9 a3 a6 10 ♖b1 ♖b8 11 b4 cxb4 12 axb4 b5 13 cxb5 axb5 14 ♕e2 e5 (14...♕b6) 15 ♘fd5 ♘xd5 16 ♘xd5 ♘e7 17 ♗b2 ♗b7 18 ♕d3 ♘xd5 19 ♗xd5 ♕d7 20 ♖fc1 ♖fe8 21 ♕b3 (Ermenkov-Radulov, Bulgarian Championship, 1988), when White has a slight advantage.

b) 8...a6 and now White plays b2-b3, ♗c1-b2, d2-d3 and allows ...b7-b5 rather than try and prevent it. This looks like his best plan.

b1) 9 ♖b1 b5 10 b3 ♖b8 11 ♗b2 d6 12 d3 ♕c7 13 ♕e2 ♖d8 14 ♗a1 (pre-empting

Black's queenside attack with ...♕c7-a5. White is slightly better according to Istratescu) 14...♕a5 15 ♘e4 e5 16 ♘d5 ♘xd5 17 cxd5 ♘e7 18 ♘c3 (18 f4!?) 18...♘f5 19 ♖be1 ♖b7 20 ♕c2 ♖c7 21 ♘e4 ♗b7 22 ♘d2 ♖e8 23 ♖e2 ♖ce7 24 ♖fe1 ♕d8 25 ♘f1 ♕a8 26 ♕d1 ♘h6?! (26...h5 is better) 27 e4 when White is clearly better, Istratescu-Milu, Bucharest 1998.

b2) 9 b3

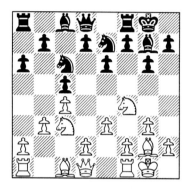

and now:

b21) Black goes for straightforward queenside expansion: 9...b5 10 ♗b2 ♖b8 11 d3 d6 12 ♕e2 (Perhaps 12 ♕d2 to more directly support d3-d4, and if 12...b4 13 ♘ce2) and here Black has tried:

b211) The immediate 12...b4 was played in Miles-Akesson, FIDE World Championship, Las Vegas 1999, which continued 13 ♘b1 (13 ♘e4 is answered by 13...e5 14 ♘d5 ♘xd5 15 cxd5 ♘e7 when White does not have 16 d4) 13...♗xb2 14 ♕xb2 e5 15 ♘e2 ♗f5 16 ♕c2 ♖c8 17 ♖e1 ♗h3 18 ♗h1 g5 19 ♘d2 f5 20 f4 and the h3-bishop is uncomfortably placed. White has a slight advantage.

b212) 12...♕c7 13 ♖fd1 b4 14 ♘e4 and it is not clear what Black's queenside expansion has achieved. If Black's b-pawn was back on b6, he would have the option of ...d6-d5 (after say ...♘c6-e5), which is not feasible now due to the weakness of the c5-pawn. Meanwhile, White has used the extra

time to prepare for the d3-d4 thrust. 14...e5 15 ♘d5 ♘xd5 16 cxd5 ♘e7 17 d4 cxd4 18 exd4 ♘xd5 19 ♖ac1 and White has an edge, Spraggett-Rogulj, Zagreb Vukovar 1993.

b22) Black plays ...b7-b5 and ...♕d8-b6 to discourage a later d3-d4: 9...d6 10 ♗b2 b5 11 d3 ♗b7 12 ♕d2 (12 ♕e2) 12...♕b6 13 ♘e4 e5 14 ♘e2 (14 ♘d5 ♘xd5 15 cxd5 ♘e7 16 ♘c3 b4 17 ♘a4 ♕c7 and now 18 e4 f5, or 18 d4 exd4 19 exd4 ♗xd5 20 dxc5 ♗xb2 21 cxd6 ♕xd6 22 ♘xb2 is equal) 14...♖ad8 15 ♘4c3 f5 16 f4 b4 17 ♘a4 ♕a7 18 ♖ac1 ♘a5 19 d4 cxd4 20 exd4 ♘ac6 21 ♔h1 ♘xd4 22 ♘xd4 exd4 23 ♖fe1 ♖fe8 24 ♖e6 ♗e4 25 ♖e1 d5 26 c5 ♖c8 27 ♗xd4 ½-½ Gulko-Psakhis, Sochi 1985.

c) 8...b6 looks to be a good approach for Black – adopting the same set-up that has worked for White – (...b6, ...♗b7, ...d6 and ...♕d7) and here:

c1) Copying the queenside fianchetto with 9 b3 ♗b7 10 ♗b2 d6 did not work out well for White after 11 h4 h6 12 ♕e2 ♕d7 13 ♖ad1 ♖ad8 14 d3 ♖fe8 15 ♖d2 d5! 16 cxd5 exd5 17 ♘cxd5 ♘xd5 18 ♗xd5 ♗xb2 19 ♖xb2 ♘d4 with an edge for Black, Turner-Andersson, European Championship (rapid), Athens 1997.

c2) 9 a3 ♗b7 10 d3 (If White tries 10 b4 then 10...d6 11 ♗b2 ♕d7 12 bxc5 (12 ♕b3!?) 12...dxc5 13 ♖a2 ♖ad8 14 d3 ♘e5 is good for Black) 10...d6 11 ♗d2 (an insipid continuation) 11...♕d7 12 ♖b1 ♘e5 13 e4 ♘7c6 14 ♗e3 (Polugaevsky suggests 14 ♘ce2 followed by 15 ♗c3 with equality) 14...♘d4 and Black is slightly better, Karlsson-Polugaevsky, Haninge 1988.

8 d3 ♘f5 9 ♕c2 h5 10 h3 ♖b8 11 b3 b5 12 ♗b2 bxc4

Black clarifies the pawn structure. He can now aim for a possible ...d7-d5 break, or an eventual minority attack with ...a7-a5-a4, while White gets some pressure on the d-file and slightly freer piece play.

13 dxc4 ♗a6 14 ♖d1 d6 15 0-0 ♕e7 16 ♘e4 ♗b7 17 h4 0-0

This game contains some good examples of 'prophylactic thinking' (for readers unfamiliar with this concept, I would recommend the book *Positional Play* by Dvoretsky and Yusupov). Black is almost ready (after say ...♖f8-d8 and ...♖b8-c8) to gets his pawns rolling with ...d6-d5. So White relocates his queen 'Reti-style' to a1 to press along the long diagonal.

18 ♕c1 ♖fd8 19 ♕a1 ♘g4 20 ♗xg7 ♘xg7 21 ♕c3

Preventing the immediate ...a7-a5, and setting up a possible later f2-f3 (after moving the e4-knight).

21...♘f5 22 ♖fe1 ♗a8 23 ♖e2 ♖b6 24 ♖ed2 ♖db8 25 ♕d3 a5 26 ♘c3 ♗xg2 27 ♘xg2 ♖b4 28 ♕e2 ♘e5 29 ♘e1 ♕b7 30 e4

After a protracted manoeuvring phase, White makes an interesting exchange sacrifice.

30...♘d4 31 ♖xd4 cxd4 32 ♖xd4 ♕e7 33 ♘c2 ♖4b6 34 ♖d1 ♔g7 35 ♘d4

White has good compensation for the material, as Black's rooks have little scope. Now, however, in a bid for activity, Black lashes out in disastrous fashion. This happens so often in the run-up to the time-control!

35...g5?? 36 ♘d5! ♕d8 37 ♘xb6 ♖xb6 38 c5 ♖b4 39 f4

White concludes the game energetically.

39...gxf4 40 gxf4 ♘g4 41 ♘c6 ♕c7 42 ♖xd6 e5 43 ♕d3 ♔h7 44 ♕d5 ♖b7 45 ♘xe5 ♘e3 46 ♕d4 1-0

Game 43
Istratescu-Fominyh
Elista Olympiad 1998

---

1 c4 c5 2 ♘c3 ♘c6 3 g3 g6 4 ♗g2 ♗g7 5 e3 e5

a) 5...♗xc3!? is played rather rarely, but has actually scored well for Black. It certainly creates opportunities for original play by both sides, and some weird and wonder-

ful schemes of development have been seen. Both recaptures have been tried:

a1) 6 dxc3 d6 7 e4 ♕d7 and now:

a11) 8 ♘f3 ♘f6 9 ♕e2 ♕c7 10 h3 h6 11 ♘d2 b6 12 ♘f1 ♗b7 13 ♘e3 e6 14 ♘g4 (White's direct approach looks promising) 14...♘g8 15 ♗f4 0-0-0 16 0-0-0 f6 17 h4 ♖h7 18 ♗h3 ♔b8 19 f3 ♗c8 20 h5 g5 21 ♗d2 ♕b7 22 ♘e3 ♕a6 23 ♔b1 ♖e7 24 ♕f1 ♖b7 25 ♗c1 ♕a5 26 ♖h2 a6 27 ♖hd2 ♔c7 28 f4, Kveinys-S.Hansen, Hamburg, with a continuing initiative for White.

a12) 8 ♘e2 b6 9 ♘f4 ♗b7 10 ♕e2 e6 11 ♘d3 h6 12 ♗d2 ♘ge7 13 0-0-0 0-0-0 14 ♖he1 ♕c7 15 h4 ♗a6 16 b3 b5 17 cxb5 ♗xb5 18 ♔b2 ♕b6 and Black is a bit better, Benko-Tarjan, Lone Pine 1979.

a2) 6 bxc3

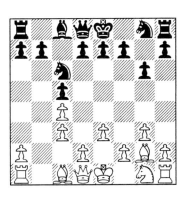

when a couple of moves have been tried:

a21) 6...b6 7 h4 ♘f6 8 e4 ♗b7 9 ♘e2 d6 10 d3 ♕d7 11 ♗g5 ♘g4 12 d4 ♘a5 13 h5 f6 14 ♗c1 g5 15 f3 ♘h6 16 ♗h3 g4 17 ♗xh6 gxh3 18 d5 ♘xc4 19 ♘f4 ♕b5 (Groszpeter-Schlosser, Lippstadt 1991) and Black is material to the good, though the position is very messy.

a22) 6...f5 7 ♘e2 b6 8 h4 ♘f6 9 h5 ♔f7 10 d3 ♗b7 11 ♘g1 ♕c7 12 ♘f3 ♖ag8 13 e4 fxe4 14 ♘g5+ ♔e8 15 ♘xe4 ♘xe4 16 ♗xe4 ♘e5 17 ♕e2 ♗xe4 18 ♕xe4 ♕c6, Kosten-Miles, British Championship 1997, and Black has neutralised White's pressure.

b) 5...♘h6 is another way of avoiding the

main lines, though play is fairly similar in character to Game 42. Black routes his knight to f5, where it is ready for active duty and prevents an early d2-d4. A couple of examples: 6 ♘ge2 ♘f5 7 0-0 0-0 8 b3 d6 9 ♗b2 ♖b8 10 d3 a6 11 ♕d2 ♗d7 and then:

b1) 12 ♘e4 ♗xb2 13 ♕xb2 b5 14 ♖fd1 bxc4 15 dxc4 ♘e5 16 ♘xc5 ♘xc4 17 ♕c1 ♘e5 18 ♘xd7 ♘xd7 19 ♘d4 ♘xd4 20 ♖xd4 a5 with equality, Knott-Emms, British League 2000.

b2) 12 ♘d5 b5 13 ♗xg7 ♘xg7 14 ♖ad1 bxc4 15 dxc4 ♘b4 16 ♘dc3 ♗c6 17 ♗xc6 ♘xc6 18 ♘f4 ♕d7 19 ♕e2 ♕b7 20 ♘d3 f5 21 f4 ♘e8 22 ♘f2 ♘f6 23 h3 ♖f7 24 g4, Spraggett-Leko, Cienfuegos 1997, with perhaps a small edge for White.

6 ♘ge2 d6 7 0-0 ♘ge7 8 a3

8 b3 0-0 9 ♗b2 is also possible. This is a good set-up for Black when played in this position with colours reversed, but less good for White as an attempt to gain the advantage, e.g. 9...♗e6 10 ♘d5 ♕d7 11 ♘ec3 ♗h3 12 ♕f3 ♗xg2 13 ♕xg2 ♖ab8 14 ♖ad1 ♘xd5 15 ♘xd5 b5 ½-½ Davies-Maksimenko, Vrnjacka Banja 1991.

8...0-0 9 d3 ♖b8 10 ♖b1 a5

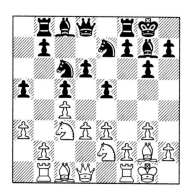

11 ♗d2

11 ♕b3 ♗e6 12 ♘d5 ♘a7 13 ♘xe7+ ♕xe7 14 ♕b6 ♘c6 15 ♗d2 e4 16 ♗xe4 ♗xc4 17 ♘f4 g5 18 ♘d5 ♕e6 19 ♘c7 ♕e7 20 ♗xa5 (rejecting the repetition of moves with 20 ♘d5) 20...f5 21 ♘d5 ♕f7 22 dxc4

fxe4 23 ♗c3 ♗xc3 24 bxc3 ♕h5 with play for the pawn, Gretarsson-Salmensuu, Reykjavik 2000.

11...♗f5

11...♗e6 is probably somewhat better. White needs to prevent ...d6-d5:

a) 12 e4 h6 13 ♘b5 f5 14 b3 ♔h7 15 f4 ♕d7 16 ♘ec3 exf4 17 gxf4 ♘d4 18 ♘xd4 ♗xd4+ 19 ♔h1 ♘c6 20 ♘b5 ♗f6 21 a4 ½-½ Spassky-Degerman, Malmo 1998.

b) 12 ♘d5 b5 13 cxb5 ♖xb5 14 ♘ec3 (14 ♘xe7+ ♘xe7 15 b4 is equal) 14...♖b8 15 ♕a4 ♗d7 16 ♕c2 ♗e6 17 ♖fc1 ♕c8 18 ♕a4 and White has a slight edge, Hjartarson-Gonzalez, Linares 1995.

12 ♕c2 ♘a7

12...♕d7 13 ♘d5 b6 14 ♘ec3 ♘xd5 15 cxd5 ♘e7 16 e4 ♗h3 17 b4 ♗xg2 18 ♔xg2 axb4 19 axb4 left White better in Radulov-Martin, Torremolinos 1974.

13 b4 axb4 14 axb4 b5 15 e4 ♗g4

Provoking h2-h3, which slightly weakens White's pawn structure.

16 h3 ♗d7 17 bxc5 dxc5 18 ♗e3 ♕c7 19 ♘d5 ♘xd5 20 cxd5 ♖fc8 21 ♖fc1 ♗f8 22 f4

White has pressure on both sides of the board.

22...b4!

Black needs to get his queenside moving, even at the expense of the exchange: 22...f6 23 d4 exd4 24 ♗xd4 is very good for White.

23 fxe5 ♕xe5 24 ♗f4 ♕e8 25 ♗xb8 ♖xb8 26 d4

White also needs to move quickly, as Black has threats of ...♘a7-b5, for example. White decides to trade in his queen to clarify the situation.

26...♖c8 27 dxc5 ♗xc5+ 28 ♕xc5 ♖xc5 29 ♖xc5

This ending should be quite good for White as his pieces are active and Black's b-pawn is weak.

29...♕b8 30 ♔h2 h5

This weakens the g5-square rather needlessly. White later posts a knight there to pressurise f7.

31 h4 ♕d6 32 ♖c2 ♘b5 33 e5 ♕xe5 34 ♖xb4 ♗f5 35 ♖cb2 ♘d6 36 ♘d4

With ideas of both ♘d4-b5 and ♖b2-e2.

36...♗d3 37 ♘f3 ♕e7

Of course not 37...♕xd5?? 38 ♖d4 winning either the bishop or the knight.

38 ♖d2 ♗f5 39 ♘g5 ♔g7 40 ♖a4 ♕e3 41 ♖da2 ♘b5 42 ♖b2 ♗d3 43 ♖f4 ♘d6 44 ♖b3 ♕e2 45 ♖b6?

Letting the advantage slip. Istratescu gives 45 ♖c3 ♗f5 46 ♖c7, followed by ♖a4-a7 with a big plus for White.

45...♕e5 46 ♖c6 ♘f5

Now White's rooks cannot get to the seventh rank easily, and White is also tied to the defence of his kingside.

47 ♖c8 ♘h6 48 ♖c1 ♗f5 49 ♖cf1 ½-½

Game 44
M.Gurevich-Filippov
Bugojno 1999

---

1 c4 c5 2 ♘c3 ♘c6 3 g3 g6 4 ♗g2 ♗g7 5 a3

Or 5 e4 e6 6 a3, transposing to the game.

5...e6 6 e4

A favourite of players who play the Botvinnik against 'everything'.

6...♘ge7

In Nogueiras-Garcia Martinez, Cuban Championship 2000, Black tried to accelerate his queenside play by delaying ...♘ge7: 6...a6 7 ♘ge2 ♖b8 8 ♖b1 b5 9 cxb5 axb5 10 b4 cxb4 11 axb4 e5?! (11...♘ge7) and after 12 d4 exd4 (12...♘xd4 13 ♘xd4 exd4 14 ♘d5 ♘f6 15 ♕xd4 0-0 16 ♗b2 is strong for White) 13 ♘d5 h6 14 ♗b2 ♘ge7 15 ♘xd4 0-0 16 ♘xc6 dxc6 17 ♘f6+ ♔h8 18 ♕c1! ♘g8 19 ♘xg8 ♔xg8 20 ♗xg7 ♔xg7 21 0-0 ♕f6 22 ♕c5! ♗e6 23 e5 ♕f5 24 ♖bd1 White has a big advantage.

7 ♘ge2 0-0

Black has two main plans in this position, one being queenside expansion, and the other starting 7...b6 8 ♖b1 ♗b7 9 b4 d6 10

d3 ♕d7 11 0-0 0-0 which reaches a standard position in this line. Black's development scheme of ...b6, ...♗b7, ...d6 and ...♕d7 has proved extremely reliable in a large number of games. Some examples:

a) 12 h4 h6 13 ♗d2 ♖ad8 14 b5 ♘e5 (thanks to the insertion of h2-h4 the g4-square is available after f2-f4, so Black does not need to play ...♘d4) 15 ♘f4 f5 16 exf5 ♘xf5 17 ♘e4 d5 18 cxd5 exd5 is good for Black, Aronian-Stohl, Portoroz 1999.

b)12 ♗e3 ♘d4 (see the rule of thumb described in the introduction to this chapter) 13 f4 (13 ♕d2 is also equal after 13...♖fd8 or 13...♘ec6) 13...f5 14 ♗f2 ♖ae8 15 ♘xd4 cxd4 16 ♘e2 e5 and Black has equalised (at least), Williams-Leko, Canaries 1995.

c)12 ♕a4 is not an inspiring attempt to gain a plus, e.g. 12...♖fd8 13 ♖d1 ♘d4 14 ♕xd7 ♘xe2+ 15 ♘xe2 ♖xd7 16 ♗e3 ♖c8 17 f4 f5 18 exf5 gxf5 19 ♗xb7 and a draw was agreed in Rogers-Novikov, Budapest 1991.

d) 12 b5 (putting the question immediately to the c6-knight enables White to play ♘e2xd4 in response to ...♘c6-d4; White's dark-squared bishop looks better placed on d2 than on f2 – as in Williams-Leko in 'b' above, for example) 12...♘d4 13 ♘xd4 cxd4 14 ♘e2 f5 15 f3 e5 16 ♗h3 ♔h8 17 ♗d2 ♕c7 18 ♘c1 a5 19 bxa6 ♖xa6 20 ♕b3 ♖fa8 21 ♖a1 ♗c8 22 ♗g2 fxe4 23 fxe4, Miezis-Malakhov, Porto San Giorgio 2000, with a tough manoeuvring battle in prospect, where chances are roughly balanced.

8 d3 a6 9 ♗e3

A new approach.

A key theme for Black, when playing the ...a6 set-up is to break early with ...b7-b5 without waiting for ...♖b8. Two examples:

a) 9 ♖b1 d6 10 0-0 transposes to Makarychev-Kasparov, Tbilisi 1978, which continued: 10...b5 11 cxb5 axb5 12 b4 cxb4 13 axb4 e5 14 ♗g5 ♕b6 15 ♘d5 ♘xd5 16 exd5 ♘d4 17 ♘xd4 ♕xd4 with equality.

b) 9 0-0 b5 transposes to Rogers-Christiansen, San Francisco 1991: 10 cxb5 axb5 and now, according to Christiansen, White should try 11 ♗e3 (the game went 11 ♘xb5 ♗a6 12 ♘bc3 ♘e5 13 ♘f4 ♕c7 14 h4 ♖fb8 when Black had good pressure) 11...d6 12 ♘xb5 ♗xb2 13 ♖b1 ♗g7 14 d4 with a balanced position.

9...d6

Black opts out of the 'automatic' 9...♘d4 after which Gurevich gives 10 b4 cxb4 (10...♘xe2 11 ♘xe2 ♗xa1 12 ♕xa1, but 10...d6 seems okay?) 11 ♗xd4 ♗xd4 12 ♘xd4 bxc3 13 ♕b3 ♕a5 14 0-0 followed by ♖f1-c1, with a promising position for White.

10 ♖b1

This game has some interesting 'exceptions that prove the rule'. If White plays the natural 10 d4 then 10...cxd4 11 ♘xd4 ♘xd4 12 ♗xd4 ♗xd4 13 ♕xd4 ♘c6 with counterplay (Gurevich). White's c-pawn is a touch weak, and if 14 ♕d1 ♕f6 followed by ...♘c6-d4 and ...♗c8-d7.

10...b5!?

A thematic Benko-like sacrifice as we saw in the notes to White's 9th move.

11 cxb5 axb5 12 b4!?

An unusual combination of moves means that the a3-pawn is en-prise. 12 ♘xb5 ♗a6 13 ♘bc3 ♘e5 14 ♘c1 ♕a5 15 0-0 ♖fb8 gives Black the typical compensation.

12...♘d4!?

12...♖xa3 13 ♘xb5 ♖a2 14 ♘ec3 is a bit better for White according to Gurevich, but 12...cxb4 13 axb4 ♖b8 14 d4 d5 is unclear.

13 e5! ♖xa3?!

Here Black should choose 13...♘xe2 14 ♕xe2 ♗xe5 15 ♘xb5 ♗a6 and if 16 bxc5 ♗xb5 17 ♖xb5 ♗c3+.

14 ♗xd4 cxd4 15 ♘xb5 ♖a2!? 16 ♕b3 ♖xe2+ 17 ♔xe2 dxe5 18 ♖hc1 ♘d5 19 ♔f1

White has made his king safe, so he is well on top.

19...♗d7

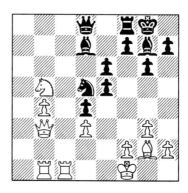

20 ♘d6?!

20 ♖c5 ♗xb5 21 ♗xd5 ♗xd3+ 22 ♕xd3 exd5 23 ♕b3 e4 24 ♕xd5 keeps White's advantage.

20...♘c3?!

Tempting, but Black should have attacked the b4-pawn with 20...♕e7! 21 ♘c4 ♖b8, which would have given White some problems.

21 ♖a1 ♕e7 22 ♘e4 ♗b5 23 ♘xc3 dxc3 24 ♖xc3 e4 25 ♗xe4

White can return the exchange and still keep an edge due to the passed b-pawn.

25...f5?!

25...♕d7 26 ♖ac1 ♗xc3 27 ♖xc3 ♖d8 28 ♔g1 ♕d4 limits Black's disadvantage.

26 ♗f3! f4 27 g4 ♕d7

27...♗xd3+ 28 ♖xd3 ♗xa1 29 b5 and the b-pawn gives White a winning position.

28 ♔g2!?

Rather than try and defend the extra pawn, say by ♖a1-d1, White switches to attack.

28...♗xc3 29 ♕xc3 ♗xd3 30 ♕e5 ♕c4 31 ♖e1 ♖e8

31...♗c6 32 ♕xe6+ ♕xe6 33 ♖xe6 ♗xf3+ 34 ♔xf3 is a winning rook ending.

32 ♕d6! ♔g7 33 g5 h6 34 h4 ♔h7 35 ♗e4 f3+ 36 ♔g3 ♕c3 37 ♖e3 ♕c1

37...♕a1 38 ♗xg6+ ♔xg6 39 ♖xe6+ ♖xe6 40 ♕xe6+ ♔g7 41 gxh6+ ♔h7 (41...♔h8 42 ♕c8+ ♔h7 43 ♕b7+) 42 ♕f5+ ♔xh6 43

♕xb5 wins.

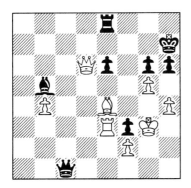

38 ♗xg6+!

White calculates that he can clean up the kingside pawns, and eventually win the b5-bishop by checking the black king.

38...♔xg6 39 ♖xe6+ ♖xe6 40 ♕xe6+ ♔g7 41 ♕xh6+ ♔g8

Or 41...♔f7 42 g6+.

42 ♕g6+ ♔h8

If 42...♔f8 43 ♕f5+.

43 ♕f6+ ♔g8 44 ♕e6+ ♔g7 45 ♕e5+ ♔g6 46 ♕xb5 ♕g1+ 47 ♔xf3 ♕h1+ 48 ♔e3 ♕c1+ 49 ♔e4 ♕h1+ 50 ♔e5 ♕e1+ 51 ♔d6 1-0

Game 45
Aleksandrov-Krasenkow
New York 1997

---

1 c4 c5 2 ♘c3 ♘c6 3 g3 g6 4 ♗g2 ♗g7 5 d3 e6 6 e4 ♘ge7 7 h4

In this game we examine attempts by White to create kingside play with an early h2-h4.

Also possible is 7 ♘ge2 0-0 (Black can try 7...b6, delaying castling until White declares his hand) and now:

a) 8 a3 d6 9 ♖b1 b6 10 h4 ♗b7 11 h5 ♘d4 12 ♘f4 ♘ec6 13 hxg6 fxg6 14 ♗e3 ♕f6 15 ♘h3 ♘e5 16 f4 ♘f7 17 0-0 ♕e7 18 b4 ♖ab8 19 ♘e2 ♗a8 20 ♘xd4 cxd4 21 ♗d2 ♖fe8 22 ♖f2 ♗c6 23 b5 ♗d7 24 ♗b4 ♗c8 25 e5 ♕c7 26 ♘g5 ♗f8 27 ♗c6 ♗d7

28 ♗e4 ♘xg5 29 fxg5 dxe5 30 ♕f3 winning, Miezis-Mikanovic, North Bay 1999.

b) 8 h4 h6 9 h5 g5 10 f4 g4 11 ♗e3 ♘d4 12 ♗f2 (a typical manoeuvre to enable White to play ♘e2xd4) 12...♘ec6 13 ♘xd4 ♘xd4 14 ♗xd4. In this position White doesn't mind exchanging the bishop, as with both Black knights off, he can combine kingside pressure with the threat of dropping his own knight into d6. 14...cxd4 15 ♘b5 ♕b6 16 e5 f6 17 0-0 fxe5 18 ♕xg4 e4 (18...a6 19 fxe5) 19 f5 with a strong attack, Jirovsky-Shulman, Pardubice 1999. The game continued 19...exf5 20 ♖xf5 ♖e8 21 ♕f4 d5 22 ♖xd5 exd3 23 ♖d6 ♕c5 24 ♗d5+ ♔h7 25 ♕f7 and White was winning.

7...h6 8 ♗e3 ♘d4 9 ♘ge2 ♘ec6 10 a3

Perhaps White should try 10 h5 g5 11 f4, though this is obviously less effective when Black has not castled kingside: 11...gxf4 12 gxf4 followed by ♗e3-f2.

10...d6 11 ♖b1 a5 12 ♘f4?!

It is not clear what White's set-up has achieved.

12...♖b8 13 0-0 0-0 14 a4 ♘b4 15 ♘b5 b6 16 ♕d2 ♔h7

Black is already slightly better.

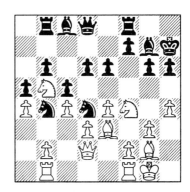

White should normally avoid capturing on d4 with the bishop as he now has potential dark square weaknesses, on e3 and c5 for example. The way Krasenkow exploits this is instructive.

17...cxd4 18 ♘e2 e5 19 f4 h5 20 ♖f2

♗h6 21 ♖bf1 ♗g4

Black has a tangible advantage, with pressure against White's centre pawns.

22 ♗f3 ♗xf3 23 ♖xf3 f5 24 ♘c1 ♖b7 25 ♕g2 ♖bf7 26 ♘b3 ♕e7

Threatening ...e5xf4, winning the e-pawn.

27 ♖e1 fxe4 28 ♖xe4 ♕d7 29 ♘d2 exf4?

Black begins to lose the thread of the game. Krasenkow gives 29...♘c6 30 fxe5 ♘xe5 31 ♖xf7+ ♖xf7 32 ♘xd4 ♘xd3 as winning for Black.

30 ♘xd4 d5?

30...fxg3 31 ♘e6 ♖e8 32 ♘g5+ ♗xg5 33 hxg5 ♖ef8 and Black is still better.

31 cxd5 ♕xd5 32 ♘e6 ♖c8 33 ♘xf4 ♗xf4 34 ♖fxf4 ♖c1+ 35 ♘f1 ♘xd3 36 ♖xf7+ ♕xf7 37 ♕e2 ♘c5 38 ♖f4 ♕d7 39 g4?

A time trouble blunder. White should just play 39 ♕f2.

39...♘d3!

White is not able to keep the g4-pawn sufficiently defended.

40 ♖e4 ♖e1 41 ♕g2 ♖xe4 42 ♕xe4 ♘c5 43 ♕e5

The a4-pawn drops off after 43 ♕c4 ♕xg4+ 44 ♕xg4 hxg4.

43...♕xg4+ 44 ♘g3 ♕xh4 45 ♕c7+ ♔h6 46 ♘f5+

Or 46 ♕e5 ♕d8.

46...gxf5 47 ♕xb6+ ♔g5 48 ♕xc5 ♕e1+ 49 ♔g2 h4 50 ♕a7 ♕e4+ 51 ♔f2

♕c2+ 52 ♔e3 f4+ 53 ♔f3 ♕d3+ 54 ♔f2 ♕e3+ 55 ♕xe3 fxe3+ 56 ♔xe3 ♔g4 57 ♔f2 h3 0-1

58 ♔g1 ♔g3 59 b3 h2+ 60 ♔h1 and White is forced to give up his b-pawn, when Black will queen first – with mate.

Game 46
S.Williams-Emms
British Championship 2000

---

1 c4 c5 2 ♘c3 g6 3 g3 ♗g7 4 ♗g2 ♘c6 5 d3

If the move order permits it, the knight tour ...♘f6-e8-c7-e6-d4, which is a typical idea in this set-up, is good for an equal position, e.g. 5 e4 ♘f6 6 ♘ge2 0-0 7 0-0 ♘e8 8 d3 ♘c7 9 ♗e3 ♘e6 10 ♕d2 d6 11 ♗h6 ♘ed4 etc.

5...♘f6 6 e4 0-0 7 ♘ge2 d6

The inclusion of an early d2-d3 by White means that it is harder for Black to complete the knight tour ...♘f6-e8-c7-e6-d4, for example 7...♘e8 8 ♗e3 ♘d4 9 ♘d5!? (an original idea – White loses time in order for Black to block the e6-square with a pawn) 9...e6 (if 9...♘c7 Gurevich gives 10 ♗g5 ♘xd5 11 exd5 with pressure on e7) 10 ♘dc3 ♘c7 11 0-0 ♖b8, M.Gurevich-Rashkovsky, USSR 1981, and now Gurevich suggests 12 a4 a6 13 a5 with a slight advantage for White.

8 0-0 a6

Black initiates queenside play while keeping ...♘f6-e8-c7 in reserve. There is a little cat-and-mouse that goes on here. White's natural plan is ♗c1-e3 and d3-d4. However, if Black's knight remains on f6, White will have to play h2-h3 if he wants to avoid the sequence ♗c1-e3 ...♘f6-g4. Black reckons that ...a7-a6 is a more useful move than h2-h3, and as we shall see, there is a tactical element that comes into play as well.

a) 8...♘e8 9 ♗e3 and now:

a1) Of course a key plan is for Black to answer ♗c1-e3 with ...♘c6-d4: 9...♘d4 10

♜b1 a5 (10...♞c7 11 b4 b6 12 ♛d2 ♝b7 13 a4 ♜b8 14 ♞b5 ♞cxb5 15 axb5 is a bit better for White according to Ribli) and now White has tried:

a11) 11 h3 ♝d7 12 f4 ♜b8 13 a4 f5 14 ♞b5 e5 15 ♛d2 fxe4 16 dxe4 ♝e6 ½-½ Ribli-Hug Altensteig 1994.

a12) 11 ♛d2 ♞c7 12 ♝h6 e5 13 ♝xg7 ♚xg7 14 f4 f6 15 a4 ♝g4 16 ♞xd4 cxd4 17 ♞b5 ♞a6 with equal chances, Sunye-Casafus, Buenos Aires 1994.

a13) 11 a3. White is now poised to play b2-b4 and get pressure down the b-file, so Black gives up the d4-square: 11...♞xe2+ 12 ♞xe2 a4 13 d4 cxd4 14 ♝xd4 ♝g4 (14...♝d7 15 ♞c3 ♜c8 may be better) and now 15 ♜e1 ♛c7 16 ♜c1 ♝h6 17 ♜c2 ♞g7 18 f3 ♝e6 19 ♞c3 ♜fc8 20 ♞d5 ♝xd5 21 exd5 e5 22 dxe6 ♞xe6 23 ♝f2 left White better, Votova-Rogers, German Bundesliga 1996.

a2) 9...♞c7 10 d4 (if Black allows this, it is not the end of the world, but White does seem to have good chances of an edge) 10...cxd4 11 ♞xd4 ♞e6 12 ♞de2 ♝d7

and now White has done well with either:

a21) 13 ♜c1 a6 14 a4 ♞c5 15 b3 ♜c8 16 h3 ♛a5 17 ♞d5 ♚h8 18 ♜b1 ♛d8 (Black's play is very passive) 19 b4 ♞e6 20 f4 ♛e8 21 ♝b6 f5 22 ♛d3 ♞ed8 23 b5 (Leitao-Nijboer, Wijk aan Zee 1999), and Black is in danger of being pushed off the edge of the board.

a22) 13 f4 a6 14 a4 ♜b8 15 ♜b1 ♞a5 16 b3 b5 17 f5 ♞c7 18 c5 dxc5 19 ♝xc5 ♞c6 20 axb5 axb5 21 ♞d5 ♞xd5 22 exd5 ♞e5 23 fxg6 hxg6 24 ♞d4 ♜c8 25 b4 and White is pressing, Schlosser-Movsesian, Tegernsee 1999.

b) 8...♝d7 is similar to 8...a6, though 8...a6 seems slightly more constructive.

c) 8...♜e8 The last two editions of ECO quote the game Temirbaev-Lanka, Moscow Olympiad 1994, which supposedly continued 9 ♝e3 ♞d4 10 ♛d2 a6 11 ♝h6 etc. But I suspect Black 8th move was a misprint (or database error) for 8...♞e8, since in the line quoted White could simply take the pawn on d4 with 10 ♞xd4 cxd4 11 ♝xd4.

9 h3

Of course White can play other moves, but then he has abandoned his key idea of fighting for the d4-square. For example 9 a3 ♜b8 10 ♜b1 b5 11 cxb5 axb5 12 b4 cxb4 13 axb4 ♝e6 14 h3 ♛d7 15 ♞f4 ♜fc8 16 ♞xe6 ♛xe6 17 ♞e2 ♜a8 18 ♝e3 ♜a4 19 ♛d2 ♜a2 20 ♞f4 ♜xd2 21 ♞xe6 ♜c2 with a complex ending, Salov-Shirov, Moscow 1992.

9...♜b8 10 a4 ♞e8 11 ♝e3 ♝d7

A natural developing move, but one which contains a well-disguised trap. Instead 11...♞d4 is also a sound equalising move. After 12 ♜b1 ♝d7 13 b4 ♞xe2+ 14 ♞xe2 cxb4 15 ♜xb4 b5 16 cxb5 axb5 17 axb5 ♛a5 18 ♛b3 ♜xb5 19 ♜b1 ♜xb4 20 ♛xb4 ♛xb4 21 ♜xb4 ♞f6 22 ♜b7 White has only a token initiative, Williams-Bekker Jensen, Witley 1999.

12 d4!?

12 ♜b1 ♞c7 13 d4 is safer. Then if Black wants to keep it simple, he can play 13...cxd4 14 ♞xd4 ♞xd4 15 ♝xd4 ♝xd4 16 ♛xd4 b5 (16...♛c8 17 ♚h2 ♞e6 18 ♛d3 ♞c5 19 ♛c2 b5 keeps slightly more play in the position, and Black even won – eventually – in Jacoby-Hebden, Copenhagen 1985) 17 cxb5 axb5 18 axb5 ♞xb5 and a draw was agreed here in M.Gurevich-El Taher, Tanta

1997.

12...cxd4 13 ♘xd4 ♕c8!

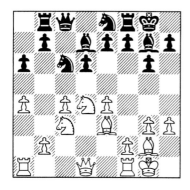

This is the point! Black hits both the h3-pawn and, indirectly, the c4-pawn. I found 11 games in the database (including an earlier game of Williams) where White had allowed this position, but Black had missed 13...♕c8. Having said that, White does get compensation for the pawn, so objectively 12 d4 is probably not a dubious move.

14 ♘d5

Or 14 ♔h2 ♘xd4 15 ♗xd4 ♕xc4 16 ♗xg7 ♘xg7 (16...♔xg7!?) 17 ♘d5 ♖fe8 18 ♕d2 ♘e6 19 ♖fc1 ♕d4 20 ♕xd4 ♘xd4. White won the pawn back after 21 ♖c7 ♗e6 (21...♗c6 22 ♘xe7+ ♖xe7 23 ♖xe7 ♔f8) 22 ♘xe7+ ♔f8 23 ♖d1 ♖xe7 24 ♖xe7 ♔xe7 25 ♖xd4 a5 26 b4 b6, but Black retains a small edge in the ending, Kanellopoulos-Mastrovasilis, Patras 1999.

14...♗xd4 15 ♗xd4 ♗xh3 16 ♗c3 f6

Black is a solid pawn up, and constructs a pawn barricade on the 3rd rank to limit White's attacking potential. Perhaps Black should, however, take a more active approach with, for example, 16...♗xg2 17 ♔xg2 ♕e6 (17...f5!?) 18 ♖h1 f6 when White needs to attend to the e4-pawn.

17 f4 ♗xg2 18 ♔xg2 e6 19 ♘e3 ♘e7 20 ♕g4 ♘g7 21 ♖ae1 ♕c6 22 ♔h2

Williams has made it difficult for Black to consolidate, and maintains annoying threats against the Black pawns. White now

threatens ♕g4-h4 and ♘e3-g4.

22...e5

If 22...♕xa4 then 23 ♕h4 ♘e8 24 ♘g4.

23 ♕h4 ♔h8 24 fxe5 dxe5 25 ♗b4 g5 26 ♕g4 ♖f7 27 ♖d1 ♖e8 28 ♖d6

White would actually be somewhat better after 28 b3!

28...♕xa4

Grabbing a second pawn and hoping to weather White's initiative.

29 ♗c3 ♘g8 30 ♖fd1 ♖ef8 31 ♕h3

31 ♖d7 is answered by 31...h5.

31...b5 32 ♖d7 b4 33 ♖xf7 ♖xf7 34 ♕c8 bxc3

After this move, White can force a draw. The winning attempt 34...♖e7 is, however, risky, e.g. 35 ♖d8 ♖e8 36 ♖xe8 ♘xe8 37 ♗d2 when although Black has a two-pawn advantage, his pieces very awkwardly placed, while White has a dangerous c-pawn and powerful outposts for the knight on f5 and d5. Nevertheless, there is nothing clear for White after 37...a5, e.g. 38 c5 (38 ♘f5 ♕c2 39 ♕xe8 ♕xd2+ 40 ♔g1 ♕c1+) 38...♕b5 39 c6 ♕e2+ 40 ♘g2 ♘d6 41 ♕d8 ♕xd2 42 c7 ♕d4 etc.

35 ♖d8 ♘e8 36 ♖xe8 ♖g7 37 ♕e6! cxb2 38 ♖xg8+ ♖xg8 39 ♕xf6+ ♖g7 40 ♕f8+ ♖g8 41 ♕f6+ ½-½

Game 47
Csom-Adorjan
Hungarian Championship 1993

---

1 c4 c5 2 g3 g6 3 ♗g2 ♗g7 4 ♘c3 ♘c6 5 ♘f3 e6 6 0-0

If White wants to spice up the position, he can try the 6 d4 sacrifice (covered in Game 48) or alternatively there is 6 a3 ♘ge7 7 b4!?. Black now has several valid replies:

a) 7...cxb4 8 axb4 ♘xb4 9 ♗a3 ♘ec6 (9...♘bc6 10 ♘b5 0-0 and now Watson recommends 11 ♗d6 – instead 11 ♘d6 a6 12 0-0 b5 Caoili-Wohl, Gold Coast 2000, is good for Black) 10 ♕a4 a5 11 ♖b1 ♖b8 12 0-0 0-0 13 ♘a2 d5 14 ♘xb4 axb4 15 ♗xb4

♘xb4 16 ♕xb4 dxc4 17 ♕xc4 ♗d7 ½-½ J.Watson-Antunac, New York 1981.

b) 7...♘xb4 8 axb4 cxb4 9 ♘e4 ♗xa1

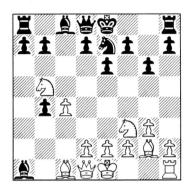

and here:

b1) 10 ♕a4 ♗g7 11 ♘d6+ ♔f8 12 ♕xb4 ♔g8 (12...h6 leaves White struggling for compensation – 13 ♗a3 ♔g8) 13 ♘g5 ♘c6 14 ♗xc6 ♕xg5 15 ♗f3 h5 16 h4 ♕d8 17 c5 a5 18 ♕a4 ♖b8? (18...♕f6 is still very good for Black) 19 ♘xf7 ♔xf7 20 ♕f4+ ♕f6 21 ♕xb8 ♕e5 22 ♕xe5 ♗xe5 23 e3 ♗c7 24 ♗b2 and White is slightly better, Pavlovic-Fominyh, Stary Smokovec 1990.

b2) Watson's suggestion 10 d4 still awaits practical tests. Watson analyses 10...♗c3+ 11 ♔f1 0-0 12 ♗g5 f5 13 ♘d6 a5 14 ♕a4 but here 14...♔g7 (instead of Watson's 14...b3) allows Black to start unravelling his pieces. The threat is ...h7-h6 and if 15 ♘e5 ♗xd4 16 ♗h6+ ♔g8 17 ♗xf8 ♗xe5 etc.

b3) 10 ♗a3 (an original tactic) 10...♗g7 (10...bxa3 11 ♕xa1) 11 ♘d6+ ♔f8 12 ♗xb4 h6 13 0-0 ♔g8 14 ♕a4 ♘f5 15 ♖b1 a5 16 ♗a3 ♘xd6 17 ♗xd6 ♖a6 18 c5 b6 19 d4 bxc5 20 dxc5 ♔h7 21 ♘d2, Marin-Kolev, Ubeda 1996. White has managed to get some play, but the whole line feels very speculative, as if White is just trying to hold on.

c) 7...b6 (7...d6 8 ♖b1 b6 is also playable) 8 ♖b1 0-0 9 bxc5 (9 ♘a4 cxb4 10 axb4 d5 11 b5 ♘a5 12 cxd5 ♘xd5 13 e4 ♘c7 14 d4 ♗b7 15 ♘c3 a6 16 bxa6 looks quite nice for

Black, though a draw was agreed here in Huzman-Zagorskis, European Team Championship, Pula 1997) 9...bxc5 10 ♘e4 d6 11 ♗b2 f5 12 ♘c3 ♖b8 13 ♕c2 a6 14 0-0 ♘d4, Van Wely-Leko, Wijk aan Zee 1996, and White has achieved nothing from the opening.

6...♘ge7 7 d3 0-0 8 ♖b1

a)8 ♗g5 h6 9 ♗d2 b6 10 ♖b1, which is similar to the main game.

b) 8 ♗f4 d5 (also possible is 8...e5 with a likely transposition to Game 49) 9 ♖b1 b6 10 ♕c1 ♗a6 11 ♖d1 d4 12 ♘b5 e5 13 ♗h6 ♕d7 14 ♗xg7 ♔xg7 15 e3 dxe3 16 fxe3 ♖ad8 17 a3 ♘f5, Enigl-Leko, Germany 1998, and here 18 b4!? would have led to an unclear outcome.

8...b6 9 ♗d2 ♗b7 10 a3 d5

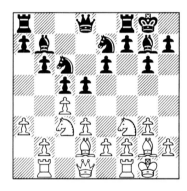

11...♘xd5 is also perfectly reliable, e.g. 12 ♘xd5 ♕xd5 13 ♗c3 (13 b4 cxb4 14 axb4 ♘d4 is equal) 13...♘d4 14 ♘e1 ♕d7 15 ♗xb7 ♕xb7 16 e3 ♘b5 17 ♗xg7 ♔xg7 18 a4 ♘d6 19 b4 ♖ac8 20 b5 ♖fd8 21 ♕f3 ♖c7, Wohl-Emms, England 2000, with equality.

12 b4 cxb4

12...c4 is overambitious. After 13 b5 ♘a5 14 ♘a4 ♖c8 15 d4 ♘b3 16 ♗b4 ♖e8 17 e3 a6 18 bxa6 ♗xa6 19 ♘d2, Speelman-Chandler, Hastings 1989/90, leaves White a bit better due to pressure on Black's weak pawns on b6 and d5.

13 axb4 d4 14 ♘a4 ♘d5 15 ♕b3

Or 15 b5 ♘ce7 16 ♕b3 ♕d7 17 ♖fc1 ♖fe8 18 ♘g5 ♖ad8 19 ♗h3 ♘f5 20 ♘e4 h6, Cuellar-Bilek, Sousse 1967, with balanced chances.

15...♖e8 16 ♘g5 ♘e5

Instead after 16...♘ce7 Adorjan gives 17 e4! dxe3 18 fxe3 ♖f8 19 e4 ♗d4+ (19...♘f6 20 ♗c3) 20 ♔h1 ♘f6 21 ♗c3 with a big plus for White.

17 b5 ♕d7 18 ♘e4

Threatening 19 ♘ac5.

18...♖ad8 19 ♗g5 ♖c8 20 ♖fc1 ♔h8 21 ♗d2

21 ♘ec5 bxc5 22 ♘xc5 ♖xc5 23 ♖xc5 ♘c3 is good for Black.

21...♗a8

Black avoids the ♘c5 tactics once and for all.

22 ♘g5 h6 23 ♘f3 ♘xf3+ 24 ♗xf3 ♗b7 25 ♖c4 ♔g8

Black is preparing his ...♘d5-c3 'shot', and so improves his piece placement to make the tactics work for him. The light-squared bishop is needed on b7 to defend the c8-rook, while the king is better placed on g8, both defending the f7-pawn, and avoiding any intermediate ♗xg7 (this is relevant on the note to White's 27th).

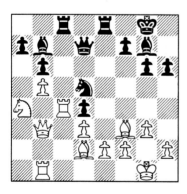

26 ♖bc1

If 26 ♔g2, trying to avoid the Black knight coming to e2 with check, Black has the spectacular 26...♖xe2! 27 ♖xc8+ ♕xc8 28 ♗xe2 ♘e3+ 29 ♔g1 ♕h3.

26...♘c3 27 ♘xc3?

White should go for 27 ♗xc3 ♗xf3 28 ♗xd4, e.g. 28...♗d5 29 ♗xg7 ♗xc4 30 ♕b2 ♗xb5 31 ♗xh6 f5 32 ♘c3 ♗c6 when Black is only slightly better, since his own king is exposed.

27...♗xf3 28 ♖xc8

If 28 exf3 dxc3 29 ♗xc3 ♕xd3.

28...♖xc8 29 ♘e4 ♖xc1+ 30 ♗xc1 ♗xe2 31 ♗xh6? ♕h3 0-1

Game 48
Nogueiras-Alvarez
Santa Clara 1999

---

1 c4 c5 2 g3 g6 3 ♗g2 ♗g7 4 ♘c3 ♘c6 5 ♘f3 e6 6 d4

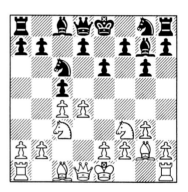

This sharp gambit has revitalised White's play in this line. The alternative, of quiet development, is simply not challenging enough. In practice, Black has had excellent results with the simple plan of ...♘g8-e7, ...b7-b6, ...♗c8-b7 and ...d7-d5 (see Game 47). 6 0-0 ♘ge7 7 d4 is also possible, though less critical than 6 d4.

6...cxd4

Black immediately has a key decision to make – how to capture on d4.

6...♘xd4 7 ♘xd4 cxd4 and now:

a) 8 ♘b5 ♕b6 9 ♕a4 (9 e3 ♘e7 10 ♘xd4 – 10 b3!? – 10...0-0 11 0-0 d5 12 cxd5 ♘xd5 and Black has equalised, Bunzmann-Sutovsky, Polanica Zdroj 1999) 9...a6 10 e3 d3 11 0-0 ♘e7 12 ♖d1 axb5! 13 ♕xa8 bxc4 14 ♖b1 0-0 15 ♗d2 d5 16 ♖dc1 ♕c7, Markowski-Macieja, Warsaw 1998, and Black is better with a huge pawn mass in return for the exchange.

b) 8 ♘e4

b1) 8...d6 9 ♕a4+ ♔e7 10 ♗d2 a5 11 ♕a3 f5 12 ♗g5+ ♘f6 13 ♗xf6+ ♗xf6 14 ♘xf6 ♔xf6 15 0-0 gives White some compensation for the pawn because of Black's displaced king and lag in development. In this game Black never solved the problem of developing his c8-bishop: 15...♕b6 16 ♖ad1 ♖d8 17 e3 dxe3 18 fxe3 ♕b4 19 ♕d3 ♕c5 20 ♔h1 ♕e5 21 e4 ♔g7 22 exf5 gxf5 23 g4 f4 24 ♕d2 ♕e3 25 ♖xf4 winning the pawn back with a better ending in prospect, Schwartzman-Fedder, Copenhagen 1990.

b2) 8...d5 9 cxd5 exd5 10 ♕a4+ ♔f8 and now:

b21) 11 ♕a3+ ♕e7 12 ♘d6 d3 13 0-0 ♗e5 (13...dxe2 14 ♖e1) 14 ♘b5 ♕xa3 15 ♘xa3 ♔g7 16 exd3 ♘f6 17 ♘b5 a6 18 d4 ♗b8 19 ♘c3 ½-½ Chernin-Macieja, Budapest 2000.

b22) Here 11 ♘c5!? is a possible improvement, for example:

b221) 11...♗g4 12 0-0!? (12 ♘d3 ♘e7 13 h3 ♗f5 14 0-0 ♗e4) 12...♗xe2 13 ♖e1 d3 14 ♘xd3 ♗xd3 15 ♕a3+ ♘e7 16 ♕xd3. White will follow up with ♗e3-c5 or -d4 (or ♗d2-b4 or -c3). He is likely to win back the d-pawn and can try and exploit his bishop v knight advantage: 16...♕d7 17 ♗g5 f6 (17...♖e8 18 ♖e2) 18 ♗d2 ♘c6 and now 19 ♗xd5 or 19 ♗e3.

b222) 11...♕e7 12 ♘d3 ♗g4 13 0-0; it will be hard for Black to retain both d-pawns, and he has to spend time getting his king safe.

7 ♘b5 d5

A rare alternative is 7...e5, e.g. 8 e3 (8 ♘d6+ ♔e7) 8...d6 9 exd4 a6 10 ♘c3 exd4 11 ♘d5 ♘ge7 12 0-0 ♘xd5 13 cxd5 ♘e5 14 ♘xd4 ♕b6 15 b3 ♗g4 16 ♕d2 h5 17 ♗b2 h4 18 f4 h3, A.Ledger-Gufeld, Hast-

ings 1992, with unclear complications.

8 cxd5 ♕a5+

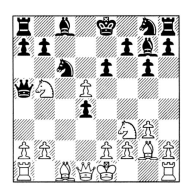

9 ♕d2

9 ♘d2 (this is a major alternative) 9...♕xb5 10 dxc6 ♘e7 11 a4 ♕b6 12 cxb7 ♗xb7 13 ♘c4 ♕b4+ 14 ♗d2 ♕xc4 15 ♗xb7 ♖b8 16 b3 and now:

a) 16...♕c7 17 ♗g2 0-0 18 0-0 ♖fd8 19 ♖c1 ♕d6 20 ♗a5 ♖dc8 21 ♕d3 h5 22 b4 ♘d5 23 b5 ♕e5 24 ♗xd5 ♕xd5 25 ♖c2 ♖xc2 26 ♕xc2 e5 27 ♖c1 e4 28 ♕c7 ♖e8 29 ♕c6 ♕xc6 30 bxc6 and White's c-pawn proved to be more dangerous than Black's central pawns, Markowski-Sriram, Calcutta 2001.

b) 16...♕c5 17 ♖c1 (better than 17 ♗g2 ♘d5 18 ♖c1 ♘c3 19 0-0 ♕b6 and Black has the advantage, Markowski-Bologan, Koszalin 1999) and now:

b1) 17...♕b6 18 ♗e4 0-0 19 b4 ♖fd8 20 0-0 ♘d5 21 ♗xd5 ♖xd5 22 b5 h5 23 ♖c6 ♕d8 24 ♕c2 ♗e5 25 ♖c1, Sulava-Hauchard, Gonfreville 1999, and White is much better – he dominates the c-file, and Black's e- and d-pawns have not got moving yet.

b2) On b6 the queen is a target for White's queenside expansion. Instead Bologan analyses 17...♕d6, where the queen stays in touch with the d5-square, so that Black can play ...♘e7-d5 quickly: 18 ♗g2 ♘d5 19 0-0 0-0 20 ♗xd5 ♕xd5 and Black's queen is ideally posted here, e.g. 21 b4 ♖fc8 with equality.

9...♕xb5 10 dxc6 ♕xc6

The counter-sacrifice 10...♘e7 is perhaps where Black should look for an improvement: 11 ♘xd4 (following 11 cxb7 Ribli gives 11...♗xb7 12 ♘xd4 ♕b6 13 ♗xb7 ♕xb7 14 ♘f3 0-0 15 0-0 ♖fd8 with compensation for the pawn) 11...♕b6 12 e3 bxc6. Now both Jansa and Gonzalez recommend 13 0-0 (instead of 13 b3 ♗a6 14 ♗a3 ♖c8! 15 ♖d1 c5 16 ♘e2 0-0 17 0-0 ♖fd8 18 ♕c2 ♘d5 19 ♗xd5 exd5 20 ♖fe1 d4, Fishbein-Jansa, Herning 1991, which is very good for Black) 13...♗a6 14 ♖d1 ♖d8 15 ♕c2 0-0 16 b4!?, with the idea of 16...♕xb4 17 a4. But here 16...e5 looks good, and if 17 ♘b3 ♕xb4 18 a4 ♕c4.

11 0-0 ♕b6

11...♕d6 is often recommended but White got a slightly better ending after 12 b3 ♘e7 13 ♗b2 0-0 (if 13...e5 14 e3) 14 ♗xd4 ♗xd4 15 ♕xd4 ♕xd4 16 ♘xd4 ♖d8 17 ♖fd1 ♖b8 18 ♖ac1 in Vaulin-Shabtai, Ajka 1992.

12 b3 ♘f6 13 ♘e5!

This is an improvement over 13 ♗a3 ♘e4 14 ♕f4 ♘c3 15 ♖fe1 and now both 15...♘d5 (Abramovic-Matulovic, Yugoslavia 1992) and 15...♘b5 (I.Almasi-T.Horvath, Austrian League 1997) give Black good play.

13...♘e4

Or 13...0-0 14 ♗a3 ♖e8 (14...♖d8?! 15 ♕f4!) 15 ♖ac1, followed by ♗a3-c5 when White is much better.

14 ♗xe4 ♗xe5 15 ♗a3

15...f5

Nogueiras suggests 15...♗d6, when 16 ♗xd6 (16 ♗b2 e5) 16...♕xd6 17 ♖ad1 e5 18 f4 looks a little better for White.

16 ♗g2 ♗d7 17 ♖ac1

Planning ♗a3-c5 followed by the capture of the d4-pawn. White's goal is to win his pawn back and retain an advantage due to his control of the h1-a8 diagonal and Black's lack of development.

17...♖c8 18 ♖xc8+ ♗xc8 19 ♖c1 ♔f7

20 ♗c5 ♕a6 21 f4!

The immediate 21 ♗xd4 is met by 21...♖d8.

21...♗f6 22 ♗xd4 ♕d6

22...♖d8? 23 ♖c7+ ♔g8 24 ♖xc8 and White wins material.

23 e3 ♗xd4

23...♖d8 is answered by 24 ♖c4.

24 ♕xd4 ♕xd4 25 exd4

White's advantage in this ending lies in the relative activity of his pieces compared to Black's. His g2-bishop dominates its opposite number, while the white rook will reach the 7th rank.

25...♖d8

If 25...♔e7 26 ♗xb7 ♗xb7 27 ♖c7+.

26 ♖c7+ ♔f6 27 ♔f2! a5 28 ♔e3 b6 29 ♖xh7

With an extra pawn in the bag, the ending is technically winning. Nogueiras concludes matters smoothly.

29...♖d7

If 29...♗d7 then White plays 30 h3, threatening g3-g4-g5 mate!

30 ♖xd7 ♗xd7 31 ♗f3 ♔e7 32 d5 ♔d6 33 ♔d4 ♗c8 34 dxe6 ♗xe6 35 ♗e2 ♗d5 36 ♗c4 ♗f3 37 a3 ♗d1 38 b4 axb4 39 axb4 ♗f3 40 ♔e3 ♗h5 41 h3 ♔c6

If Black avoids the bishop exchange, then White finally gets his kingside majority moving: 41...♗d1 42 ♗e2 ♗b3 43 ♔d4 followed by g3-g4.

42 ♗e2 ♗xe2 43 ♔xe2 ♔b5 44 g4 fxg4 45 hxg4 ♔c4 1-0

Game 49
Oll-P.Cramling
Dos Hermanas 1992

1 c4 c5 2 ♘f3 ♘c6 3 ♘c3 e5 4 g3 g6 5 ♗g2 ♗g7

This line often results from the move order 1 c4 c5 2 ♘c3 ♘c6 3 g3 g6 4 ♗g2 ♗g7 5 ♘f3 e5.

6 0-0

6 a3 a5 7 d4!? is another unclear pawn sacrifice. Delchev-Lazarev, Italy 2000 continued 7...cxd4 8 ♘b5 d6 9 e3 ♗e6 10 b3 ♘f6 11 exd4 e4 12 ♘g5 ♗g4 13 ♕c2 ♗f5 14 0-0 0-0 15 ♘xe4 ♘xe4 16 ♗xe4 ♘xd4 17 ♘xd4 ♗xd4 18 ♖b1 ♗xe4 19 ♕xe4 ♕b6 20 ♗h6 ♖fe8 21 ♕d3, and now 21...♖e6 gives Black reasonable play.

6...d6 7 ♖b1

Many ideas are of course, the same as in this line with colours reversed (Game 46). White's other main plan is to complete the knight-tour ♘f3-e1-c2-e3 as quickly as possible, before Black can prepare ...d6-d5: 7 ♘e1 ♘ge7 8 ♘c2 0-0 9 ♘e3 ♗e6 10 d3 ♕d7. Black has a straightforward equalising plan – swap the light-squared bishops and then any knights that land on d5! For example 11 ♘ed5 ♗h3 12 ♗h6 (this 'trick' doesn't achieve anything but the fact that White has no advantage has been proven in many other games) 12...♗xg2 13 ♔xg2 ♘xd5 14 ♘xd5 ♘e7 15 ♘xe7+ ½-½ Kharitonov-Belov, Moscow 1989.

The accelerated queenside expansion 7 a3 ♘ge7 8 b4 can be met by 8...e4!?, for example 9 ♘g5 f5 10 ♗b2 0-0 11 d3 h6 12 ♘h3 exd3 13 exd3 g5, with chances for both sides, Leski-de Firmian, Las Vegas 1996.

7...♘ge7 8 a3 a5 9 d3 0-0

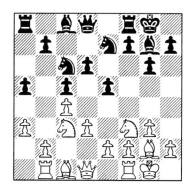

10 ♘e1

Alternatively:

a) 10 ♗g5 h6?! is a positional error (10...f6 usually transposes to the lines examined below with 11 ♗g5, as Whites next move is usually ♘f3-e1). After 11 ♗xe7 ♘xe7 12 b4 White has very good play on the light squares, while Black's kingside pawn-storm is a long way from having any bite.

b) With 10 ♗d2, White hopes that Black will waste a tempo on ...h6 in order to prepare ...♗e6 without allowing ♘f3-g5. However, after 10...♖b8 11 ♘e1 ♗e6 12 ♘c2 d5 13 cxd5 ♘xd5 Black equalises comfortably, and in fact Black has scored well from this position, for example 14 ♘xd5 ♗xd5 15 ♗xd5 ♕xd5 16 b4 axb4 17 axb4 cxb4 18 ♘xb4 ♘xb4 19 ♖xb4 ♖fc8 20 ♕b3 ♕xb3 21 ♖xb3 ♖c2 ½-½ Ivkov-Brodsky, Wijk aan Zee, 2001.

For this reason, the insertion of ♗g5-d2 and ...f7-f6 is an attempt for White to squeeze something out of the position.

10...♗e6 11 ♗g5

White provokes the slightly weakening ...f7-f6, which introduces a few tactical resources.

Leaving the bishop at home is also possible: 11 ♘c2 d5 12 cxd5 ♘xd5 and here:

a) 13 ♘e3 ♘de7 14 ♘c4 ♖b8 15 ♗g5 f6 16 ♗e3 b6 17 ♕a4 ♕c7 18 ♖fc1 ♔h8 19 ♕d1 ♕d8 ½-½ Ruck-Huzman, Istanbul Olympiad 2000.

b) 13 ♘e4 b6 14 ♘g5 ♗c8 15 ♘e3 ♘xe3 16 ♗xe3 ♗d7 17 b4!? cxb4 18 axb4 axb4 19 ♕d2 ♖c8 20 ♖fc1 ♘d4 21 ♖xc8 ♕xc8 22 ♗xd4 exd4 23 ♕xb4 ♕c2 with counterplay, Lesiege-Moldobaev, Istanbul Olympiad 2000.

11 ♘d5 ♖b8 12 ♘c2 b5 is fine for Black.

11...f6 12 ♗e3

The aim of this move is to prevent the immediate ...d6-d5. Instead 12 ♗d2 is more common. Now Black has a choice:

a) The idea of leaving the rook on a8, to support the a-pawn, is interesting: 12...♔h8 13 ♘d5 ♗xd5 14 cxd5 ♘b8 15 b4 (maybe

White should play on the kingside instead) 15...cxb4 16 axb4 a4 17 b5 ♘d7 18 ♗b4 ♘c5 19 ♘c2 f5 20 ♘a3 ♘c8 21 ♘c4 ♘b6 22 ♗a5 ♖xa5 23 ♘xa5 ♕a8 (Van der Sterren-Gdanski, Novi Sad Olympiad 1990), when Black's a-pawn 'runner' compensates for the exchange.

b) The main point of provoking ...f7-f6 is supposed to be that 12...d5? is met by 13 cxd5 ♘xd5 14 ♕b3 with a big advantage according to several books. As no analysis is given, the implication is that White is winning the b-pawn (for example). However it is not so clear after:

b1) 14...♘d4 15 ♗xd5 ♘xb3 16 ♗xe6+ ♔h8 17 ♗xb3 with three pieces for the queen, or, more to the point:

b2) 14...♕b6 15 ♕c2 (15 ♕xb6 ♘xb6 with ...c5-c4 to follow) 15...♘de7 16 ♘a4 ♕b5 with no particular problems for Black, because of the threat of ...♘c6-d4.

c) 12...♖b8 13 ♘c2 d5 14 cxd5 ♘xd5 15 b4 axb4 16 ♘xd5 ♗xd5 17 ♗xd5+ ♕xd5 18 axb4 cxb4 19 ♘xb4 ♘xb4 20 ♖xb4 b5 (but even here 20...♖fc8 would render the queen exchange moot because of 21 ♕b3 {21 ♕b1!?} 21...♕xb3 22 ♖xb3 ♖c2) 21 ♕b3 (the fact that White can exchange queens gives him a slight edge in the ending – compare this to note 'b' to White's 10th move) 21...♕xb3 22 ♖xb3 ♖fc8 23 ♖b2 ♗f8 24 ♖fb1 ♖b7 25 ♔f1 ♖cb8 26 ♗b4 ♗xb4 27 ♖xb4 ♖b6 28 ♖c1 ♖8b7 29 ♖c5 Speelman-De Firmian, New York 1995. White's active rooks give him an edge, which he later exploited to win.

12...♕d7

Or 12...b6 13 ♘d5 ♖b8 14 ♘xe7+ ♘xe7 15 b4 axb4 16 axb4 ♕d7 17 ♘c2 f5 18 ♗g5 ♘c6 19 ♗d2 cxb4 20 ♘xb4 ♘xb4 21 ♖xb4 d5 22 cxd5 ♗xd5 23 ♗xd5+ ♕xd5 24 ♕b3 ♕xb3 25 ♖xb3 ♖fc8 with a level ending, Pigusov-Mochalov, Katowice 1991.

13 ♘c2 ♗h3

This is an improvement over the earlier 13...a4 14 b3 axb3 15 ♖xb3, which was a bit

better for White in Andersson-Seirawan, Linares 1983. This game is actually a great example of how to exploit the open lines on the queenside and the light-squared weaknesses in Black's position, and is well worth playing over in full: 15...♖fb8 16 ♕b1 ♖a6 17 ♖b6 ♕c7 18 ♖b2 b6 19 ♗d2 ♕d8 20 a4 f5 21 ♘e3 ♗b4 22 ♖xb4 (the classic positional exchange sacrifice) 22...cxb4 23 ♕xb4 ♕d7 24 ♖b1 ♖d8 25 ♕b3 ♔h8 26 ♘c2 h6 27 ♘b4 ♖a5 28 h4 f4 29 ♔h2 ♔h7 30 ♘bd5 ♘xd5 31 cxd5 ♗f5 32 ♕xb6 ♖c5 33 a5 ♖dc8 34 ♖b3 fxg3+ 35 fxg3 e4 36 ♘xe4 ♖c2 37 ♕e3 ♕a4 38 ♖b7 ♖8c7 39 ♖xc7 ♖xc7 40 ♘xd6 ♖c2 41 ♘xf5 1-0

14 ♗xh3

14 b4 ♗xg2 15 ♔xg2 cxb4 16 axb4 d5 looks good for Black.

14...♕xh3 15 ♘e4 ♕d7 16 f4 f5 17 ♘g5 h6 18 ♘h3 b6

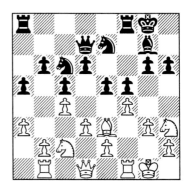

The artificial placements of White's minor pieces make Black at least equal here.

19 b4 axb4 20 axb4 ♔h7 21 ♘f2 ♘g8 22 bxc5 bxc5 23 fxe5 ♘xe5 24 ♗f4 ♘c6 25 e4 g5 26 ♗c1 ♘ge7 27 ♘e3 f4

This pawn proves to be a thorn in White's kingside.

28 gxf4 gxf4 29 ♘d5 f3 30 ♔h1 ♘xd5 31 cxd5 ♘d4 32 ♗e3 ♘e2 33 ♕b3 ♖f7 34 e5 ♗xe5 35 ♕c4 ♖a4 36 ♖b7 ♕xb7 37 ♕xa4 ♕xd5 38 ♕h4 ♗f4 39 ♗xf4 ♖xf4 40 ♕e7+ ♕f7 41 ♕xf7+ ♖xf7 42 ♘e4 d5 43 ♘xc5 ♖g7 0-1

Summary

Black should be able to equalise after 5 a3 a6. 5 e3 has the (perhaps deserved) reputation as being the most sedate line. After 5 ♘f3 Black is well advised to play either ...e7-e6 or ...e7-e5 and not allow the lines in the next Chapter where White gets in d2-d4 after ...♘g8-f6. 5 ♘f3 e5 is very popular and is perhaps even more solid than 5...e6. White can try and extract a small edge with the ♗c1-g5 idea, but right now he is looking for inspiration. After 5 ♘f3 e6 the 6 d4 sacrifice scores well for White, while if White plays the routine (but extremely common) 6 0-0 ♘ge7 Black has nothing to worry about.

1 c4 c5 2 ♘c3 ♘c6 3 g3 g6 4 ♗g2 ♗g7 (D) 5 ♘f3

     5 a3

         5...a6 – *Game 40*; 5...e6 – *Game 39*

     5 e3

         5...e5 – *Game 43*

         5...e6 6 ♘ge2 ♘ge7

             7 ♘f4 – *Game 42*

             7 d4 – *Game 41*

     5 e4

         5...♘f6 (D) – *Game 46*

         5...e6 6 ♘ge2 ♘ge7

             7 a3 – *Game 44*; 7 h4 – *Game 45*

5...e6

     5...e5 – *Game 49*

6 0-0 – *Game 47*

     6 d4 (D) – *Game 48*

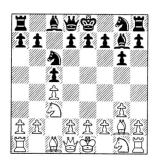

4...♗g7

5...♘f6

6 d4

CHAPTER SIX

Symmetrical English
Main Line with 5 ♘f3 ♘f6

1 c4 c5 2 ♘c3 ♘c6 3 g3 g6

3...♘f6 4 ♗g2 g6 5 ♘f3 d5 is another move order to reach the lines covered in Games 53-55.

4 ♗g2 ♗g7 5 ♘f3 ♘f6 6 0-0 0-0

6...d5 is covered in Games 53-55.

7 d4

7 d3 d5 is the move order given in ECO to reach the lines with ...d7-d5 and ...g7-g6 covered in this chapter. In practice, Black usually plays ...d7-d5 on an earlier move.

7 b3 can be found in the notes to Game 51.

7...cxd4 8 ♘xd4 ♘xd4

At this point Black has a couple ways of avoiding the main line:

8...♘g4, which is dealt with in Game 52.

For 8...d6 offering a pawn see the notes in Game 51.

9 ♕xd4 d6 10 ♕d3

This position is the starting point for the (traditional) main line. Left to his own devices, White will complete his development and then start to turn his space advantage into more tangible pressure. If Black plays too passively or casually, he can easily find himself badly clamped down in a nagging 'bind'.

So Black needs to play actively, and in fact he has a number of typical ideas:

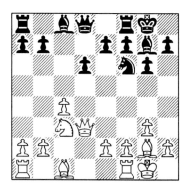

1) His key pawn break is ...b7-b5, which is prepared by ...a7-a6 and usually supported by ...♖a8-b8.

2) Black's knight can hassle White's queen with ...♘f6-d7-c5 (or -e5) or sometimes ...♘f6-g4-e5.

3) His light-squared bishop is usually developed (after securing the b7-pawn, or sacrificing it) by ...♗c8-e6 or ...♗c8-f5 to provoke e2-e4 which in turn blocks the g2-bishop's attack on the b7-pawn.

4) The queen can come into play by ...♕d8-a5 and sometimes across to h5 or back to a6 (see Game 51). Alternatively, ...♕d8-c8 is possible to support a later ...♗e6-♗h3.

This all sounds pretty dynamic and

promising, so why does White generally do well in this line?

White's initial task is to contain Black's short-term activity. It turns out that it is somewhat easier to play the White side, since he is usually playing fairly natural moves, while Black has to be pretty resourceful even to come close to equality. One very important point is that, even if Black achieves his ...b7-b5 break, it does not mean he can breathe easily. White can often get play on the newly opened c-file (after c4xb5) or generate a passed queenside pawn later on. All is not lost, however. If Black is prepared and plays accurately, there are several lines that are okay for him.

I would recommend trying to pick up the 'feel' of the opening by playing through the examples given in the notes to Games 50 and 51.

Other specific devices which White has at his disposal are:

1) A well-timed ♘c3-d5 is a key move in this position, hitting a number of potentially vulnerable points (e7, f6, b6, c7). If Black exchanges the knight, White can often get control of the c-file or e-file depending on how he recaptures (c4xd5 or e4xd5).

2) White often adopts a 'scorched earth' policy on the a1-h8 diagonal, moving his a1-rook and playing b2-b3 so that Black's g7-bishop has nothing to bite on. White's g2-bishop, meanwhile, is a powerful piece, and not so easily neutralised.

3) The c4-c5 thrust is an important factor in many lines. This can be supported by b2-b4 or played to exploit a pin on the d-file, while it is also sometimes played as a temporary sacrifice.

Game 50
Gulko-Khalifman
Yerevan 1996

---

1 c4 c5 2 ♘f3 ♘f6 3 ♘c3 ♘c6 4 g3 g6 5 d4

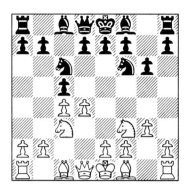

There are some advantages to playing d2-d4 sooner rather than later. Apart from the obvious point of getting this in before Black plays ...d7-d5, a delayed d2-d4 does give Black a few more options. For example after 5 ♗g2 ♗g7 6 0-0 0-0 7 d4 Black could choose either 7...d6 leading to a line of the Fianchetto King's Indian, or 7...d5 which is a Grünfeld. But note that Gulko prefers to wait until Black has at least committed himself to ...g7-g6. That way he avoids the anti-Benoni lines after say 3 d4 cxd4 4 ♘xd4 e5 or 4 d4 cxd4 5 ♘xd4 e6. Of course whether all of this is considered good or bad is a matter of personal taste, but I want to show how a knowledge of the move order nuances, especially when combined with knowledge of your opponent's preferences, can be a useful tool in the opening battle.

5...cxd4 6 ♘xd4 ♗g7 7 ♗g2 0-0 8 0-0 ♘xd4 9 ♕xd4 d6 10 ♕d3

The queen gets out of the line of fire of the g7-bishop, and prepares to quarterback the play from her central location. This move has been the main line for many years, and it has proved particularly hard for Black to find any clear path to equality. 10 ♗g5 ♗e6 11 ♕f4 ♕a5 12 ♖ac1 ♖ab8 13 b3 ♖fc8 14 ♕d2 a6 is the famous game Fischer-Spassky, Reykjavik (8th match game) 1972, where Black soon lost material with a couple of howlers, but in this position he has equality.

10...a6

Black has a number of alternatives at this point:

a) 10...♛a5 and

b) 10...♝e6 are covered in the next game.

c) 10...♝f5 is a typical device in this line – Black provokes e2-e4. Although this is not a bad move for White (it often forms part of his longer-term plan in any case), this does blunt the pressure on the h1-a8 diagonal and enables Black to develop his c8-bishop without first defending the b7-pawn: 11 e4 ♝e6 12 b3 and now:

c1) 12...a6 13 ♝d2 ♞d7 14 ♖ac1 b5 15 cxb5 axb5 16 ♛xb5 ♝xc3 17 ♖xc3 ♖xa2 18 ♝h6 ♛b8 19 ♛d3 ♖c8 20 ♖xc8+ ♛xc8 21 ♖c1 ♛b8 22 b4 ♖a7 23 b5 f6 24 ♝e3 and White retains an edge, Ivanchuk-Andersson, Reykjavik 1991.

c2) 12...♞d7 13 ♝e3 a6 14 ♖ac1 ♛a5 15 ♛d2 ♖fe8 16 ♞d5 ♛xd2 17 ♝xd2 ♖ac8 18 ♞f4 ♞c5 19 ♞xe6 fxe6 20 ♝e3 b5 21 cxb5 axb5 22 ♖fd1 and White is better thanks to the two bishops and better pawn structure, Bacrot-Kempinski, Yerevan Olympiad 1996.

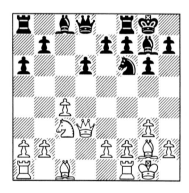

11 ♝d2

Others:

a) Watson's recommendation was 11 ♖d1 and now:

a1) After 11...♝f5, 12 ♛f3 is better than the reflex 12 e4, which has also been played several times. 'Is it the refutation of 10...a6?'

– Watson. White threatens both c4-c5 and to simply take the b7-pawn: 12...♖c8 (12...♖b8 13 c5) 13 ♛xb7 ♖xc4 14 ♛xa6 ♖b4 15 ♛a7 (but not 15 a4 ♛b8 when White's queen is in a tight spot – 16 e3 ♝e6 17 ♞d5 ♞xd5 ½-½ D.Anderton-Twyble, British League 1998) 15...e6 16 a3 ♖c4 17 ♛a6 and White is winning, Preiss-Schuh, Buehl 1992.

a2) The oldest recipe may be the best: 11...♛a5 (instead of 11...♝f5) 12 h3 ♝f5 13 e4 ♝e6 14 ♝d2 ♛h5 15 g4 (15 ♛f1!?) 15...♛c5 16 b3 ♖ab8 17 ♖ac1 ♖fc8 18 ♞a4 (18 ♝e3 ♛a3) 18...♛a3 19 ♞b6 ♖c6 20 ♝e3 ♞d7, Averbakh-Forintos, Budapest 1970, and Black held the balance.

b) 11 ♝e3 is also an important try:

b1) 11...♝f5 12 ♛d2

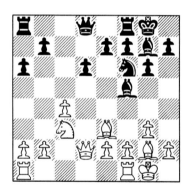

with the further branch:

b11) 12...♖b8 13 a4 ♝e6 14 b3 ♛a5 15 ♖ac1 ♖fc8 16 ♖fd1 ♞d7 17 ♝a7 ♞c5 18 ♛c2 ♖a8 19 ♝xc5 ♖xc5 20 ♝xb7 ♖b8 21 ♝d5 ♝f5 22 ♝e4 ♝xc3 23 ♝xf5 ♖xf5 24 ♛xc3 ♛b6 25 ♛e1 h5 26 ♖c3 was played in Pigusov-Vasiukov, Russian Championship 1996, and White eventually managed to consolidate his extra pawn.

b12) 12...♛d7 13 ♝d4 ♝h3 14 ♝xf6 ♝xf6 15 ♝xh3 ♛xh3 16 ♞d5 ♛f5 17 ♛d3 ♛xd3 18 ♞xf6+ ♔g7 19 ♞h5+ ♔h6 20 exd3 ♔xh5 21 ♖fe1 and the ending is a touch better for White, Bareev-Smirin, Soviet Championship 1990.

b2) 11...♘g4 12 ♗d4 ♘e5 13 ♕d1 ♖b8 and:

b21) 14 ♖c1 ♗e6 15 ♘d5 ♗xd5 (15...b5 16 c5 ♗xd5 17 ♗xd5 e6 transposes to Kirov-Schinzel below) 16 ♗xd5 ♕d7 17 ♗b6 and the b6-bishop sticks in Black's throat, leaving White slightly better, Wojtkiewicz-Adamson, Philadelphia 1995.

b22) 14 ♘d5 b5 15 c5 ♗b7 16 ♖c1 ♗xd5 17 ♗xd5 e6 18 ♗g2 d5 19 f4 ♘c6 20 ♗xg7 ♔xg7 21 e4 dxe4 22 ♗xe4 ♖c8 23 ♕xd8 ♖fxd8 24 ♖fd1 ♖xd1+ 25 ♖xd1 a5 was Kirov-Schinzel, Polanica Zdroj 1977. The ending looks pleasant for White, though probably Black has sufficient resources to hold on (the game itself was drawn), e.g. 26 ♖d6 ♘b8 27 ♖b6 ♘d7 28 ♖xb5 ♖xc5.

11...♖b8

The most direct plan, aiming for a quick ...b7-b5 before White is fully developed. Other lines tend to allow White to consolidate and achieve a small but persistent advantage. It has a similar feel to some lines of the King's Indian Defence, Fianchetto Variation, where after containing Black's temporary initiative, White is often able to get a lasting grip on the game. 11...♗f5 12 e4 ♗e6 13 b3 ♘d7 transposes to Ivanchuk-Andersson, given in the notes to Black's 10th move.

12 ♖ac1

12 c5!? is an interesting try, e.g.

a) 12...dxc5 13 ♕xd8 ♖xd8 14 ♗f4 ♖a8 15 ♖fd1 ♖e8 16 ♖ac1 e5 17 ♗e3 and White wins the pawn back with interest, Jirovsky-Piesnack, Berlin 1997.

b) 12...♗f5 13 e4 and Black can choose between:

b1) 13...♗e6!? 14 cxd6 ♘e8 15 ♘d5 (maybe White can try to improve here with 15 ♗g5 ♘xd6 16 ♖fd1 but then 16...♘c4 is unclear) 15...♘xd6 16 ♗f4 ♗xd5 17 ♕xd5 ♗xb2 with balanced chances, Tal-Neverov, Moscow 1990.

b2) 13...dxc5 14 ♕xd8 ♖bxd8 15 ♗g5

♗c8 16 e5 ♘g4 17 ♗xe7 ♗xe5 (17...♘xe5) 18 h3 ♘h6 19 ♗xd8 ♖xd8 20 ♖ad1 ♖f8 21 ♘a4 b5 22 ♖d5 leaves White better, Vaganian-Heinemann, German Bundesliga 2000.

12...b5

Alternatively:

a) 12...♗e6 13 b3 ♘d7 14 e4 ♘c5 15 ♕e2 ♕d7 16 ♘d5 b5 17 b4 ♘a4 18 cxb5 ♗xd5 19 exd5 axb5 20 ♖c6 gives White a nice position – he has pressure on both the c-file and along the e-file, Markowski-Gdanski, Polish Championship 1996.

b) 12...♗d7 13 c5 with:

b1) 13...♘e8 14 ♗g5 h6 15 ♗e3 ♗e6 16 b4! when White is better, Ye Rongguang-Gelfand, Novi Sad Olympiad 1990.

b2) 13...♗f5 ½-½ Drasko-Ye Rongguang, Belgrade 1988, but White can continue with good chances, e.g. 14 e4 dxc5 15 ♕xd8 ♖fxd8 16 ♗g5 ♗e6 17 e5 ♘d7 18 ♗xe7.

c) 12...♘d7 13 b3 ♘c5 14 ♕e3 b5 and now:

c1) 15 ♘d5 ♗e6 16 ♖fd1 ♗xd5 17 cxd5 b4! 18 ♗h3 a5 19 ♖c4 ♗b5 is okay for Black – his c5-knight is impossible to dislodge, Ki.Georgiev-Gdanski, Budapest 1993.

c2) 15 cxb5 axb5 16 ♘d5 ♗e6 17 ♘b4 ♕d7 18 ♗c3 ♗xc3 19 ♖xc3 ♖bc8 20 ♖fc1 ♖c7 21 ♕d4 ♖fc8 22 h4 and White is a bit better, Kantsler-Blees, Tel Aviv 1999.

13 cxb5!?

13 b3 ♗f5 14 e4 ♗d7 15 h3 bxc4 16 ♕xc4 and now:

a) 16...♕b6! 17 ♕d3 ♖fc8 18 ♖fe1 ♗c6 19 ♗g5 ♕a5 is equal according to Shneider.

b) 16...♕a5?! 17 ♕d3 ♕a3 18 ♖c2! ♗b5 19 ♘xb5 axb5 20 ♖c7 e6 21 ♗e3 ♖bc8?! 22 ♖a7 ♕b4 23 ♖d1 was very good for White in Shneider-Kasparov, Lyon 1994, which led to a rare loss for the World Champion against a non 'top-10' player. Perhaps this is an indication of how tricky this whole line is to play for Black.

13...axb5 14 ♘xb5 ♗f5

14...♗a6 15 a4 ♕b6 (15...♘d7 16 b3) 16 ♗c3 is equal according to Curt Hansen, but the ending (if Black takes on b5) has some resemblance to that in the main game – see the position after move 20 in Gulko-Khalifman. 16 b4!? ♗xb5 17 axb5 ♕xb5 18 ♕xb5 ♖xb5 19 e4 is also very similar.

15 e4

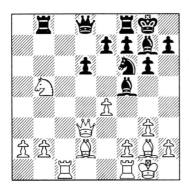

15...♗d7

The alternative, recommended in several reference books, is the forcing 15...♘xe4 16 ♗xe4 ♗xe4 17 ♕xe4 ♖xb5 18 b4 d5 (the pawns roll forward quickly after either 18...♕a8 19 ♕xa8! ♖xa8 20 a4! ♖bb8 21 a5 or 18...♕d7?! 19 a4 ♖h5 20 b5) and now:

a) 19 ♕e2 may save a tempo later when the black pawns advance, e.g. 19...♖b7 20 a4 e5 21 b5 ♕d7 22 ♖c6 e4 23 ♖fc1 ♖e8 24 a5 d4 25 b6 e3 26 fxe3.

b) 19 ♕d3 and here:

b1) 19...♕d7 20 a4 ♖bb8 21 b5 e5 22 ♖c6 was the continuation played in Ki.Georgiev-Gufeld, Calcutta 1992. White soon got an unstoppable pawn roller after 22...e4 23 ♕c2 ♖fe8 24 ♗f4 ♖a8 25 b6 d4 26 ♖c7 ♕f5 27 b7 etc.

b2) 19...♖b7!? with a further choice:

b21) 20 ♖c5 ♖d7 is given as unclear by Gufeld but I feel that White must still be a bit better. He can hold up the black central pawns while gradually advancing his unopposed a- and b-pawns.

b22) Perhaps more accurate is 20 b5 e5 21 a4 e4 22 ♕e2 ♖e8 23 a5 d4 24 b6 e3 (24...d3 25 ♕d1 ♗d4 26 ♕b3 ♕e7 27 ♖c4 or 24...♕d5 25 ♗b4) 25 fxe3 dxe3 26 ♗b4, which is better for White, despite the double-edged position.

The significance of this sub-variation (which is the mainstay of the assessment of 'unclear' for 10...a6 in *ECO* and elsewhere), together with the main game Gulko-Khalifman, is that if White can prove an advantage in these forcing lines (where Black plays an early ...b7-b5 sacrifice), then Black has to revert to the quieter approaches. However, a review of the notes to the earlier moves in the main game reveal slim pickings for Black, who usually ends up slightly worse out of the opening.

16 a4!

16 ♘c3 ♖xb2 17 ♖b1 ♖xb1 18 ♖xb1 ♗c6 is equal according to Gulko.

16...♕b6

16...♘g4 17 b4 ♕b6 was worth trying, e.g. 18 ♘c3 ♕xb4 19 ♘d5 ♕d4 20 ♘xe7+ ♔h8 with an unclear position.

17 h3!?

White stops any counterplay based on ...♘f6-g4 and aims for an ending with level material where he still holds some trumps.

17...♗xb5 18 axb5

18 ♕xb5!? would practically force the exchange on b5, since 18...♕d4 runs into 19 ♗c3.

18...♕xb5

Dolmatov gives 18...♘d7!? 19 b4 ♘e5 20 ♕e2 ♕xb5 21 ♕xb5 ♖xb5 22 ♖c7 e6 with some counterplay.

19 ♕xb5 ♖xb5 20 b4 d5

Perhaps this should be prefaced by 20...e6!?.

21 exd5 ♘xd5 22 ♖c5! ♖xc5 23 bxc5

White's passed c-pawn and two bishops give him good winning chances, despite the reduced material.

23...e6 24 ♖c1 ♖c8 25 c6 ♗b2 26 ♖c2 ♗e5 27 ♔f1 ♘e7?!

Black should instead try 27...f5!?. After 27...♔f8, Gulko's analysis runs: 28 ♗xd5! exd5 29 ♗b4+ ♔g7 30 f4 ♗a1 31 ♔e2 ♔f6 32 ♔d3 ♔e6 33 ♖e2+ ♔f6 34 ♗e7+ ♔f5 35 c7 ♖xc7 36 g4+ ♔xf4 37 ♗d6+ winning the rook.

28 g4?

28 ♗a5! ♗c7 29 ♗c3 leaves White clearly better.

28...♘d5 29 ♗xd5! exd5 30 ♔e2 30...f5 31 gxf5 gxf5 32 ♔d3 ♔f7 33 ♗c3! ♗xc3?

33...♗f4! put up stiffer resistance.

34 ♖xc3 ♔e6 35 ♔d4 ♔d6 36 c7! f4 37 ♖c5 ♖xc7 38 ♖xc7 ♔xc7 39 ♔xd5 ♔d7 40 ♔e4 ♔e6 41 ♔xf4 ♔f6 42 h4 ♔e6 43 ♔g5 ♔f7 44 ♔f5 ♔e7 45 ♔e5 ♔f7 46 h5! ♔e7 47 f4 ♔f7 48 ♔d6! ♔f6

48...h6 49 ♔e5 ♔e7 50 f5 ♔f7 51 f6 ♔f8 52 ♔e4 ♔e8 53 ♔f4 ♔f8 54 ♔e5 wins.

49 h6 ♔f7

49...♔g6 50 ♔e6 ♔xh6 51 f5 ♔g7 52 ♔e7 wins.

50 ♔d7 1-0

A sample line is 50 ♔d7 ♔f6 51 ♔e8 ♔f5 52 ♔f7 ♔xf4 53 ♔g7 ♔f5 54 ♔xh7 ♔f6 55 ♔g8.

Game 51
Lagunow-Löffler
Berlin 1994

---

1 c4 c5 2 ♘f3 ♘f6 3 ♘c3 g6 4 g3 ♗g7

5 ♗g2 ♘c6 6 d4

If White prefers a quieter and somewhat more offbeat life, he can try the 'g3-b3' combo with 6 0-0 0-0 7 b3, when Black has:

a) 7...d5 8 cxd5 ♘xd5 9 ♗b2 ♘xc3 10 ♗xc3 e5 11 ♖c1 ♗e6 12 d3 b6 13 ♕d2 ♖c8 14 ♘g5 ♗d7 15 f4 ♘d4 is given as equal in ECO, though Black faltered in the next few moves: 16 e3 ♘f5 17 ♘e4 exf4 18 ♖xf4 ♗c6?! 19 ♗xg7 ♔xg7 20 ♗h3 and White was better, Smyslov-Ivkov, Havana 1962.

b) 7...b6 is a Double Fianchetto – see Chapter 2.

c) 7...d6 8 ♗b2 e5 9 d3 and now:

c1) 9...♘e8 10 e3 ♘c7 11 ♘e1 ♗e6 12 ♘d5 ♗xd5 13 cxd5 ♘e7 14 e4 ♘b5 15 ♘c2 ♕d7 16 ♘e3 ♘d4 with equal chances, Spraggett-Becerra Rivero, Cienfuegos 1997.

c2) 9...h6 10 ♘d2 ♗e6 11 ♘d5 with a further split:

c21) 11...♗xd5 can be answered by 12 cxd5 ♘b4 13 a3 ♘bxd5 14 b4.

c22) 11...♖b8 12 a3 a5 13 e3 ♘h7 14 ♕c2 f5 15 f4 ♕d7 16 ♗c3 ♗f7 17 ♖ae1 ♖be8 18 b4 was a bit better for White in Hickl-Lutz, Nussloch 1996. The attempt to slow down the queenside expansion with ...a7-a5 has in fact given White more to 'bite on'.

c23) 11...♘h7 12 a3 f5 13 b4 ♖c8 14 b5 ♘e7 15 f4 g5 16 e3 ♖f7 17 ♖a2 ♗xd5 18 cxd5 exf4 19 exf4 ♗xb2 20 ♖xb2 gxf4 with an unclear position, Carlier-Glek, Schaan 1998.

6...cxd4 7 ♘xd4 0-0 8 0-0 ♘xd4

After the gambit continuation 8...d6, White can play the fairly harmless 9 ♘c2 or take the pawn with 9 ♘xc6 bxc6 10 ♗xc6 ♖b8 11 ♗g2 ♕a5 12 ♕c2 which should give him the edge, e.g. 12...♗f5 (or 12...♗e6 13 ♗d2) 13 e4 ♗e6 14 b3 ♘xe4 15 ♘xe4 ♗xa1 16 ♗g5 and here instead of 16...f6 17 ♗e3 trapping the bishop on a1 (Wojtkiewicz-Wahls, Geneva 1995), Black should play 16...♗f6 17 ♘xf6+ exf6 18 ♗xf6 ♕f5 19 ♕xf5 ♗xf5 20 ♗e7 ♖fe8 21 ♗xd6 ♖bd8 when White is somewhat better.

9 ♕xd4 d6 10 ♕d3 ♕a5

After the alternative 10...♗e6, White has:

a) 11 ♗d2 (!) ♘d7 12 b3 ♖b8 13 ♖ac1 a6 14 e4 transposes to Markowski-Gdanski quoted in the previous game (note 'a' to Black's 12th) 14...b5 15 cxb5 axb5 16 ♘d5 ♘c5 17 ♕e2 ♕d7 18 b4 ♗xd5 19 exd5 ♘a4 20 ♖c6 with an edge for White.

b) 11 ♗xb7 gives Black more scope, e.g. 11...♖b8 12 ♗g2 ♕a5 13 b3 ♖xb3 14 axb3 ♕xa1 and now:

b1) 15 ♗d2 ♕a6 16 ♘b5 ♖b8 17 ♗c3 d5 18 ♘c7 ♕a3 19 ♘xe6 ♖xb3 20 ♗xd5 ♖xc3 21 ♕d4 ½-½ Lagunow-Teske, Binz 1995.

b2) 15 ♘b5 ♕a2 16 ♘d4 ♗d7 17 ♗d2 ♕a6 18 b4 ♘g4 and Black has reasonable play, Filippov-Nay Oo Kyaw Tun, Shanghai 2000.

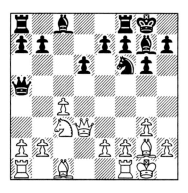

11 h3

11 ♘b5 ♗f5 and 11 ♗d2 ♕h5 are both okay for Black.

11...♗e6 12 ♗d2 ♕a6

In a bid to avoid the normal white build-up, Black has a quick ...d6-d5 in mind. An alternative way of continuing the 'direct' approach is 12...♕h5 13 g4 ♕e5 and now:

a) The opening worked out well for Black after 14 ♖ac1 ♘d7 15 b3 ♘c5 16 ♕c2 f5 17 f4 ♕d4+ 18 e3 ♕d3 19 ♗f3 ♕xc2 20 ♖xc2 ♔f7 21 b4 ♗xc3 22 ♗xc3 ♘e4 23 ♗d4 ½-½ W.Schmidt-Dvoirys,

Dortmund 1991.

b) 14 b3 is more challenging:

b1) 14...♖ab8 15 ♖ac1 a6 16 ♘a4 ♘e8 17 e3 b5 18 f4 ♕f6 19 g5 was a disaster for Black in Ricardi-Scarella, Argentinean Championship 1994.

b2) 14...♘d7 is better when:

b21) 15 e4 h5 16 f4 ♘c5 gives Black counterplay, Gottschlich-Mattick, Seefeld 1996.

b22) 15 ♗xb7 ♘c5 16 ♕f3 ♘xb7 17 ♕xb7 f5 is unclear.

b33) 15 f4 ♕c5+ 16 ♔h1 f5!? may give Black sufficient counterplay, e.g. 17 ♗xb7 ♖ab8 18 ♗d5 ♗xd5+ 19 ♕xd5+ ♕xd5+ 20 cxd5 ♘b6.

13 b3 ♖ad8

Black's play is direct and has a slightly crude feel to it. However, given that 'pretty' play in the main lines give White an edge both theoretically and statistically, it may be worth a try. 13...♖fd8 is the older move, but because of some nuances highlighted below, may offer Black better chances than 13...♖ad8.

After 13...♖fd8:

a) 14 ♖ad1 ♖ac8 (14...d5 15 ♗g5) 15 ♗e3 was played in Gheorghiu-Sahovic, Mendrisio 1987, but now Black could play 15...d5 and here:

a1) 16 cxd5? ♕xd3 17 ♖xd3 ♗f5 wins material.

a2) 16 ♘xd5 ♘xd5 17 cxd5 ♕xd3 18 ♖xd3 ♗f5 19 ♖d2 ♗c3 20 ♖dd1 ♗c2 21 ♖c1 ♗b2 22 ♗xa7 ♗xc1 23 ♖xc1 and White has two pawns for the exchange, but the position is roughly equal.

a3) 16 ♕d2 d4 17 ♗xd4 ♖xd4 18 ♕xd4 ♘d5 19 ♘xd5 ♗xd4 20 ♘xe7+ ♔g7! 21 ♘xc8 ♗c5 and White needs to spend time extricating his knight, which gives Black reasonable play, e.g. 22 ♖d8 ♕xa2 23 ♘d6 (23 ♗xb7 ♕xb3 24 ♗f3 ♕b8 wins for Black) 23...♗xd6 24 ♖xd6 ♕xb3 with approximately equal chances.

b) 14 e4 d5 15 exd5 ♗xd5 16 ♗xd5 e6

17 ♗g5 exd5 18 ♖ad1 d4 and:

b1) If now 19 ♘d5 ♘xd5!? 20 ♗xd8 ♘c3 21 ♖c1 ♘xa2 22 ♖a1 ♖xd8 23 ♕d2 ♕e6 24 ♖xa2 a6 25 ♔h2 d3 should be sufficient for Black. If White's queen moves, Black may be able to play ...d3-d2 and defend the pawn with the bishop, when he should not lose.

b2) 19 ♖fe1 and here:

b21) Black should play 19...♖e8 when White is no more than a shade better after 20 ♗xf6 ♕xf6 21 ♘d5.

b22) Instead 19...h6 20 ♗xf6 ♕xf6 21 ♘d5 ♕d6 22 ♖e7 as in Castro Rojas-Garcia, Winnipeg 1974, gives White a dominant rook .

14 e4

14 ♖ad1!? is interesting.

14...d5 15 exd5 ♗xd5

15...♘xd5 16 ♗xd5 ♗xd5 17 ♘xd5 e6 and here 18 ♘e7+ (instead of the tame 18 ♖ad1 ♖xd5 ½-½ Franco Ocampos-Hernandez, Havana 1998) 18...♔h8 19 ♕e3 is strong according to Lagunow, e.g. 19...♖fe8 20 ♘xg6+ hxg6 21 ♗c3.

16 ♗xd5 e6

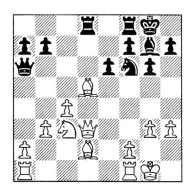

17 ♗xb7?!

The critical line is 17 ♗g5 exd5 18 ♖ad1 d4. A draw was agreed here in Arsovic-Vratonjic, Nis 1996. White should definitely play on with 19 ♘d5 (19 ♗xf6 ♗xf6 20 ♘d5 is also possible) and now:

a) 19...♖d7 20 ♗xf6 ♗xf6 21 ♖fe1. This

suggestion of Carsten Hansen indeed seems to give the more comfortable game. If Black can achieve ...b7-b5 he can probably equalise, but it seems he will have to defend a tricky position (the line given by Lagunow is 21 ♕f3 ♗g7 22 a4 claiming a slight edge for White, though after 22...♕e6 23 ♔h2 ♖e8 Black is okay). 21...♗g7 22 ♖e2 b6 23 a4 (Not 23 ♖de1?? ♖xd5) 23...♕b7 24 ♖de1 a6 25 ♖e7 ♖xe7 26 ♖xe7 ♕c6 27 ♖a7 is very strong for White.

b) 19...♘xd5!? is an exchange sacrifice worth looking at, since Black wins a pawn in return, though it seems to fall short of full compensation: 20 ♗xd8 ♘c3 21 ♗e7 (but note this move has no point if the rook is on a8 – as a result of an earlier 13...♖fd8 instead of 13...♖ad8 – so perhaps 13...♖fd8 is better after all! Instead 21 ♖c1 ♘xa2 22 ♖a1 ♖xd8 23 ♕d2 ♕e6 24 ♖xa2 a6 25 ♔h2 d3 is as above) 21...♖e8 (or 21...♖c8 22 ♖a1 ♕e6 23 ♖fe1 ♕xh3 24 ♗b4 h5 25 ♖e7) 22 ♖de1 ♕xa2 23 b4 and Black does not have quite enough play to compensate for his material deficit.

17...♕xb7

17...♖xd3 18 ♗xa6 ♖xd2 19 ♖fd1 ♖fd8 20 ♖xd2 ♖xd2 21 ♖c1 leaves White with a winning endgame.

18 ♕e2 ♘d7!

Black now has an initiative to compensate for the sacrificed pawn.

19 ♖ad1

19 ♘e4!?.

19...♘e5 20 ♕e4

Lagunow gives 20 f4 ♖d3 21 ♘e4 (21 fxe5 ♖xg3+ 22 ♔h2 ♗xe5 wins) 21...f5 22 fxe5 fxe4 (22...♕xe4!?) 23 ♖xf8+ ♗xf8 24 ♗e3 ♕d7 with play for the pawn.

20...♕xe4 21 ♘xe4 ♖d4! 22 ♗b4

Otherwise Black has ...♘e5-f3+.

22...♖xe4 23 ♗xf8 ♗xf8 24 ♔g2 ♗b4 25 ♖d8+ ♔g7 26 ♖c1 ♖e2 27 c5

White's passed pawn gives him compensation for the material.

27...♖xa2

27...♗a3 28 ♖c3 (28 c6 backfires: 28...♗xc1 29 c7 ♗e3 30 c8♕ ♖xf2+ 31 ♔h1 ♖f1+ 32 ♔g2 ♖g1+ 33 ♔h2 ♘f3 mate) 28...♗b4 29 ♖c1 repeats moves (now 29 c6 fails to ♗xc3 30 c7 ♗d4 31 ♖xd4 ♖c2 32 ♖c4 ♘xc4 33 c8♕ ♘e3+).

28 c6 ♘xc6 29 ♖xc6 ♗e1 30 ♖d7!
♖xf2+ 31 ♔g1 ♖f6 32 g4 g5 33 ♖c1
♗f2+ 34 ♔g2 ♗b6 35 ♖f1

The dust has settled, and the ending is level.

35...♖xf1 36 ♔xf1 ♔g6 37 ♔g2 ♗c5 38 ♔f3 ♔f6 39 ♔e4 ♗b6 40 ♔d3 ♗f2 41 ♔e4 ½-½

Game 52
Mikhalchishin- Sale
Nova Gorica 1999

---

1 ♘f3 c5 2 c4 ♘c6 3 d4 cxd4 4 ♘xd4 ♘f6 5 ♘c3 g6 6 g3 ♗g7 7 ♗g2 0-0 8 0-0 ♘g4

After the frustration of defending the main line (8...♘xd4 9 ♕xd4 d6 10 ♕d3 – see Games 50 and 51), players of the Black side developed this line, which aims for more active counterplay against White's centre. After a subsequent e2-e3, ...♘c6xd4, Black typically routes his knight with ...♘g4-h6-f5 to put pressure on d4. If White then pushes d4-d5, he will block his g2-bishop and create some holes on the dark squares.

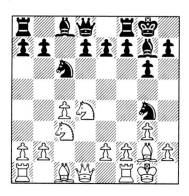

9 e3 d6

9...♘xd4 10 exd4 ♘h6 is an inaccurate move order (10...d6!? is possible, when 11 b3 ♘h6 transposes to the main game), since White can play 11 ♗xh6 ♗xh6 12 c5 d6 13 b4 when White has got his queenside moving without wasting a tempo on b2-b3. After 13...♗g7 14 ♖c1 ♖b8 15 ♕a4 a6 (15...♗xd4 16 ♕xa7 ♗d7 17 ♘e2 dxc5 18 ♘xd4 cxd4 19 ♕xd4 ♗b5 20 ♖fd1 ♕xd4 21 ♖xd4 gives White a slightly better endgame) 16 d5 White had a large advantage in Bakic-Petronic, Budva 1996.

10 b3

There are several alternatives:

a) White can ensure that he is able to recapture on d4 with a piece with 10 ♘ce2 but then Black can switch plans with 10...♘xd4 (! according to Delchev) 11 ♘xd4 (perhaps White should try 11 exd4 after all) 11...♘e5 12 ♕c2 ♕b6 13 ♗d2 ♗d7 14 ♖ac1 ♖fc8 and Black is fine, Dizdarevic-Delchev, Kastel Stari 1997.

b) Similarly, 10 ♘de2 ♕a5 (threatening ...♕a5-b4) 11 ♘d5 (11 ♗d2 ♕h5) 11...♖b8 (11...e6 12 ♗d2 ♕d8 13 ♘dc3 ♖b8 14 ♖c1 a6 15 b3 is a little better for White, though Black can try and stir things up with 15...♘ce5 16 ♘d4 ♘d3!?) 12 ♗d2 ♕d8 13 h3 ♘ge5 14 b3 e6 15 ♘dc3 d5!? 16 cxd5 and a draw was agreed in Stohl-Delchev, Croatian Team Championship 1997. Black has sufficient counterplay, e.g. 16...exd5 17 ♗c1 ♗f5 18 ♗a3 (18 ♕xd5 ♕xd5 19 ♘xd5 ♗d3) 18...♖e8 19 ♕xd5 ♕c8 20 ♗d6 ♖d8 21 ♕c5 b6 22 ♕a3 ♖b7.

Grabbing the pawn is not particularly promising:

c) 10 ♘xc6 bxc6 11 ♗xc6 ♖b8 (Saadi-Fischer, Mar del Plata 1960) or

d) 10 ♗xc6 bxc6 11 ♘xc6 ♕d7 12 ♘d4 ♗b7

both give Black some compensation for the pawn.

e) Kicking the knight with 10 h3 is possible and now:

e1) 10...♘ge5 11 b3 and White already has a pleasant position, B.Lalic-Krasenkow, Neum 2000.

e2) 10...♘xd4 11 exd4 ♘h6 12 g4 is very good for White according to Lalic.

e3) Mikhalchishin suggests 10...♘h6 11 g4 f5 12 g5 ♘f7 13 f4 with an unclear position.

10...♘xd4

An important alternative is 10...a6 when:

a) Delchev recommends 11 ♘de2 'which makes 8...♘g4 a shot in the dark' (certainly 11...♕a5 has less point than in the line 10 ♘de2 ♕a5 analysed above, because of 12 ♗b2 or 12 ♕d2). White was better after 11...♖b8 12 h3 ♘ge5 13 ♗d2 ♗f5 14 e4 ♗c8 15 ♗e3 ♕a5 16 ♗d2 ♕d8 17 f4 ♘d7 18 ♗e3 ♘c5 19 ♕d2 ♕a5 20 ♖ab1, Wojtkiewicz-Jung, Wuerzburg 1996.

b) The standard 11 ♗b2 ♘xd4 12 exd4 ♖b8 13 ♖e1 was played in Timman-Khalifman, Amsterdam 1995, when Topalov gives 13...b5!? 14 c5 dxc5 15 dxc5 ♕d4! with counterplay.

c) Also possible is the untested 11 ♘ce2, intending 11...♘xd4 12 exd4.

11 exd4 ♘h6

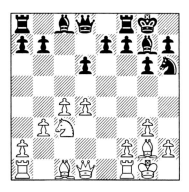

12 ♗xh6!

An unstereotyped move, giving up the two bishops. White removes Black's most active piece, in order to build on his space advantage without interference from the pesky horse. Other approaches have pre-

sented Black with few problems.

a) 12 ♗d2 ♖b8 13 ♖c1 a6 14 ♘e4 ♗g4 15 ♗f3 ♗xf3 16 ♕xf3 d5 17 cxd5 ♘f5 and Black is fine, Dizdarevic-Leko, Moscow Olympiad 1994.

b) 12 ♗b2 ♘f5 13 ♘d5 ♗d7 14 ♘e3 ♘xe3 15 fxe3 ♗c6 with equality, Khurtsidze-Delchev, Linares 1997.

12...♗xh6 13 ♕e2

13 ♖e1 is less accurate, as after 13...♗g7 White's queen is employed in defensive duties, looking after the d4-pawn: 14 ♖c1 ♖b8 15 b4 ♗e6 16 d5 (White's pawn structure loses its flexibility) 16...♗f5 17 ♕d2 a5 18 a3 axb4 19 axb4 ♕b6 20 ♘e4 ♕d4 21 ♕xd4 ♗xd4 ½-½ Akopian-Kramnik, Kazan 1997.

13...♗g7

13...♖b8 14 ♖fd1 ♕a5 15 b4! ♕a3 (15...♕xb4 16 ♘d5) 16 ♖ab1! ♗e6 (16...♕xc3 17 ♖b3 ♗g4 18 f3 ♗e3+ 19 ♔h1 wins) 17 ♖b3 ♕a6 18 ♗d5 ♗f5, Mikhalchishin-Krivoshey, Bled 1999, and now Mikhalchishin gives 19 a4 as much better for White.

14 ♖fd1

Or 14 ♖ad1 ♖b8 15 ♖fe1 ♖e8 16 h4 – Mikhalchishin.

14...♖e8

After 14...♖b8:

a) Cosma-Moraru, Romania 1998, continued 15 ♖ac1 ♕e8?! (15...e6 is better) 16 b4 e5 17 dxe5 dxe5 18 c5 ♗d7 19 ♖d6 ♗e6 20 ♖cd1 ♕c8 21 ♗d5 ♖e8? (21...♗f5) 22 ♕c4 ♗xd5 23 ♕xd5 ♖e7 24 ♘e4 ♕f5 25 ♔g2 h6 26 ♖d3! ♖f8 27 g4! winning.

b) 15 b4 ♖e8 16 ♖ac1 e6 17 ♕c2 a6 18 ♕b3 ♗d7 19 d5 exd5 20 ♘xd5 ♖e2 21 ♖c2 ♖xc2 22 ♕xc2 ♗c6 23 ♖e1 ♗xd5 24 ♗xd5 ♕d7 25 ♖e3 ½-½ Cvitan-Delchev, Kastel Stari 1997. Delchev points out that White is still slightly better, e.g. 25...♗f6 26 ♖f3 ♔g7 27 ♕e4 b6 28 ♕f4 ♕e7.

15 ♖ac1 ♖b8 16 c5!

White's trump in this position is his queenside majority, and he intends to use it!

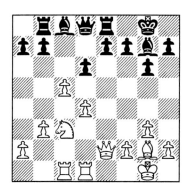

16...♗d7

If 16...e6 17 ♘b5 and the knight penetrates.

17 b4 dxc5

Carsten Hansen suggests 17...a5 18 a3 e5 19 d5 e4 as an improvement, but Mikhalchishin dismisses this idea with 17...e5 (the insertion of 17...a5 18 a3 seems to make little difference) 18 dxe5 ♗xe5 19 ♕c4 with a big plus for White.

18 dxc5

18 bxc5!? was also possible.

18...♕c8 19 ♘d5 ♗g4

White's pieces are very well co-ordinated. If 19...♗e6 20 c6! bxc6 21 ♖xc6.

20 ♘xe7+ ♔f8 21 ♘xc8 ♗xe2 22 ♘d6 ♗xd1 23 ♘xe8 ♖xe8 24 ♖xd1

White has a sound extra pawn. The opposite coloured bishops should be no obstacle to White (but of course he must keep the rooks on!).

24...♗c3 25 b5 ♖e5 26 ♗d5 ♗b4 27 c6 bxc6 28 bxc6 ♗a5 29 ♔f1 ♗b6 30 ♖d3 h6 31 g4 ♖e7 32 ♖b3 ♖e5?

A blunder, but Black's position is looking sad in any case.

33 ♖xb6 1-0

Game 53
Andersson-Timman
Ubeda 1997

---

1 ♘f3

Typical English move orders to reach the ...d5 lines are 1 c4 c5 2 ♘c3 ♘c6 (or 2...♘f6 3 ♘f3 d5 4 cxd5 ♘xd5 5 g3 ♘c6 6 ♗g2 g6) 3 g3 g6 4 ♗g2 ♗g7 5 ♘f3 ♘f6 6 0-0 (6 d4!) 6...d5 (or 6...0-0 7 d3 d5) 7 cxd5 ♘xd5 8 ♘xd5 ♕xd5. Black seems fine in this main line with ...d5. So it's surprising that Black does not choose this line more often, especially given that when White plays d4, he has a heavy plus score in practice. In turn, White should try for d4 early (e.g. before castling) if the move order allows it.

Going back to that last line, by analogy with Tal's 1 c4 c5 2 ♘f3 ♘f6 3 ♘c3 ♘c6 4 g3 d5 5 d4 (Games 34-35) and Kramnik's 1 c4 c5 2 ♘f3 ♘f6 3 g3 d5 4 d4 (Game 36), perhaps 7 d4!? (instead of 7 cxd5) deserves more tests. Play will often transpose to a line of the Fianchetto Grünfeld. An example is 7...dxc4 8 ♕a4 cxd4 9 ♘xd4 ♕xd4 10 ♗xc6+ ♗d7 11 ♖d1 ♗xc6 12 ♕xc6+ bxc6 13 ♖xd4 ♘d5 14 ♖xc4 ♗xc3 15 bxc3 ♔d7 16 ♗a3 ♖hc8 17 ♗c5 ♔e8 18 ♖b1 1-0 Karlsson-Degerman, Borlange 1992.

1...♘f6 2 c4 g6 3 g3 ♗g7 4 ♗g2 0-0 5 0-0 d5 6 cxd5 ♘xd5 7 ♘c3 c5 8 ♘xd5

8 d3 ♘c6 9 ♗d2 is possible, but tame.

8...♕xd5 9 d3 ♘c6 10 ♗e3 ♗d7

For 10...♗xb2 see the next game.

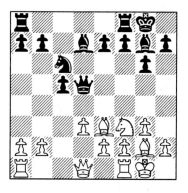

11 ♘d4

Other moves have not yielded White an advantage:

a) 11 ♕d2 ♕d6 12 ♖fc1 b6 13 ♗h6

♖ac8 14 ♗xg7 ♔xg7 15 a3 ♖fd8 16 ♖ab1 a5 17 ♖c4 h6 with equal chances, Gausel-Ribli, Slough 1997.

b) 11 d4 cxd4 12 ♘xd4 ♕c4 13 ♘xc6 ♗xc6 14 ♗xc6 bxc6 15 b3 ♕a6 16 ♖c1 ♕xa2 17 ♖xc6 ♖fd8 18 ♕c2 ♕xc2 19 ♖xc2 ♖db8 20 ♖fc1 ♗e5 21 ♖c5 ½-½ Kacheishvili-Smejkal, Mlada Boleslav 1993.

11...♕d6 12 ♘xc6 ♗xc6 13 ♗xc6 ♕xc6 14 ♖c1 ♕e6 15 ♖xc5 ♕xa2 16 ♖b5

This position is objectively quite equal, and Black should be able to hold a draw without difficulty, provided he navigates the next few moves carefully.

16...♕a6

Alternatives seem to be equally valid:

a) 16...b6 and now:

a1) 17 ♕a1 with a further split:

a11) 17...♕xa1 18 ♖xa1 ♖fb8 19 ♖a6 ♔f8 20 ♖b4 ♗e5 21 ♖ba4 leaves White with a small but nagging edge, Karpov-Ribli, Amsterdam 1980.

a12) 17...♕e6! 18 ♕a6 ♕d7 19 ♖a1 with the choice:

a121) 19...h5 20 ♖b4 ♖fc8 21 ♕a4, and here Ivanov gives 21...♕xa4 22 ♖bxa4 ♖c2 as equal. Instead, after 21...♕b7 22 h4 ♗e5 23 ♕b3 ♖c6 24 d4 White was beginning to get an edge in I.Ivanov-Timman, Lucerne Olympiad 1982.

a122) 19...♕g4 20 ♖e1 ♕d7 21 ♖a1 ♕g4 22 ♖e1 ½-½ Ftacnik-Langeweg, Dortmund 1981, though White does not need to repeat.

a2) 17 ♕b3 and again Black needs to be careful not to trade queens as 17...♕xb3 (17...♕a6! transposes to the main game) 18 ♖xb3 ♖fc8 19 ♖a1 is awkward for Black, e.g. 19...♖c2 20 ♖xb6 ♖xe2 21 ♖xa7 ♖e8 22 b4 with an extra, passed pawn, Vaganian-Mikhalchishin, Tallinn 1988.

b) 16...a6 17 ♖b6 ♖ac8 18 ♖xb7 ♖b8 19 ♖xe7 ♖xb2 20 ♗f4 a5 and now:

b1) 21 d4 ♗f6 ½-½ Damljanovic-Winants, Wijk aan Zee 1990.

b2) 21 ♖a7 ♖e8 22 e3 ♖d2 23 ♕c1 ♖xd3 24 ♕c6 ♖f8 25 ♕a6 ♖d5 26 ♗d6 ♖e8 27 ♗b4 is analysis by Ostojic. White wins the a-pawn and so retains some slim winning chances.

17 ♕b3 b6 18 ♖b4

White needs to generate some threats down the a- and b-files or Black will develop his rooks and avoid any pins. After 18 ♗g5 (Hansen and Watson), Black can simply (apart from anything else such as 18...e6) play 18...♖ac8 with ...♖c8-c7 to follow, and if 19 ♗xe7 ♖fe8 followed by ...♖e8xe2, is quite good for Black, e.g. 20 ♗a3 ♖xe2 21 ♖d5 ♕b7.

18...♖fb8

Or 18...♖fc8 19 ♖a4 ♕b7 20 ♖fa1 h5 21 h4 e6 22 ♖a6 ♖c6 23 ♕a2 ♖c2 24 ♖xb6 ♕c8 25 ♔f1 a5 26 d4 a4 27 ♕a3 ♕d8 28 ♖b5 ♗xd4 29 ♗xd4 ♕xd4 ½-½ Andersson-Cu.Hansen, Helsingor 1999.

19 ♖c4

Or 19 ♖a4 ♕b7 20 ♖fa1 a6 21 ♕a2 a5 22 ♖c1 ♗e5 23 ♖e4 ½-½ Ribli-Timman, Tilburg 1980.

19...b5

19...♕b7 20 ♖fc1 ♖c8 21 h4 h5 22 ♕b5 ♖xc4 23 ♖xc4 a6 ½-½ Andersson-Smejkal, Moscow 1981. One gets the picture!

20 ♖c7 e6 21 ♖fc1 h5 22 ♕b4 ♕a4 23 ♕e7 ♖f8 24 b4

24 ♖xa7 ♖xa7 25 ♕xa7 ♗xb2 is similar to the game.

24...a5 25 bxa5 ♕xa5 26 ♖b7 ♕a2 27 ♖xb5

27 ♔f1 ♕d5! is annoying for White.

27...♕xe2 28 ♖b3 ♖ad8 29 ♕b7 ♖xd3

Black scores a moral victory by winning a pawn, though he only has very slim winning chances, particularly against an endgame maestro such as Andersson.

30 ♖xd3 ♕xd3 31 h3 ♕f5 32 ♔g2 ♕d5+ 33 ♕xd5 exd5 34 ♖c7 ♗f6 35 ♖d7 ♖d8 36 ♖xd8+ ♗xd8 37 ♔f3 ♔f8 38 g4 ♔e7 39 ♗d4 ♔e6 40 ♔e3 ♗f6 ½-½

Game 54
Marin-Kempinski
Krynica 1998

1 c4 ♘f6 2 ♘f3 g6 3 g3 ♗g7 4 ♗g2 d5 5 cxd5 ♘xd5 6 0-0 c5 7 ♘c3 ♘c6 8 ♘xd5 ♕xd5 9 d3 0-0 10 ♗e3 ♗xb2

Or 10...♕h5 11 ♖c1 ♘d4 12 b4 ♘f5 and now:

a) 13 ♖xc5 ♘xe3 14 fxe3 ♕h6 15 ♕d2 leaves Black a pawn down for nothing.

b) 13 ♗d2 cxb4 14 ♗xb4 ♗e6, Gormally-Afek, Oakham 2000, and Black is fine.

11 ♖b1

Instead, 11 ♘d4 ♕d6 12 ♘xc6 ♗xa1 13 ♕xa1 bxc6 14 ♗h6 f6 15 ♗xf8 ♔xf8 16 ♖c1 ♖b8 17 ♕c3 ♗g4 18 ♗f1 ♖b5 19 ♕a3 ♕b8 leaves Black a bit better, Reich-Mikhalchishin, Kecskemet 1991.

11...♗f6

11...♗g7 is also common, and leads to similar play, but experience has shown that it is beneficial to Black to defend the e-pawn in a number of lines.

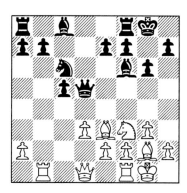

12 ♕a4

After 12 ♘d4 Black should carry on grabbing pawns with 12...♕xa2 and then:

a) In Norris-Gormally, Oakham 2000, White tried to repeat moves with 13 ♖a1?! ♕b2 14 ♖b1 ♕a3 15 ♖a1 ♕b4 16 ♖b1 but was hit with 16...♘xd4! 17 ♖xb4 cxb4 and

Black was on top.

b) 13 ♘xc6 bxc6 and now:

b1) 14 ♖c1 is Bagirov's untried suggestion (also quoted by ECO and NCO). One idea is that 14...♗g4 can be answered by 15 ♖c2. However it's not clear what the intention was after 14...♗d4, for example:

b11) 15 ♗xd4 cxd4 16 ♖xc6 should not worry Black – after all he is still a pawn up, and his formation has been straightened out.

b12) 15 ♗h6 ♖d8 16 e3 ♗f6 17 ♗xc6 ♖b8 18 ♖xc5 ♗a6 looks good for Black.

b2) 14 ♗xc5 ♗g4 15 f3 ♗e6 and Black was fine in Jirovsky-Babula, Czech Championship 1994.

b3) After 14 ♗xc6 ♗h3 15 ♗xa8 ♖xa8 16 ♖e1 ♗c3 Black has no problems.

12...♕d6

Or:

a) 12...♕d7 13 ♗xc5 b6! (13...♘d4? 14 ♕d1 ♘xf3+ 15 ♗xf3 ♖b8 16 ♗xa7 with a big plus for White, Tal-Pribyl, Tallinn 1973) 14 ♗xb6 ♘d4 is unclear according to Gipslis.

b) 12...♘b4 13 a3 ♘a2 14 ♘g5 ♘c3 15 ♗xd5 ♘xa4 16 ♘e4 ♘b6 17 ♘xf6+ exf6 18 ♗f3 looks like a good ending for White.

13 ♖fc1

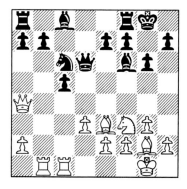

Given that Black has a likely improvement on the next move, White should try to improve here with 13 ♘d2 ♘d4 (13...♗d4!?), when 14 ♗xd4 ♗xd4 15 ♗xb7

is critical – Watson.

13...♘d4

Instead:

13...b6 is dismissed by Marin on the basis of 'a', but things are not so clear:

a) After 14 d4 ♘xd4 15 ♘xd4 cxd4 16 ♗h6 (16 ♗f4 is equal according to Carsten Hansen) 16...♗d7 White is best advised to bale out with a repetition of moves with 17 ♕a6 ♗c8 etc.

b) 14 ♖xb6 axb6 15 ♕xa8 ♗h3 16 ♕a6 is Ribli's recommendation, but it also seems ineffectual: 16...♗xg2 17 ♔xg2 ♘b4.

c) 14 ♘d2 is answered by 14...♗d7 15 ♘e4 ♕e6 16 ♗xc5 ♘e5 17 ♘xf6+ exf6 (17...♕xf6 18 ♕f4) 18 ♕b3 bxc5 19 ♗xa8 ♖xa8 20 ♖xc5 etc, when Black should be fine.

14 ♘xd4 cxd4 15 ♗h6 ♖d8

Or 15...♗g7 16 ♗xg7 ♔xg7 17 ♗xb7 ♗xb7 18 ♖xb7 is better for White.

16 ♗xb7 ♗xb7 17 ♖xb7 a6 18 ♖c6 ♕e5 19 ♖xa6 ♖ac8

After 19...♖xa6 20 ♕xa6 ♕xe2 21 ♕b6 Black cannot defend against the back-rank threats; ♖b7-b8 will follow.

20 ♖c6 ♕xe2 21 ♖xc8 ♖xc8 22 ♕d7 ♕e6 23 a4 ♕xd7

After 23...♗g7 White can retain his advantage with 24 ♕xe6 fxe6 25 ♗d2! according to Marin.

24 ♖xd7 ♗g7 25 ♗d2 ♔f8

Perhaps 25...e5 was better.

26 a5?

Dissipating most of White's advantage. Instead, White can improve the position of his bishop before pushing his a-pawn: 26 ♗b4 ♗f6 27 ♖a7 ♖b8 28 ♗c5 ♖c8 29 ♗b6. Here Marin gives the following line: 29...e5 30 ♗c7 e4 31 dxe4 d3 32 ♔f1 ♗d8 33 ♗f4 ♔e8 34 a5 ♖c2 35 ♗e3 ♖a2 36 a6 ♗f6 37 ♖a8+ ♔d7 38 a7 winning.

26...♔e8 27 ♖b7 ♖c6 28 ♗g5 ♗f6 29 ♗xf6 ♖xf6 30 ♖b4

The rook ending gives far fewer winning chances ('all rook endings are drawn').

30...♖a6 31 ♖a4 e5 32 f4 exf4 33 gxf4 ♔e7 34 ♔f2 ♔e6 35 ♔f3 f5

Creating unnecessary play for White; more accurate was 35...♔f5 followed by ...f7-f6 and ...g7-g5.

36 h4 h6 37 ♔g3 ♔f6 38 ♖a2 ♔f7 39 ♖a1 ♔f6 40 ♖a2 ♔f7 41 ♔f2 ♔f6 42 ♔e1 ♔f7 43 ♔d1 ♔f6 44 ♖a1 g5 45 hxg5+ hxg5 46 fxg5+ ♔xg5 47 ♔e2 ♔g4 48 ♔f2 f4 49 ♖g1+ ♔f5 50 ♖h1 ♔g5 ½-½

Game 55
Lputian-Timman
Wijk aan Zee 2000

---

1 ♘f3 ♘f6 2 c4 c5 3 ♘c3 d5 4 cxd5 ♘xd5 5 g3 ♘c6 6 ♗g2 g6 7 ♕a4

7 0-0 ♗g7 8 ♘xd5 ♕xd5 9 d3 is the main line (see Games 53-54).

Since the lines given in the last two games have proven rock solid for Black, White has explored ways of changing the character of the position with an early ♕d1-a4.

After the move order 7 0-0 ♗g7 8 ♕a4

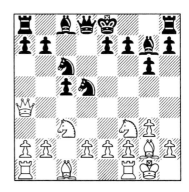

Black can choose:

a) 8...0-0?! 9 ♕c4 ♘xc3 10 dxc3 ♕b6 (10...b6 11 ♘g5 ♕c7 12 ♕h4 h6 13 ♘f3 g5 14 ♗xg5 {14 ♕h5 followed by h2-h4 is good for White according to Beliavsky and Mikhalchishin} 14...hxg5 15 ♘xg5 ♗f5 16 e4 ♗g6 17 f4 f6 18 ♘e6 ♕d7 is unclear,

Hertneck-Miles, Dortmund 1986) 11 ♕h4 ♖e8 12 ♖b1 ♘e5 13 ♘xe5 ♗xe5 14 b4 cxb4 15 ♗e3 ♕a6 16 ♕xb4 gives White a small advantage according to Uhlmann.

b) 8...♘b6 is given as equal by ECO, but with no analysis. The theoretical significance of the Kasparov-Kramnik game given below was perhaps overshadowed by the impression that Kasparov had yielded another soft draw with White (after making no progress against the Berlin defence in the other games). However, Kramnik's notes in *Informator* indicate that White has good chances of extracting an advantage from this line.

b1) 9 ♕b5 and now:

b11) 9...♘d7 10 d3 0-0 11 ♗e3 ♘d4 (or 11...♕b6 when White is slightly better after 12 ♕xb6 – or 12 a4 – 12...axb6) 12 ♗xd4 cxd4 13 ♘e4 ♕b6 14 a4! a6 15 ♕xb6 ♘xb6 16 a5 (16 ♖fc1!?) 16...♘d5 17 ♘c5 ♖d8 18 ♘d2 ♖b8?! (18...e6 19 ♘c4 ♖b8 is stronger) 19 ♘c4 (19 ♖a3 followed by ♖a3-b3 gives White a big plus according to Shipov) 19...e6 20 ♖fc1 ♗h6 21 ♖cb1 ♗f8 22 ♘b3 ♗g7 23 ♗xd5 ♖xd5 24 ♘bd2 e5 (24...♖b5! is equal – Kramnik) ½-½ Kasparov-Kramnik, London (5th match game) 2000. In the final position White is still better according to Kramnik, e.g. 25 ♘e4 ♗f5 (or 25...f5 26 ♘b6 ♖d8 27 ♘c5 and Black is tied down, or 25...♗e6 26 b4) 26 b4 ♗xe4 27 dxe4 ♖dd8, which keeps White's advantage to a minimum.

b12) 9...c4 had been played before; perhaps Kasparov had an improvement ready... 10 ♘e5 ♗xe5 11 ♗xc6+ bxc6 12 ♕xe5 f6 13 ♕e4 ♕d6 14 ♖d1 ♗f5 15 ♕f3 ♕e6 16 ♖e1 ♔f7 17 b3 ♖hd8 18 ♕e3 cxb3 19 axb3 ♕xb3 20 ♗a3 ♕e6 21 ♕xe6+ ♗xe6 22 d3 a5 23 ♗c5 ♘d7 24 ♗e3 ♖db8 ½-½ Lobejko-W.Schmidt, Koszalin 1998.

b2) Alternatively White can try 9 ♕h4 and then:

b21) 9...0-0 10 d3 f6 11 ♗h6 e5 12 ♘e4 ♕e7 13 ♖ac1 ♘d7 14 a3 ♖b8 15 e3 ♗xh6

16 ♕xh6 f5 17 ♘eg5 ♘f6 18 h3, Krasenkow-Brynell, Malmo 1995, with chances for both sides.

b22) 9...h6 may be more awkward for White: 10 ♘e1 ♘d4 11 d3 f5 12 f4 0-0 13 e3 ♘c6 14 ♗f3 ♗e6 15 ♕h3 ♕d7 16 ♕g2 ♖ac8 17 ♗d2 ♖fd8 as in Znamenacek-Szymczak, Warsaw 1987, and Black is a bit better.

7...♗g7 8 ♘g5 e6 9 ♘ge4 ♘b6 10 ♕b5

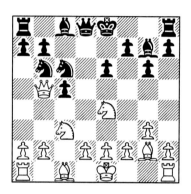

10...0-0!

An enterprising pawn sacrifice, which Timman had prepared as an improvement over earlier games, where White had managed to get a small edge. 10...c4 and now:

a) Going after the c-pawn is not very fruitful, e.g. 11 ♘a4 0-0 12 ♘xb6 axb6 13 ♕xc4 e5 14 d3 ♗e6 15 ♗g5 ♕b8 16 ♕c1 ♘d4 17 ♘c3 ♖c8 18 ♕b1 b5 with sufficient play for the pawn, A.Petrosian-Piesina, USSR 1979.

b) 11 b3 0-0 12 bxc4 ♘d4 13 ♕b1 ♘xc4 with:

b1) 14 d3 ♘d6 15 ♘xd6 ♕xd6 16 0-0 ½-½ A.Petrosian-Jelen, Bled 1999.

b2) 14 0-0 f5 15 ♘c5 ♕b6 16 ♘b3 and now:

b21) 16...♘c6 17 ♕d3 ♘4e5 18 ♕b5 ♖d8 19 ♖b1 ♕c7 20 ♕a4 a6 21 ♗b2 ♖a7 with a complex position, A.Petrosian-Lau, Lippstadt 1993.

b22) 16...♘b5 17 ♘xb5 ♕xb5 (17...♗xa1 18 ♘xa1) 18 d3 ♘b6 19 ♗b2 ♗xb2 20

♕xb2 ♗d7 21 ♕a3 ♘a4 22 ♖ab1 ♕a6 (22...♘c3) 23 ♘d4 and White is better, Lputian-Krasenkow, European Team Championship, Batumi 1999.

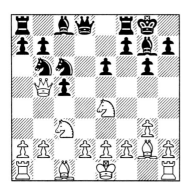

11 ♘xc5 ♘d4 12 ♕d3 ♕e7 13 ♘b3 e5 14 0-0 ♗e6 15 ♕b1 ♖fc8 16 d3
16 ♖d1!?.
16...♖xc3! 17 bxc3 ♘xe2+ 18 ♔h1 ♘xc3 19 ♕c2 ♖c8

Black has a pawn for the exchange and active pieces, so is already slightly better.
20 ♕d2

Artificial. White should try 20 ♗e3.
20...e4 21 d4 ♘b5 22 ♕g5 ♕e8 23 ♗e3 f5 24 ♕h4 ♗d5 25 g4 ♘d6 26 ♕g3 ♘bc4 27 ♗f4 ♕e7 28 ♖ac1 ♖f8 29 ♖fe1 g5 30 ♗xd6 ♘xd6 31 gxf5 ♖xf5

Timman gives 31...♘xf5 32 ♕g4 ♘d6 followed by ...♖f8-f4, gaining a tempo against White's queen.

32 ♖c2 ♖f4 33 ♖ec1 h6 34 ♕c3

White now has counterplay on the queenside.

34...♘c4 35 ♘d2 b5 36 ♘xc4 ♗xc4 37 a4 a6 38 axb5 axb5 39 ♕e3 ♕d6 40 ♖d2 ♗f6 41 ♖a1 ♗d8 42 ♖a7 ♗c7 43 ♕h3 ♖f7 44 ♖d1 ♔g7 45 d5 ♗d3 46 ♕g3?

White should play 46 ♖c1 ♗c4 47 ♖d1.

46...♕b6 47 ♕e3 b4 48 ♕xb6 ♗xb6 49 ♖xf7+ ♔xf7 50 ♗f1 ♗c2 51 ♖d2 b3 52 ♗c4 e3

Avoiding the trick 52...b2 53 ♗a2 b1♕+ 54 ♗xb1 ♗xb1 55 ♖b2.

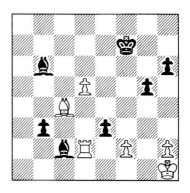

53 d6+ ♔f6 54 fxe3 ♗e4+ 55 ♖g2 b2 56 ♗a2 ♗xe3 57 h4 g4 58 d7 ♔e7 59 ♔h2 ♗f4+ 60 ♔g1 ♗xg2 61 ♔xg2 h5 0-1

Summary

White continues to score well in the main line with 7 d4, though Game 51 contains some resources for Black which are worth considering. It is surprising that more people do not opt for 6...d5 as Black (since this does so well in practice), and that White, in turn does not make sure of getting in an early d2-d4!. After the early ... d7-d5, the main line, covered in Game 53, is bone dry, but there are some new ideas in the notes to Game 55 (and the notes at the start of Game 53) which may give White improved prospects.

1 c4 c5 2 ♘c3 ♘c6 3 ♘f3 ♘f6 4 g3 g6 5 ♗g2 ♗g7 *(D)*

    5...d5 6 cxd5 ♘xd5 7 ♕a4 – *Game 55*

6 0-0 0-0

    6...d5 7 cxd5 ♘xd5 8 ♘xd5 ♕xd5 9 d3 0-0 10 ♗e3 *(D)*

        10...♗d7 – *Game 53*; 10...♗xb2 – *Game 54*

7 d4 cxd4 8 ♘xd4 *(D)* **♘xd4**

    8...♘g4 – *Game 52*

9 ♕xd4 d6 10 ♕d3 a6 – *Game 50*

    10...♕a5 – *Game 51*

 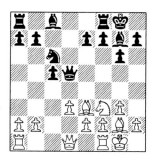 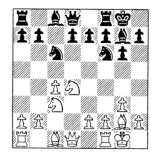

5...♗g7   *10 ♗e3*   *8 ♘xd4*

CHAPTER SEVEN

Breaking the Symmetry

This chapter covers several systems in which the symmetry is broken in the first few moves, but without an immediate d2-d4 or ...d7-d5.

1 c4

The lines in this chapter often crop up via a 1 ♘f3 move order, for example 1 ♘f3 c5 2 c4 ♘c6 3 ♘c3.

1...c5 2 ♘f3

2 ♘c3 ♘c6 ♘f3 transposes, while 3 g3 of course is Chapters 5-6.

2...♘c6

2...♘f6 3 ♘c3 b6 is covered in Game 63.

White could now choose 3 d4 if he doesn't fancy some of the lines in this chapter (e.g. 3 ♘c3 ♘d4 or 3...e5). After 3...cxd4 4 ♘xd4, Black can go for the lines in Chapter 3 with (e.g.) 4...♘f6 5 ♘c3 e6, though the inclusion of an early ...♘c6 restricts his options somewhat. Black can also choose 4...g6, and if White is not ready for the Accelerated Dragon after 5 e4 he has to go for something like 5 ♘c3 ♗g7 6 ♘c2 (which is covered in the notes to Game 27) or 5 g3 ♗g7 6 ♘c2 which should present Black with few difficulties.

3 ♘c3

Now we cover four different lines, each of which is quite distinct, though 'c' and 'd' sometimes come to the same thing, with colours reversed!

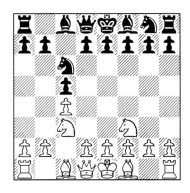

a) 3...♘d4 – Games 56-57
b) 3...g6 – Games 58-59
c) 3...e6 – Games 60-61
d) 3...e5 – Game 62

Game 56
Van der Sterren-Timman
Rotterdam 1998

---

1 ♘f3 c5 2 c4 ♘c6 3 ♘c3 ♘d4

'A provocative move but not easy to refute' according to Anand.

4 g3

Other moves will be discussed in Game 57.

4...♘xf3+

Black may as well disrupt White's structure while he has the chance. 4...g6 5 &g2 &g7 leads to a fairly normal position.

5 exf3 ♘f6 6 d4 cxd4

Instead 6...e6 7 &g2 d5 8 cxd5 ♘xd5 and here:

a) 9 ♘xd5 and Black can play either:

a1) 9...exd5 10 0-0 c4 11 f4 (Kramnik-Anand, Frankfurt 1998) and now (instead of 11...&e7? 12 ♕f3 0-0 13 ♕xd5 as played) Seirawan suggests 11...&e6 followed by ...g7-g6.

a2) 9...♕xd5 10 &e3 cxd4 11 ♕xd4 ♕xd4 12 &xd4 &b4+ 13 &e2 b6!? 14 f4 (14 &xg7 &a6+ 15 &e3 &c5+ 16 &d4 is the critical test; it remains to be proven if Black has enough for the pawn) 14...&a6+ 15 &e3 ♖d8 16 ♖hd1 0-0 with an equal ending, Vaganian-Gulko, Novgorod 1995.

b) 9 0-0 ♘xc3 10 bxc3 and now:

b1) 10...&d6 11 f4 0-0 12 c4 ♕b6 13 &e3 ♖b8 14 dxc5 &xc5 15 ♖b1 ♕c7 16 &xc5 ♕xc5 17 ♕a4 a6 18 ♖fd1 with an edge for White, Ribli-Wells, Austrian League 1998.

b2) 10...cxd4 11 cxd4 &d6 12 ♕b3 0-0 13 f4 ♖b8 14 &b2 ♕b6 and Black is close to equalising, Ribli-Emms, German Bundesliga 1996.

7 ♕xd4 g6

7...b6 has also been tried, e.g. 8 &g2 &b7 9 0-0 e6 10 ♘e4 ♘xe4 11 fxe4 f6 12 ♕d1 &c5 13 ♕h5+ g6 14 ♕h6 and here:

a) 14...&f7 15 ♖d1 &c6 16 b3 ♕f8 17 ♕d2 ♕e7 18 e5 fxe5 19 &b2 ♖ad8 20 ♕e2 &xg2 21 ♕xe5 and White dominates the a1-h8 diagonal, Ribli-Ivanisevic, Szeged, 1997.

b) 14...&f8 15 ♕d2 &g7 16 ♖d1 &c6 17 b3 0-0 18 &b2 ♕c7 19 ♖e1 ♕b7 20 b4 is also slightly better for White, Gulko-Krasenkow, Polanica Zdroj 1996.

8 &g2

Possibly a more promising approach is the double fianchetto with 8 b3 &g7 9 &b2 b6 (9...d6 looks like a better development

scheme) 10 &g2 &b7 11 0-0 0-0 12 ♕d2 d6 13 ♖fe1 ♖e8 14 ♖ad1 a6 15 ♘d5 ♘xd5 16 &xg7 &xg7 17 cxd5 ♖c8 18 f4 a5 19 f5 (Vaganian-Izoria, Yerevan 2000) and White is better. He has kingside attacking prospects while Black's pieces are very cramped.

8...&g7 9 0-0 0-0 10 f4

10 &g5 d6 11 ♖ac1 &e6 12 ♕d3 a6 13 f4 ♖b8 14 b4 b5 15 cxb5 axb5 16 ♖fe1 &c4 was fine for Black, Akopian-Qin Kanying, Calcutta 2000.

10...d6 11 &d2 a6

Also reasonable is 11...&f5 12 ♕e3 ♕d7 13 ♖fe1 ♖fe8 14 ♕f3 ♖ab8 15 ♖ac1 a6 16 b3 e5 17 fxe5 dxe5 18 &g5 ♕e6 ½-½ Nielsen-Schandorff, Roskilde 1998.

12 ♖ac1 ♖b8

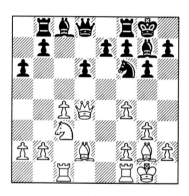

13 a4

13 ♕d3 is better, with an equal position according to Timman. If White could move his f4-pawn back to e2, he would have the pleasant position analysed in Game 50, but as it stands he has fewer dynamic prospects.

13...&e6 14 ♕d3 ♘d7

With the awkward threat of 15...♘c5 16 ♕c2 &f5. Black already has a slight plus.

15 b4 a5

Creating weaknesses in White's pawn front.

16 ♘b5 axb4 17 &xb4 ♘c5 18 ♕a3 ♘a6 19 &d2

Timman suggests 19 ♖fd1.

19...♕d7 20 ♖fe1 ♖fc8 21 &d5

In order to defend his weak c-pawn, White has to trade his strong bishop, and he is still left with an isolated pawn on d5.

21...♗xd5 22 cxd5 ♖xc1 23 ♗xc1 ♘c5 24 ♗e3 ♖c8 25 ♘a7 ♖a8

Black avoids the repetition with 25...♖c7 26 ♘b5 at the cost of a temporary pawn sacrifice.

26 ♗xc5 dxc5 27 ♕xc5 ♗f8

Black could try to win the knight with 27...b6, but Timman gives the riposte 28 ♖xe7 ♕xa4 29 ♕c6! ♖xa7 30 ♖xa7 ♕xa7 31 ♕e8+ ♗f8 32 d6 and surprisingly, Black has no way of stopping the d-pawn.

28 a5?

Now the knight really does get stuck on a7. Instead after 28 ♘b5 ♖xa4 Black has a slight edge, due to his passed b-pawn and bishop v knight.

28...e6 29 dxe6 ♕xe6 30 ♕c3 ♕d7 31 ♕e3 ♗g7 32 ♕c5

32 ♖b1 was a better defence according to Timman, e.g. 32...♗d4 33 ♕d2 ♖xa7 34 ♖d1 ♗xf2+ 35 ♔xf2 ♕xd2+ 36 ♖xd2 ♖xa5 37 ♖b2 b5 with excellent winning chances in the rook ending.

32...♗d4 33 ♕b5

White can wriggle, but there is no escape...

33...♕d8 34 ♔g2 ♗xa7 35 ♕xb7 ♗c5 36 a6 ♖a7 37 ♕c6 ♕d6 38 ♕c8+ ♔g7 39 ♖e8 ♕d5+ 40 ♔g1 ♕d1+ 41 ♔g2 ♕d5+ 42 ♔g1 ♖d7 0-1

Game 57
Karpov-Anand
Linares 1991

---

1 ♘f3 c5 2 c4 ♘c6 3 ♘c3 ♘d4 4 e3

If White gets frustrated by the lines that follow, he can always try:

a) 4 ♘g1 when:

a1) 4...♘c6 starts the game again, maybe this time White can try 5 g3.

a2) Or 4...e6 when White can continue with 5 g3 or 5 e3 ♘c6 6 ♘f3.

a3) 4...g6 5 e3 ♘c6 6 ♘f3 transposes to Games 58-59.

b) After 4 ♘e5:

b1) Black can continue the dance with 4...♘c6 5 ♘xc6 dxc6 6 g3 e5 7 ♗g2 ♘f6 8 d3 ♗e6 (8...h6 should be solid enough) 9 ♕b3 ♕d7 10 ♗g5 ♗e7 11 ♕a3 ♗h3 12 ♗xh3 ♕xh3 13 ♗xf6 gxf6 14 0-0-0 ♕d7 15 f4 and White has generated play against Black's inferior pawn structure, Boissonet-Milos, Buenos Aires 1991.

b2) 4...g6 5 e3 ♗g7 (5...♘c6 6 ♘f3 again transposes to Game 58-59) 6 exd4 cxd4 7 ♘xf7 ♔xf7 8 ♘e4 ♘f6 9 ♗d3 ♖f8 10 0-0 ♖b8 11 ♘xf6 ♗xf6 12 ♗e4 b5 13 ♕b3 ♔g7 14 cxb5 a6 with an unusual and double-edged position, Ki.Georgiev-Miles, Komotini 1992.

4...♘xf3+ 5 ♕xf3 g6

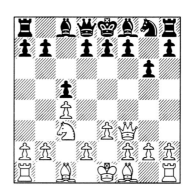

6 b3

White also has:

a) 6 d4 and after 6...♗g7:

a1) White usually plays 7 ♕d1, e.g. 7...d6 8 ♗e2 cxd4 9 exd4 ♘h6 10 0-0 ♘f5 11 d5 0-0 12 ♗f4 e5 13 dxe6 ♗xe6 14 ♖c1 ♘d4 15 ♗d3 d5 with an equal game, Panchenko-Balashov, Moscow 1991.

a2) But Benjamin's move 7 dxc5 deserves further investigation. After 7...♗xc3+ (7...♕a5 has been suggested as an improvement, though I'm not sure it makes that much difference after 8 e4) 8 bxc3, of course White's pawn structure looks horrendous, but the specific line up of minor pieces remaining does not make it easy for Black to exploit this. Benjamin-Wolff, New York 1992 continued 8...♕a5 9 e4 ♕xc5 10 ♗d3 d6 11 ♗e3 ♕a5 12 0-0 ♘f6 13 ♗d4 and White is a little better, though Black drew the ending that arose after 13...0-0 14 ♗xf6 exf6 15 ♕xf6 ♕e5 16 ♕xe5 dxe5 17 ♖fb1 ♖d8 18 ♗f1 b6 etc.

b) 6 g3 ♗g7 7 ♗g2 d6 8 0-0 ♖b8 and now:

b1) 9 ♕d1 (the loss of time inherent in this somewhat inevitable regrouping is one of the reasons that White finds it hard to extract an advantage from this variation) 9...a6 10 d4 cxd4 11 exd4 ♘f6 (11...♘h6!?) 12 h3 0-0 13 a4 ♗d7 14 ♕e2 ♖e8 15 ♗e3 e6 16 ♖fc1 ♗c6 17 d5 exd5 18 cxd5 ♗d7 and Black can maintain the balance, San Segundo-Emms, Escaldes 1998.

b2) 9 d3 a6 10 a4 ♘h6 11 ♕d1 ♘f5 12 ♗d2 0-0 13 a5 ♗d7 14 ♖a2 e6 15 ♘a4 ♗xa4 16 ♕xa4 b5 17 axb6 ♕xb6 18 ♕xa6 ♕xa6 19 ♖xa6 ♖xb2 with a level ending, Makarov-Zviaginsev, Elista 1998.

6...♗g7 7 ♗b2 d6 8 g3

An interesting recent development is 8 g4!? when Black has tried:

a)8...♖b8 9 ♗g2 ♗d7 10 ♕e2 a6?! (this justifies White's g-pawn thrust; instead 10...♘f6 11 g5 ♘h5 is unclear according to Krasenkow) 11 g5! b5 12 d3 ♕a5 13 ♖c1 h6 14 h4 and Black's g8-knight is boxed in, leaving White better, Krasenkow-Macieja, Plock 2000.

b) 8...♘f6 9 g5 ♘d7 10 h4 ♘e5 11 ♕g2 ♗g4 12 ♗e2 ♗xe2 13 ♔xe2 ♘c6 14 ♖ab1 h5 15 ♘d5 0-0 16 f4 ♗xb2 17 ♖xb2 e6 18 ♘f6+ ♔g7 19 a3 ♖b8 20 b4, and White has a strong initiative, Van Wely-Akopian, Enghien-les-Bains 2001.

8...♖b8 9 ♗g2 ♘f6

The most precise move order according to Anand. Instead, Black has tried:

a) 9...♗d7 10 0-0 ♗c6 11 ♕e2 ♗xg2 12 ♔xg2 ♘f6 13 ♘e4 and White is slightly

better as he can damage Black's pawn structure, Andersson-Ljubojevic, Brussels 1988.

b) 9...♘h6 10 ♕d1 a6 11 0-0 0-0 12 d3 b5 13 ♕d2 ♗b7 14 ♗xb7 ♖xb7 15 ♘d5 ♗xb2 16 ♕xb2 ♘g4 is okay for Black, Ftacnik-Miles, Manila 1990.

10 h3

Or 10 ♕d1 0-0 (10...♗g4!?) 11 d4 ♗g4 12 ♕d2 ♕c8 13 0-0 ♗h3 14 ♖fe1 ♗xg2 15 ♔xg2 a6 16 a4 ♖d8 17 e4 cxd4 18 ♕xd4 e6 19 ♖ac1 ½-½ Ribli-Miles, Wijk aan Zee 1989.

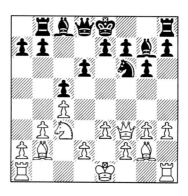

10...0-0

10...b5 11 ♘xb5! ♗b7 12 ♕xb7 ♖xb7 13 ♗xb7 0-0 14 ♗g2 is a good queen 'sacrifice' according to Karpov.

11 0-0 a6 12 ♕e2 b5! 13 d3 b4 14 ♘d1

14 ♘b1 is worth considering.

14...a5 15 a4 e5 16 e4

16 d4 should be answered by 16...e4 which emphasises the immobility of the knight on d1.

16...h5 17 h4 ♘e8

Here Anand gives 17...♗h6 18 ♘e3 ♖b7 as equal.

18 ♘e3 ♘c7

Again 18...♗h6 should be tried.

19 ♔h2 ♘e6 20 ♗h3 ♗h6?

Now this is inaccurate, since White has arranged his pieces to prepare for f2-f4.

21 ♘g2 ♗g7

This retreat is essential, to oppose bishops on the a1-h8 diagonal.

22 ♖ae1

The immediate 22 f4 can be met by 22...exf4 23 gxf4 ♗xb2 24 ♕xb2 ♘d4.

22...♖b7 23 ♗xe6! ♖xe6 24 f4 ♗g4 25 ♕d2 ♖e7 26 ♘e3

Black can hang on after 26 f5 gxf5 27 exf5 f6 28 ♘e3 ♗h6 29 ♕f2 ♗xe3 30 ♕xe3 ♖h7 (Ribli), when White has no way of breaking through.

26...f5 27 exf5 gxf5 28 ♘d5 ♖e6

28...♖ee8 is preferable.

29 ♕f2

According to Anand, White should have played 29 d4! e4 (29...cxd4 30 ♗xd4) 30 ♕e3 with the plan of ♖f2-d2, ♕f2 and ♘e3, which leaves White much better. The bishop on g4 is just a spectator.

29...♖fe8 30 ♗c1?

And here 30 fxe5 ♗xe5 31 ♗xe5 ♖xe5 32 ♖xe5 ♖xe5 33 ♕f4 ♔g7 34 ♖f2 is still good for White.

30...e4 31 dxe4 ♖xe4 32 ♖xe4 ♖xe4 33 ♖e1??

Trading the rooks is a big misjudgement. 33 ♗e3 is equal.

33...♖xe1 34 ♕xe1 ♔f7 35 ♕d2 ♗f3 36 ♘e3 ♗e4 37 ♗b2 ♗xb2 38 ♕xb2 ♕f6

This is an exception to the 'rule' that queen and knight are better than queen and bishop, in fact Black is winning because of White's weak queenside pawns on light squares.

39 ♕xf6+

Or 39 ♕e2 ♔g6 40 ♕d2 ♕d4, when White must agree to the queen trade or he will lose his queenside pawns in any case, e.g. 41 ♕e2 ♕c3.

39...♔xf6 40 ♔g1 ♗b1 41 ♘f1 ♗c2 42 ♘d2 ♔e6 43 ♔f2 d5 44 cxd5+ ♔xd5 45 ♔e3 ♗d1! 46 ♔d3 ♗xb3 0-1

Game 58
Lechtynsky-Sherbakov
Pardubice 1999

1 ♘f3 c5 2 c4 ♘c6 3 ♘c3 g6 4 e3

To paraphrase an apocryphal chess saying 'Every Russian schoolboy (or at least, the positional players among them) knows that 3...g6 is bad because of 4 e3.' Since Black cannot oppose d2-d4, his knight will often be embarrassed by d4-d5. Indeed, in the more than 660 games in my database starting from this position, White has scored close to 70%, while almost all the lines in ECO (for example) end in a white advantage. Given the verdict of both theory and practice, the reader may be surprised that GMs such as Bologan and Sherbakov have, in fairly recent times, defended the Black side. Indeed the game below ends in 0-1, so the line should not be underestimated.

Alternatively, White can try 4 d4 cxd4 5 ♘xd4 ♗g7 6 ♘c2 ♗xc3+ 7 bxc3 ♕a5 8 ♗d2 ♘f6 9 f3 d6 10 e4 which transposes to Game 27 with colours reversed. This is not a great winning attempt for White.

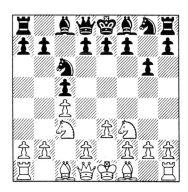

4...d6

4...♘f6 is covered in the next game, while Black often plays the move order 4...♗g7 5 d4 d6 when White can try:

a) 6 d5 is a natural move, but justifies Black's set-up somewhat.

a1) 6...♘e5 7 ♘xe5 ♗xe5 8 ♗d3 ♗g7 9 e4 (9 0-0 ♘f6 10 e4 e5!? should transpose, unless White tries 11 dxe6 ♗xe6 12 ♗g5) 9...e5! 10 f4 (Bologan suggests 10 0-0) was Akopian-Bologan, Elista 1998, and here

10...exf4 11 ♗xf4 ♘f6 12 0-0 ♘g4 is good for Black in view of the juicy e5-square.

a2) 6...♘a5 and here:

a21) 7 ♗d3 ♗xc3+!? (7...♘f6 8 0-0 0-0 9 e4 a6 10 ♖e1 is a little better for White due to the offside knight on a5) 8 bxc3 e5 9 e4 h6 10 0-0 ♘e7 11 ♘e1 g5 12 ♘c2 ♘g6 13 g3 ♗d7 14 ♘e3 ♕f6 15 ♘f5 0-0-0 16 ♗e2 ♘e7 with roughly balanced chances, Potapov-Timofeev, Russian Championship 2001.

a22) 7 ♗d2 ♘f6 8 a3 b6 9 b4 ♘b7 10 ♗d3 0-0 11 0-0 e6 12 e4 exd5 13 cxd5 a5 14 ♖b1 axb4 15 axb4 ♗d7 16 h3 ♖a3 17 ♕c2 ♕c8 18 ♖fc1, M.Gurevich-Bologan, Belfort 1998, and here Black should try 18...♗xh3 19 gxh3 ♕xh3 20 ♕d1 ♕g4+ 21 ♔f1 ♕h3+ 22 ♔e1 ♖e8 with an attack against White's king.

b) 6 ♗e2 with a split:

b1) 6...♘f6 (6...cxd4 7 exd4 ♗g4 transposes to the main game) 7 0-0 0-0 8 d5 ♘a5 9 e4 leads to a King's Indian which should yield White a slight edge (despite the tempo lost in playing e2-e3-e4) because of the offside a5-knight, e.g. 9...e5 10 ♗g5 h6 11 ♗d2 b6 12 g3 ♗h3 13 ♖e1 ♔h7 14 ♘h4 ♘g8 15 ♗d3 with good play for White, Stohl-Tolnai, Austrian League 1993.

b2) 6...♗g4 (...♗c8-g4 works best when prefaced by ...c5xd4, as in the main game, as this gives Black better counterchances against the white centre) 7 d5 ♗xf3 8 ♗xf3 ♘e5 9 ♗e2 ♘f6 10 0-0 0-0 11 e4 a6 12 ♗g5 ♖b8 13 f4 ♘ed7 14 a4 ♕c7 15 ♕d3 ♖be8 16 ♖ad1 and Black is tied down, Popov-Sivokho, St Petersburg 2000.

5 d4

5 h3 is perhaps White's best try, to rule out ...♗c8-g4. After 5...♗g7 6 d4 Black can play ...cxd4 or avoid the exchange on d4 and play a Kings-Indian style set-up.

a) 6...cxd4 7 exd4 ♘f6 (Black has mixed his plans) 8 d5 ♘b8 9 ♗e2 0-0 10 0-0 ♘a6 11 ♗e3 ♗d7 12 ♘d4 ♘c7 13 ♕d2 a6 14 a4 a5 15 f4 ♘a6 16 f5 ♘c5 17 ♕c2 ♕b6 18

♖f3 ♖ae8 19 ♘cb5 ♕d8 20 ♖af1 and White has a powerful build-up in place, Goldin-Macieja, Krynica 1997.

b) Kratochwil-Sturua, Baden-Baden 1993 saw an interesting plan for Black: 6...♗d7 7 ♗e2 cxd4 8 exd4 ♖c8 9 0-0 ♘h6 10 ♗g5 (maybe the immediate 10 d5 is better) 10...♘f5 11 d5 ♘e5 12 ♘xe5 dxe5 13 ♘e4 0-0 14 ♖c1 h6 15 ♗d2 ♘d4 16 ♗c3 e6 and Black is doing fine.

c) 6...♘f6 7 d5 ♘a5 8 ♗d3 0-0 9 e4 e5 10 g4! (a neat idea, justifying h2-h3) 10...h5 11 ♘h2 hxg4 12 hxg4 ♘h7 13 ♗e3 a6 14 ♕d2 b5 15 0-0-0 ♘xc4 16 ♗xc4 bxc4 17 f3 f5 18 gxf5 gxf5 19 exf5 ♗xf5 20 ♖dg1 with good kingside attacking chances for White, Kustar-Vaulin, Zalakaros 1999.

d) Another set-up is 6...e6 7 ♗e2 ♘ge7 8 0-0 0-0 9 ♖e1 b6 10 d5 ♘a5 11 e4 a6 12 ♗d2 ♖b8 13 a4 e5 14 ♘h2 f5 with reasonable play for Black, as White has weakened his kingside somewhat, Chloupek-Cvek, Czech Republic, 1997.

5...cxd4

5...♗g7 transposes into lines covered in the note to Black's fourth move.

6 exd4 ♗g4 7 ♗e2 ♗g7

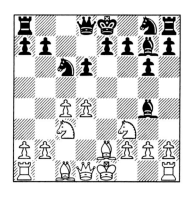

8 0-0

8 h3 ♗xf3 9 ♗xf3 ♘h6!? 10 g4 0-0 11 ♗e3 ♔h8 12 ♕d2 ♘g8 13 0-0 ½-½ Pigusov-Sherbakov, Koszalin 1999. A draw was agreed here, though anything could happen after 13...f5.

8...♘h6 9 d5 ♗xf3 10 ♗xf3 ♘e5 11 ♗e2

White has two issues to deal with – the threat to the c4-pawn (after Black has castled) and the activity of the Black knights, which can control a lot of squares from f5 and e5. To that end, White has tried several alternatives:

a) 11 b3 0-0 (11...♘f5 is better, with similar play to the main game) 12 ♗d2 a6 13 ♗e2 ♘f5 14 ♖e1 ♕b8 15 ♖c1 with an edge for White, Smejkal-Zinn, Lugano 1968.

b) 11 ♗e4 and now:

b1) 11...0-0 12 b3 f5 13 ♗f3 (the fact that the a1-h8 diagonal was opened by b2-b3 makes things more awkward for White than in the Speelman game below – 13 ♗c2 f4 14 ♘e2 f3 15 ♘d4 fxg2 16 ♔xg2 ♕b6 gives Black counterplay) 13...f4 14 ♖b1 ♘f5 and White has an uncomfortable position, Trifunovic-Portisch, Oberhausen 1961.

b2) This is more accurate than 11...f5 12 ♗c2 0-0 13 ♘e2! ♘xc4 14 ♘d4 when the weak e6-square and uncoordinated pieces hurt Black more than the loss of the c-pawn hurts White, Speelman-Xu Jun, World Team Championship, Lucerne 1989.

11...♘f5 12 ♗d2 ♖c8

After 12...0-0 13 ♖c1 a6 (13...♖c8) 14 b4 Black is a bit short of good ideas. The following kingside sortie with the queen was no exception: 14...e6 15 a3 ♕h4 16 g3 ♕h3 17 ♘e4 ♘d4 18 f4 ♘xe2+ 19 ♕xe2 ♘g4 20 ♘g5 1-0 Vaganian-Handke, Porz 2001.

13 b3 h5!?

This adds another dimension to the position. The immediate 13...♕b6 is also possible.

14 ♘e4

One of the ideas behind 13...h5 is 14 f4 ♘g4 15 ♗xg4 ♗d4+ 16 ♔h1 (16 ♖f2 ♗xf2+ 17 ♔xf2 ♕b6+ 18 ♔f1 hxg4) 16...♘g3+ 17 hxg3 hxg4 mate.

Instead, Sherbakov gives 14 ♕b1, presumably to support the plan of ♘c3-e4 and ♗d2-c3 without allowing the tactic that

occurs on move 15. This seems a bit long-winded, however, as Black can initiate counter-play with, for example, 14...a6 15 ♘e4 b5.

14...♕b6

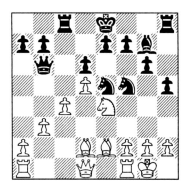

15 ♗c3

If 15 ♗g5 then simply 15...0-0 or 15...♕d4, or if White tries 15 ♔h1 then 15...h4 16 f4 ♘d7.

15...♘e3! 16 ♗d4

The point is 16 fxe3? ♕xe3+ 17 ♔h1 ♕xe4.

16...♘xd1 17 ♗xb6 axb6 18 ♖axd1 ♘d7 19 f4 ♘c5 20 ♗f3 ♖a8

After Black's simplifying combination, he is the one trying to extract something from an almost even position.

21 ♖f2

21 ♘xc5 bxc5 22 a4 is slightly better for Black according to Sherbakov, but this would be a much tougher nut to crack. As it stands, Black gets the a-file to play with.

21...♖a3 22 ♖e2 ♔d7 23 ♘g5 ♖ha8! 24 ♖de1

Sherbakov analyses 24 ♘xf7 ♖xa2 25 b4 ♖xe2 26 ♗xe2 ♘e4 27 ♗d3 ♗d4+ 28 ♔f1 ♘f2 29 ♗f5+ gxf5 30 ♖xd4 ♘g4 and Black retains the initiative.

24...♗f6 25 ♘h7 ♗d4+ 26 ♔f1 e5 27 dxe6+ fxe6 28 ♖d1 ♗c3 29 ♖e3 ♗b4!?

29...♗g7 is more conventional.

30 ♘f6+ ♔c7 31 ♘e4 ♖xa2 32 ♘xd6 ♖d8 33 ♘b5+ ♔c8 34 ♖xd8+ ♔xd8 35

g3?

Instead White can try 35 ♗d1; or 35 ♖e2 ♖a1+ 36 ♔f2 and Black has not proved anything yet.

35...♖xh2 36 ♗g2 h4 37 g4 ♗d2 38 ♖f3 h3 39 ♗xh3 ♗xf4 40 b4 ♘d7

Black has freed his rook and has good winning chances with the extra pawn.

41 g5 ♗xg5 42 ♗xe6 ♘e5 43 ♖a3 ♖b2 44 ♘c3 ♔e7 45 ♗d5 ♘g4!

Going for the king!

46 ♗xb7 ♘e3+ 47 ♔g1 ♘xc4 48 ♘d5+ ♔e6 49 ♖g3 ♘e5 50 ♘xb6 ♗h4 51 ♗d5+ ♔f5 52 ♖g2 ♖b1+ 53 ♔h2 ♘g4+ 54 ♖xg4

Otherwise it is mate.

54...♔xg4 55 ♘c4 ♔f4 56 ♗f7 ♖xb4 57 ♔g2 g5 58 ♗d5 g4 59 ♔f1 ♗f6 60 ♔g2 ♗d4 0-1

Game 59
Riumin-Kan
Moscow 1932

---

1 e4 c6 2 d4 d5 3 exd5 cxd5 4 c4 ♘f6 5 ♘c3 ♘c6 6 ♘f3 g6

The English Opening move order to reach this position is 1 c4 c5 2 ♘c3 ♘c6 3 ♘f3 g6 4 e3 ♘f6 5 d4 cxd4 6 exd4 d5.

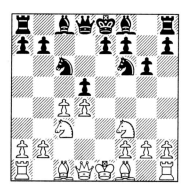

7 ♗g5

This moves casts doubt over the 4...♘f6 line. 7 cxd5 is a popular alternative, but gives Black better chances of equalising. For

example 7...♘xd5 8 ♕b3 ♘xc3 9 ♗c4 e6 (9...♘d5 10 ♗xd5 e6 11 ♗xc6+ bxc6 12 0-0 is quite good for White) 10 bxc3 and now 10...♗d6 (an improvement over the earlier tries 10...♗g7 and 10...♗d7) 11 ♗h6 ♗f8 12 ♗xf8 (12 ♗g5 ♗e7 13 ♗h6 repeats moves) 12...♔xf8 13 0-0 (Van der Sterren suggests 13 ♗e2 ♘a5 14 ♕b2) 13...♘a5 14 ♕b4+ ♔g7 15 ♗e2 b6 16 ♖fd1 ♗b7 with a balanced position, Van der Sterren-Agdestein, German Bundesliga 1998.

7...♘e4

Black has a few alternatives:

a) 7...♗e6 is perhaps Black's best chance to revive this line, e.g. 8 ♗xf6 exf6 and now:

a1) 9 ♗e2 ♗g7 10 0-0 0-0 11 ♕d2 (11 c5!?) 11...dxc4 12 d5 ♘e5 13 ♘xe5 fxe5 14 ♗xc4 with a double-edged position, Speelman-Korchnoi, Reykjavik 1988.

a2) 9 c5 a6 (otherwise ♗f1-b5 is good for White) 10 h3 ♗g7 11 ♗e2 g5!? and a draw was agreed here in Sermek-Dizdarevic, Ljubljana 1997. Black needs to play energetically to avoid being overrun on the queenside, e.g. 12 ♕a4 h5 13 b4 ♗d7.

a3) 9 cxd5 ♗xd5 10 ♗b5 ♗b4 11 0-0 and now:

a31) 11...0-0 12 ♘xd5 ♕xd5 13 ♕a4 ♗d6 14 ♖ac1 ♘e7 15 ♖fe1 a6 16 ♗c4 ♕h5 17 ♕d7 and White is in control, Ehlvest-Lyly, Jyvaskyla 1991.

a32) Van der Sterren's suggestion 11...♗xc3! 12 bxc3 0-0 followed by ...♘c6-a5 is a better attempt, and if 13 ♘d2 ♗xg2 14 ♔xg2 ♕d5+.

b) According to Van der Sterren, 7...♗g7 8 ♗xf6 ♗xf6 9 cxd5 'looks absurd when compared to similar pawn sacrifices in the Grünfeld or Caro-Kann' while

c) 7...dxc4 8 ♗xc4 ♗g7 9 d5 is also strong: 9...♘b8 10 0-0 0-0 11 ♖e1 ♘bd7 12 ♕d2 with a very good position for White, Pachman-Uhlmann, Sarajevo 1963.

8 cxd5 ♘xc3 9 bxc3 ♕xd5 10 ♕b3!

This is more clear-cut than the common

alternative 10 c4 ♕d6 11 ♕d2 ♗g7 12 ♗f4 e5 13 dxe5 ♕xd2+ 14 ♘xd2 ♘xe5 15 0-0-0 0-0 and Black is at least equal, Beim-Afek, Herzliya 1993.

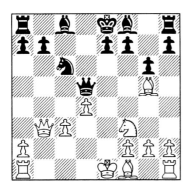

10...♕f5?!

Alternatively:

a) 10...♕xb3 is Black's best, though the ending is unpleasant for him, e.g. 11 axb3 ♗g7 and here:

a1) 12 b4 b6 13 ♗b5 ♗d7 14 ♗a6 ♗c8 15 0-0 ♗xa6 16 ♖xa6 e6 17 ♘d2 0-0 18 ♖fa1 ♖ac8 19 ♘e4 h6 20 ♗f4 e5 gave Black counterplay, Makarov-Kozlov, St Petersburg 2000.

a2) 12 ♗b5 0-0 13 0-0 h6 14 ♗e3 ♖d8 15 ♗xc6 bxc6 16 ♖a5 ♖b8 17 b4 a6 when White has a terrific grip on the position, Dautov-I.Horvath, Halle 1987.

b) 10...♕e4+ 11 ♗e3 (threatening ♕xf7+) 11...♗e6 12 c4 ♗g7? (12...♗c8 was essential) 13 ♗d3 ♕g4 14 ♕xb7 ♖c8 15 0-0 ♘xd4 16 ♗xd4 ♗xd4 17 ♖ae1 1-0 Magomedov-Kotsur, Kurgan 1993. White threatens ♖e1-e4 and if 17...♗g7 18 h3 ♕h5 19 ♖xe6.

11 d5 ♘e5 12 ♗b5+ ♗d7

12...♔d8 13 ♘xe5 ♕xe5+ 14 ♗e3 ♗h6 15 0-0 leaves White better because of Black's permanently displaced king.

13 ♗xd7+

Also strong is 13 ♘xe5 ♕xe5+ 14 ♗e3, e.g. 14...0-0-0 15 ♗e2.

13...♘xd7 14 0-0 h6 15 ♗h4 ♗g7 16

♘d4 ♕h5 17 ♗xe7! ♗e5

17...♗xe7 18 ♕b4+ ♔d8 19 ♕xb7 wins for White.

18 ♘f3 ♔xe7 19 ♘xe5 ♘xe5 20 ♕b4+

A good old-fashioned slugfest!

20...♔d8 21 ♕xb7 ♖c8 22 ♕xa7

With three pawns for the piece, and Black's king not getting any safer.

22...♘d7 23 ♖fe1 ♕xd5 24 ♖ad1 ♖a8 25 ♕e3 ♕c6 26 ♕e5 ♖g8 27 ♖d6 ♕c7 28 ♖ed1 ♔c8 29 ♕e4 ♕b7 30 ♕c4+ ♔b8 31 ♖xd7 ♕b6 32 ♕xf7 ♖c8 33 ♕f4+ ♖c7 34 ♖xc7 1-0

34...♕xc7 is answered by 35 ♖d8+.

> # Game 60
> # **Rublevsky-Sax**
> # *Neum 2000*

1 e4 c5 2 ♘f3 e6 3 c4 ♘c6 4 ♘c3 e5

1 c4 c5 2 ♘c3 ♘c6 3 ♘f3 e6 4 e4 e5 is an English move order to reach this position..

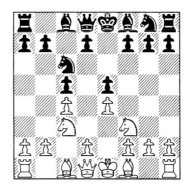

Black locks the pawn structure, reckoning that the loss of tempo (in playing ...e7-e6-e5) is less important in this kind of position. Practically unknown before the 1990s, this line has grown in popularity, with a number of GM games in the last few years. More often than not, this position is reached via the 1 e4 c5 move order used in this game. However, the play has a definite 'English' flavour.

Alternatively, 4...♘f6 would transpose to Game 61, while 4...g5!? is an off-beat try, e.g. 5 d3 h6 6 ♗e3 d6 7 h3 e5 8 ♘d5 ♗g7 9 a3 ♘ge7 10 b4 b6 11 ♗e2 ♘xd5 12 cxd5 ♘d4 13 bxc5 bxc5 14 ♘d2 and White has good play on the light squares, Rublevsky-Mochalov, Kurgan 1994.

5 a3

The first decision point. Other important choices are:

a) 5 d3 g6 6 ♘d5 ♗g7 7 ♗g5 f6 8 ♗e3 ♘ge7 9 a3 d6 10 b4 b6 11 bxc5 dxc5 12 ♗e2 0-0 13 0-0 f5 14 a4 ♘d4?! (14...h6 would be equal according to Rublevsky) 15 ♗xd4 exd4 16 ♘xe7+ ♕xe7 17 ♘d2 ♗h6 18 exf5 ♗xf5 19 ♗f3 and White is a bit better due to his light square control, Rublevsky-Solak, Herzeg Novi 1999. Note that Black cannot play 19...♗xd3 because of 20 ♗xa8 ♖xa8 21 ♕f3.

b) 5 ♘d5 d6 6 d3 and now:

b1) 6...♗e7 7 g3 and here:

b11) 7...♘f6 8 ♘xe7 ♕xe7 9 ♗g2 h6 10 0-0 g5 11 ♘e1 ♖g8 12 ♘c2 ♗g4 13 f3 ♗d7 14 b4 h5 15 bxc5 dxc5 16 ♖b1 b6 17 ♘e3 and White is a little better, Zviaginsev-Gdanski, Kazan 1997.

b12) 7...f5!? 8 ♗h3 fxe4 9 ♗xc8 ♖xc8 10 dxe4 ♘f6 11 ♘xf6+ ♗xf6 12 0-0 ♕d7 13 ♗e3 ♘d4 14 b3 b5 15 cxb5 ♕xb5 16 ♘d2 0-0 17 ♘c4 ♕c6 18 ♗xd4 exd4 19 ♕d3 d5 and Black's energetic play has prevented White from exploiting his superior structure, Nevednichy-Shchekachev, Creon 2000.

b2) 6...g6 7 b4!? cxb4 (but not 7...♘ge7?? 8 ♘f6 mate) 8 a3 bxa3 9 ♖xa3 ♗g7 10 ♗e3 ♘d4 11 ♘xd4 exd4 12 ♕a1! ♗e6 13 ♗xd4 ♗xd4 14 ♕xd4 f6 15 ♖xa7 and White is on top, Maljutin-Magerramov, Moscow 1992.

b3) Blatny suggests 6...♘ge7 as an improvement.

5...d6 6 d3

Instead:

a) 6 ♖b1 a5 7 d3 f5 (7...g6 8 ♘d5 ♗g4 9 ♕b3 ♖b8 10 ♗e2 ♗h6 11 ♗e3 ♗xf3 12 ♗xf3 ♗xe3 13 fxe3 when White is slightly better, S.Marjanovic-Pavlovic, Subotica 2000) 8 g3 ♘f6 9 ♗h3 (9 ♗g5!?) 9...fxe4 10 ♗xc8 ♕xc8 11 dxe4 ♗e7 12 0-0 0-0 13 ♗g5 ♘e8 14 ♘d5 ♗d8 15 ♗xd8 ♕xd8 16 ♔g2 ♘c7 17 b4 axb4 18 axb4 ½-½ Ivanchuk-Lautier, Belgrade 1997.

b) 6 g3 ♘ge7 7 ♗g2 g6 8 0-0 ♗g7 9 b4 cxb4 10 axb4 ♘xb4 11 ♗a3 ♘ec6 12 d4! exd4 13 ♘d5 ♘a6 14 e5 dxe5 15 ♘xe5 ♘xe5 16 ♖e1 ♗e6 17 f4 and White has a strong attack in return for the piece, G.Mohr-Maksimenko, Graz 1998.

6...g6 7 b4!

The thematic Benko-style gambit which we saw in some examples above.

7...♗g7

Black declines and tries to keep a solid position.

8 ♖b1 ♘ge7 9 g3 0-0 10 ♗g2

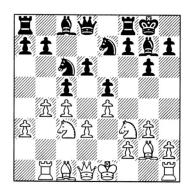

10...f5

In a later game between the same opponents, Black improved by not allowing the exchange of bishop for his e7-knight. After 10...♖b8 11 0-0 h6 12 ♗d2 ♗d7 13 ♘d5 b6 14 b5 ♘d4 15 ♘xd4 exd4 16 ♘xe7+ ♕xe7 17 a4 f5 18 f4 ♔h7 19 ♖e1 ♕f7 20 a5, Rublevsky-Sax, Istanbul Olympiad 2000, White still got a slight pull, though Black managed to hold a draw this time.

11 0-0 ♖b8 12 ♗g5

Swapping the dark-squared bishop for a black knight is a thematic way of increasing the pressure on the light squares. For a similar idea, see the ♗g5 lines in Game 49.

12...h6

After 12...♗f6 Rublevsky gives the forcing line 13 ♗xf6 ♖xf6 14 bxc5 dxc5 15 exf5 ♗xf5 16 ♘h4! ♗xd3 17 ♘d5 ♗xf1 18 ♘xf6+ ♔g7 19 ♘d7 ♗e2 20 ♕d6 ♘c8 21 ♕e6 ♗xc4 22 ♕g4 with a strong attack for White.

13 ♗xe7 ♘xe7 14 exf5 ♘xf5

14...gxf5 is better, though White is slightly better after 15 ♘d2.

15 ♘d2 b6 16 ♕a4 ♗b7?

After this, White really starts to dominate. Instead Black should play 16...♕e7 17 ♘b5 a6 18 ♘c3, when White is better due to his control of the light squares and Black's weak pawns on b6 and a6.

17 ♕xa7 ♗xg2 18 ♔xg2 ♖a8 19 ♕b7 ♖xa3 20 ♘de4

This game is a model example of light-squared play in the English. The g7-bishop isn't going anywhere, anytime soon.

20...♖f7 21 ♕d5 ♕d7 22 ♘b5 ♖a2 23 ♔g1

After avoiding ...♘e3+, White concludes matters efficiently.

23...♘e7 24 ♕xd6 ♕h3 25 ♖a1 ♖xa1 26 ♖xa1 cxb4 27 ♕xb6 ♕d7 28 ♘bd6 ♖f8 29 ♕xb4 ♘f5 30 ♕b7 ♕e6 31 ♖a7 1-0

Game 61
Zviaginsev-Ulibin
Russian Championship 1996

---

1 ♘f3 ♘f6 2 c4 c5 3 ♘c3 e6 4 e4

This is an independent line which avoids both the Hedgehog with 4 g3 b6, and 4 g3 d5 (the Keres-Parma/Semi-Tarrasch – Games 32-33), as well as the Tarrasch or Catalan for that matter. So obviously if you use this move order as Black to get to any of those openings, you need to have an answer to 4 e4.

4...♘c6 5 ♗e2

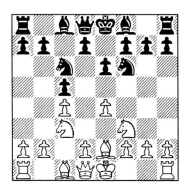

5...d5

This is not mandatory, of course. A viable alternative is 5...b6, when White has gone for:

a) 6 0-0 ♗b7 7 d4 cxd4 8 ♘xd4 ♕b8 9 ♘c2 ♘b4 10 ♗f3 ♘xc2 11 ♕xc2 ♗d6 12 g3 ♗e5 13 ♗d2 0-0 14 ♖ac1 a6 15 a4 ♕c7 16 b3 ♖ac8 17 ♖fe1 ♖fe8 18 ♕b1 d6 19 ♗g2 ♘d7 with a level position, White has a slightly passive version of a standard Hedgehog, Bareev-Adams, Sarajevo 2000.

b) 6 d4 cxd4 7 ♘xd4 ♗b7 8 ♗f4 and here:

b1) 8...♘xd4 9 ♕xd4 ♗c5 10 ♕d3 d6 11 0-0 0-0 12 ♖ad1 ♕e7!? (12...e5 is okay for Black) 13 ♗xd6 ♗xd6 14 ♕xd6 ♕xd6 15 ♖xd6 ♘xe4 16 ♘xe4 ♗xe4 17 f3 ♗b7 18 b4 ♖fc8 and Black held this ending, Zviaginsev-Leitao, Poikovsky 2001.

b2) 8...♗b4 9 ♘db5 ♘xe4 10 ♕c2 ♘xc3 11 bxc3 0-0 (Zviaginsev gives 11...♕f6! 12 ♕c1 ♗a5 13 ♗g5 ♕e5 14 ♗f4 with a repetition of moves) 12 cxb4 ♕f6 13 ♕c1 ♘xb4 14 0-0 ♕g6 15 f3 e5 16 ♗xe5 ♖fe8 17 ♕c3 1-0 was the rapid denouement in Onischuk-Leitao, Poikovsky 2001.

6 cxd5

6 e5 is an alternative move order that introduces some differences:

a) 6...♘e4 7 0-0 (an interesting try for White, as the c8-bishop has not been freed by 6 cxd5 exd5) 7...♗e7 8 ♗d3 (8 ♕c2 is answered by 8...♘g5) 8...♘xc3 9 dxc3 dxc4

---

10 ♗xc4 ♕xd1 11 ♖xd1 b6 12 ♗d3 ♗b7 13 ♗e4 ♖d8 14 ♗g5 with a slight pull for White, Glek-Van der Sterren, Breda 1999.

b) 6...♘g4 7 cxd5 exd5 (7...♘cxe5 8 ♘xe5 ♘xe5 9 d4) 8 ♗b5 transposes to the main game.

c) 6...♘d7 is best, when White has nothing better than 7 cxd5 exd5 transposing to the note 'b' to Black's next move.

6...exd5 7 e5 ♘g4

In the light of White's play in this game, Black should select one of the alternatives:

a) 7...♘e4 8 0-0 ♗e7 is equal according to Zviaginsev.

b) 7...♘d7 8 ♗b5 ♗e7 9 0-0 0-0 10 ♖e1 ♘b6 11 d4 c4 12 ♗xc6 bxc6 13 h3 ♖b8 14 ♗f4 ♘a8 15 b3 ♗e6 16 bxc4 dxc4 17 ♘e4 ♘b6 and Black has a decent position, with a firm grip on d5, Nogueiras-Delgado, Santa Clara 1999.

8 ♗b5 d4

Since White has taken two moves to get his bishop to b5 (♗f1-e2-b5), the position has now transposed into a variation which is even more important with colours reversed – 1 c4 c5 2 ♘f3 ♘c6 3 ♘c3 e5 4 e3 ♘f6 5 d4 cxd4 6 exd4 e4 7 ♘g5 (for 7 ♘e5 see Game 62) ♗b4 8 d5. This is a popular line which has been played many times. Here Gelfand-Kasparov, Dos Hermanas 1996, continued 8...♘e5 9 ♕b3 etc. However, Zviaginsev's next move is a novelty which dramatically changes the assessment both of the line he played, and the line with colours reversed! So in Gelfand-Kasparov, for example, Black should play 8...♗xc3+! 9 bxc3 ♘a5 etc. Since important games have been played with both colour orientations, it can be somewhat mind-boggling to try and figure out the theory, so I have also included the key analysis (albeit in less depth) from this game in Game 62 also.

9 ♗xc6+!

9 ♘e4 had been played before.

9...bxc6 10 ♘a4!

Black now has a weak c5-pawn to con-

tend with, and his knight is poorly placed on g4. After a later d2-d3, h2-h3 and ...♘g4-h6, White can shatter Black's kingside structure with ♗c1xh6.

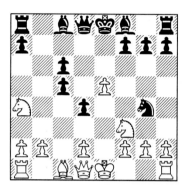

10...♗a6

Alternatively, Black can try:

a) 10...♕d5 11 0-0 ♗e7 12 ♖e1 and now:

a1) 12...♘h6 with the further choice:

a11) 13 d3 ♗g4 14 ♖e4 ♗f5 15 ♗xh6 gxh6 16 ♖f4 ♗g6 17 ♘h4 0-0 18 b3 is Gausel-Rytshagov, Asker 1997 (in reverse!) which continued 18...c4 (but why not just 18...♕xe5?) 19 bxc4 ♕xe5 with approximate equality.

a12) 13 h3 (to prevent ...♗c8-g4) is better, and then 13...d3 14 b3 c4 is a radical attempt to gum up White's development and also liquidate the weak c5-pawn. Probably White can just continue 15 ♘b2 or 15 bxc4 ♕xc4 16 ♗b2.

a2) 12...0-0 13 h3 (13 d3 is also possible as 13...f6 14 exf6 ♗xf6 15 ♕b3 is excellent for White) 13...♘h6 14 d3 ♖e8 (14...♘f5 avoids ♗xh6, though after 15 b3 White has a big advantage according to Khalifman) 15 b3 ♗a6 16 ♗xh6 gxh6 17 ♕d2 ♗f8 and Black has a gruesome position, though he eventually drew the game, Holst-Larsen, Taastrup 1998.

b) 10...c4 11 0-0 ♗f5 12 b3 ♕d5 13 ♗b2 cxb3 14 ♘xd4 ♗e6 15 axb3 ♕xe5 16 f4 ♕h5 17 h3 ♘f6 18 ♕e1 ♔d7 19 ♘b6+ axb6 20 ♖xa8 ♗d5 21 ♕e5 1-0 Adorjan-

Menyhart, Hungary 1997.

11 d3 ♕a5+

Black goes after the d3 pawn. He must try something active, or else he will be left with a positionally hopeless set-up. Zviaginsev branded 11...♕a5+ as dubious, but 11...c4 fared no better when a (poorly prepared?) opponent tried it against him the following year:

a) After 11...c4 12 0-0 (12 h3 comes unstuck after 12...♘xe5 13 ♘xe5 ♕a5+) 12...cxd3 13 e6! and now:

a1) 13...f5 14 ♗g5 (White is already much better) 14...♗e7 15 ♘c5 ♗c4 16 ♖c1 ♕d5 17 ♗xe7 d2 18 ♕xd2 ♗xf1 19 ♕g5 g6 20 ♖xf1 ♖g8 21 h3 ♖g7 22 hxg4 ♖xe7 23 ♕f6 1-0 Zviaginsev-Filippov, Elista 1997.

a2) 13...♗e7 14 h3 ♘f6 (14...d2 is not mentioned by other annotators, and could be an improvement, e.g. 15 ♗xd2 ♗xf1 16 ♕xf1 ♘f6 17 ♘g5 ♕d5 18 exf7+ ♔f8 and Black may be just about okay) 15 ♘g5 ♕d5 16 exf7+ ♔d7 17 ♖e1 with a big plus for White according to Zviaginsev.

a3) 13...fxe6 14 ♘g5 ♘f6 15 ♘xe6 leaves Black's king completely in the open.

b) White also retains a strong initiative after 11...♕d5 12 0-0 c4 13 dxc4 ♗xc4 14 ♖e1 ♖d8 15 ♗g5.

12 ♗d2 ♕b5 13 0-0

Not 13 h3 ♕xd3 followed by ...♕d3-e4+.

13...♕xd3 14 ♖e1 0-0-0

Black's king needs to get out of the way of e5-e6, but there is no hiding place.

15 h3 ♘h6 16 e6

White crashes through with powerful play.

16...fxe6

If 16...♗d6 17 ♘e5 continues the onslaught.

17 ♘e5 ♕b5

After this, White wins the exchange, but if instead 17...♕f5 18 g4 ♕f6 19 g5 Black surrenders a piece for insufficient compensation.

18 ♗xh6 gxh6 19 ♘f7 ♖g8 20 ♘xd8

♔xd8 **21 ♕f3!**

White has a winning attack.

21...♗e7

or 21...♕xa4 22 ♕f7 ♖h8 23 ♖xe6.

22 ♖xe6 ♗c8

22...♕xa4 23 ♖xe7 ♔xe7 24 ♖e1+ wins.

23 ♖xe7! ♔xe7 24 ♖e1+ ♗e6 25 ♕f5 ♖g6 26 ♘xc5 ♕c4 27 b3 1-0

White gets a winning pawn ending after 27...♕d5 28 ♕xd5 cxd5 29 ♔f1 ♔d6 30 ♘xe6 ♖xe6 31 ♖xe6+ ♔xe6 32 ♔e2.

Game 62
Marin-Movsesian
Neum 2000

1 c4 c5 2 ♘f3 ♘c6 3 e3

Or 3 ♘c3 e5 when 4 e3 transposes to the game. Another common continuation here is 4 g3, which after 4...g6 5 ♗g2 ♗g7 transposes into lines considered in Game 49 (Oll-Cramling).

3...e5 4 ♘c3 ♘f6

4...f5 is perhaps too loosening. 5 d4 and now:

a) 5...e4 6 d5 exf3 7 dxc6 fxg2 8 cxd7+ ♕xd7 9 ♗xg2 ♕xd1+ 10 ♔xd1 ♘f6 11 b3 f4!? 12 ♘d5 ♗d6, Marin-Ardeleanu, Iasi 1999, and now 13 ♘xf6+ gxf6 14 ♗b2 fxe3 15 fxe3 is slightly better for White – he controls both long diagonals.

b) 5...cxd4 6 exd4 e4 7 ♘e5 (7 d5!?) 7...♘f6 8 ♗e2 ♗b4 9 0-0 0-0 10 c5 d5 11 ♗f4 ♗a5 12 ♖c1 ♗e6 13 ♕a4 (Kharitonov-Iljushin, Novgorod 1999) and White is well placed.

5 d4

a) 5 a3 is interesting, provided White follows up with an early d2-d4 given the chance.

a1) 5...♗e7 6 d4 exd4 7 exd4 cxd4 8 ♘xd4 0-0 9 ♘c2 b6 10 ♗f4 ♗a6 11 b4 ♗b7 12 ♗e2 d6 13 0-0 when Black is hindered by his weak d-pawn, Benjamin-Kramnik, Groningen 1993.

a2) 5...d6 6 ♗e2 g6 7 d4 exd4 8 exd4

♗g7 9 ♗f4 0-0 10 0-0 ♗f5 11 d5 ♘e7, Kramnik-Kamsky, New York (match game 4) 1994, and now 12 ♕d2 gives White a slight advantage according to Kramnik.

a3) Black has had better results with 5...d5 which leads to a kind of reversed Taimanov Sicilian, e.g. 6 cxd5 ♘xd5 7 ♗b5 ♘xc3 8 bxc3 ♗d6 9 0-0 0-0 10 e4 ♘a5, and compared to the line in reverse (1 e4 c5 2 ♘f3 e6 3 d4 cxd4 4 ♘xd4 ♘c6 5 c4 ♘f6 6 ♘c3 ♗b4 7 ♗d3 0-0 8 0-0 e5 etc.), White's a-pawn may be better off on its original square. Dorfman-Yudasin, Nikolaev 1983 continued 11 d4 exd4 12 cxd4 ♗g4 13 e5 ♗c7 with an unclear position.

b) 5 b3 is playable but is no way for White to gain any opening advantage, e.g. 5...g6 6 ♗b2 ♗g7 7 ♘d5 d6 8 ♘xf6+ ♗xf6 9 d3 0-0 10 ♗e2 ♗g7 11 ♕c2 d5 12 cxd5 ♕xd5 13 0-0 b6 14 a3 ♗b7 which is obviously fine for Black, C.Horvath-Z.Almasi, Hungarian Championship 1999.

5...cxd4

5...e4 6 ♘e5 (6 d5!?) 6...cxd4 7 exd4 transposes to the game.

6 exd4 e4

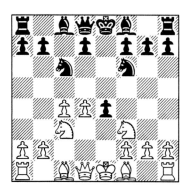

7 ♘e5

The alternatives do not look that great for White:

a) 7 ♘g5 ♗b4 8 d5 and now:

a1) 8...♗xc3+ is Zviaginsev's idea from Game 61 with colours reversed. For more details, see that game, but I have summa-

rised the main lines and conclusions below. After 9 bxc3 ♘a5:

a11) 10 ♗a3 d6 11 ♕a4+ (or 11 c5 0-0 12 cxd6 e3 13 f4 ♗g4 with a big plus for Black) 11...♗d7 12 ♕b4 0-0 13 ♕xd6 ♖e8 14 0-0-0 h6 15 ♘h3 e3 and Black is breaking through.

a12) 10 ♕d4 0-0 11 ♗e2 ♖e8 12 0-0 (12 ♘h3 h6) 12...h6 13 ♘h3 d6 14 ♖e1 b6 and Black is somewhat better.

a2) 8...♘e5 9 ♕b3 a5 10 ♗d2 0-0 11 0-0-0 d6 12 ♘gxe4 ♘xe4 13 ♘xe4 ♗f5 14 ♘g3 ♗d7 15 ♔b1 ♕e8 (Gelfand-Kasparov, Dos Hermanas 1996) and here Gelfand gives 15...♘g4 16 ♕f3 ♕b6 17 ♗d3 ♕xf2 18 ♘e4 ♕xf3 19 gxf3 f5 20 fxg4 fxe4 21 ♗xe4 ♗xg4 22 ♖dg1 with an equal position.

b) 7 ♘d2 ♗b4 8 ♘db1?! d5 9 a3 ♗xc3+ 10 bxc3 ♗e6 11 cxd5 ♕xd5 and White has yet to develop any pieces, Speelman-Ivanchuk, Linares 1992.

7...♗b4

Alternatively 7...♗d6!? 8 f4 0-0 9 ♗e2 b6 10 ♗e3 (Not 10 0-0 ♘xd4 11 ♕xd4 ♗c5) 10...♘e7 11 0-0 (Avrukh gives 11 g4 ♗b4 12 ♕b3 ♗xc3+ 13 ♕xc3 d6 14 g5 ♘e8 15 ♘g4 as unclear) 11...♘f5 12 ♗f2 ♗b4 13 ♖c1 ♗b7 14 a3 ♗xc3 15 ♖xc3, Mikhalchishin-Avrukh, European Team Championship, Batumi 1999, and here 15...d6 16 ♘g4 ♘xg4 17 ♗xg4 ♕f6 is equal according to Avrukh.

8 ♗e2 ♕a5 9 ♘xc6 dxc6 10 ♗d2

White can also offer a pawn sacrifice with 10 0-0 ♗xc3 (10...0-0 transposes to the main game after 11 ♗d2 ♖e8) 11 bxc3 ♕xc3 12 ♖b1 0-0 13 ♖b3 ♕a5 14 ♖g3 with compensation for the pawn, Bertholee-J.Polgar, Amsterdam 1990.

10...0-0 11 0-0 ♖e8 12 a3 ♗xc3 13 ♗xc3 ♕g5 14 ♕c1 ♕g6 15 ♕f4

White can also try 15 ♖e1 or 15 ♕e3.

15...h5 16 ♖fe1 ♗g4 17 ♗f1?!

White plans to try and oust the g4-bishop with ♖e1-e3 and h2-h3, followed by ♖a1-

d1. However he does not get time for this unravelling exercise. Marin gives 17 d5 as an improvement, assessing the position as equal.

17...h4 18 h3

Marin gives 18 d5 ♘h5 19 ♕c7 cxd5 20 cxd5 ♖ac8 21 ♕xb7 ♘f4 when Black has attacking chances in return for the pawn. Now Black can answer 18 ♖e3 with 18...♘h5. Black already has a promising position.

18...♗xh3 19 ♕xh4 ♗g4 20 ♖e3 ♘h5 21 ♖ae1 f5 22 d5 c5!

Not 22...f4 23 ♖xe4 ♖xe4 24 ♖xe4 ♕xe4 25 ♕xg4, which is good for White.

23 g3 ♔f7

White's queen is stranded, and can only spectate while the black artillery is moved across to the h-file.

24 ♗g2 ♖h8 25 ♗xe4

White's counterplay comes a move too late.

25...♘f6

In response to 25...fxe4 Marin gives 26 ♖xe4 ♘f6 27 ♗xf6 (27 ♖xg4 ♘xg4) 27...♖xh4 28 ♗xh4 but isn't Black winning in any case?

26 ♗xf5 ♗xf5 27 ♖e7+ ♔g8 28 ♗xf6

Or 28 ♕f4 ♕h5.

28...gxf6

Or 28...♖xh4.

29 ♕f4 ♕h5 30 ♔g2 ♗h3+ 31 ♔g1 ♗g4 32 ♕e4 ♔f8!

A precise move to finish things off .

33 ♖e3 ♗f3 0-1

34 ♖xf3 ♕h1mate or 34 ♕xf3 ♕xf3 35 ♖xf3 ♔xe7.

Game 63
Kramnik-Adams
Tilburg 1997

---

1 ♘f3 ♘f6 2 c4 b6

2...c5 3 ♘c3 e6 is a more flexible 'Hedgehog-friendly' move order, although of course Black still has to contend with 4

d4 or 4 e4.

3 ♘c3 c5

This move order is often chosen by players that like the Hedgehog set-up as Black. However the option of 4 e4 gives White some aggressive options not normally available in the Hedgehog-proper.

4 e4

4 d4 cxd4 5 ♘xd4 ♗b7 is a closely related line, which is covered in Game 16.

4 e3 should be fairly harmless, e.g. 4...g6 5 d4 ♗g7 6 d5 0-0 7 ♗d3 e6 8 0-0 d6 9 e4 exd5 10 exd5 ♗g4 11 h3 ♗xf3 12 ♕xf3 ♘bd7 13 ♕d1 ♘e8 with equality, P.Nielsen-S.Hansen, Taastrup 1998.

Instead 4 g3 ♗b7 5 ♗g2 e6 will lead to a Hedgehog (see Chapter 1).

4...d6

The immediate 4...♗b7 does not enjoy a great reputation. After 5 e5 Black has:

a) 5...♘g8 gives White a bit too much leeway: 6 d4 ♗xf3 7 ♕xf3 ♘c6 8 d5! ♘xe5 9 ♕e2 d6 10 f4 ♘d7 11 g4 g6 12 h4 h6 13 ♗h3 ♗g7 (instead 13...♘gf6 14 ♗d2 followed by 0-0-0 is slightly better for White according to Djuric) 14 g5! and the g8-knight is completely stymied, Djuric-Marinkovic, Svetozarevo 1990.

b) 5...♘g4 6 h3 ♘h6 7 d4 and now:

b1) After 7...cxd4 White can try 8 ♘b5 (instead of the regular 8 ♘xd4) 8...♘c6 9 ♘bxd4 ♘xd4 10 ♘xd4 g6 11 ♗f4 ♕c8 12 ♕d2 with a very pleasant position for White, B.Lalic-Samovojska, Makarska Tucepi 1995.

b2) 7...♗xf3 8 ♕xf3 ♘c6 9 dxc5 (Mestel suggests 9 d5!? and indeed it looks quite promising after 9...♘xe5 {or 9...♘d4 10 ♕e4} 10 ♕e4 d6 11 ♗f4) 9...♘b8 10 cxb6 axb6 11 ♕e4 e6 12 ♗e2 ♕xe5 13 ♕xe5 ♘xe5 14 ♗e3 ♗c5 15 ♗xc5 bxc5 16 ♘e4 and White is a little better in the endgame, Mestel-Ftacnik, Hastings 1983/4.

5 d4 cxd4 6 ♘xd4 ♗b7 7 ♕e2

This tends to be regarded as the main line, but 7 ♗d3 might be even more direct, and has enjoyed strong success in practical play. Black has:

a) 7...e6 8 0-0 ♗e7 9 b3 0-0 10 ♗b2 ♘bd7 11 ♕d2 ♖e8 12 ♖fe1 ♗f8 13 ♖e3 g6 14 ♖h3 ♘c5 15 ♖e1 ♘xd3 16 ♖xd3 ♘d7 17 f4, when White is well placed for central and kingside action, Suba-Yudasin, Cala Galdana 1994.

b) 7...g6 8 0-0 ♗g7 9 ♗g5 ♘bd7 10 ♕e2 0-0 11 ♖ad1 and it is difficult for Black to undertake anything active: 11...a6 12 ♗b1 ♕b8 (here Tal suggests 12...e6 13 f4 ♕c7 14 ♘f3 when White is only slightly better) 13 ♖d2 ♖a7 14 ♘d5 ♖e8 15 ♗c2 e6 16 ♘xf6+ ♘xf6 17 ♖fd1 and White has strong pressure on the d-file, Tal-Shvidler, Berlin 1986.

Meanwhile 7 f3 would transpose to Game 16.

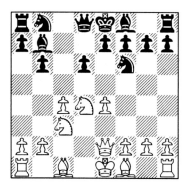

7...♘c6

Alternatively:

a) 7...g6 8 g3 and now:

a1) 8...♗g7 9 ♗g2 0-0 10 0-0 ♘c6 (this is a necessary expedient in a number of these positions – 10...♘bd7 is a bit too passive) 11 ♘xc6 ♗xc6 12 ♖d1 ♘d7 13 ♘d5, Gulko-D.Gurevich, US Championship 1994, and here Gulko gives 13...e6 14 ♘c3 ♕e7 15 ♗f4 ♘e5 with equality.

a2) 8...♘bd7 9 ♗g2 ♖c8 10 0-0 a6 (very provocative; Black should complete his development) 11 ♖d1 ♕c7 12 b3 e6 (otherwise ♘c3-d5 is strong) 13 ♗a3 ♘c5 14 ♖ac1 ♗e7 15 b4 ♘cd7 16 ♘d5! (a classic

♘d5 sacrifice) 16...exd5 17 cxd5 ♕b8 18 ♘c6 ♗xc6 19 dxc6 ♘e5 20 f4 b5 (20...♘xc6 21 e5 gives White a strong initiative) 21 fxe5 dxe5 22 ♗b2 is Salov-Yudasin, St Petersburg 1997. White has regained his piece and emerged with a better position due to the passed c-pawn and two bishops.

b) 7...e6 and now:

b1) 8 g4 h6 (8...♗e7 9 g5 ♘fd7 10 h4 a6 11 ♗e3 ♘c6 12 ♗g2 ♖c8 13 ♖c1 0-0 14 0-0 ♘xd4 15 ♗xd4, Cu.Hansen-Borge, Aarhus 1999, with a fairly promising attacking position for White) 9 ♗g2 ♗e7 10 f4 ♘bd7 11 0-0 ♕c8 12 ♗e3 g6 13 ♖ac1 h5 14 gxh5 ♖xh5 15 ♘d5 (unlike Salov-Yudasin in 'a2' above, this ♘d5 sacrifice is less well timed) 15...exd5 16 cxd5 ♘c5 17 b4 ♗a6 and White's aggression has backfired, Poluljahov-Simantsev, St Petersburg 2000.

b2) 8 g3 a6 9 ♗g2 ♕c7 10 0-0 ♗e7 11 ♗e3 with a further choice:

b21) 11...♘bd7 12 ♖ac1 ♖c8 13 b3 ♕b8 14 ♗d2 0-0 15 g4 (this game can be compared to those in the Hedgehog chapter) 15...g6 (15...h6!? could be better) 16 g5 ♘e8 17 ♗h3 ♘g7 18 f4 and White is better since he has disrupted Black co-ordination, Korchnoi-Csom, Rome 1981.

b22) 11...♘c6 (once again this move can be used to relieve some of the pressure; although Hedgehog purists generally prefer to play ...♘b8-d7 to retain more dynamic potential, White's set-up here is fairly dangerous, so pragmatism is called for) 12 ♖ac1 ♘xd4 13 ♗xd4 0-0 14 e5 dxe5 15 ♗xe5 ♕c8 16 ♘e4 ♘xe4 17 ♗xe4 ♗xe4 18 ♕xe4 ♖d8 19 ♖fd1 ♖a7 20 ♖xd8+ ♕xd8 21 ♕g4 ♗f8 22 ♖d1 ½-½ Wirthensohn-Mascarinas, Switzerland 1990.

8 ♘xc6 ♗xc6 9 ♗g5 ♘d7

Or 9...e6 10 0-0-0 ♕c8 11 ♗xf6 (this is a bit hasty; White can continue the build-up with 11 f4) 11...gxf6 12 ♔b1 ♗b7 13 f4 ♕c5 14 ♘b5 a6 15 ♘d4 ♖c8 and Black is fine. White's queen is awkwardly placed blocking the bishop and defending the c-pawn, Gasanov-Nedobora, Kharkov 1999.

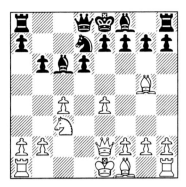

10 0-0-0 h6

Or 10...♕c8 11 ♔b1 ♘c5 12 f3 a5 13 h4 ♕b7 (Gheorghiu suggests 13...h6 though White is still slightly better) 14 h5 h6 15 ♗h4 e6 16 ♕d2 ♕c7 17 ♘d5 Korchnoi-Gheorghiu, London 1980, and White has the initiative.

11 ♗e3 e6 12 ♗d4 e5

Otherwise the threat to the g7-pawn makes it hard for Black to complete his development.

13 ♗e3 ♗e7 14 ♔b1 0-0 15 f3 a6

Kramnik suggests 15...♘c5!?.

16 ♘d5 ♗xd5 17 ♖xd5

White has a solid grip on the light squares.

17...♕c7 18 g3 ♘f6 19 ♖d2 b5

Black has to generate some counterplay before White completes his development and swings the h1-rook into the centre.

20 ♗h3?!

20 cxb5 axb5 21 ♕d1 is better according to Kramnik – White retains a clear edge.

20...bxc4 21 ♖c1 d5!

Freeing his e7-bishop. White cannot hold on to the extra pawn.

22 exd5 ♖fd8 23 d6

23 ♕xc4 ♕xc4 24 ♖xc4 should give White a small edge in the endgame.

23...♖xd6 24 ♕xc4 ♕xc4 25 ♖xc4 ♘d5 26 ♗f2

26 ♗c5 can be answered by 26...♘b6!.

26...♘c3+ 27 ♔c2 ♖xd2+ 28 ♔xd2 ♘xa2 29 ♖c8+ ♖xc8

White's two bishops give him the edge, despite his pawn deficit, however Black has good drawing chances.

30 ♗xc8 ♘b4 31 ♗c3 a5 32 ♗b7 ♗d8 33 ♗e4 g6 34 g4 ♔f8 35 ♔c4 ♔e8 36 h4 ♔d7 37 h5 gxh5 38 ♗f5+ ♔c7 39 gxh5 ♗g5 40 ♔b5 ♘c6 41 ♗b6+ ♔d6 42 ♗c5+ ♔c7 43 ♗b6+ ♔d6 44 ♗e4 ♘d4+ 45 ♔xa5

Winning the pawn at last, but meanwhile Black's pieces are actively placed and he can quickly get a passed pawn.

45...f5 46 ♗a8 ♗e3 47 ♔a4 e4 48 fxe4 ½-½

Black draws after 48 fxe4 f4 49 b4 ♘c6.

Summary

3...♘d4 continues to do well without quite becoming mainstream. 3...g6 4 e3 still should give White an edge, though don't underestimate Black's game. 3...e5 has its own nuances but is fairly promising for Black.

1 c4 c5 2 ♘c3 ♘c6
> 2...♘f6 3 ♘f3 b6 – *Game 63*

3 ♘f3 ♘d4 (D)
> 3...g6 4 e3
>> 4...d6 – *Game 58*; 4...♘f6 – *Game 59*
>
> 3...e5 4 e3 ♘f6 5 d4 cxd4 6 exd4 e4 (D)
>> 7 ♘e5 – *Game 62*; 7 ♘g5 – *Game 61* (reversed colours)
>
> 3...e6 4 e4
>> 4...e5 – *Game 60*; 4...♘f6 – *Game 61*

4 e3
> 4 g3 – *Game 56*

4...♘xf3+ 5 ♕xf3 (D) – *Game 57*

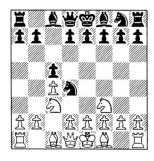

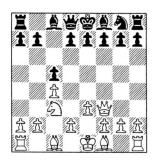

3...♘d4   *6...e4*   *5 ♕xf3*

INDEX OF COMPLETE GAMES

Akopian-Gulko, *Yerevan Olympiad 1996*.. 23

Aleksandrov-Krasenkow, *New York 1997*...113

Anand-Adams, *FIDE World Ch., Groningen 1997*... 77

Andersson-Polgar.J, *Malmo 2000*... 36

Andersson-Timman, *Ubeda 1997*...134

Beliavsky-Adams, *Dortmund 1998*... 47

Csom-Adorjan, *Hungarian Championship 1993*..116

Dyachkov-Aseev, *Russian Championship 1996*... 49

Ftacnik-Pinter, *Prague 1985*... 93

Georgiev.Ki-Topalov, *Sarajevo 2000*... 55

Gulko-Khalifman, *Yerevan 1996*...125

Gurevich.M-Filippov, *Bugojno 1999*..111

Hansen.Cu-Schandorff, *Stockholm 1996*... 70

Hauchard-Kinsman, *French League 1998*... 81

Hjartarson-Arnason, *Reykjavik 1995*... 63

Ionov-Yudasin, *Vilnius 1997*... 43

Istratescu-Fominyh, *Elista Olympiad 1998*...109

Ivanchuk-Khalifman, *Elista (3rd match game) 1998*... 66

Karpov-Anand, *Linares 1991*...143

Karpov-Csom, *Bad Lauterberg 1977*... 13

Karpov-Kasparov, *Moscow (13th match game) 1984*... 33

Karpov-Topalov, *Linares 1994*... 58

Kasparov-Kramnik, *New York (rapid) 1995*..103

Komarov-Del Rio Angelis, *Italy 1999*.. 22

Korchnoi-Brunner, *Bern 1996*.. 84

Korchnoi-Grosar, *Ptuj 1995*... 80

Korchnoi-Ponomariov, *Donetsk (8th match game) 2001* 52
Kramnik-Adams, *Tilburg 1997* 155
Kramnik-Karpov, *Dos Hermanas 1999* 29
Kramnik-Kasparov, *Linares 2000* 91
Kramnik-Timman, *Wijk aan Zee 1999* 89
Kramnik-Topalov, *Linares 1999* 87
Krasenkow-Brynell, *Copenhagen 1996* 101
Krivoshey-Shipov, *Yalta 1996* 20
Lagunow-Löffler, *Berlin 1994* 129
Lautier-Kasparov, *Tilburg 1997* 96
Lechtynsky-Sherbakov, *Pardubice 1999* 145
Lputian-Leko, *Wijk aan Zee 2000* 75
Lputian-Timman, *Wijk aan Zee 2000* 137
Makarov-Mikhailov, *Kemerovo 1995* 31
Marin-Kempinski, *Krynica 1998* 136
Marin-Movsesian, *Neum 2000* 153
Mednis-Ernst, *Gausdal 1990* 106
Mikhalchishin- Sale, *Nova Gorica 1999* 132
Mikhalchishin-Kasparov, *Soviet Championship 1981* 40
Nogueiras-Alvarez, *Santa Clara 1999* 118
Oll-Cramling.P, *Dos Hermanas 1992* 120
Piket-Kasparov, *Internet 2000* 72
Riumin-Kan, *Moscow 1932* 148
Rublevsky-Sax, *Neum 2000* 149
Sorokin-Rodriguez, *Villa Gesell 1998* 56
Spraggett-Ivanisevic, *Istanbul Olympiad 2000* 107
Summerscale-Adams, *British Championship 1997* 35
Tal-Short, *Naestved 1985* 17
Timman-Alterman, *European Team Ch., Pula 1997* 61
Tukmakov-Gheorghiu, *Crans Montana 2000* 24
Uhlmann-Priehoda, *Wattens 1995* 11
Vaganian-Planinc, *Hastings 1974/5* 51
Van der Sterren-Timman, *Rotterdam 1998* 141
Williams.S-Emms, *British Championship 2000* 114
Yermolinsky-Salov, *Wijk aan Zee 1997* 9
Zifroni-Kaspi, *Tel Aviv 1998* 15
Zviaginsev-Ulibin, *Russian Championship 1996* 151